Microprocessor-Based Systems

Microprocessor-Based Systems

Richard C. Seals BSc(Hons), PhD

Principal Lecturer
School of Engineering, Thames Polytechnic

Stanley Thornes (Publishers) Ltd

First published in 1992 by:
Stanley Thornes (Publishers) Ltd
Old Station Drive
Leckhampton
CHELTENHAM GL53 0DN
England

A catalogue record for this book is available from the British Library.

ISBN: 0 7487 1533 9

Typeset by Florencetype Ltd., Kewstoke, Avon
Printed and bound in Great Britain at The Bath Press, Avon

Contents

Foreword

In 1982 Hutchinson Educational Publishers, now part of Stanley Thornes, published on behalf of the Business Technician Education Council (BTEC), a series of books designed for use as learning packages in association with the published standard units in Microelectronic Systems and Microprocessor-Based Systems.

The last decade has seen the transformation of industrial computing with the explosion in personal computing. The reduction in price complemented by a significant increase in computing power has extended the application of personal computers so that microelectronics is now a realistic tool in all sectors of industry and commerce. The need for adequate training programmes for technicians and engineers has increased and the BTEC units have been revised and updated to reflect today's needs.

Stanley Thornes have produced a series of learning packages to support the updated syllabuses and numerous other courses which include Microelectronics and Microprocessor-Based Systems. There are five books in the series:

Microelectronics Systems	Level F	by G. Cornell
Microelectronics NII	Level N	by D. Turner
Microelectronics NIII	Level N	by D. Turner
Microprocessor-Based Systems	Level H	by R. Seals
Microcomputer Systems	Level H	by R. Seals

The two books titled *Microprocessor-Based Systems* and *Microcomputer Systems* emphasise task based learning approaches and are targetted at the first two years of undergraduate study programmes. The content is designed to give the essential foundation for final year lecture programmes and project studies.

Two additional books which complement the five above are:

Microprocessor Interfacing	Level N	by G. Dixey
Practical Exercises in Microelectronics	Level N	by D. Turner

Interfacing is an essential, but often neglected, stage in the application of microprocessors and microelectronics to any process. This book follows the BTEC unit and supports the first three titles above. *Practical Exercises in Microelectronics* is a series of exercises which complement the two Microelectronics Level NII and Level NIII books with a programme of relevant laboratory-based exercises.

Andy Thomas
Series Editor

Preface

We live in exciting times! Computers are everywhere, increasingly being included in domestic and industrial applications without the user being aware of their presence. They make machines and appliances much easier to use and understand and our lives more comfortable and productive.

This text considers some of the requirements, methods and implications of designing such microprocessor-based systems. It follows the syllabus for the **BTEC** unit of the same title and is also suitable for first and second year students on Electronic, Electrical/Electronic and other **degree courses** which include microprocessor design and programming. The text will be popular with students as it contains **sample programs** and a considerable amount of detailed information on **peripheral devices** as well as **microprocessors**.

A feature of the book is that the information is presented in a sequence which builds up into a PC-like system and shows why the original **personal computer** had many of the features we see today. Other practical treatment of everyday microprocessor-controlled electronics includes an in-depth treatment of an **automatic car park barrier control** and an **alarm clock circuit** which forms the basis of domestic and industrial timers.

The main microprocessor discussed throughout the book is the **8086** as this is the most popular in the world, thanks to the millions of personal computers in use today. However, information on the **68000** is included to enable a comparison between the two main 16-bit microprocessor families.

Throughout the text, emphasis is placed on 'doing' rather than just reading or listening to a lecturer, which is achieved through **worked examples**. The student is encouraged to collect, process and apply information as a prelude to gaining 'hands-on' experience. The method used is known as **task-oriented learning** (TOL) which avoids gaining knowledge without an identified task set to complete. TOL also provides the benefit of learning how to solve problems which will be applicable in other areas of knowledge.

This book therefore encourages the ability to think clearly about a problem or a design specification by using a **system or 'black box' approach** to define a solution and then to find ways of implementing the solution. Some of the hardware/ software solutions are considered in detail with many example **algorithms** and **program listings** written in 8086, 68000 assembler or **Pascal**. The general philosophy of design, documentation and testing is maintained alongside the detailed explanation of microprocessor applications so that the thought is conveyed that the design method is but loosely coupled to the actual devices used. At times readers are invited to supply material and ideas considered to be the most suitable for their own systems.

Chapter 1 encourages a systems view of hardware and software design. **Chapter 2** goes on to discuss relative merits of 8- and 16-bit microprocessors, CPU and memory control, the 8086 instruction set and the 68000 microprocessor.

Chapter 3 deals extensively with types of memory and memory addressing, programmable input/output devices (PIO), serial communications and the programmable interface (PSCI), the programmable interrupt controller (PIC), direct memory access (DMA), floppy disk systems and the floppy disk controller (FDC), the programmable interval timer (PIT), concluding with a review of peripheral devices available to the PC user.

Chapter 4 takes the reader through the various stages of a top-down microcomputer design process, using the everyday electronic alarm as a practical example.

Chapter 5 covers software development using a multi-storey car park entry/exit control system as an example.

Chapter 6 deals with emulation and simulation in program testing and debugging as a prelude to **Chapter 7** which covers systems testing: typical hardware and software faults are discussed including bugs specific to C, Pascal and Assembler programming.

R Seals
1992

Acknowledgements

With thanks to Jane who did all the typing and never gets a mention, and also to Ruth and Timothy.

Trademarks

Intel® is a registered trademark of Intel Corporation. IBM® is a registered trademark, and PC/AT™ and PC-DOS™ are trademarks of International Business Machines Corporation. Microsoft® and MS-DOS® are registered trademarks of Microsoft Corporation. Motorola® is a registered trademark of Motorola Corporation.

ONE

A systems approach to design

1.1 INTRODUCTION

The aim of this chapter is to analyse the basic requirements of a microcontroller and a microcomputer. This is often separated into two parts: the factors affecting product production, and the functional design.

Product production considers the factors which influence the quality of design, commercial considerations and reliability rather than the purely technical design considerations. **Functional design** uses a top-down design methodology in order to deduce the separate sub-functions required to implement the specification.

The **specification** is a description of the product that is given to the designers that enables them to make production and functional design decisions.

1.2 FUNCTIONAL DESIGN SOLUTION

It is not necessary to decide on any of the software and hardware solutions before starting the **design process**, provided the function of the product can be deduced. By a simple consideration of the operation of the system, a **set of requirements**, and the initial specification can be generated.

The product that will be described throughout is the design of a system which has the ability to produce, save, and execute computer programs. A block diagram, see *Figure 1.1*, illustrates the main functions.

This consists of four main blocks separated into two areas, the user and the computer, which meet at the user/computer interaction plane. The user is outside the solution area and has therefore been represented as a single block which cannot be altered. It is necessary to consider how the user affects the design of the computer. This is handled by the **user interface** block

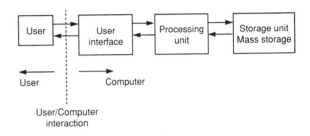

Figure 1.1 System block diagram

which performs two communication tasks. These are the conversion of user command instructions into a format understandable by the computer, and the conversion of the computer response into a format understandable by the user.

The computer must also have the ability to store large quantities of user-generated data and programs. This requires a **storage unit**. This could be considered to be similar to a library where books are stored on shelves. They are usually not read (that is, executed) until after they have been removed from the library.

The final block in the computer system is the **processing unit**. This responds to user command instructions via the user interface. This may result in a user-specified program being transferred from the storage unit, into the execution unit. Execution of programs may then be initiated which might result in further accesses to the user interface. Any results can be displayed and new user command instructions obtained.

The ideas produced are known as the **design solution**. Although these may not seem particularly useful at this stage three separate areas have already been identified and the interfaces between them given.

(a) **User interface**: accepts user command instructions as input, then outputs any available results.

1

This performs the necessary user-to-computer and computer-to-user translations.

(b) **Execution unit**: receives translated user command instructions, executes them and transfers any relevant results to the user interface, where they are translated into a user-understandable format. This also has to be capable of transferring the selected data and programs to and from the storage unit.

(c) **Storage unit**: this is capable of storing large amounts of user-generated data and programs on a long-term basis, even when power is removed. Programs need to be transferred as quickly as possible to the execution unit ready to be executed. Also, it may be necessary to transfer data to and from the storage unit during program execution, and again this should take place as quickly as possible.

System Design

Initially, the system design will be considered as outlined in *Figure 1.2*, and the general parameters discussed to consider how they interrelate.

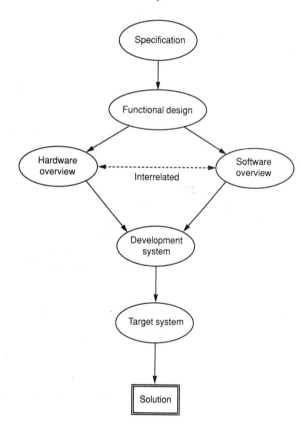

Figure 1.2   System design

There are a variety of concepts which have to be considered when a project is first being proposed, which may appear to have little to do with the functional solution; things such as reliability and maintainability – ideas which are not part of the initial concept, but which need to be considered in order to produce a product which will be attractive to the user. In the product that will be considered throughout this book, the development of a simple personal computer, there are two major elements in the design: the hardware and the software.

The **hardware** can be considered to be the physical electrical, electronic and mechanical components that can actually be seen. Various solutions will be considered in some detail at block diagram level, in order to illustrate the interaction between the hardware and software functions. Only the functional operation of the electronic components will be considered, and the electrical and mechanical components almost ignored.

Software can be considered to be that which controls the hardware and can be changed by altering the program, hence the name software and the aim is to be able to design, write, test and maintain software. The task of building a personal computer provides a flexible subject and covers almost every area of re-programmable components. Obviously, the software requires hardware to operate on and control and the functional operation of the hardware will be considered in detail to be able to operate and control it from within a program.

1.3   HARDWARE OVERVIEW

The hardware overview will consider various different alternatives, and decide which might be the optimum solution. This will involve some detailed overviews of the required topics, before the selection of one particular solution.

The hardware design process has been split into three sections as illustrated in *Figure 1.3*, called design, implementation and prototype testing.

Design

The system **specification** is that as supplied by the user and will outline the functional requirement of the entire system. This may be altered during the design process to accommodate additional detailed specifications. However, the specification should be complete and formalised before the final stages of the design process take place, and should be considered to be unalterable. Sometimes it may be absolutely necessary to make changes to the specification but this should not be a normal requirement.

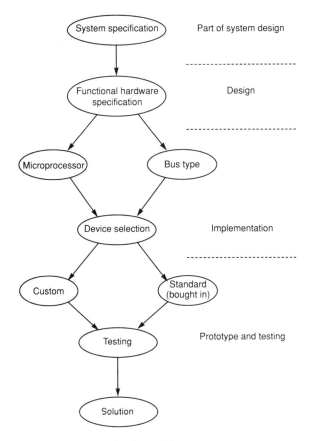

Figure 1.3 System implementation

cation, and not just to verify that the hardware is working.

Implementation

Having decided what functions the hardware should perform, the next stage is to decide what components should be used. For example, the **microprocessor** in the execution unit has to be selected based upon an optimisation of various parameters. These might include speed of execution, data bus size, and so on, which can be considered to be the technical considerations. These are relatively easy to decide unless the product being designed is a very special one requiring, for example, a very high speed of execution or a very high accuracy.

However, there are non-technical parameters which influence these decisions and often these parameters are considered first, and can be termed the product production considerations. These include the non-ideal parameters related to cost. If an investment has previously been made in a particular type of microprocessor development aid, then unless there is some extremely important overriding technical reason, such as those given above, then that microprocessor will be used in all new products.

The system specification is then separated into hardware and software components. The software/hardware separation is determined by optimising a variety of parameters, such as speed of execution, memory size, program size and so on, as determined by the user.

The separation into hardware and software is a difficult task as there are many possible solutions and, depending upon the specifications, one product may implement a function in software, another may implement it in hardware. An example might be the conversion of binary coded decimal (BCD) into signals for a seven segment display. This function can be performed using a software look-up table, or by hardware using the appropriate logic decoder.

Once the hardware requirement has been identified, its specification can be detailed. This will describe what functions have to be performed, what interfaces will be used, how fast they are and so on. This enables the test procedure that will be used on the completed prototype to be identified, and the test parameters determined. Testing should always be performed to the initial specifi-

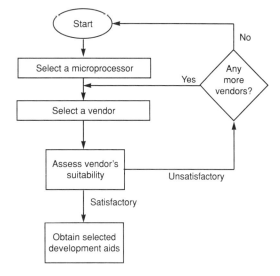

Figure 1.4 Selecting new microprocessor development aids

The only time a decision is made as to which microprocessor to use in future products, is when new microprocessor development aids are being selected. Then parameters such as the stability of the vendor become important and questions might be asked such as:

(a) 'Will the vendor still be trading in 3–5 years and therefore be able to support the equipment through maintenance and upgrades?'

(b) 'Will the microprocessor be suitable in 3–5 years time to cope with predicted trends in products?'

(c) 'Are there sufficient support staff?'

(d) 'Has the company supplied satisfactory equipment before?'

(e) 'Is the microprocessor available from alternative sources to prevent sudden changes in availability and price?'

(f) 'Are there a variety of programming languages available?'

These concepts are illustrated in *Figures 1.4 and 1.5*. For example, if a microprocessor is chosen which is already available in its maximum speed, how can the 20 per cent improvement in execution speed predicted in the future for competitors' products, be achieved? (An explanation of flow charts is provided in Chapter 5.)

Most of these questions have little to do with purely technical questions, but are guided more by speculative answers to 'what if?' type questions. Often the decision is made to use what everybody else uses, so that at least you will not be at a disadvantage and skilled staff can be obtained. This is one reason why standards, such as the IBM PC, are preferred. Everyone knows what goes on

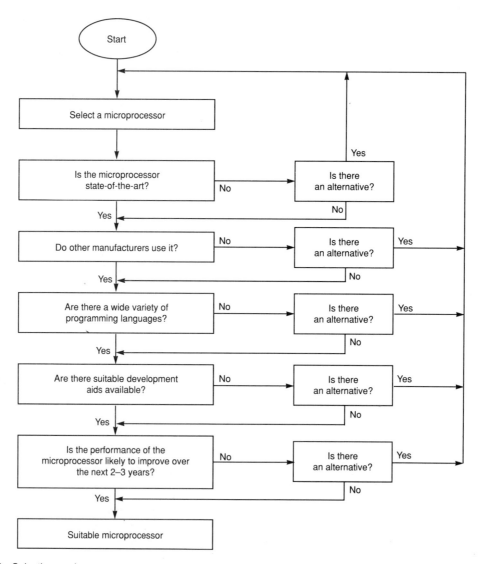

Figure 1.5 Selecting a microprocessor

inside, there are many of them so that the market is large and will be around for several years, and there are plenty of skilled users.

Prototyping and Testing

Once the devices have been selected the initial **proto-type** has to be put together and tested. This can involve two levels of prototyping: the functional and the physical, as illustrated in *Figure 1.6*.

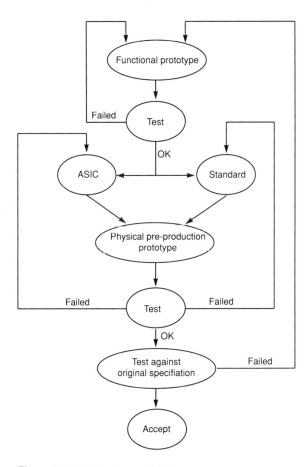

Figure 1.6 Prototyping and testing

Functional prototyping involves implementing the functions of the product to ensure that it operates correctly. This may not be in the final physical form. For example, a complex electronic and logical function containing many logic gate equivalents, may be implemented using discrete logic gates, whereas for the final production version a single custom component would be made. This would incorporate the same functional logic devices but in a more compact and cost-effective

package. These devices are generally known as application-specific integrated circuits (**ASICs**). This type of component is not often used for functional prototyping due to the cost of making only a small number: the functional prototyping may identify some problems requiring a re-design and hence a new ASIC. It is more cost-effective to perform functional prototyping using standard components, which can then be condensed into an ASIC when correct.

The use of hardware **simulators** when designing ASICs is becoming more important as the simulators become more accurate. This method uses a computer to simulate the physical and logical characteristics of all components in the product, in order to perform functional testing. Some simulators also allow physical simulation of devices such as ASICs. In this way functional prototyping can be performed without any physical devices being put together. This has the advantage of flexibility as the circuits can be changed easily if a problem is identified, and avoids a physical functional prototype. It is also possible to go directly to an ASIC after successful simulation.

The disadvantages are that the computer systems used for the simulation are expensive and complex, and that the success of the simulation depends upon the accuracy of the modelling of the physical and logical characteristics of the components. However, due to the increasing use of ASICs in products, simulation enables the physical functional prototyping stage to be avoided. This enables the operation of the ASIC design to be tested without constructing either a functional equivalent or a test ASIC, so that faults and errors can be detected. The ASIC can then be made with a high degree of confidence that it will work first time.

Physical prototyping considers the electrical and mechanical connections. Should the circuit be soldered together using a standard printed circuit board or should wire wrap be used? Wirewrap is easier to construct, quicker and easier to make changes to, but the sockets are expensive and the method has a maximum useful frequency of 8–10 MHz before signals become corrupted. It is also a method which can not be used for the final product as once the design is finalised and no more changes are to be made, it takes a long time to produce a completely connected circuit, when compared to using a PCB.

Alternatively a custom printed circuit board (PCB) could be produced if high frequency operation is required, although the cost involved means that it would usually only be used for the production version, and not just for functional testing. This would mean producing any ASICs before final prototype testing which would require parts of the product to be developed in isolation, converted into ASICs, tested, and then placed into the complete product for final prototyping and testing.

Finally the product has to be tested against the original specification, as that is the measure of the success of the technical design. Commercial considerations involved in the marketing of products are not considered here. At this stage, testing will revert to the black box approach, see *Figure 1.7*, where the product is considered only in terms of its inputs and outputs. Following this stage of testing, there will be further product testing when the software and hardware are combined into the final complete product.

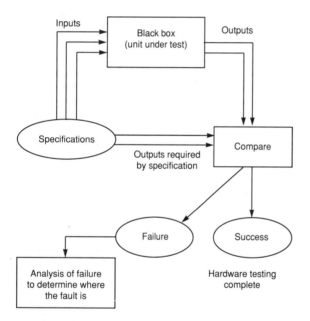

Figure 1.7 Black box testing

1.4 SOFTWARE DESIGN

Software design has much the same approach as hardware design in that the functional software description is derived from the system specification. This is then followed by the implementation stage and finally the prototype and testing stages.

Functional Software Specification

The functional software specification details the functions to be performed by the software and the **interfaces** between functions. As a general rule it can be said that software is best designed using a block structured approach, independent of the language used.

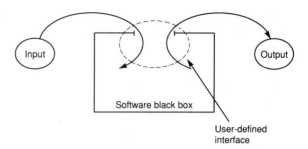

Figure 1.8 Block-structured software

When using a block structured approach, it is only necessary to specify what actions are to be performed by a particular section of software, what goes in, and what comes out, as in *Figure 1.8*. The internal operation of the software should be invisible to the rest of the program and should only communicate to the rest of the program via the defined interface.

Block structuring makes testing easier as each software black box can have its internal operation tested in isolation and then when working, it can be added to the system. When system testing takes place the data and results passing through the software program then need only be tested for correctness on entering and exiting the individual software black boxes. In this way the number of tests required can be reduced and errors pinpointed quickly. There is also the advantage that if a problem has been identified in a particular software black box, then that piece of software can be replaced with an improved version, without affecting the rest of the program provided that the interface is maintained the same.

There are a variety of functional software design techniques available, such as Jackson structured programming, data flow, flowcharts and pseudo-code to name a few, each of which has its own advantages and disadvantages. Only two will be used throughout this book which are simple to understand, flexible, and easy to use. They are a simplified version of **flowcharts**, and **pseudo-code**. There are two main types of software languages available for microprocessors, **low level languages**, (LLL) and **high level languages** (HLL). The simple flowchart technique is suitable for low level languages and pseudo-code for high level languages.

A low level language is one in which each language statement is converted into one microprocessor-executable instruction and the conversion is performed by what are known as **assemblers**. Because of the one-to-one relationship, the reverse process of converting from the microprocessor-executable format into the language statements is also possible and is known as disassembly. This type of language allows direct control over the microprocessor registers and hardware and enables fast executing programs to be produced. The disadvantages are that it is difficult to create error-free programs, and that the programs produced cannot be transferred to other computers and microprocessors. This therefore requires new programs for each new microprocessor and computer.

For high level languages, each statement is converted into several, possibly several hundred, microprocessor-executable instructions. The conversion is performed by what are known as **compilers**. As there is not a one-to-one relationship the reverse of compilation is not possible. This type of language is designed to be more general purpose than LLLs and independent of the microprocessor or computer on which it will be executing. This enables programs to be developed once and then transferred to other computers with only minor modifications, as illustrated in *Figure 1.9*. HLLs have an additional advantage in that the language constructs have been designed to support block structured programming. This simplifies the writing of programs and produces fewer errors. The disadvantages are that the resulting programs are longer due to the need to be more general purpose (a requirement of HLLs), therefore occupying more of the computer memory and taking longer to execute.

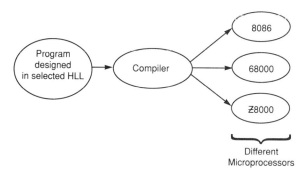

Figure 1.9   Software designed for hardware independence

The result is that for functionally-equivalent programs written in a LLL and a HLL for the same computer, the LLL program will in general, execute much more quickly. The result of this is that it is more advantageous to use a LLL for functions which must execute quickly and a HLL for the rest.

Due to the use of two functional design techniques which are related to the type of language used, the decision as to which type of programming language is to be used, has to be made early on, although it is not necessary to select the particular language until later.

Implementation

Once the functional design has been completed then the implementation can be performed. This involves the selection of the appropriate assembler and/or compiler(s). A microprocessor will generally only have one assembly language so that most assemblers will be similar. However, as there are a variety of high level languages, a decision has to be made as to which HLL to choose, and then which compiler to select and from which company. Although nominally all compilers for a particular HLL are the same, there are considerable differences in speed of compilation, the size and speed of execution of the code produced, and other factors, such as the ability to link easily to assembly language programs. Some of these decisions are also similar to those used for selecting the microprocessor and its development aids, and are based on commercial as well as technical considerations.

Each HLL has its own advantages; for example, Fortran is good for programs involving large amounts of calculations, Cobol is good for management-type business programs, Pascal is good for block structured programs and C is good for maintaining close control of the hardware of the computer, and for producing compact, fast-executing programs.

A large program which has several of these characteristics could be written in several HLLs as well as a LLL. This would enable the most efficient language to be used in different parts of the program in order to produce the optimum solution. However this would be unusual and normally the most appropriate HLL would be chosen for the complete program.

Prototyping and Testing

If two or more types of language are being used each would be produced separately and then linked together. Once this has been achieved system testing can be performed. There are a variety of testing strategies for testing each software black box as it is produced and then gradually connecting the blocks together to build up the complete system. The system testing compares the complete program operation against that required by the initial functional software specification. As with the hardware this can be achieved using two different techniques, **simulation** and **emulation**.

When simulating the operation of a program the target microcomputer is not used, instead the target system is simulated by producing a model that is equivalent. There are two basic levels of simulation, functional and detailed.

A **functional simulation** will have the same interfaces between blocks as the real hardware but they may be implemented in a different way. For example, if the target hardware has a keyboard connected this may be simulated by a list of characters stored in a file. When the program requests an input from the keyboard a character from the file is substituted. Even in a functional simulator the microprocessor will be accurately simulated to enable register and memory contents to be examined at any point. The timing of the execution of the program can usually be obtained from the simulation although it is not possible to be 100 per cent confident of the results.

For **detailed simulation**, the internal operation of the hardware blocks are also accurately modelled. This is unusual as a great deal of extra programming is required to produce an accurate simulation and there is not a significant improvement in the quality of the results obtained.

Software simulation is not quite the same as for the hardware, in that programs can usually be made to execute on several different types of computers by using a compiler suitable for each. The operation of the program can then be tested on whatever computer is available, and any hardware functions are either simulated using software equivalents, or emulated if hardware equivalents are available. This does not completely test the software as emulation or simulation can never be 100 per cent accurate, but it is a useful method if the target system is not available.

Finally, when the target hardware is available and the software has been developed and tested it can be transferred by downloading using either **read only memory** (ROM) programming, or a communication link to the target system.

At this point complete system testing can be performed involving both the hardware and software to ensure three things:

(a) The hardware meets the functional hardware specification;
(b) The software meets the functional software specification;
(c) The system meets the original system specification.

Once the prototype has been tested, the pre-production prototype is made. In the pre-production prototype the design is re-engineered so that functionally it is the same, but that the hardware of the design is adapted for production. This may involve designing a PCB or using **programmable logic arrays** (PLA) rather than discrete logic, and using surface mount components so that automated assembly techniques can be employed and so on.

The pre-production prototype is then tested against the specifications again to ensure that it is still functionally correct. Finally the production version is made which should be identical to the pre-production version, but will be made in the numbers required. It is only when large numbers are being made that difficulties in the production version may occur, due to variations in the production processes themselves. It is the job of the production engineer to ensure that these difficulties are overcome.

It is likely there there will still be faults somewhere in the product as 100 per cent testing is difficult and expensive to achieve. These faults would either be due to an incorrect specification or an incorrect implementation of the specification, which was not detected during any of the tests performed. In practice, these will be gradually discovered by users of the product and if this information can be obtained by the manufacturer an enhanced and refined version can be produced when thought appropriate.

1.5 WHAT IS A COMPUTER?

Every process, biological, commercial or industrial, has some method of controlling it. That is, for a certain set of input and environment conditions, a specific action or set of actions is performed. For example, a central heating controller turns the heating system on when the temperature drops below the preset value.

In industrial and commercial processes the control actions are implemented by computers which come in two main categories: **microcontrollers** and **microcomputers**.

Microcontrollers

A microcontroller is a microprocessor-based system which has been designed to perform a specific task or control function or closely-related group of tasks. The program is contained in permanent memory which maintains the correct program code even after the power has been removed for long periods. Usually microcontrollers perform intensive input and output (I/O) operations.

The microcontroller has input information from the function being controlled such as sensor and switch values. The data processing element, (the **microprocessor**) then performs some alteration or tests on the data, and outputs the result. The data processing performed is fixed by the program stored in **permanent memory**. The microcontroller then forms the feedback from the process being controlled to ensure that the desired states are maintained.

If the data processing function has to be changed then the permanent memory component has to be replaced. Some modern microcontrollers use a special type of permanent memory which, under certain conditions, can be made to change what was stored. Usually this type of memory, known as electrically erasable, stores data variables and not programs. An example of this is how a television is able to remember the channels it is tuned to. If we wish to change the control program being used to something more interesting, this is achieved by replacing the control program. If the input and output are not changed, the physical components which make up the microcontroller do not need to be changed either. This assumes that there is enough permanent memory to contain the new program.

There are advantages in designing for a specific control function, as the components used can be optimised for the required task. One of the optimisations is that the number of components in the microcontroller is minimised so that each component contributes directly to controlling the task. The two main types of components have already been considered, permanent program memory and I/O. In addition, most microcontrollers will require some data memory for saving intermediate data values while performing the control function. This is not permanent memory and the data values are lost when the power is removed. This is not a problem as when the power is re-applied, the control program is able to reproduce any necessary intermediate values.

The most obvious reason for using the minimum number of components in a microcontroller is that it reduces the the materials cost. However, this objective is not quite as straightforward as it would seem. Electronic components come in two distinct categories, general purpose and specific. The general purpose components are produced by companies which consider such a device to be useful to a wide range of users. They do not have a specific microcontroller function in mind but perceive a general need. This allows them to make and sell sufficient quantities of the component to make a satisfactory profit. The difficulty is that when used in a specific microcontroller, a general purpose component will not be 100 per cent utilised. For example, a general purpose I/O component may be available which has 24 I/O lines. If the function being controlled only requires 8 I/O lines, then two-thirds of the device is surplus. Effectively, two-thirds of the cost of the device is also wasted. In addition, that two-thirds is consuming power, taking up space, and so on. Therefore, a general purpose component has to be cheap in order to compensate for

the other drawbacks. To be cheap, a large number must be sold. This can be achieved by having a large market for microcontrollers using that component, or making it so general purpose that it will fit into almost any microcontroller.

Special/Custom

Alternatively, specially made components can be used. These are known under various names such as custom devices and gate arrays, but the most descriptive name is **application-specific integrated circuits** (ASICs). These are components designed to perform part or all of a control function that could be performed by a more general microcontroller, but only sufficient I/O and interfacing for the specific task are included. These ASICs will also incorporate much of the data processing element, and sometimes the data memory as well. Permanent program memory is not usually required as the control function is designed-in to the component. The result is a component, which occupies the minimum space, uses minimum power, and has all the necessary I/O and data processing.

The disadvantage is that the cost is greater as there is a development cost incurred with every new ASIC designed, plus the cost of producing the device. The general purpose component has a lower initial development cost but a higher in-use cost than the ASIC. The result of this is that at some point as the number of controllers increases, it becomes cheaper to use ASICs rather than general purpose components.

Therefore if small numbers of microcontrollers are required for a specific control function use general purpose devices, and for larger numbers use ASICs. The cross-over point varies depending on the control function implemented so each design has to be separately analysed.

The initial cost of development of ASICs is falling all the time so that it is becoming cheaper to provide ASICs. This may result in fewer general purpose components being sold which will increase their cost, hence making ASIC's even more attractive. This means that in the near future there will probably be a change away from microcontrollers using general purpose components towards those using ASICs.

Programmable Logic Controllers

In order to improve the usefulness of microcontrollers so that they can be used in many control situations, the **programmable logic controller** (PLC) was devised. This is a microcontroller which allows the user to enter programs using a special language which is based on logic hence the name, which is independent of the microprocessor used. The PLC contains a program logic interpreter to convert the logic program into the appropriate microprocessor instructions. There must also be an area of memory which can be used to store user programs.

The PLC is a general purpose controller so that the problem of less than 100 per cent utilisation can start to occur. However, this is compensated for by being able to use the PLC in a wider range of control functions without having to re-design it. Also, it can be re-programmed should the control function be changed, or improvements to the control process be required.

Microcomputers

The function to be performed by the microcontroller may require more than simple input and output, so that the program being executed may be changed regularly and have interaction in real time with the user. Then an alternative arrangement is used called a **microcomputer**.

This is similar in many ways to a microcontroller, but has greatly extended general purpose computing ability. This is reflected in two main areas, the ability to enter general user programs from some form of secondary mass program storage, and to interact with the user in real time, via some form of data entry and display function. These are usually in the form of a keyboard and a video screen. This implies a larger temporary user program and data memory area than is required by microcomputers.

Microcomputers are designed to execute user programs by means of a general purpose computer and controller. They do not have a specific control function programmed into the permanent program memory area, but are able to execute programs which implement dedicated control functions. However, because the designed is more general purpose, less than 100 per cent utilisation is achieved. The result of this is that microcomputers are not generally used for dedicated control tasks.

The microcomputer is designed to enable the user to develop programs and to execute a wide variety of already developed programs, such as word processors, spread sheets and databases.

Mass Secondary Storage

Programs and data which are not being used are saved in what is called **secondary storage**. These programs, and the data stored there, cannot be executed or accessed directly by the data processing element, but must first be downloaded into the main temporary user program and data memory area, called primary memory. It is desirable that the user is able to store a large number of programs in the secondary storage, to obtain the maximum flexibility so that it must have a large capacity, hence the term mass secondary storage.

The most common types of mass secondary storage are **disks** and **tape**. These both use a technique similar to that used on music tapes. Disks are available in two main formats, called **hard disk**, when the magnetic material is coated onto an inflexible solid disk, and **floppy disk**, when the magnetic material is coated onto a flexible plastic disk. These are covered in more detail in a later chapter.

The hard disk has the advantage that data can be stored at a much higher density, approximately 10 to 20 times that of a floppy disk, but requires more expensive mechanical and electronic systems to access the data. The floppy disk has the advantage of cheaper and more robust mechanical and electronic systems as the data is not so densely packed and is also portable, being removable from the PC. The disadvantage is that the density of data is much reduced and the average time to access the required data is greater.

Most PCs use both systems to obtain the maximum benefit, with a large secondary storage for the majority of programs and data using a hard disk, and personal or small groups of user programs using floppy disks. Floppy disks also permit a second copy, called a **backup**, to be generated and stored separately for security.

Main Memory

As the PC is designed to be able to execute a wide variety of programs and to be able to manipulate large amounts of data, the amount of temporary memory, now called main memory, is much larger than that for the microcontroller. This memory only contains programs and data whilst the power is still applied, so that the program and data have to be downloaded from the secondary storage every time the PC is turned on. When a different program or different set of data values is required it must also be transferred from mass secondary storage. Most programs are not stored in **permanent program memory** but on floppy or hard disks. This then means that the amount of permanent program memory required is not as great since it is only required to perform two specific functions.

The first task of the permanent program is to test as much of the hardware of the computer as possible, whenever the power is turned on. This ensures that the programs and data are downloaded and executed correctly, and that the required hardware initialisation functions are performed. For example, turning on the video display, initialising the keyboard, and so on.

Following this there is a simple program which downloads a program called the **boot program**, stored at a specific place in the secondary storage. This can only be run if the disk had the special program placed there when it was created and such disks are called **system disks**. Hard disks are usually set up as system disks as they are permanently resident inside the PC.

These initialisation tasks are called **bootstrapping** and are performed by the bootstrap program. The special program that is downloaded by the bootstrap program, from the specific position in secondary storage, will usually be the bootstrap loader for the **operating system** for the PC. This is often referred to as the **disk operating system** (DOS) as most of the operations that it performs have something to do with the disk storage system. The DOS is a flexible program which the user controls in order to be able to access any program or data stored in mass secondary storage. The programs can be down-loaded or up-loaded as required by the user. It is also possible to control the hardware of the PC via the DOS so that the video display attributes can be altered, or the keyboard initialisation altered, and so on.

User Interface

As the name *personal computer* suggests, the microcomputer is usually designed to be used by one person at a time. The language the data processing element uses called **machine code**, is not one that is particularly easy for the user to understand. Therefore a translation or interpretation process must take place, in both directions between the processing unit and the user. This is called the **user interface**, or the more modern name of man/machine interface.

Summary

This chapter has shown how a consideration of the functional analysis of control problems leads to the functional specification and design of microcontrollers and microcomputers.

The basic elements of each were identified and their effect on the solution highlighted.

TWO

16-bit microprocessors

2.1 ADVANTAGES AND DISADVANTAGES OF 16-BIT MICROPROCESSORS

The advent of 16-bit **microprocessors** has led to improvements in microprocessor performance in several areas, principally increases in data word length, architectures giving increased speed of execution, higher clock rates, and more powerful instructions.

Increases in Data and Address Lengths

Most eight-bit microprocessors have a basic data length of 8 bits allowing unsigned integers in the range 0–255 to be represented directly. A more useful range using 16 bits requires 2 bytes and gives unsigned integers in the range 0–65 535. This requires the manipulation of two bytes, using the flow of operations set out below for the addition of two 16-bit numbers.

Example of an 8-bit microprocessor program operation.

(a) Get low byte of first number;
(b) Get low byte of second number;
(c) Add together and save result;
(d) Get high byte of first number;
(e) Get high byte of second number;
(f) Add together with carry and save the result;
(g) If there was an overflow, indicate the error.

For a 16-bit microprocessor, the program flow would look something like that set out below:

(a) Get first number;
(b) Get second number;
(c) Add together and save result;
(d) If there was an overflow indicate an error.

Only two memory fetches are required instead of the four required by the 8-bit microprocessor, and the two values can be added together in one operation, instead of two. Assuming that each operation takes the same time, which is an over-simplification, then the same program for a 16-bit microprocessor will execute 43 per cent faster and will be shorter requiring less memory storage.

Arithmetic functions are one important area where 16-bit microprocessors have an immediate advantage, and to obtain this improvement in performance in 8-bit microprocessors some manufacturers have added some arithmetic operations, such as add and subtract. However, very few 8-bit microprocessors implement division and multiplication directly as single instructions, and programs must be used to perform these functions. This enables 16-bit microprocessors to make even more dramatic improvements in performance in calculation-intensive programs. The result of increasing the basic data length is the ability to represent directly much larger numbers, with a corresponding increase in performance when manipulating them.

In addition to the increase in performance brought about by an increased data length, there is an increase in the maximum program size as the memory address range length has also been increased. Eight-bit microprocessors tend to have a 16-bit address system, which allows a maximum of 65 536 different memory addresses. Each address accesses an 8 bit value. All the program code and data must then fit within this range.

For 16-bit microprocessors the address length has been extended to at least 20 bits allowing 1 048 576 different memory locations to be accessed. The greatest improvement in performance is achieved when every location is 16 bits. However, a compromise was arrived at by the designers which takes into account the fact that most memory components are 8 bits per location, and that an upgrade path for programs using 8-bit data values was possible. This protected the investment made in writing programs for 8-bit microprocessors and encouraged the use of 16-bit microprocessors for new products as software investment was protected, see *Figure 2.1*. As 16-bit microprocessors have been available for several years now, the benefits have become obvious and compatibility with 8-bit devices is no longer an important factor. Some newer 16-bit microprocessors have been introduced which do not have an upgrade path from 8-bit microprocessors.

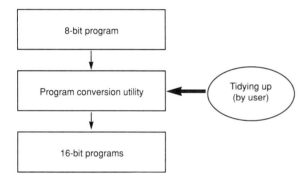

Figure 2.1 Upgrade path

The larger memory space allows larger and more useful programs to be produced. This makes 16-bit microprocessors much more useful for executing high level languages programs, as high level languages tend to produce large and complex programs. The limit of program size is being reached for 16-bit microprocessors where programs of 500 000 to 1 000 000 bytes are now commonplace, and there is an interest in using 32-bit microprocessors which have a much greater memory address space. It is now becoming more important to have a flexible operating systems which can efficiently use the available memory range rather than a large memory space.

Microprocessors are used in two main ways, either as microcontrollers when the programs are relatively small and easily fit into the available memory space, or as microcomputers, sometimes known as **personal computers** (PCs), when the programs can be larger than the available memory.

With PCs the restriction introduced by a limited memory space cannot be solved simply by increasing the available memory, as there are **operating systems** (OS) involved. These are programs which manage the available resources for the user, and interpret user commands. There is a limit on the amount of memory that they can manage. For MS-DOS this is 640 kbytes,

although newer versions are expected to overcome this limitation. Therefore as well as using a microprocessor with a larger memory space, an operating system must be available that can utilise it.

Improvements in Architecture

As well as increases in address and data lengths which lead to an improved performance, 16-bit microprocessors have improved internal architectures. The internal architecture of a microprocessor can be considered to be the organisation and control of the address and data signals, and the order in which operations are performed on these values. There are two main categories, **pipelined** and **non-pipelined**.

Non-pipelined architecture. In general, 8-bit microprocessors have a non-pipelined architecture, when only one action can be performed at any one time, and each microprocessor instruction which can consist of several operations, must complete before the next one can begin. The actions a microprocessor can perform can be generalised to:

(a) Instruction fetch;
(b) Instruction decode;
(c) Instruction execute.

When a program is being executed, the simplified general sequence illustrated in *Figure 2.2* takes place.

First the instruction has to be fetched from memory, and this operation is called the **instruction fetch**, and is the first part of any instruction. During this time, the **central processing unit** (CPU) is essentially inactive as only the communication **bus system** is being used.

Following this, there is some CPU activity when the instruction is decoded and executed. The decoded operations may be completely internal, for example, register-only versions of instructions such as add, subtract, etc.

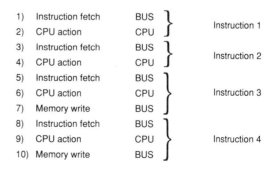

Figure 2.2 Non-pipelined microprocessor instruction sequence

During this time, the external data and bus system are inactive as in steps 2, 4, 6 and 9 in *Figure 2.2*.

At the end of the CPU activity there may be the requirement to perform memory operations, to write data to memory, as in steps 7 and 10 in *Figure 2.2*. Again, during this time, there is no CPU activity.

Pipelined Architecture. For pipelined architectures, selected operations are isolated so that they can be made to execute simultaneously. The most obvious functions which can be isolated and separated are internal CPU actions and memory operations which access the bus. The basic internal operation is *CPU action*, which is to execute the instruction. The basic memory operations are *instruction fetch*, *memory read* and *memory write*.

If the same sequence of program operations for a non-pipelined microprocessor is implemented using pipelining, the sequence of actions is similar to that illustrated in *Figure 2.3*. During step 1 an instruction is being fetched so the bus is busy, but the CPU is idle. In step 2 the CPU can now execute the instruction fetched in step 1, whilst at the same time, the next instruction is being fetched. The main point of interest is that the instruction fetch for instruction (N+1) is performed during the CPU actions of instruction N.

1) (Nothing)   Instruction 1 fetch
2) Instruction 1 cpu action   Instruction 2 fetch
3) Instruction 2 cpu action   Instruction 3 fetch
4) Instruction 3 cpu action   Instruction 4 fetch
5) Instruction 4 cpu action   Instruction 3 memory write
6) (Nothing)   Instruction 4 memory write

Figure 2.3 Pipelined microprocessor instruction sequence

Assuming that each of the operations takes the same amount of time, which is an over-simplification, then a pipelined architecture implementing two simultaneous functions leads to reduction in execution time of this program fragment of 40 per cent. That is, from 10 steps to only 6.

Improved Interrupt Structure

Interrupts provide a method of temporarily halting the execution of the main program by an unpredictable external event, so that the event can be dealt with. Eight-bit microprocessors have a small number of interrupts, between 4 and 8, although this can sometimes be extended using **programmable interrupt controllers** (PIC) to 16 or more, but usually less than 64, see *Figure 2.4*.

The more complex and sophisticated programs executed by 16-bit microprocessors allow more complex control functions to be implemented. This tends to require a greater number of interrupts in order to obtain a rapid response to external events. The drawback is that PICs have to be used, as there are insufficient connections to the microprocessor package to enable them to be connected directly.

In addition to the interrupts being initiated by external events, they can also be started by microprocessor instructions. This enables an **interrupt service routine** (ISR) to be started either by an external event (hardware) or by a program instruction (software), see *Figure 2.5* (page 16). This is achieved by using an **interrupt vector table** (IVT) which points to the location of the ISR in program memory. The interrupt then has a position in the IVT associated with it, and an interrupt, hardware or software initiated, then goes via the IVT to the location of the appropriate ISR. This allows ISRs to be placed anywhere in program memory rather than at specific addresses as required by most 8-bit microprocessors. One advantage of this is that it allows the user program to change the interrupt vector to point to a different ISR while the program is executing. This is often used in personal computers so that a users program can obtain better control of the hardware than that provided by the operating system.

Basic Input and Output Services (BIOS)

The ability to allocate interrupt vectors to interrupt service routines enables the **basic input and output services** (BIOS) to be implemented on a microcomputer. These are functions considered to be useful such as output of data to the display, input from the keyboard and secondary mass storage operations (to disk), such as save and load. The programs which perform these I/O functions are implemented in assembly language as ISRs and parameters are transferred backwards and forwards using the microprocessor registers.

The BIOS is specific to a particular manufacturer and may require a different BIOS for each new computer designed. However, the passing of parameters will be exactly the same so that provided the BIOS interface is used, programs will execute on any microcomputer.

The BIOS provides the low level control of the microcomputer hardware and is used by the disk operating system, as a standard interface to the hardware, as in *Figure 2.6* (page 16), which shows some of the computer software accessing the computer hardware of manufacturer A, via the BIOS and DOS. Provided that the DOS to BIOS interface is the same for the computer manufactured by B, the same computer software can be executed

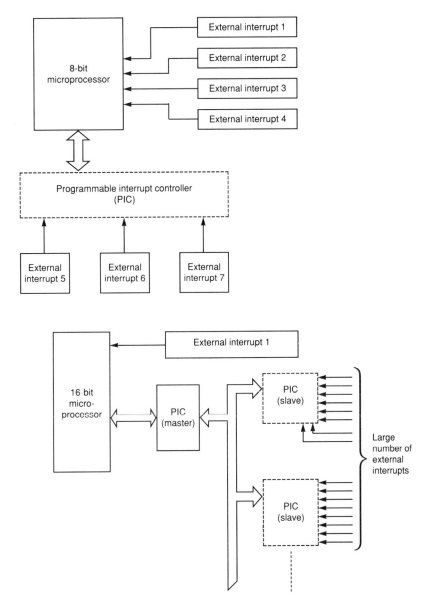

Figure 2.4 8- and 16-bit microprocessor interrupt structures

without any changes. This is advantageous for the computer software producer as a larger market is available, and is good for the user as there is a choice of computer hardware available. This encourages competition and keeps prices down.

Multi-user Systems

The larger number of memory locations available raises the possibility of having more than one program being stored in execution memory and dividing the CPU time between the programs. This enables several programs to execute apparently simultaneously and produces what is known as a multi-user system or environment.

In order to facilitate this, 16-bit microprocessors have several built-in functions which enable the resources of memory and CPU activity to be protected. CPU activity is protected by ensuring that a small period of time, called a **time slice**, can be allocated to a particular user. An interrupt is generated at regular fixed periods by a real-time clock and used to swap from one program to the next until all the programs have had a time slice. The

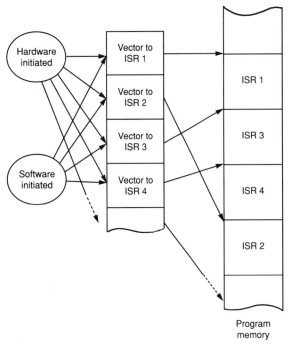

Figure 2.5 Starting an interrupt service routine

allocation of time-slices then starts again from the beginning.

Memory locations need to be protected to prevent unauthorised access and to prevent the operation of the program being affected by other programs. Program and data memory area protection is achieved by the use of segmentation.

Segmentation

Segmentation separates the available memory space into smaller areas and a user program is then allowed access to a number of them. This enables program code and data variables to be maintained in separate segments. The segments are then dedicated to one user and should not be accessible by other users. Attempts to cross the boundaries of segments by a user can then be detected as a potential clash, as in *Figure 2.7*, and prevented.

Some of these multi-user features are implemented as a combination of hardware features and software programs but have not been greatly used due to the ease with which software-based protection methods can be evaded by malicious users. This has led to the later generations of 32-bit microprocessors implementing multi-user protection in hardware only.

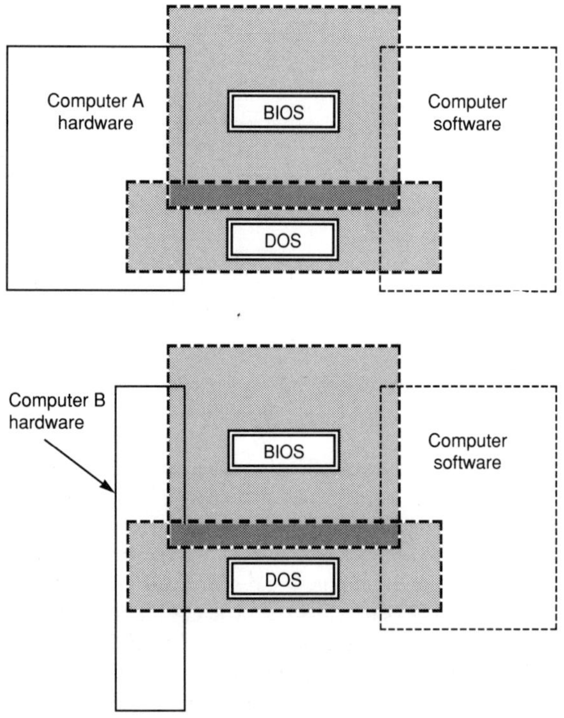

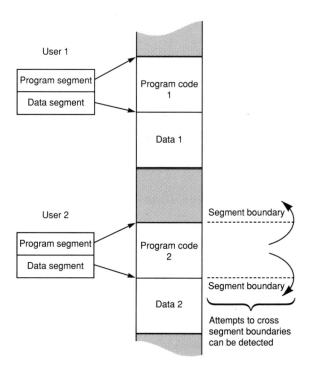

Figure 2.6 The BIOS/DOS connection

Figure 2.7 Segmentation

Semaphore Operation

If different programs share common sections of code such as mathematics operations, or controlling hardware functions such as I/O, then it may be necessary to allow only one copy of such programs. These are called critical sections of code and only one user at a time is allowed access. That user has to complete using the critical code, which could take several time-slots, before any other user can access it. This protection is achieved by the use of semaphores.

The essence of the **semaphore operation** is to access and test a memory location in one operation which cannot be interrupted, see *Figure 2.8*. The ability to do this is determined by the instruction set of the microprocessor and is only indirectly related to the architecture.

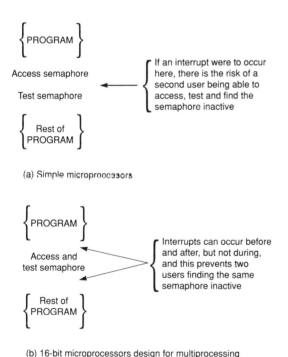

(a) Simple microprocessors

(b) 16-bit microprocessors design for multiprocessing

Figure 2.8 Multiprocessing with microprocessors

ly implement the structures used in HLLs, with the result that the compiled machine code programs are large and take longer to execute.

Some of the functions required by HLLs are direct, rather than indirect; logical operations on memory locations, local and global variables for procedures, arrays and arrays of instructions. These are features of the structure of the language which it constructs itself. In addition, surveys have indicated that an important use of computers is the transfer of long continuous sequences of data values from one area of memory to another, processing the data as it is transferred, as in *Figure 2.9*.

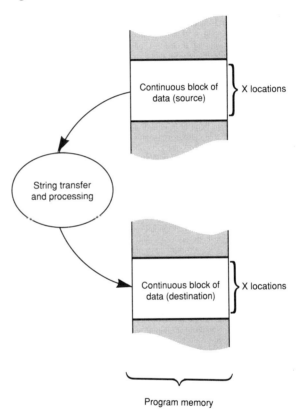

Figure 2.9 String operations

High Level Languages

It is possible to obtain compilers which convert high level language programs into machine code for execution on 8-bit microprocessors. However, 8-bit microprocessors were designed to execute assembly language programs and are not really suitable for efficiently executing programs written in high level languages. This is because the 8-bit assembly languages do not efficient-

On 8-bit microprocessors, this is achieved by using two instructions, one to get the data from memory and one to put the data in the new memory location. In addition, another two instructions are required to update the memory pointers:

(a) Get data from memory location;
(b) Put data to alternative memory location;
(c) Increment FROM memory pointer;

(d) Increment TO memory pointer;

(e) Repeat from (a) until the end of string.

On 16-bit microprocessors, the operations of (a) to (d) can be performed by a single instruction, i.e.,

(a) Transfer FROM memory TO alternative location and automatically increment memory pointers;

(b) repeat from (a) until the end of the string.

This indicates that a significant improvement in performance for this particular operation is possible when using 16-bit microprocessors rather than 8-bit devices.

Improvements in Production Technology

Another area of improvement is the use of increasingly advanced techniques of integrated circuit production which lead to increases in speed of operation due to a reduced geometry and faster transistors.

Reduced geometry.   The operation of a microprocessor is based on transistors which are operated as switches so that they are either OFF or ON. These form the logical functions from which the CPU is constructed. Each transistor consists of a geometric layout usually of rectangles of different types of semi-conductor, as in *Figure 2.10*. Making the shapes as small as possible enables more transistors to be fitted onto the semi-conductor substrate. This enables more complex functions, requiring more transistors, to be implemented. Also, the smaller the transistor, the faster it switches and the closer the transistors are together, the quicker the signals travel from one transistor to the next, hence the CPU operates more quickly. The change from 8-bit to 16-bit microprocessors occurred simultaneously with a 50 per cent reduction in transistor geometry which led to a 75 per cent reduction in size.

Further improvements in the types of semi-conductor and methods of producing them have also lead to an improvement in transistor switching speeds. These improvements in production technology can also be applied to the design of the older 8-bit microprocessors which have also led to a 60 per cent improvement in their operating frequency.

Additional Circuit Considerations

One drawback of 16-bit microprocessors is that more interface and peripheral components are required to create a complete microcontroller or microcomputer than an 8-bit microprocessor. The result of this is that 8-bit microprocessors are still preferred for micro-controllers requiring small programs and simple input and output (I/O) operations. For microcomputers with large programs and a minimum of I/O operations, 16-bit microprocessors are preferred.

If the requirement is for small programs with a lot of I/O or large programs with complex I/O requirements then the individual requirements need to be considered in order to select the most suitable type of microprocessor.

Summary

The result of all these improvements is an increase in the speed of execution of programs of between 5 and 10 times, when comparing 8- and 16-bit microprocessors. This, in turn, has allowed many more useful systems to be created which were dependent on this level of performance being achieved before they could be realistically implemented.

2.2   PROGRAMMER'S MODEL OF A MICROPROCESSOR AND MEMORY ADDRESSING MODES

The programmer's model of a microprocessor is a description of the **registers** that can be directly manipulated by a program. Registers are similar to memory locations, except that they are contained within the CPU, as shown in *Figure 2.11*, have high speed access and some additional special functions.

The registers available for each particular microprocessor, and the special functions they perform, com-

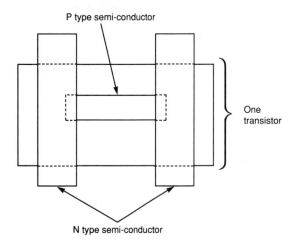

P type semi-conductor

One transistor

N type semi-conductor

Figure 2.10   Semi-conductor patterns to make transistors

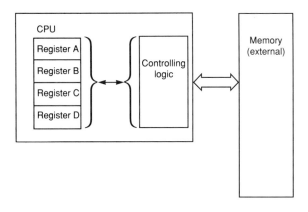

Figure 2.11 Register level of a microprocessor

pletely describe the operation of the microprocessor, as far as the programmer is concerned. The internal architecture and other hardware functions which comprise the microprocessor are invisible to the programmer and have little influence on the program. The only time it is necessary to consider the hardware of the microprocessor is when there are programs which must perform certain actions within a fixed period of time. There are two main categories of such programs:

(a) Interrupt response time;
(b) Speed of execution of certain program fragments.

These are known as time-critical or real-time programs. With **interrupt response time**, it may be important that the program performs specified actions within a given time period from the start of the interrupt. This is affected by the time taken to proceed from the interrupt to the correct **interrupt service routine**. This is called the **interrupt latency** and is very much hardware dependent. A knowledge of the hardware in these circumstances may enable the interrupt response to be within the specified period.

The execution of time-critical program fragments, such as timing loops, is dependent upon the internal architecture and hardware as these affect the speed of program execution. The speed of execution is determined by a variety of parameters such as:

(a) Number of clock pulses for each instruction;
(b) Time taken for each clock pulse;
(c) Memory and I/O access times.

The number of **clock pulses** required by each instruction is determined by the internal architecture of the microprocessor and cannot be altered by the programmer. This information is available to the programmer by reading the microprocessor data sheets and programming manuals. A program fragment can have its

time of execution calculated in terms of the clock cycles required.

General Functions of Registers

The registers within a microprocessor can be separated into three main groupings, related to their usage within programs: (a) general purpose; (b) address generation; (c) CPU control.

General purpose. General purpose registers, as the name suggests, can be used for most operations, and can be used as the source or destination of data. They can be used to temporarily store data values, which may have logical operations performed on them. These registers commonly use the first few letters of the alphabet (A, B, C, D, E) to identify them. The registers usually have the same number of bits as the data bus of the microprocessor, to enable quick and simple transfers of data.

Address generation. The larger number of memory locations and the use of segmentation enable a much greater variety of memory address generation techniques to be used. As the memory system uses 20 or more bits, then these registers either have to be longer than the general registers (i.e. 20 or more bits) in order to represent the address completely or, more commonly, two or more registers are combined to form an address of the required bit length. These are then maintained during each instruction in special temporary registers, which are not accessible directly by the programmer, and hence are invisible.

If the address registers are of a different length, or perform some special address generation function, then they often cannot be used as general registers. If two or more registers are combined to generate the address, then some of the address registers can be used as general registers.

The **instruction pointer** register contains information which is used to calculate the address of the next instruction. Depending on the type of address calculation used, the instruction pointer will have the same number of bits as the address system or if segmentation is implemented then two or more registers are used, and it will point indirectly to the next instruction.

The value contained in the instruction pointer is automatically updated when the present instruction has been fetched from memory to point to the next instruction. This enables instructions to be of a varying number of bytes which is a feature used to save program memory space.

If a non-pipelined microprocessor is being used, then the instruction pointer points to the next instruction that is going to be executed. However, if a pipelined architecture is used which can pre-fetch instructions before they are executed, it will point to the next instruction to be fetched from memory. Depending upon the size of the internal instruction queue implemented in the pipelined microprocessor, the instruction pointed at may be several instructions in front of the one being executed presently. This is demonstrated in *Figure 2.12*.

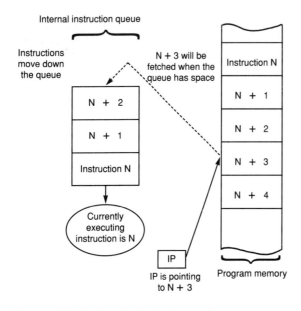

Figure 2.12   Pipelined instruction pointer

This is generally not a problem, and is invisible to the user. The only time it may cause some difficulty is when using an emulator (see Chapter 6).

The instruction pointer should not be directly altered by the user as its value is determined by the sequence of instructions being executed. The only time a programmer has to have control of its value is when starting to execute a program, to ensure that it is pointing to the beginning of the program. In the rest of the program, the programmer has only indirect control by using instructions which automatically change the instruction pointer to get to a new bit of the program.

CPU Control

There is usually a register in a microprocessor which contains information about two functions, the **CPU status and control**; this is called the **flag register**, or sometimes the machine status word.

The CPU status and control register is a register which is comprised of indicators, called flags, that are one bit long. This allows them to have two states, true or false. These are sometimes known as being set (logic 1) or not set (logic 0). This enables them to be used in Boolean logic functions.

The register usually has the same number of bits as the data system and the general registers so that it can be transferred to or from a general register, where alterations to its values can be made. Usually there are instructions to alter individual flags to a specific value, for example the 8086 instructions:

STI   set interrupt flag
CLI   clear interrupt flag

This register is used to perform two different functions, to indicate the status of various parameters within the microprocessor, and to control the manner in which certain instructions execute.

Status Operations

Status operations can be split into two different types, temporary and long-term.

Long-term **status flags** indicate to the CPU various parameters that are in force throughout program execution. For example, there may be a flag to indicate when the CPU is to operate in a multi-user mode, or perhaps a flag to indicate whether string operations are to increment automatically or decrement the memory pointers at the end of every data transfer. The state of such flags can be altered by specific instructions which determine the status of a particular flag, after which the new status is used by the CPU for all future activity until another programmed change.

Temporary status flags may be affected by the instruction presently being executed, and indicate the status of the result. These status flags usually include:

(a) **Zero flag**: this is set to a logic 1 if the result of the instruction is zero;

(b) **Non-zero flag**: this is set to a logic 1 if the result of the instruction is not zero;

(c) **Overflow flag**: this is set to a logic 1 if the result of the instruction is a number greater than that represented by the register length;

(d) **Carry flag**: this is set to a logic 1 if the result of the instruction causes a logic 1 to be transferred from the most significant bit (MSB) of the register, and is not the same as the overflow flag;

(e) **Sign flag**: this is set to a logic 1 if the MSB of the result is a logic 1; this indicates a negative number when performing 2's complement arithmetic, but can also be used as a general check on the logic value of the MSB of the register.

The zero and non-zero flags cannot both have the same logic state as this would not be logically possible, and some microprocessors only have one of these two, with the other flag being deduced when required.

Some instructions do not affect any flags, so that their status is carried over from preceding instructions which did affect them. In addition, other instructions only affect the status of some of the flags, with the remaining flags being unchanged.

Control Operations

The status flags can be used to control the flow of program execution, as there are instructions called **conditional jumps**, which divert the flow of instructions if a selected status flag is set, as in *Figure 2.13*.

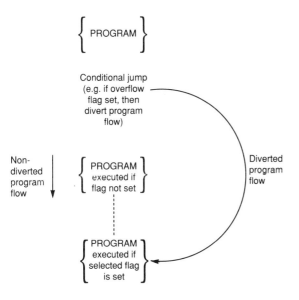

Figure 2.13 Control operations

This allows the operation of the program to be altered by testing the selected flag status at specified points in the program, and altering the program flow at those points. This enables adaptable programs to be produced which are much more useful and flexible.

By using operations which alter the status flags before a conditional jump, the program flow can be altered dynamically. That is, one execution of the program may produce one result, while a later execution with different data may result in different flag settings at important points in the program. Conditional jumps can be used to alter the program flow, see *Figure 2.14*

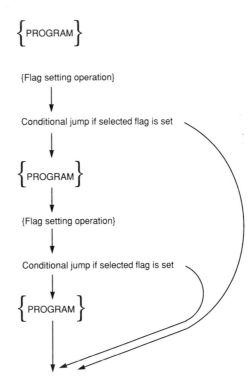

Figure 2.14 Multiple conditional jumps

The Memory Addressing Modes

When the programmer is accessing memory locations, there are a variety of different techniques for generating the required address, each of which is suited to a particular set of situations.

Immediate data. If the data values are fixed and of a limited length, usually one or two bytes, then immediate data avoids having to access data memory at all, by including the data as part of the instruction. Then, when the instruction is fetched from program memory as part of the normal program instruction fetch cycle, the data is immediately available. This is not really an addressing technique, but the end result of obtaining a data value in one of the user-accessible registers is equivalent.

Direct addressing. The simplest form of **memory addressing** is to include the address of the required memory location in the instruction. Then during program execution the address is fetched along with the instruction and forms the address of the memory location to be accessed. The data value contained in the specified memory location is transferred to the microprocessor so that it can be used in the program. This has the advantage that the value stored in the memory location has the potential to be changed and is therefore a data variable. In the immediate data mode the data value cannot be altered as it is part of the instruction, and is therefore regarded as a constant.

The technique is useful for addressing a small number of known memory locations or for accessing memory locations which are connected to input and output devices as in *Figure 2.15*, called memory mapped I/O. The addresses of memory mapped I/O locations are fixed by the hardware and are therefore particularly suitable for direct addressing as they will not change during program execution.

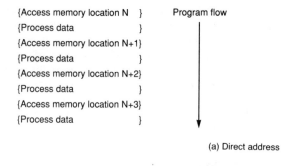

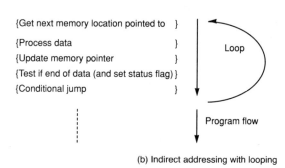

(a) Direct address

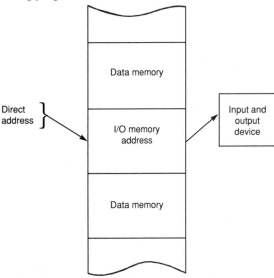

Figure 2.15   Memory mapped input and output

The disadvantage of this technique is that the data memory locations cannot be relocated. This prevents the use of such programs in multi-user environments, unless special methods are used for handling the memory locations addressed in this way. Direct addressing is unsuitable for accessing many address locations as each address has to be specifically encoded into the instruction, see *Figure 2.16*, which can make the program much larger than necessary. *Figure 2.16* illustrates that for only a few memory locations direct addressing may be preferred, but that for three or more locations, a looping technique using indirect addressing would be preferred.

Indirect addressing.   When accessing large numbers of different memory locations a looping technique should be used where memory address must not be encoded within the instruction, but must be obtained indirectly and must be alterable.

(b) Indirect addressing with looping

Figure 2.16   Memory addressing

These requirements are met by using a register to store the memory address. The value in the register can then be obtained by the program, put into the selected register and the indirect memory access made, as illustrated in *Figure 2.17*. The looping technique of *Figure 2.16* then becomes easier to understand, as illustrated in *Figure 2.18*.

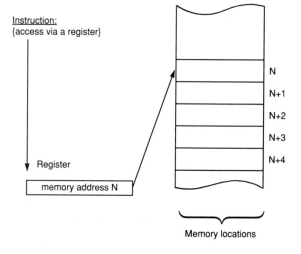

Figure 2.17   Indirect addressing

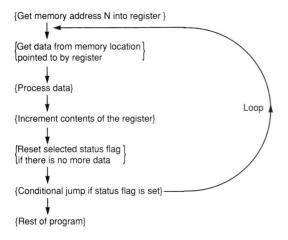

Figure 2.18 Looping using indirect addressing

More complex methods of memory address generation can be obtained by using two or more registers and a constant, which are then combined in some manner. This allows memory location addresses to be generated in a variety of flexible ways. Specific memory locations are accessed by placing the address into the register and performing an indirect access. Indirect accessing allows the memory locations to be relocated anywhere in the available memory rather than at specific locations, as with direct addressing. This is achieved through the use of segmentation by altering the segment address. Programs only infrequently alter segment addresses and it is relatively quick and easy to relocate a block of data memory locations, or even the entire program by altering the segment address.

The direct addressing technique may still be preferred if only one or two locations are to be accessed.

Summary

The programmer's model enables programs to be written using the low level language of the microprocessor, that is the assembly language, without having to know anything about the hardware or internal architecture. However, if there is a real-time speed requirement, a knowledge of the hardware which influences speed of execution is required.

There are three main techniques for obtaining data values: immediate, when the data is known and fixed, direct, when the memory address is known and fixed, and indirect, if the memory address is to be changeable or there are many of them to be accessed. Each has its own particular advantages and disadvantages and the

programmer chooses the method best suited to the program.

2.3 PROGRAMMER'S MODEL OF THE 8086 AND ITS ADDRESSING MODES

The 8086 was Intel's first 16-bit microprocessor and was designed to incorporate the features described in the previous section of this chapter, and provided an increase in performance of between 4 and 10 times that of the 8-bit 8080A. It also provided between 3 and 7 times the performance of the 8085A which is an enhanced version of the 8080A.

The instruction set of the 8086 was designed to be upwards compatible from the 8080A, as shown in *Figure 2.19*. As a result of this each 8080A instruction can be converted directly into one or more 8086 instructions to perform the equivalent operation. This provides an easy upgrade path for all 8080A-based software to 16-bit microprocessors. This protects any investment made in 8080A programs as discussed earlier.

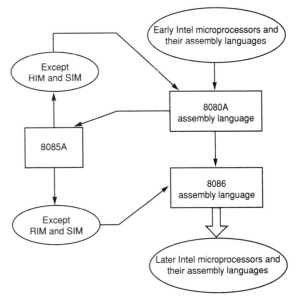

Figure 2.19 Upwards compatibility

The 8085A, which was also upwards compatible with the 8080A apart from the Serial Port and the RIM and SIM instructions, also has upwards compatibility with the 8086, see *Figure 2.19*. Upwards compatibility means a one-way conversion only, and 8086 instructions cannot always be converted to 8080A or 8085A instructions. However, there is virtually no demand for this to be done so that it is not a problem.

The following sections describe the programmer's model of the 8086 as well as the memory addressing calculation techniques.

Segmentation

Segmentation is an integral part of multi-user computer systems and software, and has been implemented in the 8086 microprocessor. This has been achieved by using a **segment register** to hold the base address of the segment, and from this an **offset pointer** which points to the physical memory location being accessed.

Memory addressing using segmentation. The segment address is 20 bits long as the 8086 has a 20-bit physical address bus, of which 16 bits are contained in the segment register with the remaining least significant four bits always assumed to be zero. The value in the segment register forms what is known as the **base address** of the segment, that is the bottom of the segment. The offset is then added to the value on the segment register to form the address pointed to. The offset value is 16 bits long, so that the maximum size of a segment is $2^{16} = 65\,356$ locations.

The offset is the part of the address that is directly produced and manipulated by programs. Segment registers which contain the segment base address cannot be directly controlled in the same way. The offsets are relative to the value in the segment register, so that changing the location of the program means that only the segment register value has to be changed. All offset addresses remain unchanged and are still valid. This makes the program easily relocatable.

If the offset is incremented to a value greater than 65 356, the overflow does not cause the value of the segment register to be changed. Instead, the overflow is ignored and the offset wraps round to the beginning of the segment. Therefore, to use segments greater than 64 kbytes, the user must ensure that the program changes the value in the segment register before the end of the segment is reached. This will also affect the value of the offset. The segment base address can start at any address divisible by 16 (with no remainder) so there could be several segments within a small area of memory. This creates 4096 ($= 2^{12}$) different logical addresses (segment and offset) for every physical location (20 bits) due to the multiple overlapping of adjacent segments.

8086 segment registers. The available memory is divided into four symbolic types: code, data, stack and extra data. The **code segment** contains the program code presently being executed, and the base address is

maintained in the CS register. The **data segment** contains any data values stored in memory that the program contained in the code segment will operate on. The base address is maintained in the data segment register. The **stack segment** contains the area of memory set aside to be used as the stack (this concept is explained later). The base address is maintained in the stack segment register. The **extra segment** can be used as a second data segment allowing twice as much data to be accessed, or is used when string operations are performed. The base address is maintained in the ES register.

8086 Offset Pointers

Offset wrap around. The offset pointers can consist of several registers and a constant in complex combinations. These combinations can create numbers greater than can be represented by 16 bits, that is, greater than 65 356. However, any overflow is lost and the offset pointer wraps around to the beginning of the segment, see *Figure 2.20*.

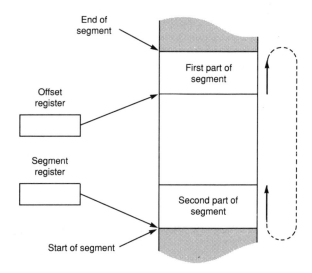

Figure 2.20 Wrap round of segments

Example: Offset Calculation

Assume that: Register 1 = 0F002H, Register 2 = 00FFFH. Then the offset = Register 1 + Register 2:

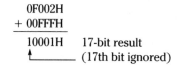

    0F002H
+ 00FFFH
‾‾‾‾‾‾‾‾‾
  10001H   17-bit result
           (17th bit ignored)

Therefore, the offset has wrapped around to the beginning of the segment to form an offset of 0001H. The segment register value is not affected by the overflow into the 17th bit.

Physical address wrap around. In addition, if the segment base address and the offset create a number larger than that which can be represented by 20 bits, then the overflow is lost, and the address wraps around to the beginning of physical memory.

Example: Different Logical Addresses

As already mentioned, each physical memory address value has 4096 different logical addresses formed by combining different values of segment base address and offset. For example, the physical address 014562H can be produced from:

Segment base address	Offset
012340H	2222H
014560H	0002H
010560H	4002H
005670H	0FFF2H
014000H	00562H

All produce the same physical address of 014562H.

Special offset registers. Two of the segments, the code segment and the stack segment, have special offset registers associated with them, whilst the other segments use more general purpose offset registers.

The Instruction Pointer (IP)

The **instruction pointer** contains the offset from the code segment base address of the next instruction to be fetched into the CPU. This is not necessarily the same as the next instruction to be executed due to the effect of pipe-lining. The instruction pointer is controlled by the CPU and is updated automatically at the end of the instruction fetch.

Example

Assume that: CS = 0FFEEH, IP = 00062H. Then the segment base address is:

CS × 10H = 0FFEEH × 010H = 0FFEE0H

Therefore, the physical memory address of the next instruction to be fetched is:

$$
\begin{array}{r}
0FFEE0H \\
+ \quad 00062H \\
\hline
0FFF42H
\end{array}
$$

The only time it is necessary to be able to control the value of the instruction pointer and also CS is when the program is started. Then CS and the instruction pointer must be initialised to point to the beginning of the program. The CPU automatically initialises CS and the instruction pointer when power is first appiied to the microprocessor. The user must then ensure that there is a program ready to execute at the power-on reset address. For the 8086 this is formed by the CS register being initialised to CS = 0FFFFH and the Instruction Pointer register to IP = 00000H.

Therefore the segment base address is:

0FFFFH × 010H = 0FFFF0H

and the power-on reset address is:

$$
\begin{array}{r}
0FFFF0H \\
+ \quad 00000H \\
\hline
0FFFF0H
\end{array}
$$

This is just 16 bytes below the top of the available memory (see *Figure 2.21*) and therefore one of the first instructions contained within those 16 bytes must be a jump to the beginning of the program.

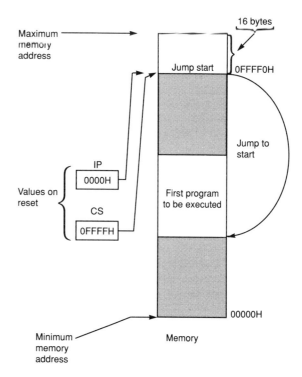

Figure 2.21 Power-on reset

Stack Segment

As with all segments, there is the **stack segment register**, SS, and the offset register, called the **stack pointer**, SP. The stack is a continuous sequence of read/write memory used to contain temporary variables such as return addresses from subroutine calls. The SP is also known as the **top of stack**, TOS. On the 8086 the stack 'grows' downwards towards low memory when items are added (see *Figure 2.22*) and 'shrinks' towards high memory when items are removed.

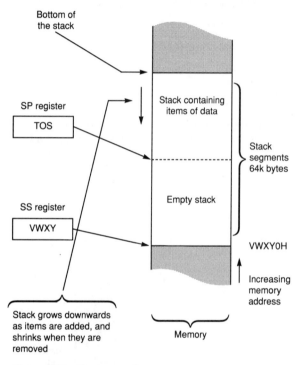

Figure 2.22 Stack operation

Stack operations. The stack pointer is controlled by stack instructions which automatically increment or decrement the SP by 2, as all stack operations are performed on words. Also the stack pointer is not normally controlled by the programmer, although it may be necessary to alter the value in the stack pointer to set aside some memory for temporary variables during program operations.

Data Segments

The **data segments** have a wider variety of methods of creating the offset values as the offset generation method is under the direct control of the program. This means that flexible and powerful methods of accessing

memory locations are available to allow the programmer to choose the most efficient technique.

There are four registers which can be used in the data offset calculations. They are all 16-bit registers, which can also be used as general purpose registers. If an index value is used in an effective address calculation, it can be obtained using the BX or BP or SI or DI register, see *Figure 2.23*, and is called single-indexed addressing. Double-indexed addressing can also be used when a register pair is selected from the same four registers. However, for double-indexed addressing one of the register pairs must be a base register, which are those

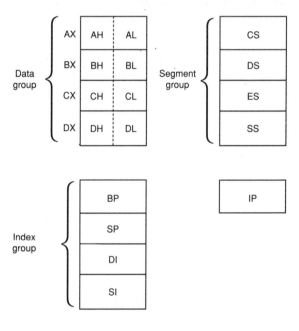

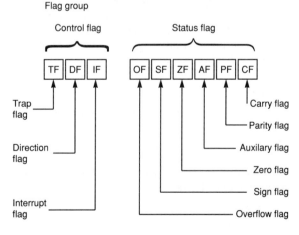

Figure 2.23 Complete programmer's model

registers beginning with a B (BX and BP), and the second register must be an index register which is those registers ending in an I (DI or SI).

This type of addressing is sometimes known as based indexing as well as double indexed, and there are four valid pairs:

[BX] [DI]
[BX] [SI]
[BP] [DI]
[BP] [SI]

The registers used, and the constant value, are specified by the instruction and are optional. There may be only a constant or only an index and this allows a flexible method of producing memory address values that meets most programming requirements.

As two 16-bit registers and a 16-bit constant can be added together, there is much more opportunity for an overflow into the 17th bit of the offset to occur. This would be ignored and cause a wrap-around to the beginning of the segment. This is not usually a problem as most data arrays are relatively small containing less than 1000 elements. However, the programmer needs to be aware that the largest data array that can be accessed as a single entity is 65 536 bytes long (i.e. 16-bit offset). Data structures larger than this would need to be accessed as two different segments.

The data segment register is DS or ES. The DS segment register is the default in data address calculations and does not have to be specified in the instruction. If the ES register is to be used as the data segment this has to be specifically encoded into the instruction using a prefix override. An example is shown below:

MOV AX, [BX] [SI]+7
               constant
               double indexed
               DS assumed

MOV AX, ES: [BX] [SI]+7
               constant
               double indexed
               ES specified in the instruction

The other segment registers, CS and SS, can also be used in this way so that accesses into the code segment and stack segment for data values can be made.

When BP is used in single-index addressing the default segment is the stack segment SS, and not the data segment DS as might be expected. This is because BP has a special usage and can be used to reserve an area on the stack for temporary data storage. This is particularly useful for structured high level languages which use procedures. The variables local to the procedure are only required while the procedure is executing, and using the stack to hold these temporary variables avoids having to specify a specific area of memory for that use.

The 8086 has no built-in method of identifying when parts of the memory space contain code, stack or data, so that all memory can be treated as data by the data-manipulating instructions. The division into different types is made when the segment registers are initialised by the program. It is the programmer's responsibility to ensure that all memory accesses to code, stack or data, are made to the memory locations containing the correct types.

General Registers

In addition to the segment and index registers, there are general purpose registers in the programmer's model, and these also have some default uses given below:

AX (16 bits)   can be accessed as AH (high 8 bits of AX) and AL (low 8 bits of AX)

BX (16 bits)   can be accessed as BH (high 8 bits of BX) and BL (low 8 bits of BX)

CX (16 bits)   can be accessed as CH (high 8 bits of CX) and CL (low 8 bits of CX)

DX (16 bits)   can be accessed as DH (high 8 bits of DX) and DL (low 8 bits of DX)

Note that BX is also an index register. Each of the 16-bit general registers can also be accessed as two 8-bit registers by identifying the register with the letters H for high byte and L for low byte, to indicate which 8 bits, see below.

AX   16-bit register
AH   Top eight bits of AX
AL   Bottom eight bits of AX

Implied uses of general registers. Each of the four general registers, AX, BX, CX and DX, also have at least one implied use. This means that the register is used in an instruction but is not always specifically identified, and that no other register can be used for that purpose. The implied use is identified from the first letter used to identify the register as outlined below:

AX: Accumulator, used for 16-bit multiply and divide instructions, and 16-bit input/output instructions

BX: Base Pointer, and also translate (see instruction set)

CX: Counter for string and loop operations

DX: Data operations, also used for 16-bit multiply and divide instructions, and as the Input and Output offset register

In addition, there are some implied 8-bit register uses:

AH: Used for 8-bit multiply and divide instructions

AL: Used for 8-bit multiply and divide instructions,

8-bit Input and Output, translate and decimal arithmetic

CL: Counter for shift and rotate instructions (see instruction set)

String Operations

String operations involve the transfer of bytes of data from one area of memory to another in a single operation. String operations require the use of two memory pointers, one to indicate the source of the data and one to indicate the destination. The default source segment is the data segment accessed by the DS register and using the SI (source index) register to form the offset. The default destination segment is the extra segment and uses the DI (destination index) register to form the offset.

Machine Status Word, or Flag Register

The remaining register is the **machine status word**, or **flag register**, containing the status and control flags. There are 6 status flags and 3 control flags, as illustrated in *Figure 2.23* which are contained in a 16-bit flag register.

Control Flags

As the name suggests, the control flags affect the way in which the instructions execute, and do not indicate the results of instruction executions. The **interrupt enable** flag, IF, allows the hardware-generated interrupts, except for NMI, to be disabled by the **clear interrupt instruction**, CLI, until the next **set interrupt instruction**, STI. The **direction flag**, DF, is used with string operations automatically, either to increment or decrement the memory pointers used. The last control flag, called the **trap flag**, TF, is used to single-step through a program during the testing stages of software development. It operates by generating an interrupt after every instruction. Then when the interrupt service routine is started the trap flag is cleared so that it will execute. The **interrupt return instruction**, IRET, at the end of the interrupt service routine then restores the original value of TF. This then allows one more instruction to execute before generating another interrupt and hence repeats the cycle.

Complete Programmer's Model. Incorporating all these elements leads to the complete programmer's model of the 8086 illustrated in *Figure 2.23*; all the implied uses have been explained. Examples of using the programmers model are given in the sections explaining the instruction set.

Although there are only 9 flags, they are contained in a 16-bit flag register, with the 7 remaining locations being undefined. The undefined flag locations may be used by later versions and generations of microprocessors. There is a direct correlation between the flags of the 8-bit 8080/5 and the 16-bit 8086/8 microprocessors (see *Figure 2.24*) so that when converting from 8080/5 assembly language to 8086/8 assembly language, the flag operations would require the minimum number of alterations to produce an equivalent result.

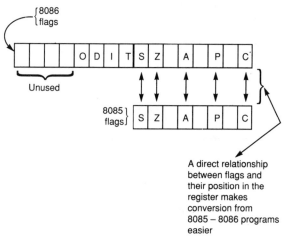

Figure 2.24 The flag registers of the 8085 and 8086

The flags can be divided into two main types: status and control flags. **Status flags** give some indication about the result of previously executed instructions and this can be used to affect the local execution of future instructions. That is, the status flags only affect the next one or two instructions to be executed. This is because most of the instructions affect the values of the status flags and as instructions are executed the flag values are frequently changing.

However, **control flags** are not affected by the results of past instructions but instead themselves affect the operation of future instructions, although generally only a small number of specific instructions are affected. For example, the direction flag only affects string instructions. These flags have a global effect and all future executions of the affected flags will be changed. The values of the control flags have to be changed by specific instructions such as:

CLI   Clear Interrupt flag
STI   Set Interrupt flag

and are therefore under direct program control.

The control flags. These involve the **direction flag** (D), **interrupt flag** (I) and **trap flag** (T)

D: 1 – Auto decrement of address,
    0 – Auto increment of address (when used)
I: 1 – Enables maskable interrupts.
    0 – Disables maskable interrupts.
T: 0 – Disables single-stepping of instructions.
    1 – Enables single-stepping of instructions by generating an INT 01H after every instruction.

The interrupt flag has no effect on non-maskable and internal interrupts.

Status Flags

C – *Carry Flag*: This flag is set if there is a carry out of or borrow into the high order bits of the 8- or 16-bit register or memory location;

P – *Parity Flag*: This flag is set if there is an even number of ones in the destination;

A – *Auxiliary Flag*: This flag is set if there has been a carry out of the low four bits into the high four bits, or vice versa for borrow;

Z – *Zero Flag*: This flag is set if the result of an arithmetic operation is zero;

S – *Sign Flag*: This flag is set if the high order bit of the destination or result is 1;

O – *Overflow Flag*: This flag is set if the most significant bit of the result has been lost due to an overflow – for 8-bit registers or memory locations this is bit 7, for 16-bit registers or memory locations this is bit 15;

U – *Undefined*: These flags have not yet been allocated a function: future generations of the Intel microprocessors may make use of these bit flag positions.

The Interrupt Structure

There are four different types of **interrupts** within the 8086 which are all handled in the same way, once the priority decision has been made. The priority of the interrupts becomes important if two or more interrupts occur simultaneously. This happens if subsequent interrupts occur during the interrupt latency period. The interrupt latency period is the time between the interrupt signal being received at the microprocessor and the start of the **interrupt service subroutine**. This delay is caused by the necessity of the presently executing instruction to complete and the interrupt service subroutine to be called.

By prioritising interrupts, a higher priority interrupt which occurs after a lower priority interrupt will be serviced first. Interrupts which have the same priority will be serviced in the order in which they were received. The priority of the interrupts is given below:

Interrupt	*Priority*
(a) Internal	Highest priority
(b) Non-maskable	Next highest
(c) External (if enabled)	Next to lowest
(d) Single step	Lowest priority

There is a maximum of 256 different interrupts, numbered 0 to 255, each of which, once generated, creates a vector address which is four times the interrupt number. Therefore interrupt 4 creates a vector address of $4 \times 4 = 16 = 010H$. Adjacent interrupts are separated by four bytes with the four bytes immediately above each vector address containing the address of the interrupt service subroutine for that interrupt. The first two bytes contain the offset address value to be put into the instruction pointer, and the next two bytes contain the segment address to go into the code segment register. All the interrupt service subroutines replace CS and IP when they are initiated.

The CPU checks for any valid interrupts after every instruction, in the order of priority, so that internals are checked first, followed by the **non-maskable interrupt** (NMI), then the external interrupts, and finally single-step. The first two types of interrupts, internal and NMI, cannot be stopped, which is why they are called non-maskable. The internals are non-maskable interrupts generated by the program using the INT instruction; the NMI is a hardware-initiated interrupt external to the microprocessor and program. The remaining two types, external and single step, can be prevented from affecting program execution, and are called **maskable interrupts**. The external interrupts use handshaking and require the presence of a programmable interrupt controller. They are enabled or disabled by the interrupt flag using the STI and CLI instructions.

The single-step interrupt is automatically generated by the microprocessor after every instruction if the trap flag, TF, is set. This flag has to be altered by manipulating the appropriate bit position in the flag register with general-purpose bit-manipulation instructions, and does not have specific instructions to control it.

Type	Source	Interrupt vector range	Maskable?	Comments
INT	internal	0–255	no	
NMI	external	2	no	
maskable	external	0–255	yes	Requires PIC
single-step	internal	1	yes	Used to single-step through programs for testing purposes.

If an external interrupt is made using the interrupt request signal, INTR, then an interrupt acknowledge is generated and the flags and the current values of CS and IP are saved on the stack. CS and IP are then updated with the address of the interrupt service subroutine fetched from the interrupt vector address, and external and single-step interrupts are disabled by resetting the appropriate bits in the flag register. The interrupt service subroutine is then executed and when the IRET instruction is encountered, the CS and IP and flag values are popped from the stack and the interrupted program is resumed. The complete interrupt sequence is illustrated in *Figure 2.25*.

Internal interrupts. These are generated internally from a special instruction:

    INT   *n*

where *n* is the interrupt number from 0 to 255. The value of *n* is encoded into the instruction and the interrupt acknowledge bus cycles are not required. *Figure 2.26* indicates which interrupts have been dedicated to 8086 actions by Intel and which have been reserved for future use.

The first five interrupts are dedicated to specific 8086 functions and should not be used for any other purpose in 8086 programs.

Reserved interrupts. *Types 5 to 31* have been reserved by Intel for future extensions to the 8086 family of microprocessors. It is advisable not to use these to ensure that future versions of the microprocessor will be compatible with existing software.

Type 0. The CPU itself generates this type of interrupt after a divide instruction (IDIV or DIV) has been executed, if the quotient has more bits than the destination register.

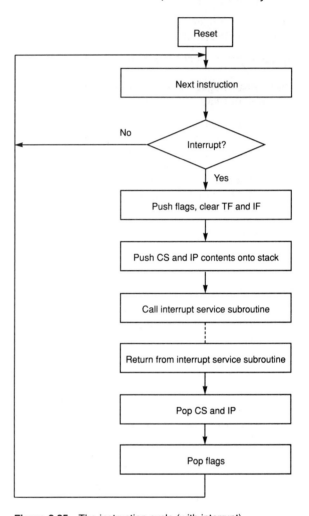

Figure 2.25 The instruction cycle (with interrupt)

Type 1. The single-step function is built into the 8086 and is turned on by setting the TF flag. When the trap flag is set, a type 1 interrupt is generated after every instruction. By writing an appropriate interrupt service subroutine, the instructions can be single stepped for test purposes. After an interrupt, the TF flag is always cleared so that the single step interrupt service subroutine is not single stepped itself. At the end of the subroutine the original values of the flags are restored into the flag register and single stepping recommences. The trap flag is set by OR-ing flag register contents with 0100H, and cleared by AND-ing with OFEFFH.

Type 2. This is generated by an interrupt signal on the NMI pin of the CPU, and as the name suggests, this

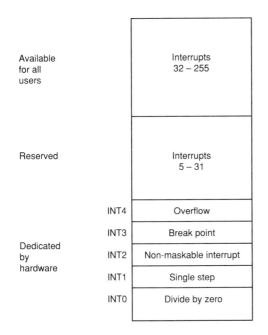

Figure 2.26 Internal interrupts

interrupt cannot be masked off. This subroutine can also be called from a program by using:

```
INT   02H   ;NMI interrupt
```

Type 3. The type 3 interrupt is a special one-byte instruction which was designed to be used to implement breakpoint functions into program debuggers. Being only one byte long it is easy to insert into a program to cause a jump-out of the normal program execution into a breakpoint interrupt service subroutine, which would allow the registers and memory to be examined.

Type 4. Type 4 interrupts can be called by using INTO, which causes an interrupt if the overflow flag is set. This type of interrupt is designed to be used after any instruction or sequence of instructions in which the occurrence of an overflow would indicate that a fatal program error had occurred. Typical uses would be after arithmetic operations.

Example

```
MUL   AX,BX    ;Critical operation, must not overflow.
INTO           ;If there is an overflow, a type 4
               ;interrupt will be generated, otherwise
               ;nothing will happen.
```

This interrupt could be initiated by the INT 04H instruction although if the ISR interrupt service routine

was implemented to handle overflow situations after arithmetic operations this would not be particularly useful.

Unreserved interrupts. *Types 32 to 255* are not reserved and can be used by the programmer for any purpose. However, some of them have uses defined by other standards such as the IBM PC. This uses some of the unreserved interrupts within its operating system which, because so many people use it, has much software written for it. If these interrupts are used for other purposes the software written for the IBM PC will be unable to execute correctly on it.

External interrupts. The INTR **interrupt request** signal is controlled by a **programmable interrupt controller** (PIC) and provides 8 interrupt inputs. The PIC encodes the interrupts and puts the interrupt number onto the data bus. The INTR signal is used to indicate to the CPU that an interrupt has occurred. *Figure 2.27* shows in outline how a PIC is connected.

If the IF flag is cleared in the microprocessor so that external interrupts are disabled, the state of the INTR signal does not affect the CPU. However if the IF flag is set and external interrupts are enabled, the CPU recognises the request and deals with it. Only currently active external interrupt requests are dealt with as this signal is not latched.

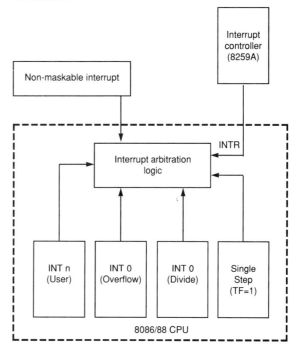

Figure 2.27 Interrupt sources

Time and Function Multiplexed Pins

The 8086 was originally designed to fit into a 40-pin package but the number of facilities and functions required by a 16-bit microprocessor were difficult to implement using only this small number. Therefore, some of the pins were time-multiplexed to carry two different sorts of data, while some pins have two different functions selected by the mode of operation selected.

Time-multiplexed pins. The address and data signals are time-multiplexed onto the same set of pins, see *Figure 2.28*. 16 address signals, A_0–A_{15}, are multiplexed with 16 bits of data, D_0–D_{15}. The resulting 16 signals are known as address data, AD_0–AD_{15}. The remaining 4 bits of the 20 bit address, A_{16}–A_{19}, are not time multiplexed with data but with internal status information.

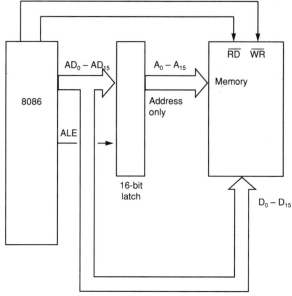

Figure 2.29   Simple multiplexing scheme

In order to be connected to standard memory and I/O components, the address data signals must be de-multiplexed and there are signals which control this function. The **address latch enable** (ALE) saves the 16-bit address into an external register, as in *Figure 2.29*. To transfer data in the correct direction at the correct time in the bus cycle, a combination of four signals is used, as in *Figure 2.30*. The two signals, DT/R (data transmit/receive) and DEN (data enable), control the direction, and RD and WR control the time of transfer. *Figure 2.31* (page 34) illustrates a fully buffered address and data bus system.

Function-multiplexed pins. As well as using time-multiplexed pins, the 8086 has function-multiplexed pins, where the function of eight pins is changed, depending upon the signal applied to the mode pin. This provides two modes of operation for the 8086, one called minimum mode when the 8086 is operating as a simple 16-bit microcontroller, and maximum mode when the 8086 implements many additional features, such as bus control, that are required by microcomputers.

The mode of operation is only tested when power is first applied to cause a power-on reset and cannot be changed during program execution. This is not a problem as the remainder of the system hardware has to be designed to implement only one of the modes. This will either be a microcontroller (minimum mode) or a microcomputer (maximum mode).

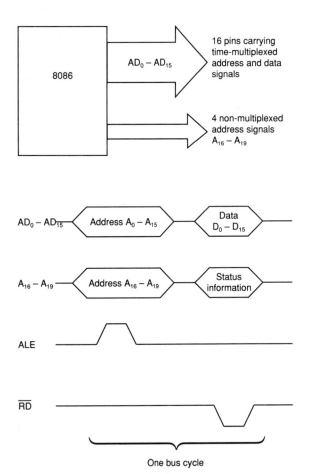

Figure 2.28   Multiplexed data and addresses with timing diagrams

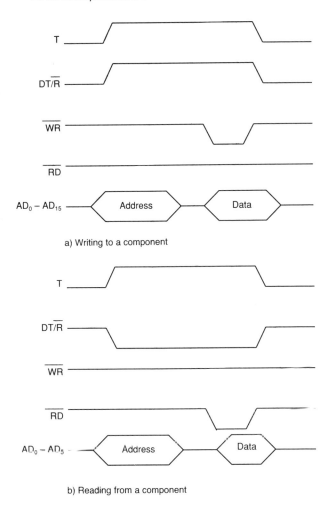

a) Writing to a component

b) Reading from a component

Figure 2.30 Data transfer between component and microprocessor

Minimum Mode Operation

When in minimum mode the 8 signals implement five functions as listed below which are illustrated in *Figure 2.32* (page 35):

(a) Bus control (2 signals), HOLD, HOLDA;
(b) De-multiplexing (3 signals), ALE, DT/R, DEN;
(c) Write control (1 signal), WR;
(d) Memory and I/O operation separation (1 signal), M/IO;
(e) Interrupt acknowledgement (1 signal), INTA.

Maximum Mode Operation

When in maximum mode the signals implement four functions, see *Figure 2.33* (page 35), some of which require additional decoding components. These are:

(a) Bus status indicators (3 signals), S_0, S_1, S_2;
(b) Bus arbitration (2 signals), RG, GTO;
(c) Bus locking (1 signal), LOCK;
(d) Queue status indicators (2 signals), QS_0, QS_1.

Three of the functions provide an enhanced and sophisticated address and data bus system. Therefore, the signals which previously controlled the de-multiplexing and buffering (ALE, DT/R, DEN, WR) have been replaced by encoded bus status signals (S_0, S_1, S_2). These signals allow the implementation of what is known as the **multibus**, which is a standard address, data and control bus. This bus is microprocessor-independent, although it was primarily designed for use with the Intel range of microprocessors, and allows other products, such as memory boards, to be developed. Because of the standardised bus system the boards can be fitted to any multibus-based microcomputer.

Bus arbitration allows several masters to be connected to a bus system and decides which master should have access to the bus at any one time. This is covered in more detail later.

Bus locking is used to prevent arbitration taking place during program-specified instructions. This therefore prevents other masters from gaining control of the bus system and enables short-term critical bus control program fragments to execute uninterrupted.

The internal queue status indicators are used to enable an external device to keep a track of exactly which instruction the CPU is presently executing. This is required when attempting to follow program execution using emulators or logic analysers. This is used to overcome the problem caused by being able to pre-fetch up to 6 bytes of instructions ahead of the instruction being executed. Because of this the IP register does not always identify the next instruction to be executed. Provided that tracking of the internal instruction queue begins immediately after a RESET, an external device will be able to deduce which instruction is executing. This knowledge may be necessary to obtain synchronisation of some event between two independent devices, such as the 8086 and a coprocessor.

Remaining Signals

There are several remaining signals concerned with power supplies and correct power on reset and initialisation. Other signals of interest are read ($\overline{RD}$) which is used to control the transfer of data from memory and I/O components and Bus High Enable ($\overline{BHE}$) which is part of the physical memory address decoding and is explained in more detail later.

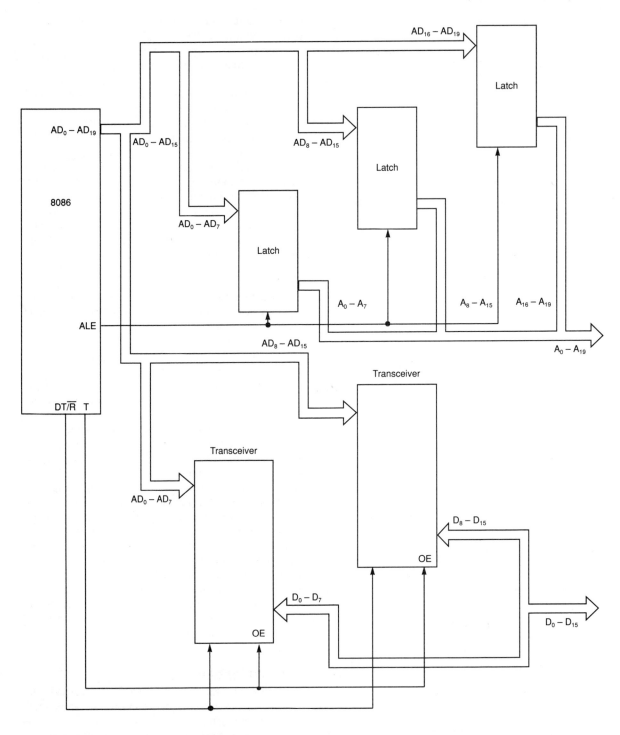

Figure 2.31   A fully-buffered system

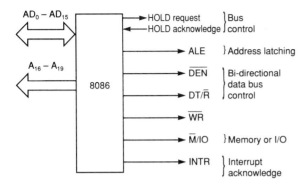

Figure 2.32 Minimum mode 8086

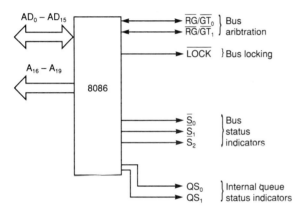

Figure 2.33 Maximum mode 8086

8- and 16-bit Versions of the 8086

So far, only the 8086 with a 16-bit data bus has been discussed, but there is an alternative microprocessor with essentially the same internal architecture, called the 8088, which has an 8-bit data bus as shown in *Figure 2.34*.

The 8-bit data bus is multiplexed with the bottom 8 bits of the address bus, otherwise the two devices are the same. They will execute the same programs with no changes, in exactly the same way, and obtain exactly the same results. The only difference is that because the 8088 has an 8-bit data bus, data word accesses take two 8-bit bus cycles and therefore programs take longer to execute.

In programs which use large amounts of word data elements, the 8086 may execute programs almost twice as fast as the 8088, whereas, if it is mostly byte data elements, the 8088 can approach within 10 per cent of the performance of an 8086. The difference is due to instructions having to be fetched as bytes instead of words as with the 8086. The 8088 only has a 4-byte instruction queue as this is the optimum size for the 8-bit data bus implemented.

The reason the 8088 was produced is that simpler microcontrollers can be produced with less components. The 8086 has a complex technique for addressing memory as either bytes or words, requiring additional decoding and buffering. The 8088 always accesses memory as bytes and this reduces the number of components required, simplifies the address decoding and allows all 8-bit I/O peripheral and memory components developed for the 8-bit 8080 and 8085 microprocessors to be used with the 8088. The 8086 has more difficulty interfacing with the majority of 8-bit I/O devices, and some components cannot be connected at all.

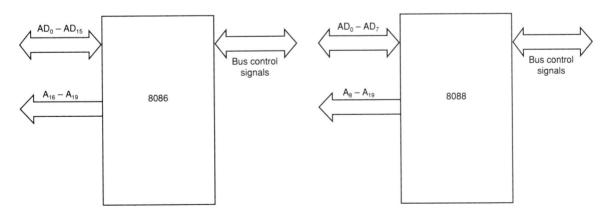

Figure 2.34 8086 and 8088 microprocessors

Summary

The main advantage of the 8086 is that programs will execute much more quickly. Therefore, if a powerful microcomputer is required the 8086 should be used. If a simple microcontroller with the minimum number of components is required which can use readily available and cheap 8-bit I/O peripheral components, then the 8088 should be used.

Physical Memory Organisation

Memory components have an 8-bit data bus, whereas the 8086 has a 16-bit data bus. Therefore two memory components are required so that word accesses can be made, and 8086 memory is organised into two blocks of 512 kbytes called odd and even. A 16-bit word then consists of a byte from the even bank and a byte from the odd bank. The 8086 can access memory as bytes in which case only one bank is accessed.

The two banks should be exactly the same, apart from the bank select signals, AO and BHE. AO enables the even bank as when AO = 0 it must be an even address, and BHE, bus high enable, selects the odd bank. The even bank is connected to the low 8 bits of the data bus, and the odd bank of bytes is connected to the high 8 bits of the data bus, as in *Figure 2.35*.

AO and BHE are independent signals controlled by the 8086 so that both bytes can be accessed simultaneously or one at a time, see the table below.

BHE	AO	*BYTE transferred*
0	0	Both
0	1	Upper byte (odd)
1	0	Lower byte (even)
1	1	None

A 16-bit word starting at an even address consists of the even byte plus the next higher address (odd) byte, and can be accessed in one 16-bit wide data bus cycle, see *Figure 2.36*.

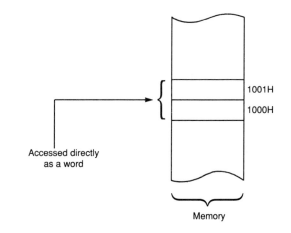

Figure 2.36 Even address word access

However, if the starting address of the word is odd, it cannot be accessed as one word. Instead it has to be accessed as two successive byte accesses, as in *Figure 2.37*, and the bytes must also be swapped over from the low 8 bits of the data bus to the high 8 bits, and vice versa, so that the destination word has the bytes in the correct order. The swapping process is invisible to the user and does not incur any additional time penalties.

The first access reads 1001H and automatically swaps the data to the low byte of the destination word (normally in a register). The second access reads 1002H and automatically swaps the data value into the high byte of

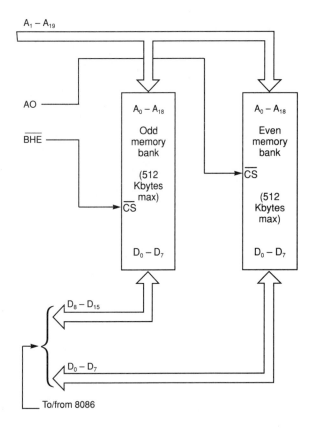

Figure 2.35 Memory addressing of odd and even memory banks

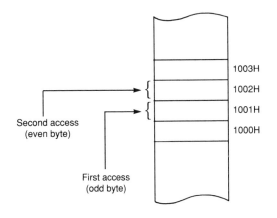

Figure 2.37 Odd address word access

the destination. The process is transparent to the user apart from the time penalty incurred due to the two memory accesses being made.

Increase in Performance over an 8-bit Microprocessor

To give some idea of the increase in performance possible over an 8-bit microprocessor, the equivalent program execution time will be calculated for an 8085. The basic clock frequency of the 8085 is 3 MHz so that one clock cycle takes 0.33 microseconds. The basic clock frequency of the 8086 is 5 MHz so that one clock cycle takes 0.20 microseconds.

8086 Instruction Sequence

A short sequence of instructions which implements a program to count from 0 to 9, will be used to illustrate the internal operation of the queue and of bus activity.

8086 Program

Assembly language		Machine Code	Clocks
	MOV AX,0000H	B80000	4
AGAIN:	INC AX	40	3
	CMP AX,0009H	3D0900	4
	JNZ AGAIN	75FA	16/4
	NOP	90	
	NOP	90	
	NOP	90	
Total = 27 clocks			

8085 Program

	MVI	A,00H	7 clocks
AGAIN:	INR	A	4 clocks
	CPI	09H	7 clocks
	JNZ	AGAIN	10 if jump taken, 7 if not
Total = 28 clocks			

The 8085 is a non-pipelined architecture so that the individual instruction execution periods include the fetching of instructions from memory. The program time for each microprocessor = number of clocks × clock period:

For the 8085 = 28 × 0.33 = 9.24 μs

For the 8086 = 27 × 0.20 = 5.40 μs

In this example, the increase in the speed of execution of the program when transferred from an 8085 to an 8086 is:

$$\frac{9.24 - 5.40}{9.24} \times 100\% = \frac{3.84}{9.24} \times 100\% = 42\%$$

This is not a particularly significant improvement in speed and is due to the basic program operation being performed on 8-bit numbers. If the original program which operated on 16-bit numbers is used, then a much more significant improvement can be identified. 16-bit registers will be used to count from 0 to 9 in the following example.

Revised 8085 Program

Program			Clocks
	LXI	B,0000H	10
AGAIN:	INX	B	6
	MOV	A,B	4
	CPI	00H	7
	JNZ	AGAIN	7/10 (always 7)
	MOV	A,C	4
	CPI	09H	7
	JNZ	AGAIN	7/10 (usually 10).
Total clocks = 55			

In this example, the program time for each microprocessor is:

For the 8085 = 55 × 0.33 = 18.15 μs

For the 8086 = 27 × 0.20 = 5.40 μs

This gives an increase in speed of program execution of:

$$\frac{18.15 - 5.40}{18.5} \times 100\% = \frac{12.75}{18.5} \times 100\% = 70\%$$

which is much more significant and is due to the inherent 8-bit data capacity of the 8085 which results in an inefficient method of handling 16-bit numbers.

It is possible to obtain versions of the 8085 8-bit microprocessor with a clock frequency of 6 MHz which would halve the execution time. However, the 8086 is also available in a 10 MHz clock frequency version, which would restore the balance. Eight-bit microprocessors are also available which have a much better capability for handling 16-bit numbers and the difference in execution of an equivalent program would not be significant. However, the 8086 has an improved performance in most areas in order to produce a sustained instruction execution. 8-bit microprocessors cannot match this performance in every area and a careful selection of the most appropriate device for each problem is helpful, in order to achieve the optimum solution.

Summary

It is necessary to consider the application that the microcomputer or microcontroller is going to be used for, and select the most appropriate device. 16-bit microprocessors are not always better than 8-bit microprocessors.

2.4 THE INSTRUCTION SET OF THE 8086

The 8086 is a **complex instruction set computer** (CISC) and attempts to provide separate and powerful instructions for each type and variation of operation required. For example, the MOV instruction has 28 different variants out of the possible 285 operation codes available. The CISC's aim is to provide the exact instruction necessary to perform the required function in order to produce compact and fast executing programs.

It has been said that a normal programmer will only use 20 per cent of a CISC's instructions in 80 per cent of the programs produced, which was one of the reasons for producing **reduced instruction set computers** (RISCs). For this reason, only 22 of the possible 71 instruction types will be considered in detail, and using these 22 instructions most programs can be written. All the examples in this book use this subset.

Introduction to Simple Subset 8086 Instructions

The number of basic instructions is limited to 71, with each instruction having a variable number of variations, producing approximately 285 possible instructions. Only a small subset of these is necessary to write assembly language programs and these are outlined in the following sections with practical examples and problems. Not all the possible variations of each instruction are explained. The remainder of the instructions are listed in the latter part of this chapter. Selected instructions are examined in detail in later chapters when their operation is essential to understanding some aspect of the 8086 operation.

The MOV Instruction

The MOV **move instruction** is one of the most versatile available and its function is to move a byte or word of data from one location to another. The source and destination can be 8 or 16 bits long, but they must both be the same length. It is not permissible to move an 8-bit source into a 16-bit destination, and it is not possible to move a 16-bit source into an 8-bit destination. The only exception is when immediate data, that is, absolute number values contained within the instruction, is to be moved to a 16-bit destination.

MOV 16-bit destination, 8-bit absolute number value

Depending upon how the programmer specified the 8-bit absolute number the assembler will try to extend it to a 16-bit absolute number by adding leading zeros.

Example

```
8_bit_abs1 EQU 027H    ;An 8- or 16-bit absolute number.
8_bit_abs2 DB 027H     ;A byte memory location.
;
;
MOV   AX, 8_bit_abs1   ;This is allowed as the 8-bit
                       ;value is extended to 16 bits.
MOV   AX, 8_bit_abs2   ;This is not allowed as the
                       ;memory location is defined as a
                       ;byte.
```

There are six possible options:

(a) Move from register to register;
(b) Move immediate data to register;
(c) Move from register to memory;
(d) Move from memory to register;
(e) Move from memory to memory string;
(f) Move immediate data to memory.

The move from memory to memory is called a **string operation** and has a special mnemonic, MOVS, meaning

MOVE STRING. Some assemblers allow this to be extended to indicate whether a byte or word move is intended as this is not always clear from the instruction MOVS.

MOVSB   move string byte
MOVSW   move string word

MOV register to register. The contents of the register on the right-hand side are copied into the register on the left-hand side:

MOV   Reg1, Reg2

The contents of Reg2 remain unchanged and the contents of Reg1 before the move are lost and replaced with a copy of the contents of Reg1. The registers can be any of the 8- or 16-bit registers outlined in the programmer's model, but both registers must be of the same size.

Correct Syntax

MOV   AX, BX   ;16-bit copy from BX to AX,
MOV   CH, BL   ;8-bit copy from BL to CH,

Incorrect Syntax

MOV   AX, BH   ;This instruction is incorrect
                        ;as AX is 16 bits, BH is 8 bits.

The general purpose registers AX, BX, CX and DX, can be used in 8-bit register moves as AH, AL, BH, BL, CH, CL, DH and DL, as well as in 16-bit register moves. The remaining registers SI, DI, BP, SP, IP, CS, DS, ES, and SS can only perform 16-bit register moves.

Example

MOV   AX, 0000H   ;Set segment address to 0000H.
MOV   SS, AX   ;Sets up segment registers at the
                           ;beginning of a program,
MOV   DS, AX   ;in this case all are set to zero so
MOV   ES, AX   ;that all segments overlap same
                           ;64 kbyte of memory. CS is not
                           ;included as this is set by reset to
                           ;0FFFFH or by the operating system to
                           ;point to the beginning of the program.

MOV immediate data to register. This variation on the instruction is to move an immediate data value into a register. The data size is fixed by the register being copied into and the data must match that. Leading zeros can be added to a number to extend it to 16 bits but a 16-bit number cannot be shortened to 8 bits.

Correct Syntax

MOV   AX, 01234H   ;16 bit immediate data value move
                           ;to AX.
MOV   BL, 027H   ;8 bit immediate data value move to
                           ;BL.

Incorrect Syntax

MOV   AH, 01234H   ;This is incorrect as 01234H cannot fit
                           ;into AH.
MOV   AX, 012H   ;This is correct as 012H can
                           ;become 00012H.

Using these two variations of the MOV instruction registers can be made to contain any value required.

Example

MOV   AX, 0000H   ;Sets up the segment registers to the
                           ;bottom 64 kbytes.
MOV   DS, AX   ;First to DS, next to
MOV   AX, 01000H   ;ES, and third to SS for
MOV   ES, AX   ;the stack. The SP is
MOV   AX, 2000H   ;then set to point to the
MOV   SS, AX   ;top of the stack (SP decrements
MOV   SP, 0FFFFH   ;when values are added to the stack).

The segment registers CS, DS, ES and SS, cannot have immediate data values moved into them and must always be accessed by a register-to-register move, as illustrated in the example above.

MOV register to memory or memory to register. These two instruction variations of MOV are similar, except that the data is copied to a register from memory or to memory from a register and allows access to the contents of memory locations. The segment containing the memory location is assumed to be the current data segment, as outlined in addressing techniques. Other segments can be accessed as required by using a segment prefix override.

The move can be 8 or 16 bits and is determined by the length of the register used in the instruction. 8-bit registers indicate 8-bit memory locations and 16-bit registers indicate 16-bit memory locations. The memory pointer can consist of a combination of:

(a) A constant offset only;
(b) A constant and/or one index register;
(c) A constant and/or two index registers.

If a constant only is being used, some way of distinguishing this from an immediate data move is required, and this is in the form of the words:

BYTE PTR   or   WORD PTR

These indicate that the constant refers to a memory offset constant and not an immediate data value.

Example

```
MOV   AX, WORD PTR 01234H   ;Moves the contents of the
                            ;word memory location
                            ;(010H × DS) + 01234H into
                            ;AX.
MOV   AX, 01234H            ;Moves 01234H into AX and
                            ;does not access any
                            ;memory locations.
MOV   CL, BYTE PTR 012H     ;The constant offset can be
                            ;8 or 16 bits and makes no
                            ;difference whether the
                            ;data is 8 or 16 bits.

MOV   CL, BYTE PTR 012H
MOV   CL, BYTE PTR 013H
MOV   CX, WORD PTR 012H
MOV   CX, WORD PTR 013H     ;As this is an odd address it
                            ;requires 2 bus cycles to
                            ;complete.
```

If WORD PTR is used then the register must also be 16 bits, and if BYTE PTR is used the register must be 8 bits. If the memory location address is an odd address then word accesses take two bus cycles rather than one as outlined in the addressing mode section. This is invisible to the programmer but it does take longer for the instruction to execute.

When copying data into memory a similar syntax for the instructions is used:

```
MOV   BYTE PTR 012H, CL
MOV   WORD PTR 012H, CX

MOV   WORD PTR 01234H, AX
MOV   BYTE PTR 05678H, BH
```

MOV using single indexed addressing. Single-indexed addressing uses an index register in the offset address calculation, and may also add an optional constant. There are four registers which can be used in single indexed addressing: BX, BP, SI and DI. Of these, BX, SI and DI use the DS register as the default segment register, whereas BP uses SS. This arrangement of default segment registers has been included to simplify the writing of programs which pass parameters via the stack.

The use of WORD or BYTE PTR need only be included in the instruction if the size of the destination cannot be determined from the instruction itself.

Example

Assume BX = 00001H, DS = 02345H. The instruction:

```
MOV   AX, [BX] + 06H
```

produces an offset value of:

$$\text{Offset} = \text{contents of BX} + 06H$$
$$= 00001H + 00006H$$
$$= 00007H$$

As the destination register is 16 bits long a word access to the following physical memory location is made (as illustrated in *Figure 2.38*):

$$\text{Memory location} = (010H × 02345H) + 00007H$$
$$= 023457H$$

As this is an access to an odd memory location it would require two bus cycles to complete.

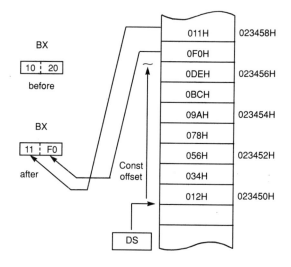

Figure 2.38 Single indexed word addressing

The opposite operation of writing from a register to a memory location is achieved by using the instruction:

```
MOV   [BX] + 0003H, DH
```

As this is an 8-bit source register, a byte is transferred and it does not matter if the address is odd or even.

$$\text{Offset} = [BX] + 00003H$$
$$= 00001H + 00003H$$
$$= 00004H.$$

Therefore the physical memory location of the destination is:

$$(010H × 02345H) + 00004H = 023454H$$

MOV using double indexed addressing. As the name suggests, double indexed addressing uses two registers with an optional constant in the offset calculation. The instruction contains sufficient information to determine if the transfer is a byte or a word. The following instruction:

MOV   AX, [BX] [DI] + 0123H

is a word transfer, as the destination register, AX, is a 16-bit register. Assume BX = 00002H, DI = 00003H, DS = 02345H. Then the offset used in the address calculation is:

Offset = [BX] + [DI] + 0123H
       = 00002H + 00003H + 0123H
       = 00128H

so that the physical memory location used as the source is:

Memory location = (010H × 02345H) + 00128H
                = 023578H

Similarly, the following instruction illustrates a byte transfer from the source register, CH, to the memory location 023578H:

MOV   [BX] [DI] + 00123H, CH

As with single indexed addressing, only four registers can be used as index registers and they are used in pairs but are restricted to using a register beginning with a B and a register ending in an I. Therefore, the allowed pairs of registers are:

[BX] [DI]
[BX] [SI]
[BP] [DI]
[BP] [SI].

For double indexed addressing the default segment register is always the data segment register, DS.

Segment prefix override instructions.

It is possible to use segments other than the default for either single or double indexed addressing by using a segment override prefix. For example:

MOV   [BX] [DI] + 0123H, CH

uses the default DS register when calculating the memory address, while the instruction:

MOV   CS: [BX] [DI] + 01223H, CH

uses the CS register, as there is the code segment prefix in front of the index registers. The prefix consists of the required segment register followed by a colon. Adding a prefix to an instruction increases the length of the assembled instruction by one byte so, wherever possible, the default segment register should be used, as this will produce the most compact and fast-executing code possible.

String movement operations (memory to memory moves).

The string movement instruction is an extension of the basic data movement instruction, MOV, and allows direct memory-to-memory byte or word transfers. For example, the instruction MOVSB is a byte transfer from the source memory location to the destination memory location. The instruction MOVSW is a word transfer from the source memory location to the destination memory location. Both these instructions execute without using an intermediate register to hold the data value. The instruction does not explicitly contain the registers used to produce the memory pointers, as there are default register combinations.

In order to achieve memory-to-memory transfers it is necessary to have two memory pointers as well as two segment registers to allow for segment-to-segment transfers. The data segment is always used as the default source segment, and the extra segment as the destination segment. The DS register can be overridden using a segment prefix instruction to enable CS, ES or SS to be used as the source segment. However, the ES register must always be used as the destination segment register and cannot be overridden.

The two segment offsets are formed from the source and destination registers, SI and DI, and alternatives are not allowed. The following is an example of a memory-to-memory transfer.

MOV	AX, SEG SOURCE	;Initialise the source
MOV	DS, AX	;segment register.
MOV	SI, OFFSET SOURCE	;Initialise the source
		;offset register.
MOV	AX, SEG DESTINATION	;Initialise the destination
		;segment register.
MOV	ES, AX	
MOV	DI, OFFSET DESTINATION	;Initialise the destination
		;offset register.
MOVSB		;A memory-to-memory
		;transfer.

The string instruction also automatically increments, or decrements the index registers SI and DI each time the string instruction is executed. The direction flag is used by the instruction to determine whether the index registers are to be incremented or decremented.

This may not seem much of an advantage due to the number of instructions required to initialise the various registers acting as memory pointers. However, string operations can be combined with the repeat prefix instruction, REP. This uses the CX register as a count down register and enables the instruction prefixed to be repeatedly executed up to 65 536 times. The contents of the CX register are decremented each time the instruction is executed until CX = 0000H. This means that strings up to 65 536 bytes can be transferred in a single instruction.

Therefore, by adding two instructions to the previous sequence, one to initialise the CX register and one as a repeat prefix, a large number of bytes can be easily transferred.

```
MOV, AX, SEG SOURCE         ;Initialise the source
MOV   DS, AX                ;segment register.
MOV   SI,OFFSET SOURCE      ;Initialise the source
                           ;offset register.
MOV   AX,SEG DESTINATION    ;Initialise the destination
                           ;segment register.
MOV   ES, AX
MOV   DI,OFFSET DESTINATION  ;Initialise the destination
                           ;offset register.
MOV   CX,BYTES_IN_STRING    ;Initialise byte counter.
REP
MOVSB                       ;A memory-to-memory
                           ;transfer of up to 65 536
                           ;bytes.
```

Input and Output Operations

The 8086 has the ability to differentiate between operations which access memory and operations which access peripheral components. The peripheral components are given the generic name of **I/O devices** as data is transferred into and out of the registers associated with the peripheral components. These peripheral registers are also known as **ports**. The registers do not just store data but use the values stored to affect the operation of the peripheral. Sometimes, the ports form a temporary **buffer** between the CPU and the external environment in order to synchronise the transfer of data.

To enable the identification of I/O operations there are two special instructions, IN and OUT. If these two instructions are not used, all instructions which involve a physical address are assumed to operate on memory locations.

The IN instruction performs the input operation and transfers the data from any one of 65 536 port addresses into the accumulator. Only the accumulator can be used for input operations, with AX used for 16-bit inputs and AL for 8-bit inputs. The port address is not segmented and is therefore limited to 16 bits allowing access to 65 536 ports. IN and OUT are the only data transfer operations which do not use segmentation, only an offset. This limits the maximum port address to 16 bits, as already mentioned.

```
IN    accumulator, port    ;Transfer from port to
                          ;accumulator.
OUT   port, accumulator    ;Transfers from accumulator to
                          ;port.
```

The OUT instruction performs the opposite operation of transferring data from the accumulator, which must be the AX or AL register, to the specified port address. Again the port address is limited to 16 bits and can be any one of 65 536 locations. The usual method of indicating the port address is indirectly using the DX register. Only the DX register can be used to contain the offset and it cannot be combined with any other register or constant. The port address is always placed directly into the DX register and the accumulator is used to distinguish between word (AX) and byte (AL) transfers. The indirect port addressing allows all the 65 536 ports to be accessed. The ports are also organised into two banks using AO and BHE to distinguish between byte and word accesses. It is common to implement only one bank of I/O addresses such as the even bank, as most peripheral devices use 8-bit data values.

This results in only four indirect I/O instructions which are listed below:

```
IN    AL,DX    ;8-bit input
IN    AX,DX    ;16-bit input
OUT   DX,AL    ;8-bit output
OUT   DX,AX    ;16-bit output
```

For port addresses greater than 255 the indirect method of addressing the port listed above must be used. However, there is an alternative shorter direct addressing version which can be used for port addresses less than 256, as illustrated below:

```
IN    AL,245    ;8-bit input from port 245
IN    AX,245    ;16-bit input from port 245
OUT   245,AL    ;8-bit output to port 245
OUT   245,AX    ;16-bit output to port 245
```

The same ports can be accessed indirectly as illustrated below, but this does take an extra instruction. However, the IN instruction is now a one byte instruction and only requires 8 clock cycles rather than the 10 required by the direct method.

Example

An example of indirect port addressing:

```
MOV   DX,245    ;3 byte instruction taking 4 clocks,
IN    AL,DX     ;1 byte instruction taking 8 clocks,
               ;making a total of 4 bytes, and takes
               ;12 clocks to execute.
```

The same port addressed directly:

```
IN    AL,245    ;2 byte instruction taking 10 clocks to
               ;execute.
```

Stack Operations

This section will consider the most commonly used operations which affect the stack and the stack pointer

(SS:IP), and are divided into two types, data storage and program address storage.

Data Storage: PUSH and POP

These two operations enable the register or memory contents to be saved onto the existing top of stack (TOS). The TOS is then automatically decremented by two to point to the next free word location on the stack. A more detailed explanation of stack operation of the **Stack Pointer** (SP) is given elsewhere.

All stack locations are 16 bits and therefore all data values saved and restored must be 16 bits. This means that 8-bit register and memory location contents cannot be directly saved but must be saved as 16-bit values. For example, the AL register contents would be saved as AX, which would also save AH which may be unwanted. Saving unwanted 8-bit register contents is not generally a problem unless there are large numbers of 8-bit values to be saved when they occupy valuable memory space.

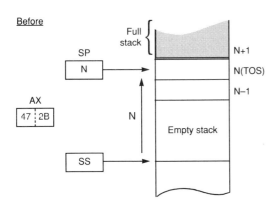

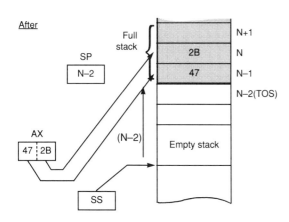

Figure 2.39 Stack operation

PUSH. The operation of the PUSH instruction is illustrated in *Figure 2.39*. When pushing memory location contents onto the stack, any of the data addressing techniques can be used; direct, single, double-indexed, and so on.

Example

PUSH   ES: [BX] [SI] + 0007H

This example uses double-indexed addressing plus a constant with a segment override prefix, so that ES is the segment register used rather than the default DS. The memory location pointed to by this address is then copied to the TOS which is always pointed to by SS and SP. It is not possible to override the stack segment when accessing the stack. Any values added to the stack during program execution by pushing are only considered to be temporarily stored, and should be removed before the program completes. This avoids the stack becoming filled with unwanted data values.

A typical short-term use would be to pass parameters to subroutines via the stack. This removes the need to use specific registers or memory locations and therefore produces more general purpose subroutines.

Example

```
PUSH   AX                   ,Save subroutine
                            ;parameters to the stack.
PUSH   ES: [BX] [SI] + 0007H
CALL   SUBR                 ;Execute subroutine, which
                            ;will fetch the parameters
                            ;from the stack.
```

Alternatively, the stack can be used within a subroutine to save values which will be required later in the subroutine. This avoids the need for dedicated memory locations and allows recursive subroutines to be written. These must be removed from the stack before the subroutine completes or all further stack operations will be operating on invalid data.

Example

The following is an example of how values can be saved on the stack at the beginning of a subroutine execution, and then correctly restored at the end.

```
SUBR:  PUSH   AX     ;Beginning of subr, save AX and BX.
       PUSH   BX
         .                 ;Rest of subroutine instructions.
         .
         .
       POP    BX     ;Restore registers from the stack in
       POP    AX     ;the reverse order.
       RET           ;End of the subroutine.
```

This technique is often used to save the contents of all the registers affected when writing subroutines so that the state of all the registers is the same after the subroutine has executed as they were before execution. This means that the programmer does not have to be concerned with whether the subroutine changes any of the register values. These values may be required later on in the program and would otherwise have to be saved to fixed memory locations.

POP. As indicated in the previous example the instruction used to copy values from the TOS is POP. This causes the TOS to be incremented by 2 and the contents of the word pointed to copied to the specified destination. This can be any valid register or memory location.

Example

```
POP   AX
POP   ES: [BX] [SI] + 0007H
```

The stack operates as a **first-in-last-out (FILO) memory**, so that words are removed in the reverse order to that in which they were added. As illustrated in the previous example, this must be remembered when saving register contents during subroutine entry and exit points.

The stack can also be used for memory-to-memory transfers which do not use intermediate registers for temporary storage and which do not treat the data as strings. This is useful for writing general purpose programs which perform memory-to-memory moves, without having to save and restore register contents, so that the registers can be used as intermediate storage.

Example

```
PUSH  ES: [BX] [SI] + 0007H   ;Transfer from the memory
POP   [BP] [DI] − 0007H        ;location to an alternative
                               ;memory location.
```

A segment override is used in the first instruction but the default segment, DS, is used in the POP instruction.

Program Address Storage

As well as being used for data storage, the stack is used to save return addresses when a subroutine or interrupt service subroutine is initiated.

CALL. A subroutine can be considered to be a section of code with an explicit beginning and end which implements some complete function, such as outputting

data values to an I/O port, but which is not included in the main code path. This enables the subroutine code to be used repeatedly within a program without having to include the complete code each time it is required. The subroutine code is placed before or after the main code path in the program memory area and a CALL is made to it, see *Figure 2.40*.

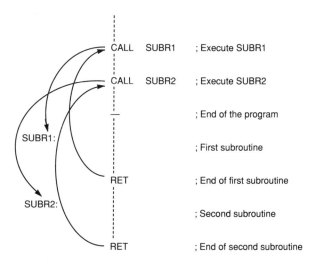

```
     ┌──→ CALL  SUBR1    ; Execute SUBR1
     │
     │ ┌→ CALL  SUBR2    ; Execute SUBR2
     │ │
     │ │   ─             ; End of the program
SUBR1: │
     │ │                 ; First subroutine
     │ │
     │ └── RET           ; End of first subroutine
SUBR2:
       │                 ; Second subroutine
       │
       └── RET           ; End of second subroutine
```

Figure 2.40 Subroutine calling

The CALL mnemonic indicates that a subroutine is to be executed, and the parameter included in the CALL instruction indicates the starting address of the subroutine. When the CALL instruction is executed, two different actions are performed. First the address of the instruction following the call is pushed onto the stack. This is performed so that when the subroutine has completed executing and returns to the calling program, the address of the instruction after the call can be retrieved and execution can continue from that address. Following this the address specified in the CALL instruction is copied into the IP register which then points to the first instruction of the subroutine. This type of subroutine call which only updates the IP register and not the CS register as well is used when the subroutine is in the same code segment as the program which called it and is known as a NEAR subroutine call. The alternative, which is known as a FAR subroutine call, updates both the CS and IP registers as the subroutine being called is in a different segment and the old CS and IP values must be saved on the stack. The CS contents are saved on the stack first followed by the contents of IP, so that the TOS is pointing to the IP value, as with near calls.

Example

```
      CS        IP
    0C000H   F007H   CALL 02204H   ;A near subroutine call.
    0C000H   0F00AH                ;The address of the next
                                   ;instruction.
```

(The next instruction is at CS = 0C000H, IP = 0F00AH.) This is a NEAR call and therefore 0F00AH is pushed onto the stack and 02204H copied into the IP register.

RET. When the subroutine has completed executing, the return instruction, RET, is used. This returns program execution to the instruction immediately following the original subroutine CALL by causing the TOS to be copied into the IP. If it is a FAR subroutine call the new TOS is copied into CS as well. These operations on the stack are performed automatically as part of the return instruction. The return instruction can therefore be a near or far return and must match the calling instruction, otherwise the correct operation of the subroutines and stack cannot be guaranteed. The incrementing of the stack pointer by two whenever a value is removed from the stack is always performed automatically as a standard stack operation. The value which is in the IP register (and the CS register if it is a FAR subroutine) are lost at the end of the subroutine as it is not necessary to save them.

It is important that any values pushed onto the stack during subroutine execution are removed by popping before the return. This is because the pushed values are added to the stack after the return address, see *Figure 2.41*, and if they are not removed before the return instruction they will be taken to be the values for CS and/or IP, instead of the correct return address.

There is a special variation of the return instruction for use when values are pushed onto the stack immediately before the subroutine CALL as parameters for the subroutine. These have to be removed after the subroutine returns, which can be achieved automatically by giving the return instruction an operand. This operand, which should be a constant, indicates by how much the TOS pointer should be incremented after the return instruction has been executed, but before the next instruction is executed.

Example

The following fragment of code illustrates how parameters pushed onto the stack before a subroutine call can be removed using POP instructions:

```
    PUSH   AX      ;Pass the parameters to the
    PUSH   BX      ;subroutine via the stack.
    PUSH   CX
    CALL   SUBR    ;Execute the subroutine.
    POP    AX      ;Discard the unwanted values from
                   ;the stack.
    POP    AX
    POP    AX
                   ;The rest of the program
                   ;instructions. Subroutine placed
                   ;after the main program code.
    SUBR:          ;The subroutine instructions.
    RET            ;An ordinary return.
```

Example

By adding an operand to the return instruction a more compact and faster executing program sequence can be written:

```
    PUSH   AX       ;The parameters are passed to the
    PUSH   BX       ;subroutine via the stack.
    PUSH   CX
    CALL   SUBR3    ;Execute subroutine SUBR3.
      .             ;It is not necessary to discard
                    ;values.
      .             ;Rest of the program instructions.
                    ;Subroutine placed after the main
                    ;program code.
    SUBR3:          ;The subroutine instructions.
    RET 6           ;The return has an operand which
                    ;automatically discards 6 bytes
                    ;from the stack after returning.
```

This time the TOS is automatically incremented by 6 before the return instruction completes. This performs the same function as the three POPs did, but much more quickly.

Interrupt Service Subroutines

As previously discussed, the 8086 has a flexible interrupt structure which allocates each interrupt a unique interrupt vector. The interrupt vector is used to generate a memory address. The four bytes following this address then contain the address of the **interrupt service**

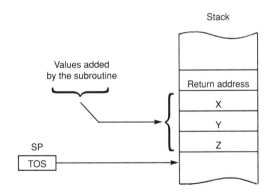

Figure 2.41 Values added to the stack by the subroutine

subroutine and consist of the CS and IP address values.

An interrupt service subroutine initiation is almost the same as a subroutine call except that the flag register is saved and all interrupts are disabled before the interrupt service subroutine starts executing. The 16-bit flag register is saved onto the stack before the CS and IP register values of the next instruction. All interrupt service subroutines are FAR subroutines because CS and IP values are saved, as it is not possible to determine whether the interrupt service subroutine is NEAR or FAR from the interrupt signal. The new values of CS and IP are obtained from the interrupt vector address.

Interrupts can be caused by asynchronous hardware-based signals which can occur at any time in a program's execution. When an external interrupt signal is received the presently executing instruction is always completed before the interrupt is acknowledged. Alternatively, interrupts can be generated internally by the instruction INT. The flag register contents are saved at the beginning of the interrupt so that the state of the microprocessor can be exactly restored to what it was before the interrupt. If the states of any of the microprocessor registers need to be saved during the interrupt service subroutine then the programmer has to ensure that instructions are placed into the interrupt service routine to do this.

As the flag register is saved at the beginning of the interrupt, the normal return instruction, RET, cannot be used as the flags would not be restored. Instead a special interrupt return instruction, IRET, is used. This instruction does not have an optional operand indicating how the TOS should be altered, as parameters are never passed to interrupt service subroutines via the stack.

When an interrupt return is executed, IP is restored first, followed by CS and finally the flag register. The program will then continue executing at the point that it was interrupted.

Conditional and Unconditional Program Jumps

Sometimes it is necessary for a program to make a test on some data value which will result in a true or false answer. The result can then be used to control whether program control is transferred to a sequential or a non-sequential memory location containing the next instruction. Such a transfer is called a **conditional jump**.

The jump can be made to an instruction further down the instruction sequence that has not yet been executed when it is termed a **feed forward**, or to an instruction back up the program that has already been executed, when it is termed a **feedback**. An alternative name for a feedback is a **loop**.

Status flags

CF Carry Flag
ZF Zero Flag
SF Sign Flag
OF Overflow Flag
PF Parity Flag

The flags can be used in two ways, directly or as a logical combination. When used directly the flag is named in the conditional jump. When a flag is not set and contains a logic zero, this means the operation has not resulted in that particular state occurring. This state can be tested for by inserting an N into the instruction mnemonic, as listed below.

Direct conditions

JC	Jump if carry flag set	$CF = 1$
JNC	Jump if carry flag not set	$CF = 0$
JZ	Jump if zero flag set	$ZF = 1$
JNZ	Jump if zero flag not set	$ZF = 0$
JO	Jump if overflow flag set	$OF = 1$
JNO	Jump if overflow flag not set	$OF = 0$
JP	Jump if parity flag set	$PF = 1$
JNP	Jump if parity flag not set	$PF = 0$
JS	Jump if sign flag set	$SF = 1$
JNS	Jump if sign flag not set	$SF = 0$

Logical Combinations

Generally, these conditions are used after an arithmetic operation on unsigned integers and this is usually a subtraction (or comparison which is equivalent but does not alter the operands). Assuming the two values are A and B and the subtraction is performed as $(A - B)$, then the following is a list of the available jumps which use a logical combination of status flags:

CF = 0 and ZF = 0

JA   Jump if above.

This can also be expressed in the opposing manner:

JNBE   Jump if not below or equal.

The jump is made if $B > A$ which is indicated by $CF = 0$ and $ZF = 0$.

CF = 0

JAE   Jump if above or equal

This can also be expressed in the opposing manner:

JNB   Jump if not below

The jump is made if B > A or B = A which is indicated by CF = 0.

These two conditional jump instructions are exactly the same as JNC, but are included to allow the most appropriate instruction to be used. This can make the program more readable and understandable by indicating what the emphasis of the test was.

CF = 1

JB   Jump if below

This can also be expressed in the opposing manner:

JAE   Jump if above or equal.

The jump is made if B < A which is indicated by CF = 1, so that this instruction is equivalent to JC.

CF = 1 and ZF = 1

JBE   Jump if below or equal

This can also be expressed in the opposing manner:

JNAE   Jump if not above or equal

The jump is made if B < A or B = A which is indicated by CF = 1 or ZF = 1.

ZF = 1

JE   Jump if equal

This can also be expressed in the opposing manner:

JNE   Jump if not equal

The jump is made if B = A which is indicated by ZF = 1. These two instructions are the same as JZ.

Conditional Jumps after Signed Integer Arithmetic

If signed integer arithmetic operations are being performed and conditional jumps made afterwards then the sign flag can be included in the condition and this is made possible by having different mnemonics.

(SF XOR OF) = 0 and ZF = 0

JG   Jump if greater than

This can be expressed in the opposing manner:

JNLE   Jump if not less than or equal

The jump is made if B > A which is indicated by (SF XOR OF) = 0 and ZF = 0.

(SF XOR OF) = 0

JGE   Jump if greater than or equal

This can also be expressed in the opposing manner:

JNL   Jump if not less than

The jump is made if B > A or B = A which is indicated by (SF XOR OF) = 0.

(SF XOR OF) = 1

JL   Jump if less than

This can also be expressed in the opposing manner:

JNGE   Jump if not greater than or equal

The jump is made if B < A which is indicated by (SF XOR OF) = 1.

(SF XOR OF) = 1 or ZF = 1

JLE   Jump if less than or equal

This can also be expressed in the opposing manner:

JNG   Jump if Not Greater than

The jump is made if B < A or B = A which is indicated by (SF XOR OF) = 1 or ZF = 1.

Example

The following fragment of program code compares the contents of two registers, the result of which sets various status flags depending upon the two values used. There are then three conditional jumps which are used to detect various flag state combinations.

```
                     ;The first value is in AX and
                     ;the second is in BX.
CMP   AX,BX          ;The test performed is AX − BX.
                     ;Neither register is altered, only
                     ;the flags.
```

The following conditional jumps could then be used to distinguish various facts about the result of the comparison.

```
                     ;The first test.
JZ   SOMEWHERE1      ;A straight forward test of ZF.
                     ;(ZF = 1 IF AX = BX).
                     ;The second test.
JE   SOMEWHERE2      ;An unsigned integer test for
                     ;AX = BX.
                     ;The third test.
JLE  SOMEWHERE3      ;A signed integer test for
                     ;BX > = AX.
```

The conditional jump taken would depend on the initial values in the registers which would depend on the actions taken previously in the program execution. Therefore the conditional jumps allow the program flow to adapt to the values of the data being used which produces a useful and flexible program. As the jumps are all relative, only the IP register is updated and the CS register contents are unaffected.

If the condition being tested for is not present then the jump is not made and the next instruction in the sequence is executed.

Example

MOV	AX, 00027H	;The first value.
MOV	BX, 00057H	;The second value.
CMP	AX, BX	;The test performed is AX − BX. ;Neither register is altered, ;only the flags.
JZ	SOMEWHERE1	;As the two values are not the
MOV	.....	;same the following instruction ;is executed and the jump is ;not made.

Unconditional Jumps

There is an unconditional jump instruction as already mentioned, which can be used for jumps within the same segment or into another segment.

Relative jump.   For jumps within the same segment the jump is relative and is a signed integer value giving a range from −32 768 to +32 767 and is therefore a relocatable instruction. The relative unconditional jump allows program control to be transferred anywhere within the existing segment, as the contents of the CS register are not altered. This is achieved by adding the offset contained in the jump instruction to the contents of the IP register. This is still relative addressing as required by segmented programs and multiprocessing applications and can be used to extend the range of conditional jumps as illustrated previously.

Unconditional absolute jump.   For jumps between segments when both the CS and IP registers are updated, the jump is an absolute one to the specified address. Absolute jumps are not directly relocatable, so any program which includes them would need to have some method of updating these absolute addresses if the program is relocated. In a multi-user system all the programs must be relocatable and even in single-user systems the maximum flexibility and usefulness is obtained by being able to relocate programs.

An absolute jump occurs when a jump is made to an alternative segment which requires completely new values for the CS and IP registers. The unconditional absolute jump instruction is now a 5-byte instruction as it contains the new values for CS and IP. The previous values which were in the CS and IP registers are lost and cannot be regained.

Example

JMP ANYWHERE	;An unconditional jump to ;ANYWHERE in the 1 Mbyte ;address space.

If the segment containing ANYWHERE was OFCOOH and the offset was 02207H, then the instruction would become:

   JMP   OFCOOH:02207H

which would encode in hexadecimal as:

0EAH	inter segment jump
007H	offset
022H	
000H	segment
0FCH	

Loops

An alternative to using a test followed by a conditional jump in a feedback to execute a section of instructions repeatedly, is to use a **loop instruction**, of which there are two types, unconditional counted and conditional counted.

Unconditional counted loops.   It is often required to repeat a section of code a fixed number of times and this could be achieved by using a register as a counter, decrementing and testing for the count being equal to zero each time, as illustrated below:

Example

	MOV AX,10	;Set the count equal to 10.
REPEAT	.	;The instructions to be
	.	;executed repeatedly.
		;
	DEC AX	;Decrement the count; this ;instruction will set the zero flag ;when AX = 0.
	JNZ REPEAT	;Repeat the instructions in the ;loop until count = 0.
		;

These types of feedback loops can be simplified by using the LOOP instruction which performs the same decrement and test function. The register CX is used to hold the count value and is automatically decremented each time through the loop instruction until CX = 0.

Example

```
        MOV   CX,10       ;Set the count equal to 10.
REPEAT  .                 ;The instructions to be
        .                 ;executed repeatedly.
                          ;
        LOOP  REPEAT      ;The CX register is
NEXT_INSTRUCTION:         ;automatically decremented by
                          ;1 each time through the loop
                          ;until CX = 0, when the next
                          ;instruction is executed.
```

The loop has to be within −128 or + 127 bytes.

Conditional counted loops. Sometimes it may be necessary to repeat a loop a fixed number of times or until a specific situation occurs. For example, if during the transfer of 20 words into a buffer, one of the words was used to indicate the premature end of the data, then the transfer can be stopped by using the conditional counted loop instruction listed below. These instructions also automatically decrement CX in the same way as the unconditional counted loop instructions.

LOOPNZ   loop while CX is non-zero and the zero flag is not set.

There is also the opposite conditional loop:

LOOPZ   Loop while CX is non-zero and the zero flag is set.

Example

```
        MOV   CX,20       ;20 words are to be transferred.
REPEAT: MOV   AX,[DI]     ;Get the word from memory.
        CMP   AX,0000H    ;Test it for zero, (zero flag
                          ;affected).
        MOV   [SI],AX     ;Move the word to the new
                          ;destination in memory. This
                          ;instruction does not affect the
                          ;flags.
        LOOPNZ REPEAT     ;Repeat the instructions in the
                          ;loop for 20 words or until a
                          ;zero value is reached.
```

Instructions Performing Logical Operations

The four basic logical operations that can be performed on binary numbers are OR, AND, NOT and XOR (exclusive OR), and these are available as 8086 instructions. These instructions can be used to perform logical operations on binary numbers, or to perform tests on data values to affect the status flags. The results can then be used to control the conditional jumps as illustrated below:

Example

```
        MOV   AX,[BX]     ;Get a value from memory.
        AND   AX,0001H    ;Check it for LSB = 1.
        JNZ   BIT_SET     ;Jump if the LSB of AX is a
                          ;logic 1.
        BIT_NOT_SET:      ;Continue executing from here,
                          ;if the LSB of AX is not a logical
                          ;1.
```

(The plus symbol, +, is used to indicate a logical OR operation, and the full stop, the logical AND operation. NOT and exclusive OR operations are identified by the mnemonics NOT and XOR respectively. Further details on the use of these instructions are given below).

OR

```
OR  reg1,reg2       ;OR the contents of reg2 with reg1,
                    ;and put the result into reg1.
                    ;
OR  mem,reg         ;OR the contents of reg with
                    ;memory, and put the result into
                    ;memory.
                    ;
OR  reg,mem         ;OR the contents of memory with
                    ;reg, and put the result into reg.
                    ;
OR  reg,immediate   ;OR the immediate value with reg,
                    ;and put the result into reg.
```

The OR Truth Table

$$0 + 0 = 0$$
$$0 + 1 = 1$$
$$1 + 0 = 1$$
$$1 + 1 = 1$$

AND

```
AND  reg1,reg2       ;AND the contents of reg2 with
                     ;reg1 and put the result into reg1.
                     ;
AND  mem,reg         ;AND the contents of reg with
                     ;memory, and put the result into
                     ;memory.
                     ;
AND  reg,mem         ;AND the contents of memory with
                     ;reg, and put the result into reg.
AND  reg,immediate   ;AND the immediate value with reg,
                     ;and put the result into reg.
                     ;
```

The AND Truth Table

$$0.0 = 0$$
$$0.1 = 0$$
$$1.0 = 0$$
$$1.1 = 1$$

NOT

NOT   reg   ;Convert all logic 1's to logic 0's,
                   ;and all logic 0's to logic 1's, in reg.
                   ;
NOT   mem   ;Convert all logic 1's to logic 0's,
                   ;and all logic 0's to logic 1's, in the
                   ;memory location pointed to.
                   ;

The NOT Truth Table

NOT 0 = 1
NOT 1 = 0

XOR

XOR   reg1,reg2   ;XOR the contents of reg2 with
                   ;reg1 and put the result into reg1.
                   ;
XOR   mem,reg   ;XOR the contents of reg with
                   ;memory, and put the result into
                   ;memory.
                   ;
XOR   reg,mem   ;XOR the contents of memory with
                   ;reg, and put the result into reg.
                   ;
XOR   reg,immediate ;XOR the immediate value with reg,
                   ;and put the result into reg.
                   ;

The XOR Truth Table

0 XOR 0 = 0
0 XOR 1 = 1
1 XOR 0 = 1
1 XOR 1 = 0

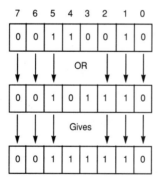

Figure 2.42   Bit operations

The logical operations are performed on the individual bit positions of the bytes and words, with each bit position combined with the appropriate bit position of the second operand, see *Figure 2.42*. The least significant bit of operand 1, LSB1, is OR'ed with the least

significant bit of operand 2, LSB2, to form the least significant bit of the results, LSB3. None of the other bits in the result are affected by this bit result, with each bit position being independent of all other bit positions. The status flags are set or reset as a result of the operation of the entire byte or word, not the individual bit positions. The zero flag would be set only if all the bits of the result were logic zeros. The other flags would also be affected.

Each instruction has two operands, except NOT which only has one. The left-most operand also forms the result with the original contents being lost. The second operand is not changed by the instruction.

Example

OR   AX,BX   ;ORs the contents of AX with BX and
                  ;the result is saved in AX. BX is
                  ;unchanged.
                  ;
AND   CX,BX   ;The contents of CX are AND'ed with
                  ;those of BX and the result saved in CX.
                  ;The contents of BX remain
                  ;unchanged.
                  ;
XOR   BX,DX   ;The contents of BX are exclusive
                  ;OR'ed with those of DX and the result
                  ;saved in BX. DX remains unchanged.
                  ;
NOT   CX   ;The contents of CX are inverted and
                  ;saved in CX. No other registers are
                  ;affected.

Memory locations and immediate data values can also be used as operands, although an immediate data value cannot form the left-most operand as it cannot store the result. The logical operations affect all the status flags, apart from the NOT operation which does not affect any flags.

Arithmetic Instructions

The final group of instructions commonly used implements the four basic integer arithmetic functions, add, subtract, divide and multiply.

Increment and decrement.   There are special versions of the add and subtract instructions when only 1 is to be added or subtracted, called **increment** and **decrement**. These have been included as adding or subtracting by 1 is a common requirement of programs and these special instructions occupy less bytes and execute more quickly.

Example

INC   AX   ;This instruction is one byte long, and
                  ;takes 3 clocks to execute.

| ADD | AX,O1H | ;This is functionally equivalent but
;occupies 3 bytes and takes 4 clocks
;to execute.
; |

These are single operand instructions which operate on registers or memory locations, byte or word, and affect the status flags.

Example

INC	AX	;The 16-bit register, AX, is ;incremented by 1.
INC	BH	;The 8-bit register, BH, is ;incremented by 1.
INC	Byte ptr [BP][DI] + 7	;The 8-bit memory location ;is incremented by 1.
DEC	DX	;The 16-bit register, DX, is ;decremented by 1.
DEC	CL	;The 8-bit register, CL, is ;decremented by 1.
DEC	WORD PTR [SI]	;The 16-bit memory location is ;decremented by 1.

Addition and subtraction. If larger amounts are to be added or subtracted the ADD and SUB instructions should be used. These are two operand instructions where the first operand is altered by the amount specified in the second.

Example

ADD	AX,0027H	;This instruction adds 0027H to ;AX.
ADD	AH,AL	;This adds contents AL to AH. ;AH is updated and AL is ;unchanged.
ADD	BX,[SI] + 7	;The contents of the word at the ;memory location pointed to by ;DS:[SI] + 7 is added to BX. BX is ;updated and the memory ;location remains unchanged. ;

The subtraction instruction is much the same except that the value of the second operand is subtracted from the first.

Example

SUB	AX,0027H	;0027H is subtracted from the ;contents of AX, AX is updated.
SUB	AH,AL	;The contents of AL are ;subtracted from AH, AH is ;updated and AL remains unchanged.
SUB	BX,[SI]+7	;The contents of the word at the ;memory location pointed to by ;DS:[SI]+7 is subtracted from ;BX. BX is updated and the ;memory location remains ;unchanged. ;

Multiplication. As the result of a binary multiplication can be twice the number of bits of the operands, default registers are used. The accumulator is always the first operand in the multiplication and also forms part of the result. If the 8-bit accumulator, AL is the first operand, then AX will contain the 16-bit result after the multiplication has taken place. The second operand can be any valid 8-bit register or memory location.

Example

MUL	BL	;The contents of BL are ;multiplied with those of AL, ;and the result is put into AX. BL ;is unchanged. ;
MUL	Byte ptr [DI]+7	;The contents of the memory ;location DS: [DI]+7 are ;multiplied by the contents of ;AL, and the result is put into ;AX. ;
MUL	CX	;The 16-bit contents of CX are ;multiplied with the contents of ;AX and the result is put into DX ;(the most significant 16 bits) ;and AX (the least significant 16 ;bits). ;
MUL	WORD PTR [SI]+14	;The 16-bit value in the memory ;location at DS: [SI]+14 is ;multiplied with the contents of ;AX, and the result is put into ;DX and AX.

Only two status flags, CF and OF are affected by these instructions with the remaining status flags left in an unknown state.

For signed multiplication, **2's complement** integers are used and the multiplication operation is performed assuming that the MSB of each operand represents the sign, and ensures that the result has the correct sign bit. The instruction used is IMUL standing for integer multiplication, and is used in the same way as MUL, except that the result will be different as 2's complement numbers are assumed.

Example

| IMUL | CX | ;This instruction performs signed integer
;multiplication of the contents of CX and
;the contents of AX, with the result put into
;DX and AX, and the sign bit which is the
;MSB of the result, correctly set.
; |

Division. Division performs the opposite operation to multiplication and the answer has less bits than the first operand. There may also be a remainder as integer division is performed. In **unsigned binary division**, if the second operand is a byte, then by default the AX register contains the first operand. After the division the result is contained in AL with the remainder in AH. If the result is larger than 8 bits a type 0 interrupt is generated and the result is invalid. For example, if AX = 0FFFFH and the divisor is 00H, the result would be infinite and the interrupt would be generated.

Example

```
DIV   BL          ;This instruction divides the contents of
                  ;AX by the contents of BL, and the result
                  ;is put into AL, and the remainder into AH.
                  ;
```

For word division, the DX:AX register pair is assumed to contain the first operand and the result is put into AX and the remainder in DX.

Example

```
DIV   WORD PTR [SI]+52H  ;The contents of DX:AX are
                         ;divided by the contents of
                         ;the memory location at
                         ;DS:[SI]+52H.
```

The flags are left in an unknown state by the division instruction.

As with signed binary multiplication, the **signed binary division** instruction uses 2's complement integers and correctly maintains the sign of the result. Apart from this the operation of the instruction is much the same as for unsigned binary division.

The Compare instruction. A useful instruction is compare, which performs the same operation as subtract except that the result is not saved. However, the flags are still set or reset correctly depending on the value of the result which enables tests to be made on register and memory location values, without changing those values.

Example

```
        MOV   MAX,0000H  ;Set a counter to zero.
REPEAT: INC   AX         ;Increment the counter.
        CMP   AX,10      ;Test for counter = 10.
        JNZ   REPEAT     ;Repeat the instruction in the
                         ;loop if the count is not 10.
                         ;The zero flag is set if AX = 10,
                         ;as 10 − 10 = 0.
                         ;
```

Remaining Instructions

The remaining 41 instructions are listed below and can be used in certain circumstances to produce more compact and faster executing code than is possible with the simpler instructions explained previously.

AAA	ASCII adjust for addition
AAD	ASCII adjust for division
AAM	ASCII adjust for multiplication
AAS	ASCII adjust for subtraction
ADC	Add with carry
CBW	Convert byte to word
CLC	Clear carry
CLD	Clear direction flag
CLI	Clear interrupt enable flag
CMC	Complement carry flag
CMPS⁻	Compare string
CWD	Convert word to double word
DAA	Decimal adjust for addition
DAS	Decimal adjust for subtraction
HLT	Halt, stop microprocessor
LAHF	Load AH from flags (for 8080 conversion)
LDS	Load pointer using DS
LEA	Load effective address
LES	Load pointer using ES
LOCK	Locks the bus
LODS	Load string
NEG	Negate
NOP	No operation (does nothing, takes 3 clocks)
POPF	POP flag register
PUSHF	PUSH flag register
RCL	Rotate through carry left
RCR	Rotate through carry right
ROL	Rotate left
ROR	Rotate right
SAHF	Store register AH into flags
SAL	Shift arithmetic left
SAR	Shift arithmetic right
SBB	Subtract with borrow
SCAS	Scan string
SHR	Shift logical right
STC	Set carry flag
STD	Set direction flag
STI	Set interrupt enable flag
STOS	Store string
TEST	Test (performs logical AND but does not save result: only the status flags are affected).
WAIT	Wait for TEST signal active
XCHG	Exchange
XLAT	Translate.

Detailed information on these instructions and those that have been covered previously can be found in the appropriate Intel assembly language manuals.

Summary

As can be seen from the variety of instructions and the variety of operations they can perform, the 8086 has a flexible and complex instruction set. Most programs, however, can be written just using the instructions explained in this section.

2.5   68000 16-BIT MICROPROCESSOR

The 68000 has many characteristics similar to the 8086 and because of this, only an overview will be given, paying particular emphasis to the interesting differ-ences. The major signals of the 68000 microprocessor are illustrated in *Figure 2.43*, and this shows one signifi-cant difference from the 8086, a demultiplexed address and data bus. This makes the 68000 inherently faster when executing instructions. The 68000 also has a much larger addressable memory range, 16 Mbytes, instead of the 1 Mbyte of the 8086. This is because the 68000 has a 24-bit address bus while the 8086 only has a 20-bit address bus. However, the 8086 does have a mechanism, albeit complex, for accessing odd addressed words in memory, while the 68000 does not allow accesses to odd addressed word memory locations.

Additionally the 68000 does not maintain complete compatibility with the earlier 8-bit microprocessor

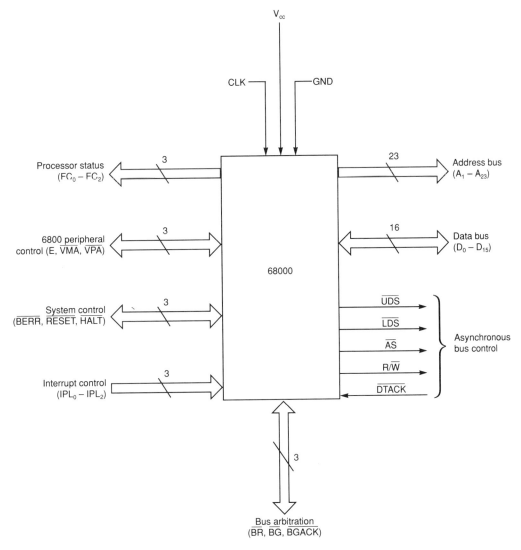

Figure 2.43   68000 signals

peripherals, designed for the 6800, instead preferring to use all new, purpose-designed 16-bit peripheral components, unlike the 8086 which even now does not have purpose-designed 16-bit peripheral components. The 68000 does have some signals which allow 6800 peripherals to be added but it is not straightforward and it is much better to use the special peripheral components.

The 68000 does not use a clock generator component but instead connects a suitable clock signal directly to the microprocessor, as is the reset signal. The method of dealing with interupts is virtually identical to the 8086 using interrupt vectors and a look-up table but is has some interesting methods of allocating priority through the use of the **interrupt priority level** signals which avoid the need for an interrupt controller. This is different to the 8086 which has to use the 8259A PIC for anything other than the non-maskable interrupt (NMI).

Memory

Physical memory is organised into even addressed words (16 bits); odd addressed words cannot be accessed although bytes can be individually accessed. The AO address signal which is not available externally, is used to produce some additional signals:

$\overline{\text{UDS}}$ – Upper Data Strobe (D_8–D_{15}) active low
$\overline{\text{LDS}}$ – Lower Data Strobe (D_0–D_7) active low

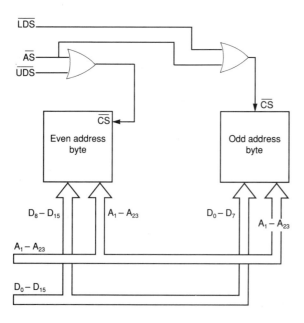

Figure 2.44   Memory addressing

which are used to enable ODD and EVEN banks of memory. In a byte access only one of the banks is activated whereas in an even word access, both signals are activated. A representation of this is show in *Figure 2.44*.

Byte and Word Access

When accessing **even addressed words** both $\overline{\text{UDS}}$ and $\overline{\text{LDS}}$ become active low. **Odd addressed words** cannot be accessed and if this is attempted it causes an **exception**. An exception is another name for interrupt.

For **even addressed bytes** (D_8–D_{15}), only $\overline{\text{UDS}}$ is active-low. Because the data is on the high 8 bits of the data bus and should be on the low 8 bits for all byte accesses, it is transferred internally from (D_8–D_{15}) to (D_0–D_7). This is performed automatically and is invisible to the programmer.

Odd addressed bytes (D_0–D_7), only $\overline{\text{LDS}}$ is active-low. As the data is already on the low 8 bits of the data bus no further action is required.

Memory layout.   Even addressed words consist of the even byte plus the next higher odd byte as illustrated in *Figure 2.45*, so that word accesses increment the address by 2, starting from the lowest address, which is zero.

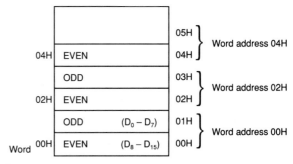

Figure 2.45   Equivalent memory layout

The READ Cycle

The bus cycle is semi-synchronous, which has the advantage of a fast transfer controlled by the clock signal but which can use the $\overline{\text{DTACK}}$ signal to extend the transfer by complete clock cycles if slow peripherals are being accessed.

The bus transfer can be considered to pass through four stages:

(a) Addressing the memory location;
(b) The memory device outputs the data;

(c) The microprocessor inputs the data;
(d) The cycle is terminated.

To address the memory location the following actions are performed:

(a) The R/$\overline{\text{W}}$ signal is set to read;
(b) The function code is placed onto the FC_0–FC_2 signals;
(c) The address is placed onto the A_1–A_{23} address signals;
(d) The address strobe ($\overline{\text{AS}}$) is activated;
(e) $\overline{\text{UDS}}$ and $\overline{\text{LDS}}$ are activated as necessary depending on whether it is a byte or word access.

These are all outputs from the microprocessor necessary to start the memory read. The memory component then responds with the following actions:

(a) The address is decoded internally to access the required location;
(b) Data is transfered from that location and placed onto D_0–D_7 and D_8–D_{15} as specified by $\overline{\text{UDS}}$ and $\overline{\text{LDS}}$ signals;
(c) The data transfer acknowledge signal ($\overline{\text{DTACK}}$) is activated to indicate that valid data is present.

$\overline{\text{DTACK}}$ is used to extend the bus cycle for slow memory components. If the memory device will always respond in the allowed period this signal need not be controlled by memory.

Following this second stage the microprocessor inputs the data from the data bus with the following actions:

(a) The data is latched internally from the data bus D_0–D_7, D_8–D_{15} as indicated by $\overline{\text{UDS}}$ and $\overline{\text{LDS}}$;
(b) $\overline{\text{UDS}}$, $\overline{\text{LDS}}$ and $\overline{\text{AS}}$ are inactivated indicating that the transfer has been successfully completed.

The bus transfer must then be terminated by:

(c) Removing the data from D_{15}–D_8, D_7–D_0, as appropriate which is a microprocessor action;
(d) De-activating $\overline{\text{DTACK}}$ if it was controlled by a memory component action.

These operations are illustrated by the read timing diagram in *Figure 2.46*.

The read cycle requires 8 clock states, (S_0 to S_7) which is four complete clock pulses. Therefore, for the 16 MHz version, a read operation takes:

$$\text{READ cycle time} = \frac{\text{Number of clocks}}{\text{Clock frequency}}$$

$$= \frac{4}{16}\ \mu\text{s} = 250\ \text{ns}$$

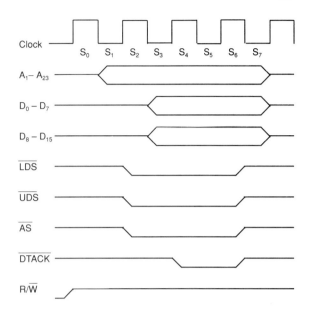

Figure 2.46 Read timing diagram

This is a fast transfer and would require high speed memory to be able to operate without wait states at that speed.

Extended READ. In the extended READ, extra clock states are inserted between S_4 and S_5 if $\overline{\text{DTACK}}$ is not activated (active-low) before the rising edge of S_4. When $\overline{\text{DTACK}}$ is activated (sometime after S_4) then S_5 will begin at the next falling clock pulse edge.

An even byte **extended read** is illustrated in *Figure 2.47* (overleaf) and is almost the same as *Figure 2.46*, except that the signals have been 'stretched' between clock states S_4 and S_5, which increases the transfer period for as long as necessary and at the same time maintains stable signal values.

The WRITE Cycle

The WRITE cycle, illustrated in *Figure 2.48*, has four steps that are similar to those in the read cycle:

(a) The memory location is addressed;
(b) The memory component inputs the data and internally decodes the address to select the correct location for data storage;
(c) The microprocessor removes the data from the data bus;
(d) The bus transfer is terminated.

To address the memory location the following actions are performed:

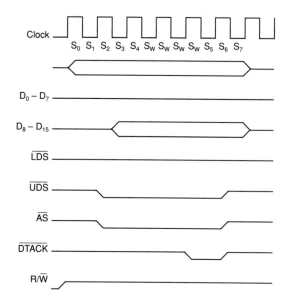

Figure 2.47   Extended byte read diagram

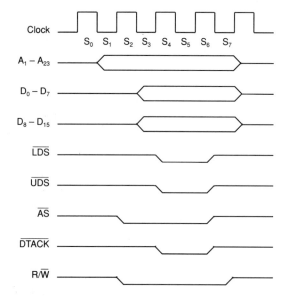

Figure 2.48   Write timing diagram

(a) The write memory function code is placed onto FC_0–FC_2.
(b) The address is placed onto A_1–A_{23}.
(c) The address strobe is activated;
(d) The $R/\overline{W}$ signal is set to write;
(e) The data to be written into memory is placed onto D_{15}–D_8, D_7–D_0 as appropriate;
(f) $\overline{UDS}$ and $\overline{LDS}$ are activated as appropriate.

The memory component then responds by:

(g) Internally decoding the address on the address bus;
(h) Stores the data on D_{15}–D_8, D_7–D_0 as selected by $\overline{UDS}$, $\overline{LDS}$ in the selected memory location;
(i) $\overline{DTACK}$ is activated to indicate a successful write.

Following this second stage the microprocessor removes the data by performing the following actions:

(j) $\overline{UDS}$ and $\overline{LDS}$ are inactivated as appropriate;
(k) $\overline{AS}$ is inactivated;
(l) Data is removed from D_0–D_7, D_8–D_{15} as appropriate;
(m) $R/\overline{W}$ is set to read which is a safety feature designed to prevent spurious writes which could change unspecified memory location contents;
(n) Inactivating $\overline{DTACK}$, to terminate the bus transfer.

Byte writes are similar to byte reads and even word, odd byte and even byte writes can be performed.

Odd word interrupt.   If an odd word read or write is attempted, an interrupt (called an **exception**) is generated and the operation prevented. A user-defined interrupt service routine is required to take care of this exception.

Extended Write.   In the extended write, clock cycles are inserted between S_6 and S_7. The wait states are inserted if $\overline{DTACK}$ is *not* activated valid before the beginning of S_7. Apart from this the extended write is similar to the extended read, with all signals remaining valid during the wait states and any number of wait states can be inserted. The timing diagram for the extended write is not included but is left as an exercise for the reader.

The Programmer's Model (68000)

The programmer's model identifies all the user-accessible registers in the microprocessor, which can be used when writing assembly language programs.

The 68000 has two similar programmer's models, the supervisor and the user models. The supervisor model is an extension of the user model which has special privileges which allow it to execute several additional instructions. These additional instructions are useful in a multi-tasking environment as they are used to protect individual user areas and programs.

The Main Privileged Instructions

STOP
RESET
RTE
MOVE to SR

AND immediate to SR
EOR immediate to SR
OR immediate to SR
MOVE USP

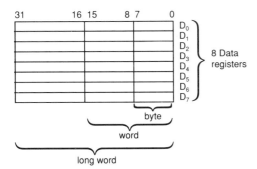

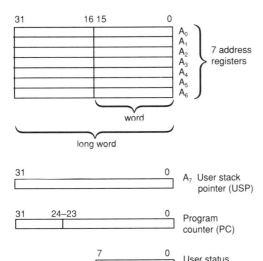

Figure 2.49   User's programmer's model

User's programmer's model.   The registers available in the user's model are illustrated in *Figure 2.49* and consist of:

- 8 × 32-bit **data registers** which can be used to manipulate byte (uses low 8 bits), word (uses low 16 bits) or longword (uses entire 32 bits) values: all data registers are equivalent and none have specialised uses but all of which are labelled logically, D_0 through D_7;
- 8 × 32-bit **address registers**, labelled A_0 through A_7 and all the address registers are the same except for A_7 which is a special case.

The address registers can manipulate word (uses low 16 bits) or longwords (uses entire 32 bits) values and can be used as data registers. However, they are primarily intended to be used to manipulate address values and they are the only registers that can be used in addressing modes. A_7 is a special register, because as well as being used as an ordinary address register it also acts as the stack pointer. Because of this special use, A_7 is not usually used as an ordinary address register unless stack manipulations are being performed, and it is given a special label, **user stack pointer** (USP). The USP is a full 32-bit register although the 68000 is limited to a maximum 24-bit physical address. This helps to maintain compatibility with later versions of the 68000 which have a full 32-bit physical memory addressing capability.

The **program counter** (PC) is used to indicate the address of the next instruction to be executed and is nominally a 32-bit register. However, because the physical address is limited to 24 bits, the top 8 bits of the PC are permanently set to zero. Again, this is to maintain compatibility with later versions of the 68000. This means that programs written for the 68000 will execute without any changes being necessary, on later versions such as the 68010, etc.

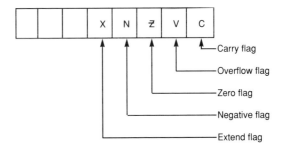

Figure 2.50   User status register

Finally there is the **user status register** (USR), illustrated in *Figure 2.50*, which is an 8-bit register containing the 5 **flags** available to the user-mode programmer. These are:

Carry;
Overflow;
Zero;
Negative;
Extend

The remaining three bits are not used in the 68000.

Supervisor's programmer's model.   *Figure 2.51* (overleaf) illustrates the supervisor's programmer's model which is similar to the user's programmer's

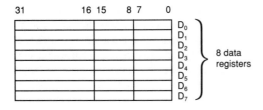

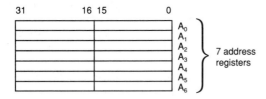

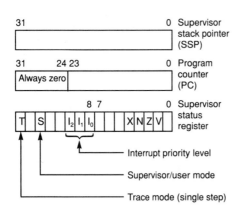

Figure 2.51 Supervisor's programmer's model

The interrupt priority level selects which of the available seven levels will be the minimum interrupt priority level which will be accepted and is usually used to prevent lower priority interrupts from interrupting an interrupt service subroutine that has already been started by an interrupt!

The supervisor/user mode flag can be used when in supervisor mode to put the microprocessor into user mode. This flag is only accessible by the programmer when in supervisor mode and this prevents the user mode programmer from ever being able to access supervisor previliges.

Finally, the trace bit is used when there is a requirement to single-step through a program as in this mode a special hardware-generated interrupt occurs at the end of every instruction. The single-step interrupt service subroutine is then used to process the results of the instruction just executed.

The third difference is the additional privileged instructions that become available to the supervisor mode programmer which are mainly concerned with manipulating the additional features available.

When first powered up, the 68000 is in the supervisor mode, which with its privileged status is designed to perform system operations (i.e. secure operations) in a multi-user system. Once these have been completed the supervisor flag is set to user mode and the 68000 reverts to the user's programmer's model.

If system operations are required, the 68000 has a safe method of temporarily returning to the supervisor mode.

In a single-user system, the 68000 can be left in supervisor mode as protection from other users is not required.

More on the Instruction Set

A byte, word or long word operation is specified by a suffix on the mnemonic.

Example

MOVE.B	move a byte (only data registers)
MOVE.W	move a word
MOVE.L	move a long word

Operand lengths must match, so for example, an immediate word cannot be moved as a byte, nor can there be byte moves involving address registers.

| MOVE.B | #$3FFF,A2 | ;Not allowed as #$3FFF is not a ;byte value. |
| MOVE.B | #$3F,A2; | Not allowed, A_2 cannot be ;accessed as a byte. |

model except for three small but significant differences. The register A_7 is now called the **supervisor stack pointer** (SSP) and is a completely different register, replacing the USP altogether. Special instructions can be used in the supervisor mode to access the USP whereas the SSP cannot be accessed at all when in the user mode. This allows the supervisor to have a completely different stack area without having to set it up every time the supervisor mode is entered. Secondly the 8-bit USR is extended to the 16-bit **supervisor status register** (SSR) of which the low 8 bits are formed by the USR. Five bits of the extra 8 are used to control three functions:

(a) Interrupt priority level;
(b) Supervisor/user mode model;
(c) Trace mode (single step).

Addressing Modes

There are a number of different addressing modes available when using the 68000 and the three main ones are described below.

Absolute addressing. With absolute addressing the address of the memory location is contained in the instruction.

MOVE $3FFF,A5

The above instruction moves the contents of memory location $00003FFF into register A_5. Note that leading zeros are assumed and a 32-bit address with the top 8 bits set to zero is always used. Absolute address values should not be used if the program is to be relocatable.

Register direct. When values are transferred from register to register this is called register direct and is illustrated by the following instructions:

MOVE.B	D3, D2	;Copies low byte of D_3 into low byte ;of D_2.
MOVE.W	D7, A2	;Copies low word of D_7 into low ;byte of A_2
MOVE.W	A5, D0	;Copies low word of A_5 into low ;word of D_0.
MOVE.L	A3, A4	;Copies 32 bits of A_3 into A_4.
MOVE.L	D2, D6;	;Copies 32 bits of D_2 into D_6.

The source register contents indicated by the first operand, is left unchanged by this operation, while the contents of the destination register, given by the second operand, are lost and replaced with the contents of the source register. This is the fastest type of data transfer as it takes place completely within the microprocessor.

Register indirect. The contents of the specified (address) register point to a memory location which contains the address of the memory location to be accessed.

Example

MOVE.L   #$3FFF, A4
MOVE.W   D6, (A4)

The first instruction puts the 32-bit address $00003FFF into A_4. The second instruction then saves the contents of D6 in the memory location specified by the contents of the register A_4, which is the memory location $00003FFF. This sequence is illustrated in *Figure 2.52*.

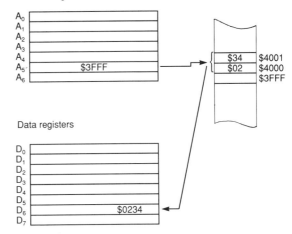

Figure 2.52   Register indirect: mover (A4), D6

Instruction Set

Most of the 68000 assembler instructions can use most of the addressing modes in most combinations. The only operation that is not allowed is a memory location to memory location, but register to register, register to memory and memory to register are all allowed. The memory location to memory location operation is produced by performing two successive operations: memory location to register followed by register to the other memory location.

The full 68000 instruction set is quite complex and only a small subset will be listed here, consisting of the most commonly used instructions which also appear in most microprocessor instruction sets. With this subset most programs can be written and they allow a good comparison between different microprocessors. However, the programs produced may not be the most compact, efficient or fast executing as might be possible if the full instruction set is used.

Instruction Subset

ADD	
AND	
BCC	Conditional branch [relative addresses]
BSR	Branch to subroutine
CMP	Compare
EOR	Exclusive OR
JMP	[Absolute addresses]
JSR	Jump to subroutine

MOVE
NOP
NOT
OR
RTS   Return from subroutine
SUB

These 14 instructions operate with bytes, words or longwords and all three addressing modes described earlier. As there are 80 basic instructions which can have B, W or L extensions and use each addressing mode, plus several others that have not been described, the full set of instructions is long and complex.

THREE

Microprocessor support circuits and peripherals

3.1 MEMORY

The size of the memory for program, data and future expansion. In the design of microprocessor systems an important consideration is the amount of memory to be included. This is selected from a knowledge of the program operation from which an estimate is made as to how much memory space each particular function will require. This can be achieved by waiting until the software has been designed and then calculating how much memory is required. This is often not possible for microcontrollers as both the hardware and software are designed simultaneously so as to be ready at the same time. Therefore during the initial specification stage of the hardware and software the amount of memory required is fixed.

There are two main types of memory required for a microcontroller or a microcomputer, called program and data memory. The program must be permanently saved when the power is removed so that it can be easily and repeatedly executed when power is re-applied. There are two main types of program memory components used to achieve this; **read only memory** (ROM) designed to execute only one program and **secondary mass storage** for microcomputers which enables many programs to be stored, selected and then executed.

Data memory must be alterable and is known as **read write memory** (RWM), and sometimes incorrectly as **random access memory** (RAM). This term is incorrect because ROM is also a random access memory, as this refers to the internal architecture of the memory which is independent of whether it is program or data memory.

RWM is used to store intermediate data values that are generated while the program is running which will not be required once the program has completed executing. There may also be a requirement for a stack and heap which are program functions described later. This need for data memory is common to both microcontrollers and microcomputers and in addition microcomputers often use RWM to store the presently executing program, as this allows new programs to be transferred into memory for execution.

The result of the different uses of memory is that microcontrollers have relatively large amounts of ROM compared to RWM as they only execute one specific program repeatedly, whereas microcomputers have a large amount of RWM, a small amount of ROM, and a large secondary mass storage device, in order to be able to execute a wide variety of programs. This section will concentrate on the choice of ROM and RWM components in a system.

The memory selected is separated into three areas, program, data and stack memory illustrated in *Figure 3.1.* (overleaf). Program memory stores the machine code binary instructions which the microprocessor will execute and which are required every time the program is executed. If the program has to be available immediately power is applied, then it has to be stored in non-volatile memory, such as **read only memory** (ROM). This is known as the power-on-reset or **boot-strap program**. The binary patterns are permanently stored in a semiconductor matrix which does not alter, even when the power is turned off and on repeatedly. If mass secondary storage is used, the boot-strap program can then be used to transfer programs from it into executable memory (RWM).

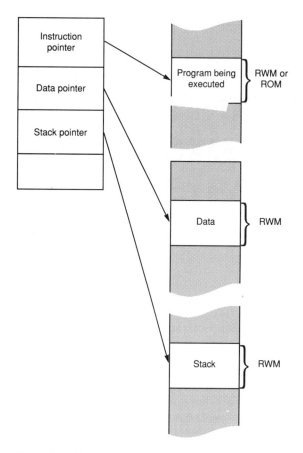

Figure 3.1 Microcomputer memory: programmer's model of the microcomputer

Memory Components

Memory components are produced in various sizes that are powers of 2 due to the addressing technique used and are measured in units of binary thousands of bytes called a kilobyte. As semiconductor technology has advanced, the average ROM component size has increased from 1 kbyte to the 1000 kbyte (1 Megabyte) or greater. The system memory is then comprised of several such memory components, each with a different starting address as in *Figure 3.2*.

The latest generation of ROM components has been designed for 16-bit microprocessors which have physical memory addressing capabilities of several megabytes, organised into 16-bit words rather than 8-bit bytes.

For small microcontrollers the memory component would be about 8 kbytes, capable of holding between 3000 and 4000 assembly language instructions. If the programs were written in a high level language such as

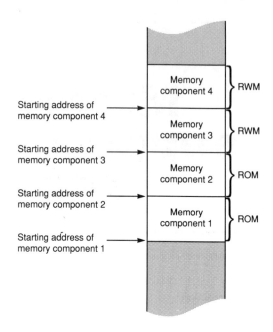

Figure 3.2 Memory components

Pascal, which produces larger programs, then a larger program memory area would be required to store them.

Data Areas

There are two types of data used in a program, variables and constants. Variable data is generated during the program execution and resides in RWM so that it can be altered. Such variable values are useful while the program is executing and are discarded when the program terminates or power is removed. They are re-initialised when the power is re-applied and the program re-executed.

Constant data values are required throughout the program execution without being changed and might take the form of look-up tables for values of trigonometric functions. This type of constant data is normally stored in ROM and is available whenever power is applied without any initialisation. The numbers of both variable and static data memory locations required are fixed when writing the program and the memory system can be designed to include them.

The Stack

In addition to the RWM locations reserved for variable data, a continuous section of RWM must be set aside for the program stack, see *Figure 3.3*. This is a mechanism whereby return addresses are saved when subroutines are called, without having specifically to denote variable data locations for that purpose. As subroutines are nested and called within the program, the stack fills and empties and depending upon the use of subroutines and the values they save onto the stack, the stack can vary in size from a few bytes to several kilobytes.

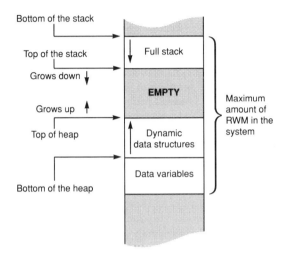

Figure 3.3 The stack and heap

As stack usage is dynamic and can only be determined accurately when the program is executing and may also vary between different executions of the same program if the input values vary, it is often difficult to estimate the size of stack required. The normal practice is to reserve some RWM locations for variable data and allocate the rest for the heap. Some checks may be included which detect when the stack is nearly full and indicate this to the user.

The Heap

When using high level languages there is often the ability to define variable data structures dynamically during the course of program execution, which is achieved using a mechanism known as the heap. This is similar to a second stack, except that it is used to define variable data elements. Once defined, such data elements remain available to the program throughout the execution of the program. It is possible to 'undefine' such structures later on in the program if the memory space is required. The heap therefore has a tendency to increase in size during program execution and again it is difficult to predict the maximum size of heap that a program may require.

To maximise the use of the available RWM, the stack and heap are initialised to the top and bottom of a continuous RWM area, so that the stack grows downwards and the heap upwards (see *Figure* 3.3). Sophisticated checking routines are required to detect a stack/heap collision and prevent the overwriting of data on either type.

Estimating the Memory Requirements

Having considered all the program code and data, stack and heap requirements, the size of the memory required for a particular function can be estimated.

Certain kinds of memory are required at specific addresses in the microprocessor memory range. For example, the 8086 starts executing the boot-strap program after a reset, at the address 0FFFF0H near the top of the available 1 Mbyte address range. To make the fullest use of the interrupt structure, the interrupt vector addresses should be maintained in RWM in the range of addresses 00000H to 0003FFH at the bottom of the memory space. Therefore different types of memory are required at each end of the 1 Mbyte address space which is shown in *Figure 3.4*, and this can cause some difficulties when producing the memory component selection signals.

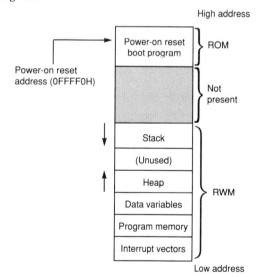

Figure 3.4 8086 memory requirements

Non-Volatile Read/Write Memory

Occasionally a function may require that some variable data values are maintained even after the power has been removed, so that when power is re-applied the values are immediately available. ROM cannot be used as the values cannot be altered. Alternatives such as battery-backed CMOS RWM or **electrically-erasable**

programmable ROM called EPROM are possible and these will be discussed later.

Future Expansion

When designing the memory system some thought should be given to the future needs of the product, as enhancements and additions to the hardware and software are a necessary and continuing part of the product's future. This is going to mean extra memory devices to contain the additional program code, ROM for a microcontroller and RWM for a microcomputer. It is normal to include a few extra chip-select signals which are valid in unused areas of the microprocessor memory space to facilitate the addition of memory components.

As the majority of products incorporate a **printed circuit board** (PCB), two options for incorporating the additional memory components are available. The PCB layout can include tracks and connections so that extra memory components can be added at the production time with very little difficulty, as in *Figure 3.5*. Alternatively, the PCB can be re-designed when necessary to add the extra tracks and pads. The majority of the PCB would remain the same with only the areas containing the extra devices being changed. This balances the extra cost of unused PCB area leading to easy upgrading, against a compact PCB design requiring costly re-design and re-production of enhanced PCBs.

Leaving tracks and pads on the PCB which do not contain any components is one example of designing for future enhancements, where each of the products contains an element of cost that is not directly related to the product function, but to future enhancements. That cost has various elements such as the original circuit design and PCB layout. The PCB initially has empty space to be included in the packaging which therefore must be larger and hence cost more. The reliability of the product is reduced as there is more of the PCB and packaging to malfunction. The major advantage of this technique is that the enhancements can be easily incorporated by adding devices at production time which requires only minor changes in production flow. There are no changes in the basic PCB and packaging so there are no major retooling costs in production. The retrofitting of components to products that have sold in the past is also possible, which maintains the usefulness of the hardware for a longer period.

The alternative method of redesigning the PCB involves major costs to change the packaging and retool the PCB and the product production processes. Also, the reliability will be significantly lower during the initial phase of production.

Including an easy path for enhancements may not always be cost effective as new techniques of design and packaging are becoming available. For example, when the original IBM PC was designed, Dual-In-Line components were used whereas the latest technique uses much smaller Surface Mount components. The result is that later generations of the PC which incorporate more functions take up less PCB space than earlier versions so that the expansion allowed for within the casing has become unnecessary, and is a cost that cannot now be recouped.

Semiconductor Memory

There are a variety of different types of semiconductor memory components which have different characteristics and which are selected to fulfil specific requirements of the microcontroller or microcomputer system. The main characteristics of interest are:

(a) Cost;
(b) Time required to transfer a byte into or out of the component, known as the access time;
(c) Power requirements;
(d) Storage density (this is related to the PCB area required).

Figure 3.6 illustrates a typical memory component with an address bus, a data bus and a control bus. The address and control buses are uni-directional from the

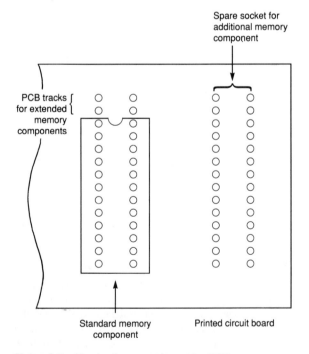

Figure 3.5 Allowing for expansion on the PCB

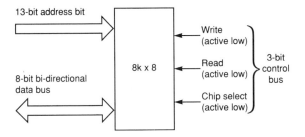

Figure 3.6 Typical memory component

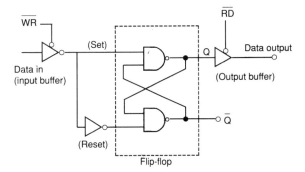

Figure 3.7 A flip-flop memory

microprocessor to the component. The data bus is bi-directional, although some components such as ROMs can only transfer data in one direction, to the microprocessor.

The 13 address bits give 2^{13} (8192) different locations within the component to be individually addressed. Each of the locations within the memory component consists of 8 parallel bits of data forming one byte. The control bus consists of three signals which are used to transfer the data correctly between the microprocessor and the memory component.

The chip select (active low) activates the complete component (i.e. I/P and O/P buffers) and can be used to power-down the memory component in order to reduce the system power requirements.

The read and write signals allow the address to stabilise before a transfer is made because if any address lines do change the wrong location might be accessed. The READ signal (active low) indicates that a transfer is to be made from the component to the microprocessor. The WRITE signal (active low) indicates that a transfer is to be made from the microprocessor to the specified location in the memory component.

Static RWM

The static RWM is not time-dependent and the transfer can be as long as required, although there is a minimum time required for any transfer. There is no clock input and each bit of data is saved on a **flip-flop**, see *Figure 3.7*, for as long as power is applied.

A flip-flop is a circuit which has two stable states, one called zero, logic 0 or false, and the other called one, logic 1 or true. The flip-flop can be stimulated to flip from one state to the other and will remain in that state until stimulated again as each of the two states is stable. *Figure 3.7* indicates how two-input NAND gates can be used to produce a flip-flop. Assume that Q is at logic 1 and the SET and RESET signals are both at logic 1 maintaining Q at logic 1. If SET is momentarily taken to

logic 0 which is equivalent to writing a logic 1, nothing will happen as Q is already at logic 1. However, when RESET is momentarily taken to logic 0 which is equivalent to writing a logic 0, the Q output will be changed to a logic 0. The logic 0 state on Q will be maintained even when the logic 0 has been removed from RESET. It can be changed back whenever SET is momentarily taken to logic 0. This type of flip-flop also produces the inverted bit, $\overline{Q}$ as well as Q, which can be useful.

The data stored on the flip-flop can be read by enabling the output buffer which transfers the data onto the data bus. For 8-bit wide data buses there would need to be eight such flip-flops for each memory location.

Bipolar, NMOS or CMOS transistors can be used to construct the flip-flops. Bipolar transistor memory components are faster than MOS devices but require larger power supplies. NMOS transistor memory components have a much lower power requirement than bi-polar transistor memory components, but are also slower. CMOS transistor memory components are replacing NMOS devices as they require even less power but still have high transfer rates.

NMOS. NMOS stands for **N-channel metal oxide silicon** and indicates the particular process by which the transistors are produced. In memory components, transistors are used as switches and are either ON or OFF. NMOS memory components use NMOS transistors as active loads instead of the large impedances used in discrete circuits, as large impedances are difficult to achieve using semiconductors. In addition, each flip-flop typically requires 10 NMOS transistors and large memory components contain many thousands of transistors. Each of the NMOS transistors consumes power and this limits the size of NMOS memory components as the power is converted to heat, and the heat has to be removed from the semiconductor to prevent damage. Standard packaging has a limit to the amount of heat it can dissipate and it is this, coupled with the large area of silicon required, which limits the memory component size. Large areas of silicon are difficult to produce without crystal defects, which would prevent the component made on that piece of silicon from working correctly.

CMOS. CMOS stands for **complementary metal oxide silicon** and avoids the need for the transistors which compose the memory cells, to have active loads consuming current continuously. Instead, the transistors are arranged such that current is only required when the transistors are changing state, from ON to OFF, and from OFF to ON, which is only for a short time. This reduces the current required for a memory component which is not being accessed to a very small amount which can in turn be supplied by a small battery. Even when a memory component is being accessed, the total current supplied is much smaller than for the NMOS transistor-based flip-flop. The reduction in the total power required by the component reduces the heat needed to be dissipated, which allows cheaper packaging to be used. As the power supply is reduced significantly for the memory component the complete system may also have a smaller power supply which would be cheaper and easier to include.

Bipolar. In bipolar transistor memory the transistors are used in their active region (rather than the saturated regions used by NMOS and CMOS, when the transistors are completely on or completely off) which enables extremely fast switching times to be achieved and this type of memory can be used with the fastest microprocessors. The drawback is that in the active regions the transistors require relatively large currents, increasing the heat to be dissipated and limiting the number of transistors in a single component package. The bipolar memory components are also relatively expensive. This prevents bipolar memory being used for general purpose memory due to the large number of components required, but it is often used to form a small high speed

memory area that can be used in conjunction with slower, cheaper memory components to increase the speed of data transfer.

Microprocessors now execute instructions faster than they can be fetched from the cheaper, slower memory components and the use of an intermediate buffer of high speed RWM enables a memory system to be constructed which increases the speed of transfer between microprocessor and memory but does not require large amounts of expensive memory.

Dynamic RWMs

The dynamic RWM was devised to reduce the number of transistors in a bit storage cell and hence the size of the silicon required, and also the power consumption. Charge is stored on a capacitor to represent a logic 1, and zero charge to represent a logic 0, see *Figure 3.8*, rather than using a flip-flop. However, because semiconductor capacitors can only store a small charge and have a high leakage resistance, the charge must be periodically 'refreshed', by reading each memory location at intervals of less than 4 milliseconds. There is a feedback circuit from the data output to the data input of the capacitor and during a READ operation this circuit is completed and the charge restored to its initial value.

To write data: S_1 is closed and S_2 and S_3 opened, so there is no feedback loop and the capacitor is charged to the input logic level.

To read data: S_2 and S_3 are closed and S_1 opened, so that there is a feedback loop and the charge is refreshed to its initial value.

It is not necessary to **refresh** each cell individually as DRWM's (**Dynamic RWM's**) are arranged in an X–Y grid, and by only enabling the 1-of-X decoders all the cells in a row can be refreshed simultaneously. For a 256 kbit DRWM arranged as 512 rows by 512 columns, only 512 refresh operations are required. Normally burst refresh is used with 512 READs sequentially performed. There is no data transferred during this process. The alternative is to use unused bus cycles to perform the refresh operations. This is more complex to implement but does improve memory utilisation. Burst refresh occupies approximately 8 per cent of the available memory bandwidth.

A typical DRWM cell consists only of a single transistor and capacitor produced from another transistor and hence requires only two transistors as opposed to 10 for the static RWM. It is therefore easier to manufacture with a large number of locations increasing the number of address lines required. For a 256 kbit device, 18 address lines are required, plus the data-in signal, the data-out signal, the read signal, the write signal, the chip select

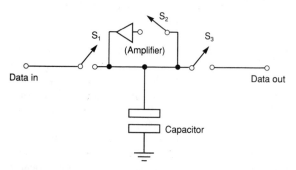

Figure 3.8   Symbolic dynamic RWM

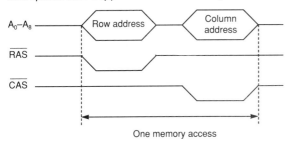

Figure 3.9 Time-multiplexed DRWM address signals

signal, and the two power supply connections, making 24 signals in all.

To reduce the number of pins required per memory component, the address is time-multiplexed, (shown in *Figure 3.9*), into two equal sized parts. For the 256 kbit memory component, the 18 address signals are divided into 2 blocks of 9 called the row and column addresses, and then multiplexed onto 9 address lines. Two additional signals, $\overline{RAS}$ (**row address select**) and $\overline{CAS}$ (**column address select**) are required for the DRWM component to internally de-multiplex the address, making a total of 18 pins. The 18-pin package is on a 0.3 inch pin row spacing, whereas 24-pin packages use a 0.6 inch pin row spacing, so 50 per cent of the PCB area can be saved by using the 18-pin package.

A special DRWM controller is used to perform the multiplexing, obtain the correct timing of the signals, and perform most of the memory refreshing actions. Therefore DRWMs are usually only used if a large memory is required to make it worthwhile adding the (expensive) DRWM controller.

ROM

This is a **read only memory** component whose contents cannot be altered, with each bit storage implemented as a transistor that is permanently ON or permanently OFF, see *Figure 3.10*. This is achieved by either the transistor being absent to indicate a logic 1 is stored, or the transistor is present to indicate a logic 0.

The presence or absence of the transistor is dependent on the **mask** used in its production, and a change in the ROM contents requires a new mask to be produced. This is an expensive process that is only used when many thousands of a particular ROM are required.

PROM (Programmable ROM)

An alternative to using a ROM if only a few are required, is a **programmable ROM** (PROM) which avoids the cost of mask production.

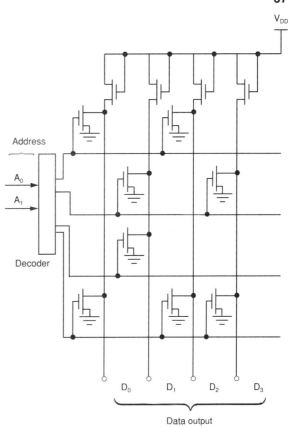

Figure 3.10 ROM layout of a 4 × 4 device

These contain fusible links of either nichrome or polysilicon which are either programmed to be an open circuit or a closed circuit, as in *Figure 3.11* (overleaf). These devices can only be programmed once and for small numbers are more cost effective than ROMs.

EPROM (Erasable Programmable ROM)

When programs are being developed there are many changes made and to overcome the problem of using only one-time programmable ROMs, which would require many ROMs, the EPROM was developed. This allows a ROM to be programmed and then, if necessary, erased by exposure to ultraviolet light. The entire program has to be erased by this process. The EPROM structure is effectively the same as the PROM structure except that the 'fuses' are erasable and reprogrammable.

CMOS Stand-By (Non-volatile) Memory

An alternative to ROM, PROM or EPROM, which allows easy changing of the program and saved data is the

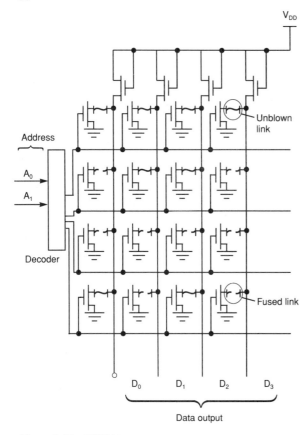

Figure 3.11   PROM layout

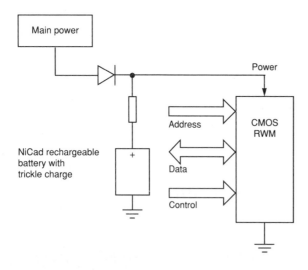

Figure 3.12   CMOS memory with battery back-up

battery-backed CMOS memory component. These are CMOS memory components with an extremely low power requirement which can be supplied by a small rechargeable battery, see *Figure 3.12*. When power is applied the CMOS memory components act as RWM devices and at the same time the battery is being charged. When power is removed, the power supply to the CMOS memory components is switched from the main supply to the battery. The data in the CMOS memory component can be retained for several weeks at a time when the rest of the microcontroller or microcomputer is switched off. The data stored in this way is then immediately available when the main power supply is restored.

The CMOS supply is isolated from the main supply by the diode so that when the main supply is removed the battery continues to supply the CMOS devices with current. When the main power is applied, the memory component has power and also the battery is trickle charged to ensure that it is always fully charged.

Electrically-Alterable ROM

An alternative to battery-backed CMOS is EAROM, which is similar to RWM but with a much longer WRITE cycle (approximately a 1 ms access time). However, when the power is removed the data is still maintained correctly. The structure is very similar to the that of the EPROM, except that the data can be altered while the device is being used. These do not require any battery back-ups to save the data when the power is removed but are much more expensive to produce.

3.2   PROGRAMMABLE INPUT AND OUTPUT (PIO)

A microcontroller and microcomputer need to transfer data to and from external devices and components. For example, there may be a series of switches, which can be either ON or OFF, used to control a device such as a lift as in *Figure 3.13*.

The method of connecting such devices to the microcontroller, which is known as **interfacing**, is by using an **input/output (I/O) port**. An I/O port is similar to a memory location in that it has a specific address and data can be transferred to or from it. Some microprocessors have separate I/O and memory address ranges, while others have only a memory address range and treat I/O ports as memory locations. The difference is that a memory location is used to store the data value placed into it, whereas a memory location used as an I/O port uses the data transferred to it. When writing to an

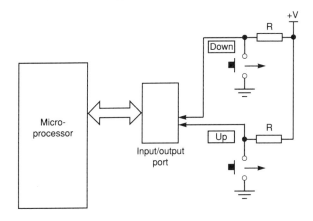

Figure 3.13 Interfacing to a microprocessor: lift control

I/O port the data can also be used to configure the operation of the peripheral component containing the I/O ports which are then called **control ports**. Alternatively, data can be transferred out of the microcontroller or microcomputer completely in order to influence external events such as switching lights on and off. When reading from an I/O port, the data value obtained can be an indication of the status of the peripheral component or alternatively, the state of external events such as whether a switch is on or off.

Table 3.1 Possible I/O port uses

State	Port	Function
OUTPUT	Control port	Controls and configures the operation of the peripheral component
	Data port	Transfers data values to external devices
INPUT	Status port	Indicates the status of the peripheral component
	Data port	Transfers data values from external devices to the microprocessor

Only a few specialised I/O ports allow data to be written to and read from the same I/O address, as is possible with most memory locations. Most are programmed for input only or for output only and are known as **programmable input/output** (PIO). This is acceptable as few external devices are bi-directional. *Figure 3.13* illustrates how to input from some switches and it can be seen that any output to the switches would not serve any useful purpose and may even cause permanent damage.

The programmer's model of a PIO is simple and consists of a command/status register used to configure the complete component and a data register for each port, as in *Figure 3.14*. Once programmed by writing the required command byte to the command register, the individual data ports can be used for input only or output only. A data port programmed for output will only transfer values from the microprocessor to the data pins on the component associated with that port. Attempting to read from a port programmed for output will not obtain any useful information. Similarly, a data port programmed for input will only transfer the data value on the pins associated with that port to the microprocessor, and writing to that port will not change any of the values.

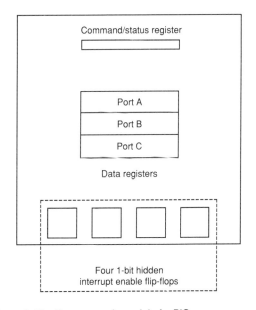

Figure 3.14 Programmer's model of a PIO

Figure 3.14 shows a PIO with three 8-bit ports, which is the usual number that can be fitted into a 40-pin integrated circuit package. Each data port requires 8 pins for byte transfers, making 24 pins. There is also an 8-bit bi-directional data bus and 2 address lines connected between the microprocessor and the PIO, making 34 pins. This leaves 6 pins for the power supply connections and other control signals, such as read, write and chip select, see *Figure 3.15* (overleaf).

The I/O addresses of the PIO ports are comprised of the chip select address plus the local I/O port offset. The chip select address is determined by the physical address decoding used and will be assumed to be PIO_CS_ADDR for the following example. The local offset is then added to this to form the I/O address of the

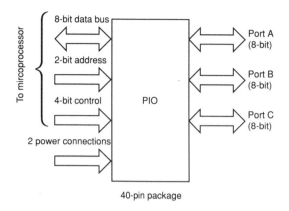

Figure 3.15   PIO package

individual ports. The 2 address bits connected to the PIO component can decode four local offsets, comprising the three data ports and the command register. This enables the port addresses to be produced as follows.

Example

```
PORTA   EQU   CS_PIO_ADDR + 0      ;Address of port A.
PORTB   EQU   CS_PIO_ADDR + 1      ;Address of port B.
PORTC   EQU   CS_PIO_ADDR + 2      ;Address of port C.
COMM_REG   EQU   CS_PIO_ADDR + 3   ;Address of the
                                   ;command
                                   ;register.
```

These I/O port addresses can then be used to access the ports required as illustrated in the following program fragment which programs, using 8086 assembly language, a PIO for PORT A as output and PORT B as input. (See chapter 5 for explanations of assembly language programming.)

Example

```
MOV   DX,COMM_REG          ;Set up command register.
MOV   AL,PA_OUT_&_PB_IN    ;Select port A as output and
                           ; port B as input.
OUT   DX,AL                ;Program the PIO.
```

Equivalent 68000 Program

```
move.1 comm_reg, A1        ;Set up command reg, A as
                           ;O/P, B as I/P.
move.b PA_OUT_&_PB_IN,(A1)
```

To output to a port, it is now only necessary to write to the port data register. The following program fragment will output the contents of the 8086 AL register to PORT A of the PIO.

Example

```
MOV   DX,PORTA         ;Set up address to port.
MOV   AL,DATA_VALUE    ;Get data byte.
OUT   DX,AL            ;Output data to port.
```

Equivalent 68000 Program

```
move.1   portA,A1      ;Set up port address.
move.b   (A1),D0
```

A similar program illustrated with 8086 assembly language is used to input data from PORT B of the PIO:

```
MOV   DX,PORTB      ;Set up address to port.
IN    AL,DX         ;Input the data from the port.
```

Handshaking

Sometimes there is a requirement to ensure that the transfer of data between the port and the external device has been correctly completed. This is known as handshaking and requires two control signals in addition to the data bits. The PIO is programmed to perform handshaking by using one of the ports for control purposes rather than data I/O. This reduces the number of 8-bit ports available from 3 to 2 when handshaking is used.

The two control signals required for handshaking are **data valid** and **acknowledge**. The data valid signal is controlled by the component transmitting the data to indicate that data is stable on the port pins, as illustrated in *Figure 3.16*. The component receiving the data recognises this signal, reads the data from the port and then, when the read operation is completed, uses the acknowledge signal to indicate a successful transfer. The transmitting component then recognises the acknowledge signal as indicating a successful transfer and the data and data valid signals can be removed. The receiving component then completes the data transfer by removing the acknowledge signal, leaving the port ready for the next data byte to be transferred.

Example

The following algorithm indicates how a port is programmed to transmit data on a port with handshaking:

(1) Initialise;
(2) Put data onto port;
(3) Activate the data valid signal;
(4) Wait for the acknowledge signal to become valid;
(5) De-activate the data valid signal;
(6) Wait for the acknowledge signal to become invalid;
(7) Transfer next byte by repeating from step (2).

It is not necessary to remove the data from the ports as deactivating the data valid signal indicates that any

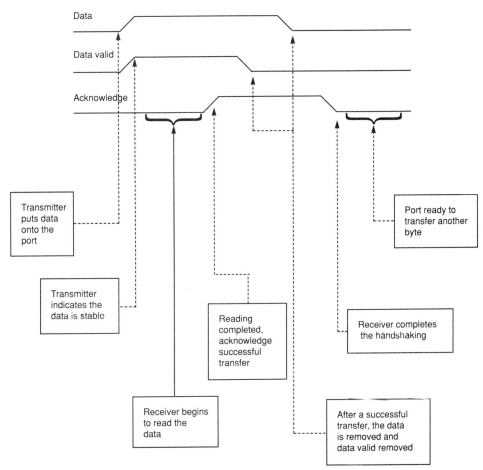

Figure 3.16 Handshaking

data present is no longer valid. The following example indicates a possible 8086 assembly language implementation of the above algorithm.

```
                            ;Initialise. Step (1)
    MOV   DX,COMM_REG
    MOV   AL,PORTA_OUT
    OUT   DX,AL
                            ;Put data onto the port. Step (2)
    MOV   DX,PORTA          ;O/P data to port A
    MOV   AL,DATA_BYTE
    OUT   DX,AL
                            ;Activate data valid signal. Step (3)
    MOV   DX, HS_PORT_OUT   ;Activate the data
    MOV   AL, DATA_VALID    ;signal bit on the
    OUT   DX, AL            ;port used for
                           ;handshaking.
                            ;Wait for acknowledge valid. Step (4)
    MOV   DX, HS_PORT_IN    ;
WAIT1:  IN  AL, DX         ;Wait until the bit
                           ;used for
    AND   AL, ACKNOWLEDGE   ;acknowledge on the
```

```
    JZ    WAITL             ;handshaking port
                           ;becomes active.
                 ;De-activate data valid signal. Step (5)
    MOV   DX, HS_PORT_OUT   ;Deactivate data
    MOV   AL, INVALID       ;valid.
    OUT   DX, AL
                    ;Wait for acknowledge invalid. Step (6)
    MOV   DX, HS_PORT_IN
WAIT2:  IN  AL, DX
    AND   AL, ACKNOWLEDGE   ;Test for
                           ;acknowledge bit
                           ;active.
    JNZ   WAIT2             ;Wait until
                           ;acknowledge is
                           ;inactive.
                  ;Transfer next byte. Step (7)
```

There must then be a similar program execution which controls the handshaking at the receiving port. This could be another 8086 controlling another PIO programmed for receiving data values using handshaking to ensure correct transfer.

Example

A typical algorithm for transmitting with handshaking is listed below. The writing of the program is left as an exercise for the reader:

(1) Initialise;
(2) Wait for the data valid signal to be activated;
(3) Read data from port;
(4) Activate the acknowledge signal;
(5) Wait for the data valid signal to become inactive;
(6) De-activate the acknowledge signal;
(7) Wait for next transfer; repeat from step (2).

If a PIO under microprocessor control was used to control the transmission of data and another microprocessor-controlled PIO was used to receive the data under handshaking control, it would enable the two microprocessors to synchronise in order to transfer data. Usually only one side of the transfer link is under microprocessor control with the other being a dedicated hardware component or device that is only able to control the handshaking signals.

The 8255 PIO

The PIO that will be considered in detail is the Intel 8255, see *Figure 3.17*, which has 24 I/O signals arranged as three 8-bit ports, A, B and C, or as two groups of 12, called ports A and B, which transfer 8-bit data values under handshaking control. This device is similar to the general I/O device described previously.

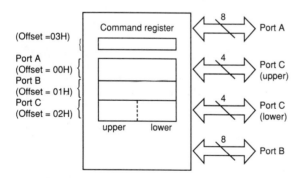

Figure 3.17   The 8255 PIO

The Command Register

The command register has a local offset address of 03H, and this is then added to the chip select address and forms the command register address. For example, assuming the chip select address was 060H, then the

command register would be addressed as: 060H + 03H = 063H.

Port A would then be addressed as: 060H + 00H = 060H.

Port B would be addressed as: 060H + 01H = 061H.

Port C would be addressed as: 060H + 02H = 062H.

The command register is a write only register and reading from it obtains invalid results. Therefore, if it is necessary to maintain a record of how the PIO was programmed, a copy of the command byte has to be separately maintained in memory.

The functions allocated to the bit positions of the command register are shown in *Figure 3.18*. Bit 7 is used to select between programming the mode definitions or for Port C individual bit programming. This means each bit position has two uses depending upon the logic value of bit 7, and this enables some complex programming to be performed using only one 8-bit command register. The 8255 does not have the status register indicated in the general PIO programmer's model, although some status information can be obtained in the handshaking modes by reading port C.

Types of Operation

The 24 I/O signals are divided into two groups of 12 and each group can be used as an 8-bit port with handshaking, or as separate 8-bit and 4-bit ports. The two types of operation are called mode 0 and mode 1, which allow uni-directional transfer of data in the programmed direction. The 12 I/O signals known as group A have an additional mode called mode 2, which allows bi-directional data transfer through the same port without having to re-program its direction. This mode of operation is not explained here as it is rarely used.

Port B: mode 0.   In this mode, the 12 I/O signals known as group B, consisting of two ports: B (8 bits) and C lower (4 bits) are used as simple I/O ports. The direction of each complete port is fixed by the direction select bits in the command register, and the four combinations are:

Command (in binary)	Selection	
1XXXX000	Port B output	Port C (lower) output
1XXXX001	Port B output	Port C (lower) input
1XXXX010	Port B input	Port C (lower) output
1XXXX011	Port B input	Port C (lower) input

X indicates a command register bit that has not yet been selected.

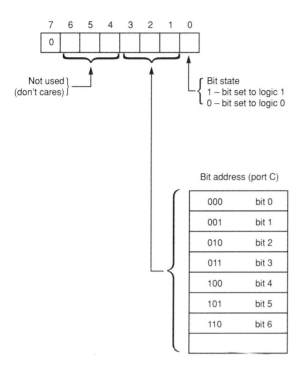

(a) Single bit programming (bit 7 = 0)

Port B: mode 1. In mode 1, the 8-bit port B has handshaking implemented using the low three bits of Port C which are used as the data valid, acknowledge (explained earlier) and interrupt request signals. In this mode, only the direction of Port B needs to be programmed as Port C (lower) is always used for handshaking and does not require programming as the signals are fixed.

Handshaking signals: Output on port B

Signal	Name	Direction	Comment
PC_0	INTRB	Output	Used as an interrupt to the transmitting CPU, to indicate that the O/P port is now empty. This signal is reset by the next write.
PC_1	$\overline{OBFB}$	Output	Output buffer full signal (active low) is connected to the receiving device to indicate that a byte is present.
PC_2	$\overline{ACKB}$	Input	Acknowledge signal (active low) from the receiving device to indicate that the byte has been correctly received.

Input on port B

Signal	Name	Direction	Comment
PC_0	INTRB	Output	Used as an interrupt to the receiving CPU, to indicate that the input port is now full. This signal is reset by the next read.
PC_1	IBFB	Output	Input buffer full signal is connected to the transmitting device to indicate that a byte has been received.
PC_2	$\overline{STBB}$	Input	Acknowledge signal (active low) from the transmitting device to indicate that the byte has been placed onto the transmitting device port and is ready to be received.

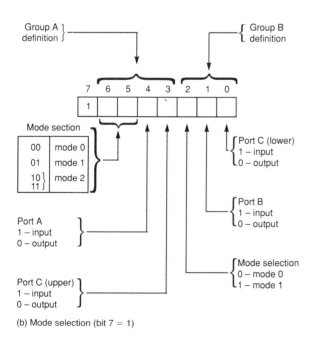

(b) Mode selection (bit 7 = 1)

Figure 3.18 Command register functions

Input in mode 1 on port B. When inputting data from port B, bit 2 of port C becomes the data valid input signal, which is active low, rather than the active high as explained earlier in the handshaking section, and Bit 1 of port C becomes the acknowledge signal. These two signals perform most of the handshaking functions that were under program control in the earlier example.

Data will be valid on the port before the data valid signal (PC_2) goes active low, so that it can be automatically saved into port B. Following this the acknowledge signal, (PC_1), is activated to indicate to the transmitting device that data has been correctly received. When the transmitting device recognises the acknowledge, the data valid signal (PC_2) becomes inactive (high state). The next read to port B will cause the acknowledge signal (PC_1) to be de-activated, which allows the next byte to be received.

There are two ways the microprocessor can be made aware that there is data in port B waiting to be read, called **polling** or **interrupt driven**.

Port C as a status register (polling). If polling is being implemented, the microprocessor has to access the status register of the port to determine whether a data byte has been received. This means the program periodically has to test the information in the status register to identify this state, and a byte may have been received for a considerable period of time before being noticed if the program is busy elsewhere.

In mode 1 operation, as well as port C acting as handshaking for port B (and port A), it also functions as the status register containing information regarding the stage of handshaking reached, see *Figure 3.19*

The interrupt request from the PIO is enabled by setting one of the hidden flip-flops, refer to *Figure 3.14*, called INTEB (interrupt enable group B). This is achieved by a bit set operation (see earlier) to bit 2 of port C. In mode 1, when a read of port C is performed the state of the interrupt request signal is indicated by PC_0:

$PC_0 = 0$ There is no interrupt request which indicates that a byte has not been received.

$PC_0 = 1$ An interrupt request is pending, which indicates that a byte has been received.

Bit 1 of port C, PC_1, indicates different status information depending on whether group B is inputting or outputting. If inputting, PC_1 indicates the state of the acknowledge signal, where:

$PC_1 = 0$ The acknowledge signal is inactive, (which indicates that the byte has not yet been received).

$PC_1 = 1$ The acknowledge signal is active, (which indicates that the byte has been received).

When outputting, PC_1 indicates the state of the data valid signal. This is an active low signal so that:

$PC_1 = 0$ indicates that data is valid on port B ready for output and indicates that the byte has not yet been transmitted.

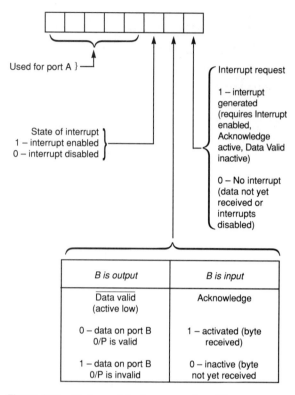

Figure 3.19   Status register for groups A and B

$PC_1 = 1$ indicates that the data is invalid on port B and shows that the data has been transmitted.

These status bits can be used by the program to determine when a byte is ready for transfer. Normally, bit PC_1 would be used in the input mode 1.

Example

In this example Port B has been programmed for input in mode 1 and demonstrates reading the status port.

```
        MOV  DX,PORTC    ;Get the status from port C.
WAIT:   IN   AL,DX
;
        AND  AL,00000010B  ;Is the acknowledge signal
                           ;active?
        JZ   WAIT          ;No, then continue waiting as
                           ;the byte has not yet been
                           ;received.
;
        MOV  DX,PORTB    ;Yes, then read the received
        IN   AL,DX       ;data from port B. This will
                         ;automatically de-activate
                         ;acknowledge.
```

As can be seen from this small example program, mode 1 operation for inputting bytes on port B with handshaking (using bits of port C) is much simplified. The disadvantage is that the response time between a byte being received by the port and then transferred to the CPU may be large, depending on the program.

Using Interrupt Request

It is possible to use the interrupt request signal (INTR) to generate an interrupt to the microprocessor, as in *Figure 3.20*. This shows that a **programmable interrupt controller** (PIC) has been used to handle the interrupt request correctly as required by the 8086. However, not all microprocessors require a PIC to be present to handle the interrupt. This has the advantage that the response time between a byte being received and then transferred to the CPU is reduced to a few microseconds, and is not dependent on what the program is doing.

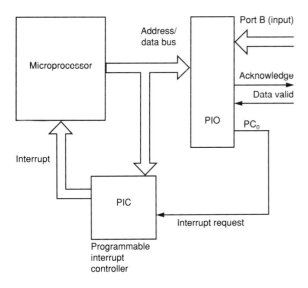

Figure 3.20   Interrupt-driven handshaking

This is particularly useful if the rate at which bytes are received at port B is irregular or infrequent, as it enables the microprocessor to execute some other part of the program, without having to interrogate the status register periodically. The interrupt is used to initiate an **interrupt service** subroutine which will read the data from port B.

The interrupt request is set if:

(a) The interrupt enable bit is active;
(b) The data valid signal is inactive;
(c) The acknowledge signal is active.

This indicates that a data byte has been received by port B and is waiting to be read. When port B is read the acknowledge signal and interrupt request signal are both cleared. Bit 2 of port C, PC_2, allows the programmer to determine the state of the **interrupt enable flag**, INTEB. This enables the interrupt request to be turned ON or OFF by the program as required.

Outputting data to port B in mode 1.   As indicated in the handshaking section, when outputting data from port B, data valid (active low) is an output now on PC_1, and acknowledge is an input now on PC_2 (also active low).

After the microprocessor has completed writing the byte, it appears on the output pins of port B and the data valid (active low) signal is activated. When the receiving device has correctly read the data, it activates the acknowledge signal (active low pulse) which will be recognised by port B, the transmitting device, and the data valid signal will be de-activated. This indicates that the transfer has been completed so that acknowledge is de-activated. At this stage the interrupt request signal (PC_0) is activated as:

(a) The data valid signal is inactive;
(b) The acknowledge signal is inactive;
(c) The interrupt enable bit is active.

This can be used as an interrupt to the microprocessor and indicates that port B is ready for another data byte. The interrupt request signal is de-activated by the start of the write operation to port B as new data is being transferred.

Port C can be used to monitor the status of the output transfer if the port is using the polling method when PC_1, data valid (active low) is used to monitor the state of the transfer. Data valid is activated by writing to port B and does not become inactive until the data has been received and the receiver has activated acknowledge. Therefore, by waiting for data valid to become inactive after a byte has been transferred to port B for output, the transfer can be identified as being successfully completed and another byte transferred to port B.

Example

The following program fragment assumes that port B is already programmed for output in mode 1 (with handshaking).

```
                          ;Example program to
                          ;output on port B in
                          ;mode 1.
    ;
        MOV   DX,PORT_B   ;Write the data to port B.
```

```
        MOV   AL,DATA_VALUE        ;This clears any
                                   ;previous interrupt
        OUT   DX,AL                ;requests and activates
                                   ;data valid signal.
;
        MOV   DX,PORT_C            ;Wait for the data valid
WAIT:   IN    AL,DX                ;signal to become
        AND   AL,00000010B         ;inactive, as this
        JZ    WAIT                 ;indicates that another
                                   ;data byte can be written
                                   ;to port B.
;
                                   ;Port B is now ready for
                                   ;another data byte to be
                                   ;written.
                                   ;
```

The Operation of Port A in Modes 0 and 1

Port A group operates in a similar way as the port B group in modes 0 and 1. The differences are that in mode 0 the upper four bits of port C are used as an I/O port whilst in mode 1 the top 5 bits of port C are used in the handshaking mode.

Full information on this mode and the complete detailed information for using mode 0 and mode 1 for groups A and B and also mode 2 operation for group A, can be obtained by referring to the appropriate data books (as some simplifications have been made and some detail omitted).

Example of mode 0 operation. *Figure 3.21* illustrates the use of a PIO to input the status of a bank of 8 on/off switches. The base address of the PIO is 060H. The straight-forward method of interfacing the switches would be to use an 8-bit port as an input port. However, if the 8 switches are organised into two banks of four switches each, the number of I/O signals required is reduced from 8 to 5. The 5 consist of the 4 input signals which can be connected to either bank, which is determined by the state of a single output signal.

The signal PB_3, which is bit 3 of port B is used as the switch bank select and when a logic 0, switch bits SW_1 to SW_4 are connected to bits PC_0 to PC_3 of port C. When PB_3 is a logic 1 switch bits SW_5 to SW_8 are connected to bits

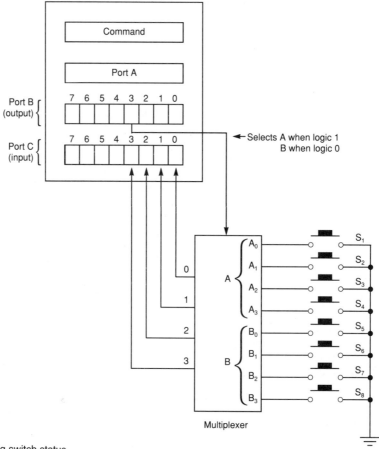

Figure 3.21   Reading switch status

PC$_0$ to PC$_3$ of port C. Therefore, port B has to be programmed for output and port C for input and this is basic input and output without handshaking. Port A will also be programmed for output, although in this example it is not used for anything, so both A and B groups will be programmed for mode 0 operation. As mode 0 operation is used the hidden interrupt enable flip-flops do not need to be programmed as they are not used. The algorithm is as follows:

(1) Initialise the PIO (program command register);
(2) Select the first bank of switches (set PB$_3$ to logic 0);
(3) Input the switch states (read SW$_1$ to SW$_4$ from port C, PC$_0$ to PC$_3$);
(4) Select the second bank of switches (set PB$_3$ to logic 1);
(5) Input the switch states (read SW$_5$ to SW$_5$ from port C, PC$_0$ to PC$_3$);
(6) Save the 8 bits of data input as the switch settings.

Example

This program will input the status of 8 switches organised as two banks of 4, with port C, bit 3, PC$_3$, acting as an output to select which bank, and port B acting as the input.

```
COMMAND_PORT  EQU  063H       ;Command port
                              ;address.
PORT_B        EQU  061H       ;Address port B.
LOW_SWITCH    EQU  00001000B  ;Bit PC3 to low for
                              ;SW1-SW4.
HIGH_SWITCH   EQU  00001000B  ;Bit PC3 to high for
                              ;SW5-SW8.
                              ;Initialise. Step (1)
MOV  DX,COMMAND_PORT;Initialise the PIO for mode 0
MOV  AL,10001001B             ;operation for groups A and B.
OUT  DX,AL                    ;Ports A and B for output and
                              ;port C for input.
                              ;Select the first bank of
                              ;switches. Step (2)
MOV  DX,PORT_B                ;Set PB3 to low to read
MOV  AL,LOW_SWITCH            ;SW1 to SW4.
OUT  DX,AL                    ;
                              ;Input switch states. Step (3)
MOV  DX,PORT_C                ;Input the switch settings of
IN   AL,DX                    ;SW1 to SW4 and save in BL
MOV  BL,AL                    ;temporarily.
                              ;Select the second bank
                              ;of switches. Step (4)
MOV  DX,PORT_B                ;Set PB3 to high to read
MOV  AL,HIGH_SWITCH           ;SW5 to SW8.
OUT  DX,AL
                              ;Input the switch settings. Step (5)
MOV  DX,PORT_C                ;Input the switch settings of
IN   AL,DX                    ;SW5 to SW8.
                              ;Save 8 bits of data as the
                              ;switch settings. Step (6)
MOV  CL,4                     ;Shift to top nibble and
SHL  AL,CL                    ;combine with SW1 to SW4
```

```
AND  AL,0F0H                  ;to create SW1 to SW8.
OR   BL,A
MOV  SWITCHES,BL              ;Save the switch settings in
                              ;memory.
```

This arrangement of switches was used in the IBM PC/XT to indicate details about the hardware of the computer required during initialisation, as illustrated in *Figure 3.22*

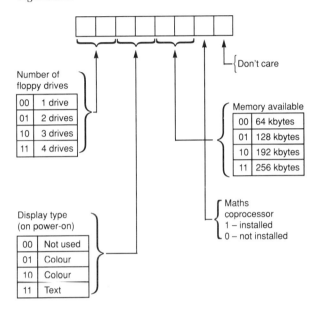

Figure 3.22 Switch settings

Summary

The PIO, although an apparently simple peripheral component which is easy to program, is a flexible device allowing the transfer of data values with or without handshaking, to or from external devices connected to the microcontroller or microcomputer.

3.3 PROGRAMMABLE COMMUNICATIONS

One of the requirements of microcontrollers and microcomputers is to be able to transfer information between two points as in *Figure 3.23* (overleaf). This can generally be described as a communication link and is normally bi-directional so that information can be transferred simultaneously in both directions.

There are a variety of methods for implementing

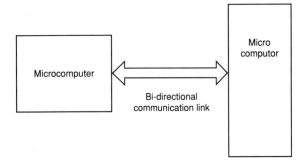

Figure 3.23   Transfer information

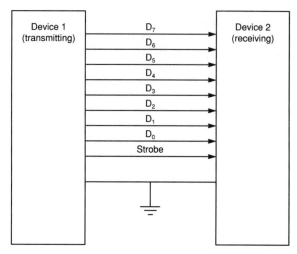

Figure 3.24   Parallel communication

communication links which can be divided into two main categories, parallel and serial. Each of these methods has some similar functions such as error detection and correction and can operate at different frequencies, so programmable communication interface components are used. These allow a range of different methods to be implemented with one component by just reprogramming it. However, as parallel and serial communication require different numbers of data transfer signals, 10 for parallel and 2 for serial, it is usual for a device to implement parallel communication methods only, or serial communication methods only. This can be used to reduce the number of pins on the component so that a serial device will typically have 28 pins and a parallel device 40 pins.

Communication links have several important requirements that affect how the link is implemented. In most circumstances, the two microcomputers will be several metres or more apart and therefore the cables used to connect them must be as cheap as possible. In addition, the longer the cables the more likely it is that the data will be affected by man-made (e.g. radio waves) and natural (e.g. lightning strikes) interference, so a method resistant to such interference should be chosen. In circumstances when the data is corrupted, the communication link should be able to detect when these events have occurred.

Parallel Communication

In parallel communication the data is transmitted as bytes, with each bit having a separate connection, as illustrated in *Figure 3.24*. Parallel communication makes sense as the data manipulated by the microcomputers is in bytes. However, such a link requires ten wires, 8 data, 1 strobe and 1 ground, and would be expensive over long distances. It is also liable to electrical interference which can corrupt the data if the cables are longer than two metres.

For parallel communication the data is placed onto the output of a parallel port, such as would be available on a programmable input/output device (PIO). When it has stabilised, a short pulse is output on the strobe connection as illustrated in *Figure 3.25* This will cause the receiving port to latch the data and complete the transfer. This is a fast, simple method that is often used over short distances such as would be required to connected a printer to a personal computer.

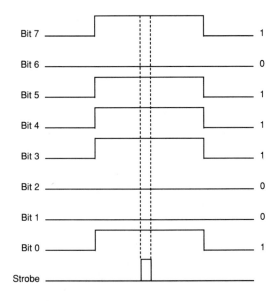

Figure 3.25   Parallel communication timing

The voltages used to represent the different logic levels in the parallel communication link are the same as those inside the computer so special buffers are not required. However, these signals have a relatively high impedance and if the cables are more than one or two metres long, they act as aerials and pick up electrical noise which can corrupt the data. It would be possible to provide special buffers to avoid this problem but this, combined with the necessity of having 10 connections, would make the parallel communication link relatively costly.

Serial Communication

The alternative to parallel communication is serial communication, illustrated in *Figure 3.26*, when a byte of data is transmitted a bit at a time rather than all at once. This requires simpler buffers to obtain interference resistant transmission, and fewer wires connecting the two devices, so that the cost is much less than that for parallel communication.

The byte is converted into a serial format using a parallel-to-serial converter and one bit is output for every bit clock pulse, *Figure 3.27*. It is necessary to add some extra bits to the data being transmitted so that the

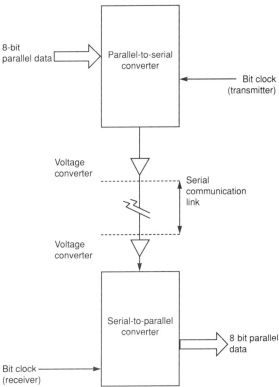

Figure 3.27   Parallel-serial-parallel conversion

beginning and end can be detected. These are called the start and stop bits. The start bit is used to indicate that a new byte of data is about to begin and the stop bits are used to indicate that the byte transmission has been completed. These are also used to detect any errors that may be introduced by electrical interference.

The rate at which bits are transmitted and received is determined by the transmitting and receiving clock signals as illustrated in *Figure 3.27*. The bit clock is not transmitted with the data so that a separate bit clock is required for the transmitter and for the receiver. It is necessary to ensure that these two clocks have the same frequency so that data is clocked in at the same rate as it is clocked out; this frequency is known as the **Baud rate**.

The timing diagram shown in *Figure 3.26* is known as an **asynchronous protocol** as bytes can be transmitted at any time. The start and stop bits then provide all the necessary information to transfer each byte correctly.

There is an alternative method known as synchronous, but that will not be covered.

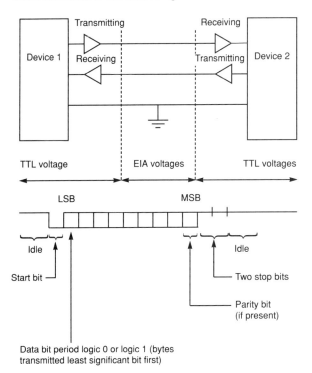

Figure 3.26   Serial communication and timing

Error Detection

In a good communication system it is expected that errors in the data caused by external interference will occur infrequently. For asynchronous communication links this means that no more than one bit may have a changed state during a byte of data, either from logic 0 to logic 1, or from logic 1 to logic 0. This allows simple error detection techniques to be used.

The correction of detected errors is possible but requires additional control information to be included with the transmitted data. This reduces the effective rate at which data is transmitted, which is a disadvantage, as illustrated below.

With no Data Correction Bits

Data bits $\quad = 8$
Control bits $= 2$ (1 start and 1 stop)
_____
Total $\qquad = 10$

At a fixed frequency, F, the effective data bandwidth is:

$$\frac{\text{Data bits}}{\text{Total bits}} \frac{8}{} \times 100\% \text{ of } F = \frac{8}{10} = 80\% \text{ of } F$$

Data Correction Bits Included

Data bits $\qquad = 8$
Control bits $\quad = 2$
Correction bits $= 4$
_____
Total $\qquad = 14$

At a fixed frequency, F, the effective data bandwidth is:

$$\frac{\text{Data bits}}{\text{Total bits}} \times 100\% \text{ of } F = \frac{8}{14} = 57\% \text{ of } F$$

As the rate at which errors occur is very low, usually less than 1 in a million bits, no error correction bits are included, only error detection bits. It is then left to the individual user to decide what to do if an error is detected.

Parity Check

The main error detection method is the parity check and this is used to detect any bit changes caused by external interference during transmission.

The communication link will be defined to use either an even or an odd parity, to ensure that all bytes are transmitted and received with the same parity. The transmitter and receiver have to be programmed to use the same parity checking. An additional bit, called the **parity bit**, is added to the data as in *Figure 3.26*.

The parity can be considered to be the sum of logic 1's

in a byte of data. If this adds up to an even number, the byte has even parity; if it is an odd number, the byte has odd parity. For an even parity communication link the parity bit is set to zero if the number of bits in the byte is even, and set to a 1 if the number of bytes is odd. The receiver calculates the parity of the received byte and checks this with the parity bit. If the two quantities disagree an error has occurred and the data has been corrupted. Parity checking is guaranteed to detect single errors and is therefore compatible with low error rate communication links.

For odd parity, the parity bit is set to zero if the number of bits in the byte is odd and set to a one if the number of bits is even.

If a parity error is detected it only applies to that particular byte and does not indicate that the communication link is faulty. Only if the rate of parity errors detected becomes relatively high may the communication link be considered faulty.

On modern microcomputers, because the communication link is very reliable, parity checking is often not used.

Two other errors that can be easily detected are **framing errors** and **overrun errors** caused by the incorrect use of the programmable serial communication interface components, rather than by electrical interference.

Frame Error

A frame error occurs when a receiver does not detect a stop bit as the last data bit received, and this will occur when the transmitting and receiving bit clock frequencies are different. As the stop bit is always a logic 1 a frame error is detected when the last sampled bit position is not a logic 1, *Figure 3.28*. For a communication link which has incorrect bit clock frequencies it is not guaranteed that a framing error will be detected on the first byte transmitted, but there is a high probability that it will be detected within a few bytes.

A frame error is a serious error which renders the communication link un-usable as no data transmitted can be considered to be correctly received.

Overrun Error

An overrun error occurs when a byte of data is received before the previous byte has been removed from the receiver. This can occur when the transmitter is transmitting a sequential string of bytes such as text, but the receiver is not ready to receive such a string. This problem can be reduced by double buffering the receiver so that as soon as a complete byte is contained in the serial-to-parallel converter it is automatically

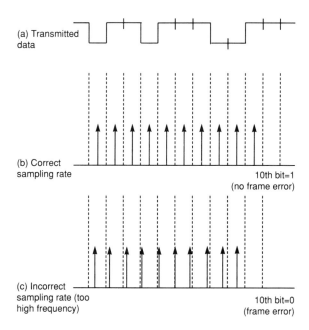

(a) Transmitted data

(b) Correct sampling rate
10th bit=1 (no frame error)

(c) Incorrect sampling rate (too high frequency)
10th bit=0 (frame error)

Figure 3.28 Frame error

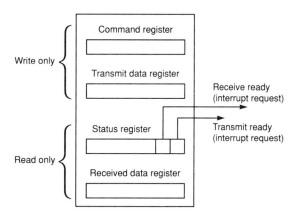

Figure 3.29 Programmable serial communication interface

transferred to a buffer register. This clears the serial-to-parallel converter so that it is ready to receive the next byte. While this byte is being received the microprocessor can be notified that a byte is ready and it can be transferred.

This usually works well because the Baud rate is a relatively low frequency when compared with the rate at which the microprocessor executes instructions. The 8086 can execute approximately 1 million instructions per second. At 9600 baud it takes:

$$\frac{\text{Number of bits per byte}}{\text{Baud rate}} = \frac{10}{9600} = 1.04 \text{ ms}$$

to receive a complete byte, in which time approximately 1000 instructions can be executed. This is usually enough to transfer the data correctly from the receiver to the microprocessor.

Also, this type of error can be avoided by using additional signals to implement handshaking. However, this requires additional wires and buffers and on many modern microcomputers handshaking is not implemented to avoid the additional cost.

Programmer's Model of a Programmable Serial Communication Interface (PSCI)

Figure 3.29 illustrates the general programmer's model of a **programmable serial communication interface** (PSCI) and this consists of 4 registers, 2 of which, the

command and transmit data registers, are write only and two read only, status and received data registers.

The command register is used to set various parameters concerning the serial communications, such as what parity is used, what Baud rate, whether asynchronous or synchronous operation is to be used, and so on. The transmit data register holds the data to be converted into serial format and transmitted. As these two registers are write only the mode and data byte transmitted cannot be read back once written, and copies of these values should be saved elsewhere in memory if it is required to know the mode.

The status register contains several flags which are used to determine the state of the transmitter and receiver and whether there are any errors, *Figure 3.30*. The frame, overrun and parity errors have an individual

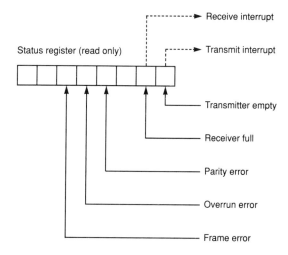

Figure 3.30 Status register flags

error flag, and there is a flag to indicate when the transmitter is empty so that another byte can be written to the PSCI, and a flag to indicate when a byte has been received so that it can be read by the microprocessor.

The status flags which indicate whether the transmit and receive data registers are empty or full are also available as interrupt signals. This allows the PSCI to be software-polled or interrupt-driven to provide the most suitable and efficient method of control. If interrupt-driven, the microcomputer or microcontroller would probably need to contain a programmable interrupt controller (PIC).

The use of interrupts in this way enables the microprocessor to be executing other useful programs while waiting for the serial communication link. This is how a PC is able to control a serial link such as a modem as a background task while still executing other user-specified programs. The use of interrupts does increase the complexity of the programming but frees the microprocessor for other tasks.

The Intel 8251A   Universal Asynchronous/Synchronous Receiver/Transmitter

One widely used PSCI is the Intel 8251A which incorporates both synchronous and asynchronous communication protocols. Only the asynchronous protocol will be considered here. Full programming and interfacing details can be obtained from the appropriate Intel data manuals.

The programmer's model is shown in *Figure 3.31* and is similar to the general PSCI programmer's model. A typical base address of the component might be 03F8H to which would be added the offset address of the registers. Only two offsets are used, 00H and 01H, as the read and write operations are used to distinguish between registers having the same offset. Reading from offset 00H reads the received data register, while writing to offset 00H writes a byte to the transmit data register. Serial transmission begins immediately after a write to the transmit data register, provided the transmitter is enabled, as described in the section about the status register.

Initialising the PSCI

The PSCI is initialised at two different levels, the mode initialisation and the command initialisation. The mode initialisation can only be performed after a reset of the component and is used to set parameters that will not change during the long-term use of the component. They are generally related to the hardware specification

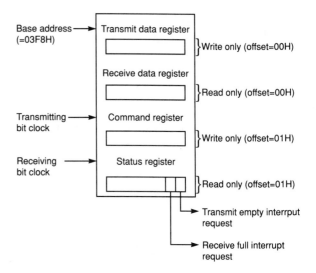

Figure 3.31   Programmer's model of the 8251A

of the communication link which will be fixed for a particular microcomputer and communication link. *Figure 3.32* illustrates the five parameters controlled by the mode which is the first byte written to the command register after a reset operation. Once programmed the mode can only be changed by producing another reset and then rewriting the mode command byte.

Mode Selection

Baud rate clock divisor (bits 0 and 1)   The basic transmission and receive bit clocks are generated externally to the PSCI by hardware-controlled clocks. Some

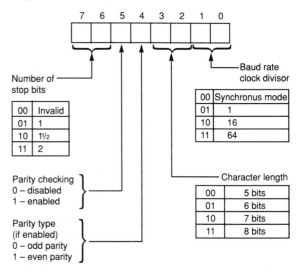

Figure 3.32   Mode command byte

programmed control over the baud rate clock is achieved by an internal programmable baud rate clock divider. This can be programmed to divide by 1, 16 or 64. For example, assuming the bits are to be transmitted at a rate of 1200 baud, the externally-generated bit clock should be 16 times this, which is 19 200 Hz. This then provides the possibility of altering the baud rate under program control to be:

300 baud (input clock frequency of 19 200 Hz divided by 64)

1200 baud (input clock frequency of 19 200 Hz divided by 16)

19 200 baud (input clock frequency of 19 200 Hz divided by 1)

The divisor value selected affects both the transmitting and receiving clock signals. If the divisor bits are both set to zero, then the synchronous communication method is selected. Information on this can be obtained from the appropriate Intel manuals. The normal divisor would be 16 so that the centre of the received signal could be accurately sampled, refer to *Figure 3.28*, as the 8th clock of each bit. For a divisor of 64 this would be the 32nd clock. If the divisor of 1 is used it is more difficult to accurately sample the centre of the received bit, and in some circumstances this can lead to incorrect data being received.

Character bit length (bits 2 and 3). The normal length of the transmitted and received data elements has been assumed to be 8 bits. However, some older microcomputers used data lengths less than this and this parameter enables compatibility with this older equipment to be achieved. For new microcontrollers and microcomputers, the data element length should always be set to 8.

Parity (bits 4 and 5). If parity checking is to be used, bit 4 of the mode byte should be set to a logic 1 to enable checking and then bit 5 is used to select either odd or even parity generation when transmitting or checking when receiving. In simple communication links parity is not used so both these bits would be set to zero.

Stop bits (bits 6 and 7). Some receivers require more than one stop bit and to provide compatibility this parameter selects either 1, 1.5 or 2 stop bits. Normal operation requires only one stop bit as this enables the maximum byte transmission rate to be achieved.

Examples of Byte Transmission Rates

For a fixed baud rate clock of 1200 baud a variety of byte transmission rates are possible. The fastest rate is

achieved for the smaller data element lengths used in the older protocols and would use:

1 start bit
5 bits per data element
1 stop bit

Total data length = 7 bits

The byte transmission rate can be calculated as follows:

$$\text{Byte transmission rate} = \frac{\text{Baud rate}}{\text{Data length}}$$

$$= \frac{1200}{7} = 171 \text{ bytes per second}$$

A typical rate for a modern system would be:

1 start-bit
8 bits per data element
1 stop bit

Total data length = 10 bits

The byte transmission rate can be calculated as follows:

$$\text{Byte transmission rate} = \frac{\text{Baud rate}}{\text{Data length}}$$

$$= \frac{1200}{10} = 120 \text{ bytes per second}$$

If two stops bits were used this would be reduced to 109 bytes per second.

A typical mode byte value. The resulting mode will usually be a bit clock divisor of 16, 8-bit data elements, disabled parity, and one stop bit. This would give a mode byte of:

01001110B = 04EH.

Command Byte Programming

Any bytes transferred to the command register after the mode has been programmed enable a variety of parameters to be controlled while a program is executing, in order to obtain an improved performance for the communication link. These are illustrated in *Figure 3.33* (overleaf) and form the command byte. The seven parameters specified by the command byte control the asynchronous and synchronous operation of the PSCI, although only one type of communication will be implemented for a specific link.

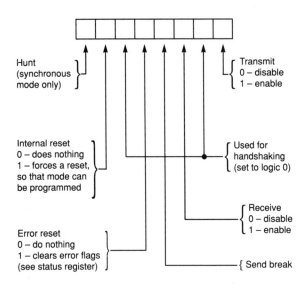

Figure 3.33   Command byte

The **hunt parameter** only applies to the synchronous method and will not be discussed further, and should be set to zero when in the asynchronous mode.

There are five minor alterations that can be made to the mode selected, by the command byte.

Transmit and receive disable (bits 0 and 2).   Before transmitting and receiving will start, these two bits must be set to a logic 1 to enable transmission and reception. These bits are useful when handshaking is used, to ensure the correct transfer of data and that the maximum rate of data transmission is not exceeded. When handshaking is not used, disabling the transmission and reception serves no useful purpose as any data received would be lost and no data would be transmitted.

Handshaking (bits 1 and 5).   Bits 1 and 5 are used to implement the two signals required for handshaking. The simplest asynchronous communication links always enable transmit and receive and do not use handshaking so these bits should be set to zero to achieve this.

Break (bit 3).   Some equipment requires a long logic 0 to be placed onto the transmitting signal connection before any transmissions will be recognised. Under normal operation the bit time is controlled by the baud rate clock signal which is hardware generated and cannot be easily changed. The break bit enables the normal timing to be extended to produce a long logic 0 which is recognised as a request by a communication link to be recognised. This is useful for mainframe computer installations which have more terminals than communication links. In normal operation not all the terminals would be in use and those not in use would be considered to have a non-active communication link. Although there is still a physical link due to the cables, the communication is electronically switched and when inactive the communication link does not operate. To activate the link the terminal indicates to the mainframe through the break operation that communication is required.

For a fixed point-to-point communication link there is no need for the break operation as the link is always active and bit 3 should be set to a logic 0.

Error reset (bit 4).   Whenever one of the three types of error occurs, an error flag is set in the status register. The errors only apply to received bytes so that the bits could be checked after every byte is received to ensure that it was correctly received. If an error is detected by the PSCI the appropriate error bits are set. These flags can only be cleared by setting the error reset bit to a logic 1. Normally it would be a logic 0. As most simple asynchronous communication links are very reliable, tests for error states are not often made.

Internal reset (bit 6).   As the mode can only be changed after a reset this bit can be used to force an internal reset. This does not affect any of the other components in the microcomputer and allows the software to change the mode. Once the reset operation has been performed and the mode re-programmed this bit should be set to logic 0. The PSCI does not differentiate between a hardware or software initiated reset. However, the software initiated reset has the advantage that other programmable components in the microcontroller or microcomputer are not affected.

Typical Command Byte Value

In normal operation, with no internal reset or error reset, no break, no handshaking, and receive and transmit enabled, the following command byte would be used:

00000101B = 05H

Example of Programming a PSCI for a Simple Asynchronous Communication Link

The following typical program fragment could be used to initialise the PSCI for simple asynchronous operation. Unfortunately, due to a fault in the design of the component, it is not possible to predict the state of the PSCI after a hardware reset, and a 'worst case' assumption must be made that it will be in synchronous mode. This must then be correctly programmed and only then can a software-generated internal reset be performed and the correct asynchronous mode be selected.

In addition, due to timing restraints, a short delay has to be inserted after every write to the PSCI to ensure correct programming. For data byte writes, this always occurs during the natural flow of the program, but for command register writes which occur consecutively it has to be programmed in. A typical algorithm and program is as follows:

(1) Send the 3 bytes required for synchronous programming;
(2) Perform an internal reset;
(3) Program the required mode programming;
(4) Program the required command byte programming.

Example

This program will perform the necessary initialisation of an Intel 8251A serial communication peripheral, and then program it for asynchronous operation:

```
        MOV   DX,03F9H      ;Move the address of the
        MOV   AL,00H        ;command register into
                            ,DX. This is a base
                            ;address of 03F8H plus a
                            ;command register
                            ;offset of 01H.
                            ;Send the three bytes
                            ;required for
                            ;synchronous
                            ;programming.
                            ;Step (1)
        OUT   DX, AL
;
        MOV   CX, SMALL_DELAY  ;Inter-write delay,
HERE:   LOOP HERE
;
        OUT   DX,AL         ;Second byte of
                            ;synchronous.
;
        MOV   CX,SMALL_DELAY
HERE1:  LOOP HERE1          ;Inter-write delay.
;
        OUT   DX,AL         ;Third byte of
                            ; synchronous.
;
        MOV   CX, SMALL_DELAY  ;Inter-write delay.
HERE2:  LOOP HERE2
                            ;Perform an internal
                            ;reset. Step (2)
        MOV   AL,01000000B  ;The internal reset byte.
        OUT   DX, AL
;
        MOV   CX,SMALL_DELAY  ;Inter-write delay.
HERE3:  LOOP HERE3
                            ;Perform the mode
```

```
                            ;programming. Step (3)
        MOV   AL,04EH       ;Mode selected is clock
        OUT   DX,AL         ;divisor is 16, 8 bit
                            ;characters, disabled
                            ;parity, and one stop bit.
;
        MOV   CX, SMALL_DELAY  ;Inter-write delay.
HERE4:  LOOP HERE4
                            ;Perform the command
                            ;byte programming.
                            ;Step (4)
        MOV   AL,05H        ;Command byte
        OUT   DX,AL         ;selected is no
                            ;handshaking and
                            ;transmit and receive
                            ;enabled.
;
        CX,SMALL_DELAY     ;Inter-write delay.
HERE5:  LOOP HERE5
                            ;The PSCI is now
                            ;initialised and ready to
                            ;transfer data.
```

Status Register

The status register enables information about the internal state of the PSCI to be obtained and has the bit allocation shown in *Figure 3.34*. The status of four different functions can be obtained.

The receiver and transmitter ready status bits are also copied onto external signals which can be used to create an interrupt-driven transmit and receive.

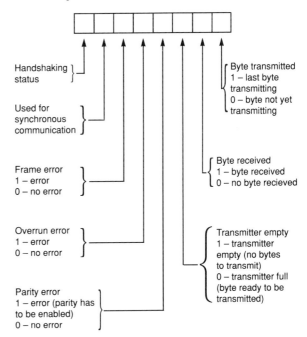

Figure 3.34 Status register

Transmitter ready (bits 0 and 2). Before a byte can be written to the PSCI so that it can be transmitted, any previously-written bytes must have been transmitted. Two status bits are used to determine the state of the transmitting data byte. Bit 0 is usually used to determine whether the last byte written is transmitting. If it is, another byte can be written as the data registers are double buffered. This status bit is used for polled control but the signal is also available as an interrupt signal for use in interrupt-controlled communication. The other transmit status bit, bit 2, is the transmitter empty bit and is used when handshaking is implemented. An algorithm and example program follow:

(1) Wait until the transmitter can accept another byte;
(2) Transfer the next byte.

Example

```
                                  ;Wait until the transmitter
                                  ;can accept another byte.
                                  ;Step (1)
           MOV   DX,03F9H         ;Address of the status
                                  ;register.
WAIT_TX:   IN AL,DX
;
           CMP AL,00000001B       ;Wait until status indicates
           JZ    WAIT_TX          ;the transmitter is ready.
                                  ;Transfer the next byte.
                                  ;Step (2)
           MOV   DX,03F8H         ;Transfer the next byte to
           MOV   AL,DATA_ELEMENT  ;the PSCI.
           OUT   DX,AL
```

Receiver ready (bit 1). Similarly, the byte received status bit can be used to detect when a complete byte has been received on the serial communication link. This can be polled by a program, or the hardware-generated copy of the status bit can be used as an interrupt signal. A second receiver empty bit is not required as it would not serve any useful purpose, even when handshaking is implemented. An algorithm and example program for this follows:

(1) Wait until a byte has been received;
(2) Transfer the byte to the microprocessor.

Example

```
                                  ;Wait until a byte has
                                  ;been received. Step (1)
           MOV   DX,03F9H         ;Address of status register.
WAIT_RX:   IN    AL, DX
;
           CMP AL,00000010B       ;Wait until status bit
           JZ    WAIT_RX          ;indicates a byte has been
                                  ;received. Transfer the byte
                                  ;to the microprocessor.
                                  ;Step (2)
```

```
           MOV   DX,03F8H         ;Transfer byte from the PSCI
           IN    AL, DX           ;to the microprocessor.
           MOV   DATA_ELEMENT, AL
```

Errors status (bits 3, 4 and 5). The three hardware-detectable errors possible in received bytes each have a status flag associated with them and these can be used by the program to handle that particular error. If an error is detected and one or more error flags set, it does not prevent further bytes from being transmitted or received. The error flags only indicate that an error has been detected and do not affect future operations as in the following example:

(1) Input the status register value;
(2) Check for any errors.

Example

```
                                  ;Input the status register
                                  ;value. Step (1)
           MOV   DX,03F9H         ;Address of the status
           IN    AL, DX           ;register.
                                  ;Check for any errors.
                                  ;Step (2)
           CMP   AL,00111000B     ;If any errors call
           JZ    NO_ERRORS        ;the error handling
           CALL  PSCI_ERROR       ;routine
NO_ERRORS:                        ;otherwise continue
                                  ;with the program.
```

Synchronous and handshaking status flags (bits 6 and 7). Bit 6 is used during synchronous communication and will not be considered here and bit 7 enables the microprocessor to determine the state of one of the handshaking signals. These status flags are not used in simple asynchronous serial communication links.

Summary

When information, usually in the form of data elements, has to be transferred between microcomputers, a programmable serial communication interface can be used to produce a communication link. The link is relatively inexpensive and easy to install, contains simple error detection hardware, and can be used in interrupt-driven, or software-polled programs.

3.4 PROGRAMMABLE INTERRUPT CONTROLLER (PIC)

A microprocessor will only have a small number of inputs dedicated to interrupts whereas both micro-controllers and microcomputers require several interrupt inputs in order to interface fully with programmable peripherals. A **programmable interrupt controller** (PIC) provides a suitable interface between the microprocessor and other interrupt sources, as illustrated in *Figure 3.35*. Eight interrupts are connected directly to the PIC, and **interrupt handshaking signals** (interrupt request and interrupt acknowledge) allow communication between the PIC and the microprocessor. Interrupts connected via a PIC are effectively indirect maskable interrupts controlled by the software. There is also a **non-maskable interrupt** (NMI) connected directly to the microprocessor, which avoids the PIC. As the name suggests, this interrupt cannot be controlled by software and is non-maskable.

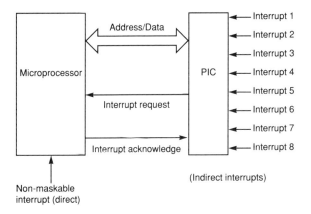

Figure 3.35 Microprocessor with a PIC

When one of the inputs to the PIC is activated the interrupt request signal is generated, which indicates to the microprocessor that an indirect interrupt has occurred. If the indirect interrupts are enabled, when the microprocessor is ready it activates the interrupt acknowledge signal. This delay is usually a short period while the presently executing instruction is allowed to complete. Indirect interrupts can be disabled as the interrupt handshaking signals are conditioned by an interrupt enable flag in the microprocessor. When disabled, none of the indirect interrupts will be recognised and acted upon.

When interrupts are activated the PIC transfers a number representing the interrupt to the microprocessor. The numbers associated with the specific interrupt inputs to the PIC are programmed into the PIC during the initialisation stages before any interrupts occur. For example, interrupt 1 into the PIC could have been programmed to pass an interrupt number of 020H to the microprocessor. This would then be used as the inter-

rupt vector to the interrupt service subroutine. This indirect method allows the hardware interrupts into the PIC to be redirected to the selected interrupt vectors simply by re-programming the PIC. If more than 8 interrupts were required, then additional PICs can be connected together.

Direct interrupts. The microprocessor will usually have one direct interrupt, sometimes more, which does not require a PIC and does not use the interrupt handshaking signals. When an interrupt signal is received on a direct interrupt input the presently executing instruction completes as with indirect interrupts and the interrupt vector associated with the interrupt is directly initiated. These interrupts cannot be associated with any other interrupt vectors, other than the specifically allocated non-maskable ones.

General Programmer's Model

The programmer's model of a general PIC is shown in *Figure 3.36* and indicates that four functions are under program control:

(a) latching the interrupt signal so that it is recognised even if the interrupt signal itself becomes inactive;
(b) prioritising the interrupts;
(c) redirecting the interrupts;
(d) controlling the interrupt request and acknowledge handshaking signals.

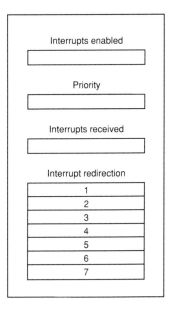

Figure 3.36 Programmer's model of a PIC

Although enabling the latching of the interrupts and the interrupt handshaking are programmable there are PIC hardware-controlled functions that are not directly visible to the programmer and are not directly controllable by the software.

As well as latching the interrupt input signals, it is possible to enable or disable individual interrupts using the **interrupts enabled register** and as this is an 8-bit register, up to 8 interrupt input signals can be controlled in this way.

It is possible to have several interrupts active simultaneously as it takes time to execute the interrupt service subroutines. The interrupt with the highest priority will be the first one acknowledged. If the interrupts all had the same priority they would be acknowledged and serviced in the order in which they were received. However, if the interrupts have different priorities then a high priority interrupt received after a low priority interrupt will be serviced first. This depends upon the interrupts still being enabled as it is normal for the microprocessor to disable the interrupts whenever a new interrupt is received.

The interrupts are latched in the PIC so that when the interrupted program is re-started the remaining interrupt with the highest priority is selected and the remainder disabled again. A typical sequence of events is:

(a) Interrupt received;
(b) The microprocessor disables all other interrupts;
(c) The interrupt service subroutine is executed, (during this, further interrupts are received but are not recognised);
(d) The microprocessor is re-enabled;
(e) The next interrupt is selected with the highest priority;
(f) Repeat from (b).

Alternatively, it might be considered a good idea to execute immediately any higher priority interrupts that are received during an interrupt service subroutine. This can be achieved by re-enabling the PIC at the beginning of each interrupt service subroutine, as illustrated below:

(a) Interrupt received;
(b) Microprocessor disables all interrupts;
(c) The interrupt service subroutine is started;
(d) Interrupts are re-enabled by the software;
(e) The rest of the interrupt service subroutine is executed.

The PIC then only allows higher priority interrupt input signals to interrupt the existing interrupt service subroutine, but not any lower or equal priority interrupt inputs.

The priority is shown as a single 8-bit register and operates by specifying which of the interrupt inputs, numbered 0 to 7, is the highest priority. The others then have a sequential descending priority with increasing interrupt number. So if interrupt 5 was chosen to have the highest priority, 6 would have the next priority followed by 7. This would then be followed by 0, 1, 2, 3 and 4, with 4 having the lowest priority. It is unusual for a PIC to allow each interrupt input to have its priority individually programmed.

The redirection registers allow the interrupt inputs to the PIC to be associated with the interrupt vectors selected by the programmer. These registers may contain an address, or an interrupt vector number, depending on the specific microprocessor the PIC is used with. The 8086 uses interrupt vectors and the PIC is therefore programmed with the interrupt vector to be associated with the input to the PIC. For example, interrupt 0 input to the PIC may be programmed to pass interrupt vector 080H to the 8086 microprocessor. The 8086 will then perform the normal interrupt handling process and multiply the interrupt vector by four to obtain the interrupt vector address, which contains the address of the interrupt service subroutine itself.

The most flexible PICs allow each interrupt input signal to be individually redirected as illustrated in *Figure 3.36*. A less flexible but easier to program method only allows the first interrupt input, interrupt 0, to be completely re-directable with the others sequentially numbered from that. For example, if interrupt 0 input to the PIC was programmed to redirect to interrupt vector 64, the other PIC interrupt inputs would be:

Interrupt 0 redirected as interrupt vector 64;
Interrupt 1 redirected as interrupt vector 65;
Interrupt 2 redirected as interrupt vector 66;
Interrupt 3 redirected as interrupt vector 67;
Interrupt 4 redirected as interrupt vector 68;
Interrupt 5 redirected as interrupt vector 69;
Interrupt 6 redirected as interrupt vector 70;
Interrupt 7 redirected as interrupt vector 71.

One difference between the PIC and most other peripheral components is that it does not directly manipulate any data or I/O values. It is simply concerned with the redirection and control of hardware-generated interrupt signals. The result of this is that most of the PIC registers are write only. The only useful information that might be obtained from the interrupt controller is how many interrupt input signals have been activated at a specific moment in time.

The Intel 8259A Programmable Interrupt Controller

The PIC that will be considered in detail is the Intel 8259A, which is a sophisticated device designed to work with both the 8-bit 8085 and the 16-bit 8086. Only the 8086 mode of operation is of interest and only the basic modes will be considered. Full programming details can be obtained from the appropriate Intel data manual.

Programmer's model of the 8259A. There are only two addressable registers in the programmer's model, as illustrated in *Figure 3.37*, the initialisation and the operation registers. These have local offset addresses of 00H and 01H from the base address of the PIC which will be assumed to be 020H. The programmer's model is quite different from the general programmer's model as the 8259A, like most other programmable peripherals, has been designed to use the minimum number of addressable registers. This is achieved by giving special significance to the sequence in which bytes are transferred to the registers, with the first byte performing one operation, the second another and so on, until all the functions of the PIC have been programmed. The result of this is that programming is not a simple process. As can be deduced from the programmer's model, there are two types of programming, initialisation and operation.

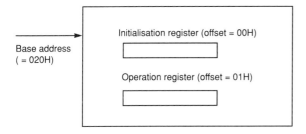

Figure 3.37 Programmer's model of the 8259A PIC

Initialisation Programming

Initialisation programming is performed after a hardware reset or whenever the mode of operation of the PIC is to be changed, and the PIC has to be completely reprogrammed from the beginning. The initialisation process consists of writing a command byte to the initialisation register followed by two successive parameter control bytes to the operation register. Some modes of operation require three successive parameter control bytes but they will not be considered.

When writing to the initialisation register, the command byte is identified as starting the initialisation process when bit 4 is a logic 1 as illustrated in *Figure 3.38*. As

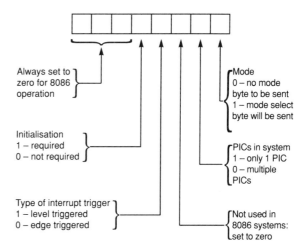

Figure 3.38 Command byte

can be seen, the command byte controls three parameters, the mode, the number of PICs in the system, and the type of interrupt inputs to the PIC. When used with an 8086, 4 of the bits, 1, 5, 6 and 7, perform no function and should always be set to zero. The remaining three bits control three parameters.

Mode (bit 0). If the mode bit is set to a logic 1, it indicates that a mode select byte will be sent to the operation register as the last part of the initialisation sequence. This is the case when used in an 8086-based system.

Number of PICs (bit 1). As there is only one set of interrupt handshaking signals available to the microprocessor and they cannot be connected in parallel to several PICs, an alternative method of connecting multiple PICs is used. The number of PICs bit is used to indicate whether only one PIC is being used, which is the normal situation, or whether there are multiple PICs. (See the appropriate data sheets if multiple PICs are required.) Multiple PICs are required when more than 8 interrupt inputs are requested.

Type of interrupt signal (bit 3). Interrupt signals can be activated in two ways, edge- or level-triggered. If edge-triggered there must be a change of the signal from a logic 0 to a logic 1 and if level-triggered then the signal has to be at a logic 1 to be recognised as an interrupt.

There is only a small difference in operation between these two types of triggering and in most instances there would be no detectable difference. However, if the signal used to initiate a level-triggered interrupt remains high for a long period, the interrupt service subroutine may finish and re-enable the interrupts and consider the signal, which is still logic 1, to be another valid interrupt and perform the interrupt service subroutine again. In that situation, edge-triggered interrupts would be used so that even if the interrupt signal remained high after the interrupt service subroutine completed, it would not be recognised as another valid interrupt. The signal would have to return to logic 0 and then back to logic 1 to be recognised as a valid interrupt. It is normal to use edge-triggered interrupts unless there are special requirements. Therefore, for a single PIC in an 8086-based system, using edge-triggered interrupts, the initialisation command byte with a mode select would be:

00010011B = 013H

Parameter Control Bytes

The two parameter control bytes are transferred to the operation register immediately following the transfer of the initialisation command byte to the operation register. The first is used to program the redirection of the interrupts. The 8259A PIC uses the block programming method and only specifies the new interrupt type for the interrupt 0 input signal. *Figure 3.39* illustrates how this address is programmed with the top five bits, bits 3 to 7, used to identify the beginning of a block of 8 interrupt vectors. The remaining three bits, which must always be set to zero, are provided by the PIC when one of the interrupt input signals is activated and means that the block of redirected vectors must start on an 8-byte boundary.

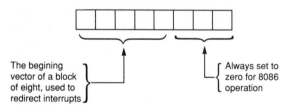

The begining vector of a block of eight, used to redirect interrupts

Always set to zero for 8086 operation

Figure 3.39 Parameter byte one

The five bits of programmed address and the three bits supplied directly by the PIC, depending on which interrupt is active, produce the 8-bit interrupt vector used by the 8086 and enable any of the possible 256 vectors to be accessed. For example, assuming that the beginning vector of the redirected block is to be 08H, the first parameter byte would have the value:

00001000B = 08H

The three least significant bits are equal to zero so that values such as 09H and so on cannot be used. When

activated, the interrupts produce the following vectors to be passed from the PIC to the microprocessor:

Interrupt 0 redirected to 08H + 0H = 08H
Interrupt 1 redirected to 08H + 1H = 09H
Interrupt 2 redirected to 08H + 2H = 0AH
Interrupt 3 redirected to 08H + 3H = 0BH
Interrupt 4 redirected to 08H + 4H = 0CH
Interrupt 5 redirected to 08H + 5H = 0DH
Interrupt 6 redirected to 08H + 6H = 0EH
Interrupt 7 redirected to 08H + 7H = 0FH

Mode Command Parameter Byte

The second parameter control byte is called the mode command byte. This byte is only required if bit 0 of the command initialisation byte was set to a logic 1. This byte controls four parameters as illustrated in *Figure 3.40*:

(a) Which microprocessor;
(b) Which end of interrupt technique;
(c) Buffered;
(d) Special fully-nested mode

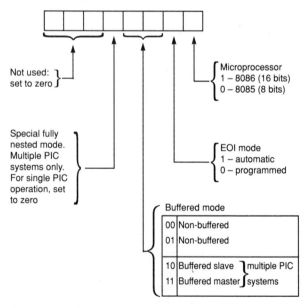

Not used: set to zero

Special fully nested mode. Multiple PIC systems only. For single PIC operation, set to zero

Microprocessor
1 – 8086 (16 bits)
0 – 8085 (8 bits)

EOI mode
1 – automatic
0 – programmed

Buffered mode	
00	Non-buffered
01	Non-buffered
10	Buffered slave
11	Buffered master

multiple PIC systems

Figure 3.40 Second parameter byte

Only the first two are of interest when the PIC is used in an 8086-based system. The special fully-nested mode and the buffered mode are only of interest in multiple PIC systems and for the systems described should be set to logic 0. The top three bits of the mode command byte, bits 5, 6 and 7, are not used and should always be set to logic 0.

Microprocessor (bit 0). As indicated previously, the Intel 8259A can be used with two different microprocessors, the 8-bit 8085, and the 16-bit 8086/88. The PIC is programmed differently depending upon the state of this bit, and only the 8086/88 mode, when bit 0 is set to a logic 1, will be considered.

End of interrupt (bit 1). Once an interrupt input signal has been activated and recognised, a bit is set in the interrupts pending latch. Once set, this prevents further interrupt input signals with the same, or any lower, priority being recognised. This enables higher priority interrupts to be recognised, as described previously. This bit has to be cleared by an **end of interrupt** (EOI) command, which can be hardware- or software-generated, before another interrupt of lower or equal priority will be recognised. The hardware-generated EOI is produced by the PIC in the automatic EOI mode (bit 3 of this parameter byte set to a logic 1), which occurs immediately following the transfer of the redirected interrupt vector to the microprocessor. This results in the PIC being ready to accept another interrupt signal before the previous interrupt service subroutine has completed. This may be necessary if interrupts have to be recognised and responded to as quickly as possible.

However, the normal method would be to prevent further interrupts being recognised until the existing interrupt has been serviced; this is achieved by using the programmed EOI mode (bit 1 set to a logic 1) which requires an EOI byte to be sent to the operation register. This would be transferred just before the interrupt service subroutine completes in order to prevent the recognition of any further interrupts with the same or lower priority, until the existing interrupt has been serviced. The result of these decisions is that the following mode command byte is selected the non-special fully-nested, non-buffered, programmed EOI and 8086 microprocessor, giving a byte value of:

00000001B = 01H

Example

A typical initialisation sequence is illustrated by the following algorithm and program:

(1) Send the initialisation command byte;
(2) Send the first parameter control byte;
(3) Send the second parameter control byte.

The following sequence of instructions implements the algorithm and performs the initialisation of an 8259A PIC.

```
                        ;Performs the 8259A PIC
                        ;initialisation programming.
                        ;Send the initialisation
                        ;command byte. Step (1)
MOV   DX, PIC_BASE + INIT_REG
                        ;Point to the initialisation
                        ;register.
MOV   AL, 13H           ;Select edge triggered, single
                        ;PIC, mode parameter byte.
OUT   DX,AL             ;Output to the PIC.
                        ;Send the first parameter
                        ;control byte. Step (2)
MOV   DX,PIC_BASE + OP_REG
                        ;Point to the operation
                        ;register.
MOV   AL,08H            ;Redirect interrupt vectors
OUT   DX,AL             ;to start at 08H.
                        ;Send the second parameter
                        ;control byte. Step (3)
MOV   AL,01H            ;The mode parameter selecting
OUT   DX,AL             ;the 8086 microprocessor,
                        ;normal EOI and non-buffered
                        ;operation, is now
                        ;transferred.
```

Operation Programming

Once the initialisation programming has been completed, the operation programming can begin. This consists of a sequence of three bytes; the first one to the operations register, followed by two bytes to the initialisation register. The swapping of registers in this way enables the PIC to identify which type of programming, initialisation or operation, is being performed.

The Interrupt Mask Byte

The first byte of the operation programming sequence is the interrupt mask byte, which can be used to enable interrupt inputs. If an interrupt is received and the interrupt is not enabled then it will not be recognised.

Each of the 8 interrupt inputs has a bit associated with it in the interrupt mask register, as illustrated in *Figure 3.41* (overleaf). If a bit is a logic 0, the interrupt input signal associated with that bit position will be enabled so that when the interrupt is activated the interrupt handshaking process is initiated. In normal operation all the interrupt inputs are enabled so that this byte would be:

00000000B = 00H

The Priority Byte

As already mentioned, the interrupt inputs have a priority associated with them which is initially specified by the initialisation programming sequence. The priority

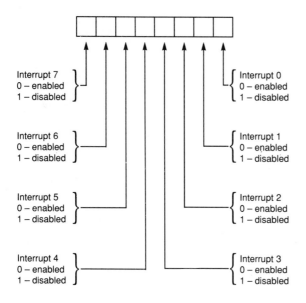

Figure 3.41   Interrupt mask

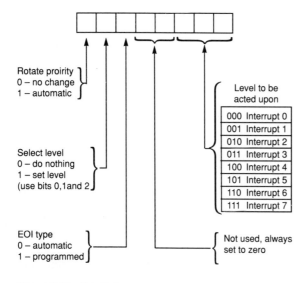

Figure 3.42   Priority byte

byte allows three more priority parameters to be controlled as in *Figure 3.42*:

(a) Rotate priority;
(b) Set priority level;
(c) End of interrupt type.

End of Interrupt

The type of EOI required, automatic or programmed, is selected by the initialisation programming sequence. If programmed EOI is selected then it is possible to select which interrupt has been ended, and this is called a specific EOI. If a non-specific EOI is selected then the highest priority interrupt recognised will be ended. Ending an interrupt consists of clearing the bit specific to that interrupt in the interrupt latch register.

A non-specific EOI is produced by setting the EOI type to programmed (bit 5 = logic 1), select level to off (bit 6 = logic 0) and no rotation of priority (bit 7 = logic 0). This combination of the three parameters, and the operation it produces, along with the others' available, are identified in *Table 3.1*

Table 3.1   Possible EOI combinations

Rotate	Select-level	EOI	Explanation
0	0	0	Stop rotate in automatic EOI mode
0	0	1	Non-specific EOI command
0	1	0	Not used – does nothing
0	1	1	Specific EOI command
1	0	0	Start rotate in automatic EOI mode
1	0	1	Rotate on non-specific EOI command
1	1	0	Set lowest priority
1	1	1	Rotate on specific EOI command

The non-specific EOI which indicates to the PIC that the highest priority interrupt which has been activated has been completed, is the normal mode of operation of the PIC and does not change the priority of the interrupt inputs. As a specific interrupt level is not selected, bits 0, 1 and 2 are not used and should be set to logic 0. The result is a priority parameter byte of:

00100000B = 020H

In some modes of operation it may be necessary to indicate to the PIC that a specific interrupt has been completed and this is achieved using the specific EOI command. From *Table 3.1*, this type of operation is achieved with programmed EOI (bit 5 = logic 1), select level (bit 6 = logic 1) and no rotation of priority (bit 7 = logic 0). Bits 0, 1 and 2 are then used to select which one of the 8 interrupts has been completed. For example, if interrupt 5 was completed, the priority byte would be:

01100101B = 065H

One of these two commands must be used if the programmed EOI mode is selected during the initialisation sequence. Otherwise the PIC will not recognise that the interrupt service subroutine has completed and will not initiate further interrupt requests.

Priority

The previous two EOI commands do not change the priority from that specified by the initialisation programming sequence, however, the remaining commands do. In normal use, commands which change priority are unnecessary except for the set priority level command.

Set Priority Level. When initialising the PIC the lowest priority interrupt is specified, rather than the highest as indicated in the general programmer's model and this is performed with the set lowest priority command byte. This command is executed when an automatic EOI is selected (bit 5 = logic 0), selected level is set (bit 6 = logic 1), and no rotation of priority (bit 7 = logic 0).

When select level is on, bits 0, 1 and 2 are used to specify the interrupt input which is to have the lowest priority. The interrupt with the next lowest number then has a higher priority and this is repeated until interrupt input 0. Interrupt input 7 is then taken as the next interrupt and has the next highest priority. This is illustrated in *Figure 3.43*, when interrupt 3 is selected to have the lowest priority and leads to interrupt input 4 having the highest priority.

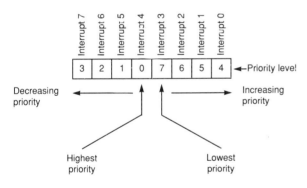

Figure 3.43 Interrupt priority

Reading The Status Registers

Status information can be obtained from the PIC from two registers, the **interrupt request** and **in-service interrupt registers**. The interrupt request register indicates which of the enabled interrupts have been activated. The in-service register indicates those activated interrupt requests which have an interrupt service subroutine presently executing.

In normal operation, to have more than one interrupt request being serviced, an interrupt input signal must have been activated and redirected into the microprocessor. This sets the appropriate bit in the in-service register. If, following this, a higher priority interrupt is

received and accepted by the microprocessor, then the first interrupt service subroutine will be interrupted and a second higher priority one started. This will be indicated by two or more bits being set in the in-service register. Remember that the microprocessor disables the interrupt request handshaking after the first request and to allow a second interrupt to occur before the IRET instruction, the interrupt service subroutine must re-enable the interrupt handshaking using the STI instruction.

If a status register read operation is required, this is indicated to the PIC by transferring a second parameter byte to the initialisation register as part of the operation programming sequence. This controls three functions as seen in *Figure 3.44*:

(a) Special mask mode;
(b) Polling;
(c) Register reading;

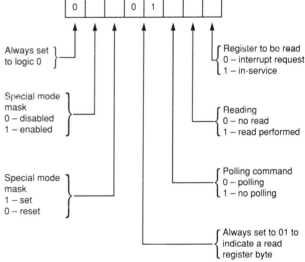

Figure 3.44 Read register parameter byte

Special mask mode allows a further variation on the priority of interrupt inputs which will not be considered further. Bits 6 and 5 are set to logic 0 to disable this function. Bits 7 and 4 are always set to logic zero, and bit 3 is set to logic 1 to indicate that this is the third byte of the operation programming sequence.

Polling. Sometimes it may be advantageous to use a software method of determining when an interrupt input signal has been activated, rather than by using the hardware interrupt request and interrupt acknowledge handshaking signals. Setting polling to be on (bit 2 = logic 1), the hardware handshaking between the PIC and the microprocessor is disabled. The microprocessor then has to read the status registers to determine which, if any, interrupt inputs have been activated. If software polling of interrupts is used, a PIC is not really necessary. Therefore, this mode will not be explained further and bit 2 should be set to logic 0 to disable this function.

Register read.   A register read is achieved by setting bit 1 to a logic 1 to indicate that a register read operation is to be performed. Bit 0 is used to indicate which register is to be read.

The register read operation is performed immediately after the third parameter byte has been transferred to the initialisation register to complete the operation programming sequence. The register status information is obtained by reading the initialisation register.

Example

The following example program indicates a typical operation programming sequence when a register read is not required. The algorithm and program listing are shown below:

(1) Send the first byte to the operation register;
(2) Send the second byte to the initialisation register;
(3) Send the third byte to the initialisation register.

```
                        ;Performs a simple operation
                        ;programming sequence.
                        ;Send the first byte to the
                        ;operation register. Step (1)
MOV   DX, PIC_BASE + OP_REG
                        ;Write the interrupts enabled
MOV   AL, OOH           ;byte to the operation
OUT   DX, AL            ;register. All interrupt
                        ;inputs are enabled.
                        ;Send the first byte to the
                        ;initialisation register. Step (2)
MOV   DX, PIC_BASE + INIT_REG
                        ;Point to the initialisation
MOV   AL, 020H          ;register.
OUT   DX, AL            ;Send the non-specific EOI
                        ;command.
                        ;Send the third byte to the
                        ;initialisation register. Step (3)
MOV   AL, 08H           ;No special mask, no polling
OUT   DX, AL            ;and no status register read.
                        ;Operation programming
                        ;completed.
```

End Of Interrupt Command

It is not necessary to send the complete three byte operation programming sequence to initiate the end of interrupt command whenever an interrupt service subroutine completes. Once the initialisation and oper-

ation programming sequences have been sent for the first time, it is only necessary to send the second byte of the operation programming sequence, the priority byte, to the initialisation register.

A typical interrupt service subroutine would then have the following instruction layout:

Example

```
DEMO_INT:   PROC FAR
            STI               ;Re-enable interrupt flag in
                              ;the microprocessor. This
                              ;will allow any higher
                              ;priority interrupts.
            PUSH  AX          ;Save the registers.
            PUSH  BX
                              ;Interrupt service
                              ;subroutine handling code.
            POP   BX          ;Restore the saved registers.
            POP   AX
            MOV   DX, PIC_BASE + INIT_REG
                              ;Point to the initialisation
                              ;register.
            MOV   AL,020H     ;Perform a non-specific EOI
                              ;command.
            OUT   DX, AL
            IRET              ;End of interrupt service
                              ;subroutine.
```

Summary

The programmable interrupt controller is an important programmable peripheral for microcomputer and microcontroller systems as it allows the easy interfacing of other programmable peripherals, such as the floppy disk controller and the direct memory addressing controller. It also enables interrupts to be connected to the system so that a very quick response to external events can be obtained.

The device can be programmed for a wide range of modes of operation such as changing priority and software polling of interrupts. However, because of the complexity of the programming sequences, if anything other than a simple interrupt handler is required, the programming of these devices can become complex. This complexity would lead to great difficulty if trying to debug a faulty system.

3.5   DIRECT MEMORY ACCESS (DMA)

One of the major requirements of a microcomputer is the transfer of large blocks of data from one location in the system to another. This may be from an I/O port to memory, memory to an I/O port, or from memory to memory. It is unusual to transfer from an I/O port to another I/O port. A typical I/O port would be a floppy disk controller, or some other mass storage media. Typical applications would be the loading of programs from the floppy disk into memory ready for execution, or saving programs or data to floppy disk.

Therefore a fast method of transferring large blocks of data is required, as this will increase the total system program execution rate. One method of transferring data between memory and an I/O port is to use the microprocessor to read data from one and write it to another.

Example

An example algorithm and program are given below:

(1) Initialise memory and I/O pointers;
(2) Read a value from memory;
(3) Write a value to the I/O port;
(4) Increment the memory pointer;
(5) Repeat from (2) until the end of the block.

A program to perform a multi-byte transfer from a block of memory to an I/O port address:

```
        MOV   SI, MEM_ADDR    ;Initialise memory
                              ;pointer to the start
                              ;of the block.
        MOV   CX, NUMB_BLOCK  ;Initialise the block
                              ;counter.
        MOV   DX, IO_PORT     ;Initialise the I/O port
                              ;pointer.
AGAIN:  MOV   AL, [SI]        ;Read from memory
                              ;pointed to.
        OUT   DX, AL          ;Write to I/O port.
        INC   SI              ;Increment the
                              ;memory pointer.
        LOOP  AGAIN           ;Repeat until end of
                              ;the block.
```

The above instructions are now shown with the number of clock cycles required:

```
AGAIN:  MOV   AL, [SI]    ;13 clock cycles.
        OUT   DX, AL      ;8 clock cycles.
        INC   SI          ;3 clock cycles.
        LOOP  AGAIN       ;17 clock cycles if
                          ;jump made,
                          ;5 clock cycles if
                          ;jump not made.
```

The total number of clock cycles per transfer can be found by adding the clock cycles required for the individual instructions, which is $13+8+3+17 = 41$ clock cycles. However, if the I/O port is capable of accepting a new data value every 5 clocks as a floppy disk controller is, then the program-controlled transfer method is much slower than the I/O is capable of.

The byte transfer time cannot be reduced significantly while the microprocessor has to execute the controlling program. Therefore, removing the microprocessor from the control of the transfer and using a faster, dedicated transfer method is a suitable alternative. This dedicated memory to I/O data transfer method is known as **direct memory access** (DMA), as the reading and writing to memory is directly controlled. A special component, known as a **DMA controller**, is used to implement this direct transfer method; this is essentially a dedicated device for executing a similar program to that shown above.

In normal operation the microprocessor controls the address, data and control buses, but in DMA mode the DMA controller assumes control of these buses. This requires a method of bus arbitration between the two bus masters. The DMA controller has to request the use of the bus system from the microprocessor and then wait until that request is granted. Normally the microprocessor is organised to respond to a bus control request as quickly as possible, so that the DMA transfers will take place as quickly as possible.

As the DMA transfers involve the I/O port, it is more efficient to use the I/O port to start the transfer when it is ready. This is because the I/O port may require a period of time before it is capable of handling the data. This can be illustrated by the floppy disk controller, which has to wait between 20–60 milliseconds for the physical head movement before the data becomes available. Therefore the I/O port will have the ability to make a DMA request to the DMA controller, which will be acknowledged when the DMA controller has been granted control of the bus system by the microprocessor.

When the microprocessor has released control of the bus, it automatically puts itself into a frozen state known as **hold**. The microprocessor will remain in the **hold state** while the hold request is maintained by the DMA controller. When the hold is removed the microprocessor will continue executing instructions. Alternatively, an interrupt can be used to force the microprocessor to exit from the hold state, although care has to be taken to ensure that it does not immediately re-enter the state by removing the hold request signal. An interrupt is usually produced by the DMA controller once the complete block of data has been transferred and this is called the **terminal count** (TC).

Figure 3.45 (overleaf) indicates how a DMA controller is connected to a microprocessor system. It is connected in parallel to the address and data buses and some of the control signals. The I/O port is also connected to the data bus but is controlled by the DMA device. The hold request and hold grant signals enable the DMA controller to gain control of the bus system, and the DMA

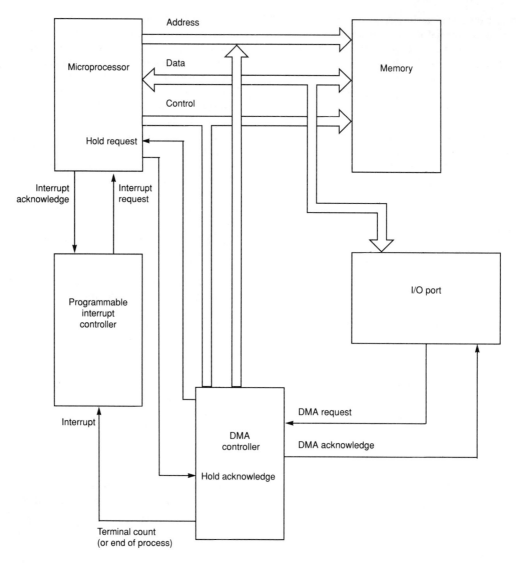

Figure 3.45   A system with a DMA controller

request and DMA grant enable the I/O port to initiate a transfer. The TC signal is used to interrupt the microprocessor when the transfer is completed.

When the microprocessor is controlling the address, data and control bus, the DMA controller is quiescent and does not affect these signals. However, when a direct memory to I/O port transfer is to be made, the microprocessor programs the DMA controller which, when ready, requests control of the bus system. At this stage two things must happen. The I/O device, which must have been pre-programmed to perform a DMA transfer, makes a DMA transfer request to the DMA

controller, using the DMA request signal. The DMA controller then has to obtain full control of the address, data and control buses, which it does by making a hold request to the microprocessor using the hold signal. The microprocessor then completes the presently executing instruction, activates the hold acknowledge signal and disconnects itself from the address, data and part of the control buses.

The DMA controller then has complete control of the bus and performs a DMA request acknowledge to the I/O device. The DMA controller then uses the two DMA handshaking signals, DMA request and DMA acknowledge, to transfer data between the I/O device and memory. The DMA controller has to perform two actions simultaneously, either:

(a) Memory read *and* I/O write, or

(b) I/O read *and* memory write.

Because of this, four control signals are required:

$\overline{\text{MRD}}$ Memory Read (active low)
$\overline{\text{MWR}}$ Memory Write (active low)
$\overline{\text{IORD}}$ I/O Read (active low)
$\overline{\text{IOWR}}$ I/O Write (active low)

These are used in pairs: $\overline{\text{MRD}}$ with $\overline{\text{IOWR}}$ and $\overline{\text{MWR}}$ with $\overline{\text{IORD}}$. This is because in microcomputer systems the memory read and write signals are separated from the I/O read and write signals, in order to improve the system performance. However, the microprocessor only needs to control memory or I/O, whereas the DMA controller has to control both memory and I/O read and write signals. Whenever the I/O port is ready for another element of data it signals the DMA controller and the next transfer is started.

The DMA controller will only transfer blocks of data to and from consecutive memory locations. If non-consecutive memory locations are to be accessed, each one has to be separately programmed as a complete DMA block transfer, perhaps of only one byte. In this situation the DMA technique has no advantages. Therefore, for block transfers the DMA controller only needs programming with two quantities, the starting address in memory and a counter containing the number of bytes to be transferred. This results in the programmer's model of the DMA controller shown in *Figure 3.46*. The I/O port does not need to be programmed as it is assumed that the I/O port being used will already have been activated and will be the only I/O port that is activated at that time. This means that only I/O ports with DMA capability, such as a FDC, can be used in this way. The TC signal can be used to complete the transfer so there is no need for a status register.

The microprocessor loads the starting address of the block into the DMA memory address pointer, and the number of bytes into the byte counter. The I/O device is then programmed to perform a DMA transfer. Every time a byte is successfully transferred, the memory address pointer is incremented and the byte counter decremented. This continues until the complete block has been transferred and the byte counter is zero. At this point the DMA controller relinquishes control of the address, data and control buses. The microprocessor must then be removed from the holding state it was put into by the DMA controller's hold request by de-activating the hold request. The microprocessor then re-asserts control over the address, data and control buses.

When the byte counter reaches zero, a signal is generated which indicates that the block transfer has been completed. This is in addition to the removal of the hold signal and is required for some DMA transfers, such as cycle stealing and transparent transfers, when a de-activated hold request does not indicate the end of the transfer. The terminal count signal is used as an interrupt to restart the microprocessor at the end of the DMA block transfer part of the program. *Figure 3.47* (overleaf) illustrates a typical sequence of events for a DMA block transfer. For an 8086-based system the DMA controller will transfer a byte every 4 or 5 clock cycles.

There are three ways of performing a DMA transfer. The first is burst mode which is exactly the same as that described above. The second is cycle stealing which treats each byte transfer as a separate DMA block transfer, allowing the microprocessor to continue executing the main program. The DMA controller then 'steals' single bus cycles from the microprocessor as illustrated in *Figure 3.48*. When this method is being used the TC signal has to be connected as an interrupt to the microprocessor to indicate the end of the DMA transfer, as the release of the bus does not indicate this as it does in burst mode. The result of the cycle stealing is to slow down both the program execution rate and the DMA byte transfer rate, but it does have the advantage that both the program execution and the DMA transfer continue without long breaks.

The third method is the transparent mode where the DMA controller detects when the address, data and control buses are not being used by the microprocessor because it is performing internal operations. It then makes use of any unused bus cycles to perform the DMA transfer, a byte at a time. The program instruction execution rate is not affected as with cycle stealing, however, the time taken to complete the DMA transfer is unpredictable and depends upon how many bus cycles are left unused by the particular program sequence. This may not be a particularly useful technique for pipelined microprocessors, which tend always to have a busy bus system.

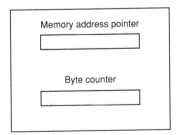

Figure 3.46   A simple model of an ideal DMA controller

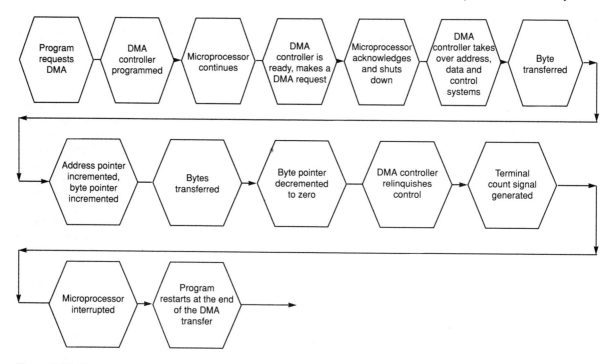

Figure 3.47   DMA sequence of events

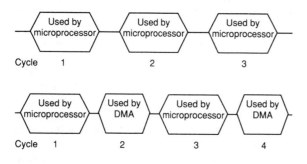

Figure 3.48   A bus system with and without DMA 'cycle stealing'

Programmer's Model of a DMA Controller (Intel 8237A)

The use of a DMA controller may be better understood by using the programmer's model of a specific device and writing a program which will perform a block DMA transfer. The device chosen is the Intel 8237A which is a readily available component and is suitable for use in personal computers such as the IBM PC.

Because of the complexity of DMA transfers and the need to reduce the number of separate addresses required to program the DMA controller, the programmer's model of the 8237A is much more complex and awkward to use than the general programmer's model shown in *Figure 3.46*. This is because the DMA controller is not an independent microprocessor, but merely an extension of the microprocessor contained in the system and therefore the minimum number of addressable locations must be used in order to allow as much flexibility in the number and type of other programmable components added to the system. *Figure 3.49* shows a simplified programmer's model of the 8237A DMA controller which consists of 8×16-bit registers and 8×8-bit registers.

All of these registers are accessed through only 16 locations which are treated as 16 write only registers and 16 read only registers. Only those details necessary to program a block burst transfer will be explained: programming information for the other modes of operation and full technical information can be obtained from the appropriate Intel data books.

Also, the DMA controller is only capable of generating a 16-bit address, whereas most 16-bit microprocessors have a 20-bit, or larger, address bus. These extra bits of address can be provided by using a separate address latch, which provides the extra 4 bits required for the 20-bit 8086 address bus. Although this produces the required size of address bus, as only 16 bits are under the direct control of the DMA controller, this limits the maximum block size that can be transferred in a single

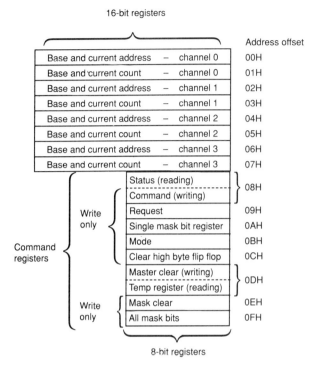

Figure 3.49 DMA registers and offsets

operation, to 64 kbytes. A similar latch would be required for each of the four DMA channels the 8237A provides.

As illustrated in the programmer's model of the 8237A, the DMA controller provides four channels, although only one can be transferring data at any one time. Because of the requirement to perform hardware-controlled handshaking to ensure correct transfer, a dedicated DMA channel is required for every I/O component capable of supporting DMA transfers. By having four channels, up to four components can be used with the minimum of handshaking. The IBM PC uses one DMA channel for refreshing the DRAM, one for the floppy disk transfers which leaves two DMA channels for general purpose use and these are connected to the PC expansion bus.

The 16 addressable locations in the DMA controller can be divided into distinct types, address and count registers which are 16-bit registers, and command and status registers which are 8-bit.

Writing to Base and Current Registers

The 16-bit registers can be controlled in a similar manner, although the requirements are slightly different. The 16-bit registers are used to hold two quantities, the

starting address of the block of data in memory, and the size of the block to be transferred in the count register.

When a write is made to one of the address registers it is actually written into two registers, the base address register and the current address register, see *Figure 3.50*. The same process happens when writing to a count register. However, when a read to the selected register is made, only the value in the current address or count register is transferred. The base address register is only used to save the starting address or the starting count value of the memory block and can be used to shorten the initialisation program code required if the same DMA transfer is to be repeated. This is achieved by simply transferring from the base registers into the current registers, thereby saving all the programming of the register contents, one at a time, by the microprocessor.

This sort of function would be useful for operations such as transferring data to and from a floppy disk controller. The floppy disk I/O address is fixed and a block of memory called a file buffer is set aside which has a fixed starting address. Whenever the program performs a disk to memory DMA transfer it is always between the file buffer and the floppy disk controller I/O

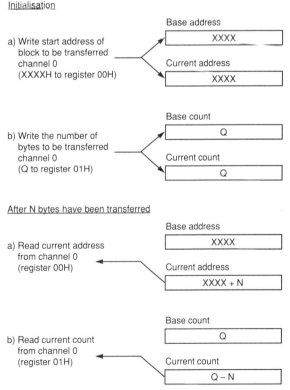

Figure 3.50 Address and count registers

address. As the address of the file buffer and the I/O port do not change, the transfer from base to current registers simplifies everything.

A program may have more than one file I/O buffer in use, as not all files are disk-based and most programs have several active at any one time for keyboard, display, data from disk, results to disk, etc. This can reduce the usefulness of the base registers for DMA transfers if different buffers are used each time.

Reading from Base and Current Registers

When a read operation is performed on a base or current register, only the value of the current register is transferred. It is not usually necessary to obtain the starting address as this should be available to the program. However, it may be necessary to obtain the next address that data is to be transferred to at some time in the program, or possibly what was the address of the last byte transferred.

The base and current address and count registers are 16-bit registers which are accessed through 8-bit I/O port locations. This is achieved by performing two consecutive 8-bit reads (or writes) to the same register address. An internal flip-flop called the high byte flip-flop is used to distinguish which of the two bytes is being transferred.

High byte flip-flop.   One of the command registers of the programmer's model in *Figure 3.49*, is called clear high byte flip-flop. The data written to this command register is irrelevant as the writing to that register address clears the high byte flip-flop. This operation is performed before each 16-bit read or write in order to obtain a correct 16-bit transfer.

Example

The following algorithm indicates how the address and count values for a DMA transfer using channel 0 are programmed.

(a) clear high byte flip-flop (write to clear high byte flip-flop register),
(b) Write low byte to address register (channel 0 low byte),
(c) Write high byte to address register (channel 0 high byte),
(d) Clear high byte flip-flop (write to clear high byte flip-flop register),
(e) Write low byte to count register (channel 0 low byte),
(f) Write high byte to count register (channel 0 high byte).

The terminal count signal is generated when the active count register underflows from 0000H to 0FFFFH. One side-effect of this is that one byte extra to the value specified in the base count register is transferred. This should be taken into account by the program before the DMA transfer is programmed and the appropriate adjustments made.

Command Registers

There are 8 command registers, six of which are write only, used to select the type of operation to be performed and to program some of the DMA functions.

The command register.   The bits in this register control 5 basic DMA parameters, as illustrated in *Figure 3.51*. Bits 0 and 1 are used if memory to memory, rather than memory to I/O or I/O to memory, DMA transfers are required. This is a special technique requiring two channels be used and will not be explained here. This technique is disabled by setting both bits to zero. The complete controller can be disabled by setting bit 2 equal to a logic 1. This can be used to prevent any DMA operations occurring during the initialisation or programming sequences. Normal operation is obtained by setting this bit to logic 0. It is possible to change the priority of the four channels after each one has performed a DMA transfer by using the rotating priority feature. This feature will not be explained as normal operation is with a fixed priority, obtained by setting bit 4 to logic 0.

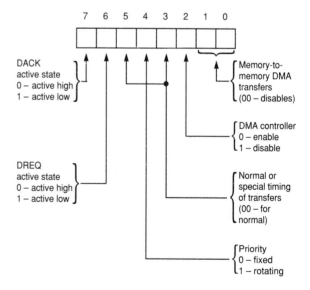

Figure 3.51   Command register

The state of the two DMA handshaking signals, DMA request (DREQ) and DMA acknowledge (DACK) are controlled by bits 6 and 7, as some microprocessors have different active states. For Intel microprocessors the normal states are DREQ active high and DACK active low obtained by setting bits 6 and 7 to logic 0. This results in a normal disable DMA control byte value of 04H (bit 2 is a logic 1) and a normal enable byte of 00H.

The request register. A DMA transfer, once programmed, can be started by the I/O port hardware using the DMA request signal (DREQ). Alternatively, software can write to the request register to initiate the DMA transfer. Once the DMA transfer has been initiated, the DMA controller performs a hold request (HOLD) to the microprocessor and then waits until it has control of the bus, by the hold acknowledge (HOLDA) signal being activated.

Only three bits of this register are used, see *Figure 3.52*, with bits 0 and 1 indicating which channel is presently being programmed and bit 2 indicating whether the DMA transfer request is being initiated (bit 2 = logic 1) or terminated (bit 2 = logic 0).

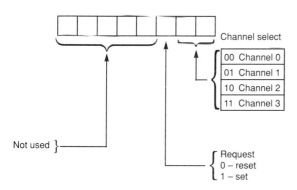

Figure 3.52 The request register (write only)

Although only one DMA channel can be actively controlling the system bus, it is possible to have between 1 and 4 channels in the process of performing transfers and just waiting for control of the bus. If four channels are active then a separate write to the request register would be required for each channel.

The mask registers. It is possible to disable the DMA requests for individual channels without disabling the entire controller, by using the mask bits. There is one bit for each channel and when the mask is set (to logic 1), the DMA requests, both the DREQ (hardware) and the request register (software), for that channel are disabled. The mask bits are set or reset using one of two registers, the single mask bit register or the all mask bits register.

The mode register. Whereas the command register controls parameters which affect the entire DMA controller, the mode register controls parameters which only affect individual channels. This enables each channel to be programmed to perform differently. There are four different parameters that can be altered, the mode, the address increment/decrement, the auto-initialisation and the transfer type, see *Figure 3.53*. The channel to be programmed is selected by bits 0 and 1 and the type of transfer by bits 2 and 3. A write operation transfers a byte from I/O to memory and simultaneously activates I/O read and memory write control signals. A read operation transfers a byte from memory to I/O and simultaneously activates memory read and I/O write. The verify transfer is a special function which activates address signals and DMA handshaking but does not actually transfer data, and is used for test purposes to ensure the correct operation of the DMA controller when connected to the microprocessor.

If a channel is auto-initialised the transfer starts automatically by copying the value from the base address and count registers into current address and count registers, at the end of the currently active channel DMA transfer. The auto initialised DMA transfer then begins

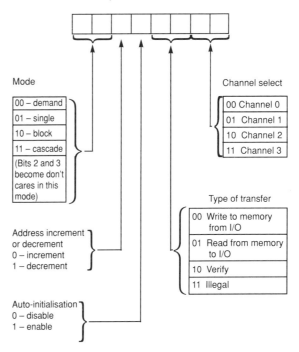

Figure 3.53 The mode register

and thereby avoids having to wait until the end of a DMA transfer before programming the start of the next DMA transfer.

So far, the current address register has been assumed to increment by one after every byte transfer. This can be changed by using bit 5 of the mode register to set a channel to decrement the value in the current address register. The current count register is unaffected and always decrements after each transfer.

There are three **DMA transfer modes** selected by bits 6 and 7, **single**, **block** and **demand** methods. Single is used when one byte at a time is transferred, after which control is returned to the microprocessor, which will execute at least one instruction before the next byte transfer takes place. This mode is used to maintain program execution during the DMA transfer, although both operations are slowed down. Block transfer is the normal method of operation and is used to transfer blocks of data between memory and I/O. In demand mode, the I/O device is unable to transfer data continuously at the same rate as the memory. For example, if the I/O device is only able to supply 1 kbyte at full speed transfer rates and a 4 kbyte block transfer is requested, then demand mode can be used, so that when the I/O is exhausted, the DMA transfer is temporarily stopped and program execution restarted. When the I/O port is ready to recommence the DMA handshaking signals are used to regain control of the bus.

The fourth mode, **cascade**, is not a transfer technique, but indicates that additional DMA controllers have been connected. Each additional DMA controller occupies one of the existing channels but provides four more, so that two DMA controllers provide seven channels, three provide 10 channels, and so on. This method of connection is necessary if more than 4 channels are required, as the microprocessor only has one set of DMA compatible handshaking signals. If the channel is in cascade mode, it cannot be programmed to control a DMA transfer so that bits 2 and 3 of the mode register become don't cares.

Other Register Commands

The remaining write only command registers, clear high byte flip-flop, mask clear, and master clear, do not program register values but perform a complete function. The clear high byte flip-flop has already been explained. A write to the mask clear register sets all four channel mask bits and therefore enables a request on any of the channels. This is a simple method of enabling all four channels. A write to the master clear register performs a similar operation to the hardware reset, but does not affect any other programmable components.

The command, status, request, temporary registers and high byte flip-flop are all cleared ready for programming, and all mask bits are set, disabling any DMA requests that may occur.

The read only command registers. Of the 8 command registers, there are only two which when read contain valid data and these are the temporary register and the status register.

The temporary register. The temporary register contains the value of the last byte transferred and is available to the programmer if required. It can also be used to perform software controlled transfers. In memory to memory DMA transfers, this register acts as the temporary byte storage in between the memory read and the memory write operations.

The status register. The status register, see *Figure 3.54*, enables the programmer to obtain two sorts of information about each of the four DMA channels, whether a channel has reached terminal count, that is, if the transfer has been completed and whether there is a request pending, either software- or hardware-generated.

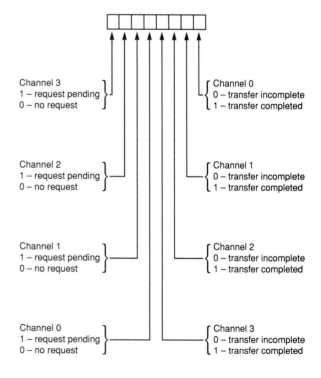

Channel 3
1 – request pending
0 – no request

Channel 0
0 – transfer incomplete
1 – transfer completed

Channel 2
1 – request pending
0 – no request

Channel 1
0 – transfer incomplete
1 – transfer completed

Channel 1
1 – request pending
0 – no request

Channel 2
0 – transfer incomplete
1 – transfer completed

Channel 0
1 – request pending
0 – no request

Channel 3
0 – transfer incomplete
1 – transfer completed

Figure 3.54   The status register

Example

The following example illustrates how to initialise a DMA controller and then program it to transfer a 4 kbyte block of data from I/O into memory using channel 1. The TC signal is used to interrupt the 8086 and restart the microprocessor and indicates that a programmable interrupt controller is available.

The algorithm of the program is shown below and assumes that there is a 4-bit latch connected to the top 4 bits of the address bus for storing the top 4 bits of the address:

(1) Initialise;
(2) Program channel 1 count registers;
(3) Program channel 1 address registers and DMA address latch;
(4) Enable the DMA controller;
(5) Program the I/O device for a DMA transfer;
(6) Wait for the end of the DMA transfer.

The program to implement this can now be written. The specific I/O device has not been identified, although on the IBM PC, DMA channel 1 is connected to the floppy disk controller. It performs a **burst DMA transfer** using channel 1 of the 8237A DMA controller:

```
COMMAND         EQU     08H       ;Command register
                                  ;address.
DMA_DISABLE     EQU     04H
MASTER_CLEAR    EQU     0DH       ;Master clear
                                  ;command address.
MODE            EQU     0BH       ;Mode register
                                  ;address.
MODE_COMMAND    EQU  10000001B    ;Perform an I/O to
                                  ;memory write using
                                  ;channel 1, with no
                                  ;auto-initialisation.
                                  ;Use incrementing of
                                  ;current address
                                  ;register, as a block
                                  ;transfer.
MASK_SINGLE     EQU  00000001B    ;Enable channel 1
                                  ;request mask bit.
MASK_ADDRESS    EQU     0AH       ;Single bit mask
                                  ;register address.
CLR_HIGH_BYTE   EQU     0CH       ;Clear high byte flip
                                  ;flop address.
BASE_COUNT      EQU     03H       ;Base count register
                                  ;address.
BLOCK_SIZE      EQU   1000H       ;4 kbyte block size.
DMA_TOP_LATCH   EQU    080H       ;Address of latch for
                                  ;A₁₆-A₁₉.
BASE_ADDRESS    EQU     02H       ;Base address
                                  ;register address.
ENABLE          EQU     00A       ;Enable DMA
                                  ;controller.
                                  ;Initialise Step (1)
        MOV   DX,COMMAND          ;Disable DMA controller.
```

```
        MOV   AL,DMA_DISABLE
        OUT   DX,AL
;
        MOV   DX,MASTER_CLEAR     ;Perform a master clear.
        OUT   DX,AL               ;The value in AL is
                                  ;irrelevant.
;
        MOV   DX,MODE             ;Set up the mode
                                  ;register.
        MOV   AL,MODE_COMMAND
        OUT   DX,AL
;
        MOV   DX,MASK_ADDR        ;Enable requests on
                                  ;channel 1.
        MOV   AL,MASK_SINGLE
        OUT   DX,AL
;
        MOV   DX,CLR_HIGH_BYTE    ;Clear high byte flip flop,
        OUT   DX,AL
                                  ;Program channel 1
                                  ;count registers.
                                  ;Step (2)
        MOV   DX,BASE_COUNT       ;Write block size to base
                                  ;and current count
                                  ;registers.
        MOV   AX,BLOCK_SIZE       ;
        DEC   AX                  ;Size is decremented by
                                  ;1 to adjust for DMA
                                  ;over-count.
        OUT   DX,AL               ;Least significant byte of
        MOV   AL,AH               ;size transferred first.
        OUT   DX,AL               ;Most significant byte of
                                  ;size transferred second.
                                  ;Program channel 1
                                  ;address register and
                                  ;DMA address latch.
                                  ;Step (3)
                                  ;First the buffer address
                                  ;is converted to an
                                  ;absolute value.
        MOV   BX,SEGMENT_BUFFER   ;Get the 4 most
                                  ;significant bits of
                                  ;the segment
                                  ;address.
        MOV   AX,BX
        AND   AH,TOP_4_BITS
        MOV   CL,FOUR_BIT_SHIFT   ;Put into the bottom
        SHR   AH,CL               ;four bits.
        MOV   CL,FOUR_BIT_SHIFT
        SHL   BX,CL               ;Multiply by 16 to
                                  ;convert to the absolute
                                  ;segment address.
        MOV   CX,OFFSET BUFFER    ;Add the offset of the file
        ADD   CX,BX               ;buffer.
        JNC   OK                  ;If there is no overflow
                                  ;then the offset is OK,
        INC   AH                  ;otherwise the top 4 bits
                                  ;of the segment need
                                  ;incrementing.
OK:                               ;AH contains A₁₆-A₁₉
                                  ;CX contains A₀-A₁₅.
        PUSH  AX                  ;Save address bits
                                  ;A₁₆-A₁₉.
        MOV   AX,CX               ;Add the block size to
```

```
        ADD   AX,BLOCK_SIZE        ;the memory offset.
                                   ;Block has to be less
                                   ;than 32 kbytes.
        JNC   NO_ALTERATION        ;Do nothing if the
                                   ;segment boundary is
                                   ;not crossed.
        POP   AX                   ;The segment boundary
                                   ;has been crossed and
        MOV   DX,MASTER_CLEAR      ;this indicates an error
                                   ;situation.
        OUT   DX,AL                ;Therefore, reset the
                                   ;DMA and stop.
        HLT
;
NO_ALTERATION:
;
        POP   AX                   ;Get A16–A19 address
        MOV   DX,DMA_TOP_LATCH     ;bits and output
                                   ;them to the latch.
        OUT   DX,AL
;                                  ;Clear high byte flip
        MOV   DX,CLEAR_HIGH_BYTE   ;flop ready for the
        OUT   DX,AL                ;least significant
                                   ;byte.
        MOV   DX,BASE_ADDRESS      ;Output the memory
        MOV   AX,CX                ;block starting address
                                   ;to the base and current
        OUT   DX,AL                ;address registers.
        MOV   AL,AH
        OUT   DX,AL
                                   ;Enable the DMA
                                   ;controller. Step (4)
        MOV   DX,COMMAND
        MOV   AL,ENABLE
        OUT   DX,AL                ;DMA controller
                                   ;enabled. I/O device will
                                   ;be programmed here to
                                   ;request and use a
                                   ;4 KByte DMA transfer.
                                   ;Step (5)
                                   ;Wait for the end of the
                                   ;DMA transfer. Step (6)
        MOV   CX,TIMEOUT           ;If the DMA transfer has
WAIT:   NOP                        ;not occurred by the end
        NOP                        ;of the count then time-
                                   ;out. This only occurs if
        NOP                        ;the DMA transfer was
        NOP                        ;not started, otherwise
        NOP                        ;the microprocessor is
                                   ;in hold and cannot
        NOP                        ;execute the time-out
                                   ;loop.
        LOOP WAIT                  ;Exit from loop by
                                   ;interrupt initiated by
                                   ;the terminal count
                                   ;signal.
;
        TIMED_OUT:                 ;To reach this point, the
                                   ;DMA transfer must not
                                   ;have taken place and
                                   ;therefore the wait loop
                                   ;has timed-out. An error
                                   ;handling routine should
                                   ;then be placed here.
```

Summary

DMA transfers using a DMA controller can be used to increase the rate of block byte transfer between memory and I/O, I/O and memory, or memory to memory. However, the DMA controller is a complex device to interface and program and generally only high performance systems, such as microcomputers or personal computers, would find it worthwhile.

3.6   FLOPPY DISK CONTROLLER (FDC)

One of the requirements of a microcomputer system is to have a secondary mass storage device for saving user programs, data and the operating system software. One common secondary mass storage device is the floppy disk with its associated **floppy disk drive**, see *Figure 3.55*. This is interfaced to the microprocessor by a peripheral component called a **floppy disk controller** (FDC), and is programmed by the microprocessor to perform the data storage and retrieval actions.

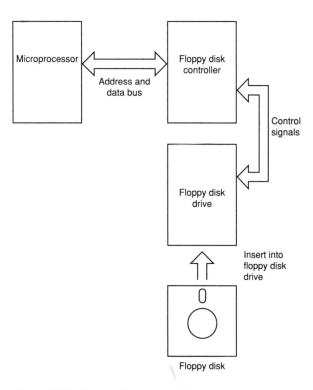

Figure 3.55   Floppy disk and disk drive

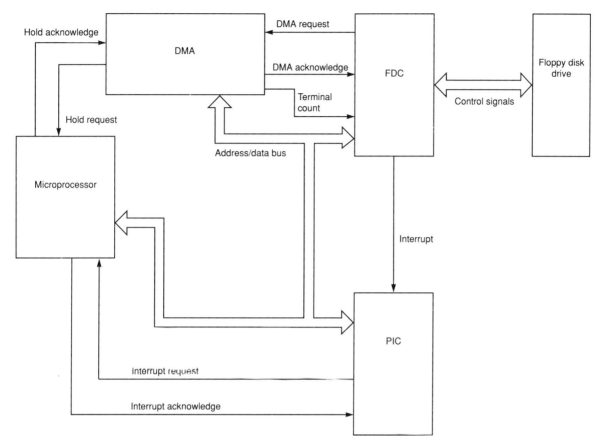

Figure 3.56 Floppy disk with DMA transfer

These actions fall into one of three categories:

(a) Reading data from the floppy disk to memory;
(b) Writing data from memory to the floppy disk;
(c) Initialising the floppy disk drive and floppy disk.

Because this device is designed for mass storage, the data transferred is in large blocks and to obtain the maximum performance DMA transfers are performed. The system must therefore also contain a DMA controller.

The FDC can be used in either a polled or an interrupt-driven mode. In an interrupt-driven mode there is an interrupt signal which is used to indicate that the presently executing command has completed; if this is used a programmable interrupt controller will also be required as in *Figure 3.56*.

A Floppy Disk

To gain a better understanding of the FDC operations the details of the floppy disk will be explained first. As the name suggests, a floppy disk is a disk of flexible material, usually plastic, which has had a flexible coating of magnetic material applied to it. This is then housed in a square protective jacket, as illustrated in *Figure 3.57* (overleaf).

A recording head similar to those used in cassette tape recorders is used to write data onto the magnetic media layer when data is being saved and reads data from the magnetic layer when data is being retrieved. Reading the data does not alter the data stored on the **magnetic media**, so that once saved the data can be restored to the microcomputer memory as many times as required. Programs can be stored in this way, as well as data values.

The two most common sizes of floppy disk are $5\frac{1}{4}$ inches diameter, and $3\frac{1}{2}$ inches diameter. The $5\frac{1}{4}$ inch disk is well established but is now becoming obsolete as it is being replaced by the smaller disk, which is designed to store larger amounts of data and is housed in a rigid plastic protective jacket so that it is more robust. The data on the disk is organised into tracks

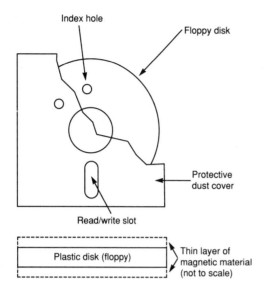

Figure 3.57 A floppy disk

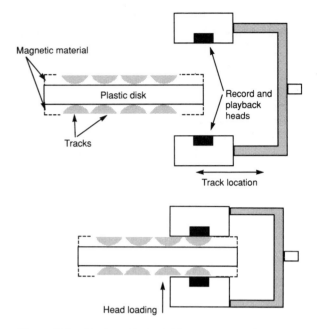

Figure 3.58 Head positioning (sideways view) and loading/unloading

similar to the tracks on an audio record, although each track on the floppy disk is completely separate from all other tracks and does not spiral in towards the centre. Each side of the disk contains a fixed number of tracks and a separate head to access each side. Each track contains a fixed number of sectors and each sector contains a fixed number of bytes of data.

The IBM PC floppy disk drives use a double-sided floppy disk, so the disk drives have dual record/playback heads, one for each side. There are 40 tracks per side, 9 sectors per track and 512 bytes per sector. This gives a total **storage capacity, S_{cap},** for each floppy disk of:

$$N \times T \times S \times B = 2 \times 40 \times 9 \times 512 = 368\,640 \text{ bytes}$$

N number of sides per floppy disk;
T number of tracks per side;
S number of sectors per track;
B number of bytes per sector.

The IBM PC/XT/AT family of personal computers also use floppy disk drives with higher densities of data storage.

Data is then accessed on the floppy disk in terms of the head used, the track number and the sector number. The record/playback head is physically moved to place it directly over the selected track, and then pressed against the track, in order to be able to read or write data, see *Figure 3.58*. The movement of the head against the floppy disk is called **head loading** and removing the head from pressing against the floppy disk, is called head unloading.

The sectors are all the same length and this is fixed when the disk is formatted. A typical value would be 512 bytes per sector, as used by the IBM PC. However, the actual number of bytes of data stored in a sector can vary from 1 to 512, as any unused byte locations are set to the null character. This can result in a 1 byte file occupying 512 bytes on the floppy disk; alternatively, if the program or data is longer than 512 bytes then several sectors are used.

Other disk formats can be used with higher densities and 720 kbytes and 1.2 Mbyte floppy disks are common. To the user, the floppy disk format used is not of great importance, except in how it affects the program used to program the FDC.

Two important parameters of floppy disks and floppy disk drives are the size of files that can be stored and the speed at which data can be transferred between the floppy disk and memory. Generally, the higher the number of bytes on a floppy disk, the larger the maximum size of files that can be stored and the higher the byte transfer rate. The disadvantage of the higher density floppy disks are that the floppy disks and the floppy disk drives cost more.

Track 0 of side 0 of the floppy disk is used to contain the directory which is a list of the files containing user programs and data that are stored on the disk. The directory also contains information which indicates where each file is physically stored on the disk, in terms of side, track and sector. The FDC has a special method of accessing track 0 of side 0 in order to obtain this very important information.

It is also possible to prevent any data that is on the floppy disk from being changed in any way so that the complete disk becomes a read-only-disk, and this is called **write protect**. On a floppy disk which can be written to, a small notch will be present which is detected by the floppy disk drive and enables new data to be written to the disk. This can be used to prevent data and programs from being accidentally overwritten by covering the notch with special stickers once it has been decided that the disk is not to be altered any more, to make it into a write-protected floppy disk. This protection applies to the whole disk and therefore cannot be used on disks which are still being used to save new data.

The Floppy Disk Controller

The general programmer's model for a FDC is shown in *Figure 3.59* and consists of the status and data registers. The FDC is different to most other peripheral components in that it does not require a programmed initialisation, as the correct initialisation takes place internally whenever there is a hardware reset.

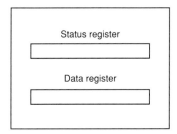

Figure 3.59 Programmer's model of a FDC

The FDC is similar to a simple co-processor as it is programmed by writing successive command bytes to the data register. The number of bytes written to the data register for a single operation can vary from one to nine bytes. The FDC independently executes the specified operation which may involve positioning the head over the correct track, loading the head and writing or reading the selected sectors. This sequence can take up to 60 or 70 ms, during which time the main microprocessor is free to perform other actions. Once the operation has been completed, the FDC has several bytes of status information which the microprocessor can read from the data register.

The data register acts as the entry point to a pop-up and push-down queue. When a data byte has been written, it is automatically popped-down and another byte can be written. When the complete sequence has been transferred the operation executes and when complete the status information is available by reading from the data register. The first byte is read from the data register and the next byte is automatically popped-up ready to be read. This process is repeated until all the status bytes have been read by the microprocessor. The FDC repeatedly executes the sequence:

(a) Program the required floppy disk operation;
(b) Execute the programmed operation;
(c) Obtain the results of selected operation.

The FDC is designed to transfer the data between execution memory and the floppy disk using DMA, as this is the fastest method of transferring large blocks of data. It is possible to transfer each byte one at a time under direct microprocessor control but this is not recommended as it takes many times longer and does not have any advantages.

As most transfers will be in DMA mode, the DMA handshaking signals are provided automatically and the data is not written to the data register. The data is transferred directly between execution memory and the floppy disk via the FDC. The DMA transfers take place between an I/O port and a block of execution memory locations. No I/O address is specified as during DMA transfers only the active I/O device is connected to the data bus. The DMA controller controls the memory address value and control signals, and this frees the FDC from the need to be programmed with this information.

Most FDC's have the ability to transfer data to any one of four floppy disk drives and some additional decoding may be required to select the correct drive as only one drive can be active at any one time.

A typical sequence of bytes required to perform a data write operation might be:

(a) The write data operation command byte;
(b) The selected drive byte;
(c) The selected track number byte;
(d) The selected head number byte;
(e) The starting sector number byte;
(f) The number of bytes per sector;
(g) The total number of bytes to be transferred.

Following the writing of the last byte of step (g), the FDC moves the head until it is over the track specified in step (c), on the drive selected in step (b). The two heads are physically dependent so they both move together until they are over the selected track, one each side of the floppy disk. This simplifies the mechanics of the floppy disk drive but it does mean that data can only be accessed from one side of the floppy disk at any one time. The selected head would then be loaded. A DMA request would be made by the FDC, and the data would be transferred to the floppy disk a sector at a time, starting with the sector specified in step (e). When a complete sector has been transferred the next sector is selected and used. Only complete sectors can be transferred, so that the total number of bytes, as given in step (g), divided by the number of bytes per sector step (f), must be an integer with no remainder. If incomplete sector transfers are required then a special format of the previous command is used.

It is the responsibility of the programmer to ensure that only complete sectors are transferred. If more than one sector of data is to be transferred then the FDC will automatically increment the sector number, so that multiple sector transfers can be automatically implemented. However, there are restrictions to this automatic sector incrementing. One restriction is that the sectors being transferred must be sequentially adjacent on the same track, so that if three sectors are to be transferred to the floppy disk starting at sector three, then sectors four and five must not contain valid data from other files, or they will be over-written. If reading, the same operation must ensure that the data in sectors four and five logically follows that in sector three. The information regarding the position of sectors which constitute a multiple-sector file, is maintained in the **floppy disk directory** and any alteration to the disk contents affecting sector positioning has to be reflected in the directory to ensure correct operation. This checking is the responsibility of the programmer, although for the majority of users, this task can be left to the **disk operating system** (DOS), as is the organisation of the data so that it is correctly transferred to the tracks and sectors without errors.

In addition, the sector number cannot be automatically incremented past the last sector on a track, so that if, for example, the starting sector was seven, then a maximum of two sectors could be transferred in one operation using automatic sector incrementing before the end of the track was reached. Any remaining sectors in the data would have to be transferred in a completely new operation which would specify the next free track and sector.

As files are transferred to and from the floppy disk, the sectors of each file can be placed on non-adjacent tracks and can be on several tracks. This is called file fragmentation. Each time a following sector is non-adjacent the file transfer time is increased, and every repositioning of the head over a different track takes 20–70 ms. Therefore, a floppy disk which is continuously used will become more and more fragmented, which in turn slows down the speed of file transfer. Significant increases in file transfer for well-used floppy disks can be achieved by transferring the files, one at a time, to a new disk where they will be automatically placed in sequentially and physically adjacent sectors.

As the head is physically pressed against the floppy disk there is a wearing action introduced and for reliable operation, the floppy disks should be periodically replaced with new ones and the old ones discarded. The disk drives themselves should also be maintained in good order and periodically cleaned. However, care has to be taken as too much cleaning can produce more head wear than just using floppy disks.

The Intel 8272A Floppy Disk Controller

The Intel 8272A FDC is almost exactly the same as the FDC used in the IBM PC, and the programmer's model shown in *Figure 3.60* is similar to the general model outlined previously. The base address of the FDC in the PC/XT is 03F4H, with the status register having an offset of 00H and the data register an offset of 01H, to give a status register address of 03F4H and a data register address of 03F5H.

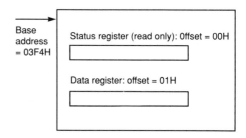

Figure 3.60   Programmer's model of the 8272A FDC

An initialisation sequence is not required for this FDC, although in the complete microcomputer system it is advisable to check that the floppy disk drive is operating correctly, by performing a simple series of tests when the power is first applied.

8272A FDC Commands Available

The 8272A FDC can execute the 15 commands listed below and detailed information on these commands can be obtained from the appropriate Intel data manuals.

(a)   Read data
(b)   Read deleted data
(c)   Write data
(d)   Write deleted data
(e)   Read a track
(f)   Read identification

(g) Format a track
(h) Scan equal
(i) Scan low or equal
(j) Scan high or equal
(k) Recalibrate
(l) Sense interrupt status
(m) Specify parameters
(n) Sense drive status
(o) Seek

Only the recalibrate, sense interrupt status, seek, read and write commands will be considered in detail as these are the minimum operands that are required by all systems, and allow 8086 assembler language programs to be written. These programs will control the transfer of data between memory and a previously formatted floppy disk.

The Recalibrate Operation

The recalibrate operation is a test that is usually performed after a system reset to ensure that the floppy disk drive can correctly position the head over the selected track. After a reset the FDC has no information regarding the track position of the heads of the floppy disk drive. To obtain the head track position, the head is moved towards track 0 on the floppy disk, a track at a time, until the track 0 sense switch on the floppy disk drive is activated. Once the track 0 sense switch has been activated the physical position of the head over track 0 is known, and this information is then available to the FDC for all future track positioning commands. If the FDC loses the correct head position the floppy disk drive will have to be recalibrated. For any position of the head after a system reset, 40 or less track steps will be needed before the track 0 sense switch is activated. If more steps are required an error has occurred.

Figure 3.61 shows the two bytes required to program the calibration operation. There are no status bytes returned after completion. However, several bits in the status bytes of other commands are affected, for example, see the SEEK command.

The FDC has a special handshaking method of transferring the sequence of command bytes to the data register and the sequence of result bytes from the data register, which involves the status register. The status register, as illustrated in *Figure 3.62*, contains information about the complete FDC rather than just the local status information obtained from the data register after a command has completed. Before a new sequence of command bytes can be transferred to the FDC, the FDC busy bit, bit 4 of the status register, is checked for not busy. When the FDC is not busy (bit 4 = 0) the FDC ready

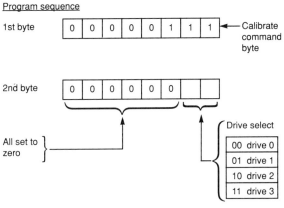

Program sequence

Execute phase
The head is moved to track 0, the outer-most track

Figure 3.61 Recalibrate command

bit, bit 7, is checked. When the FDC is ready (bit 7 = 1) the next byte in the command sequence can be transferred. This status bit becomes inactive after each byte transfer to enable the FDC to implement each specific part of the command. Therefore this bit has to be checked for the ready state before the next byte can be transferred.

The direction status bit is used in conjunction with the ready status bit to determine whether the FDC is being programmed with a command, (direction status bit = 0), or reading the status results, (the direction status bit = 1).

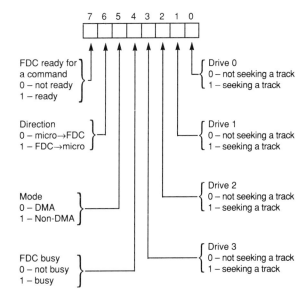

Figure 3.62 The status register

Example

An algorithm which would implement the calibrate command would contain the following sequence of actions for the recalibrate command:

(1) Check the FDC is not busy;
(2) Check the direction is correct for programming the FDC;
(3) Check the FDC is ready for the command byte;
(4) Transfer the first byte to the FDC;
(5) Wait until the FDC is ready for the next byte;
(6) Transfer the second byte of the recalibrate command.

A typical assembly language program for the recalibrate command is given below. This subroutine implements the FDC recalibrate operation on the IBM PC or close compatibles. AX and DX are used although these registers are left with their original values.

```
CALIBRATE:  PROC  NEAR
            PUSH  AX
            PUSH  DX
            MOV   DX, 03F4H    ;Set up address of
                              ;status registers.
                              ;Check the FDC is not
                              ;busy Step (1)
WAIT_BUSY:  IN    AL, DX      ;Read status byte.
            CMP   AL, 00010000B
            JNZ   WAIT_BUSY    ;Wait until not busy.
                              ;Check the direction
                              ;is correct. Step (2)
WAIT_DIR:   IN    AL, DX
            CMP   AL, 01000000B
            JNZ   WAIT_DIR     ;Check that direction
                              ;is correct for
                              ;programming.
                              ;Check FDC is ready
                              ;for the byte. Step
                              ;(3)
WAIT_RDY:   IN    AL, DX      ;Wait until FDC is
            CMP   AL, 10000000B ;ready to accept the
            JZ    WAIT_RDY     ;command byte.
                              ;Transfer the first
                              ;byte to the FDC.
                              ;Step (4)
            MOV   DX, 03F5H    ;Write calibrate
            MOV   AL, 00000111B ;command byte to
            OUT   DX, AL       ;data register.
                              ;Wait until the FDC is
                              ;ready for the next
                              ;byte. Step (5)
            MOV   DX, 03F4H    ;Status register
                              ;address.
WAIT_RDY2:  IN    AL, DX      ;Wait until FDC ready
            CMP   AL, 10000000B ;for next byte of the
            JZ    WAIT_RDY2    ;calibrate command.
                              ;Transfer the second
                              ;byte of the
                              ;recalibrate
                              ;command. Step (6)
            MOV   DX, 03F5H    ;Write drive selected
                              ;byte to data register.
            MOV   AL, 00H      ;Drive 0 selected.
            OUT   DX, AL
                              ;Calibrate command
                              ;completed.
            POP   DX          ;Restore registers
            POP   AX          ;and exit from the
            RET               ;subroutine.
                              ;
CALIBRATE:  ENDP
```

This operation does not return any status bytes when completed. Unless another command is then issued, such as sense interrupt status, the operation is always assumed to have executed correctly if the FDC exits from the busy state within a fixed time period. After this command has completed, the read/write head can be assumed to be positioned over track 0.

For most operations the interrupt signal indicates the beginning of the results stage when status registers can be read. As the calibrate command does not have any status registers to read, the interrupt signal indicates that the calibrate operation has completed. A separate sense interrupt status command is used to obtain some status information to verify that the calibrate operation has completed successfully.

Sense Interrupt Status Command

The sense interrupt status command programming sequence consists of a single byte of value 08H, and a result sequence of two bytes. The first result byte indicates the contents of the status register and the second results byte, the present track position of the head, see *Figure 3.63*. These values enable the calibrate operation to ensure that there are no faults, that track 0 was found and that the operation terminated normally.

Example

The transfer of the command byte sequence to the FDC can be represented by the following algorithm:

(1) Check that the FDC is not busy;
(2) Check that the direction is correct for programming;
(3) Send the sense interrupt status command byte sequence;
(4) Read the status information;
(5) Check the status information for correct termination;
(6) Check that the floppy disk drive is functioning correctly;
(7) Save the head position.

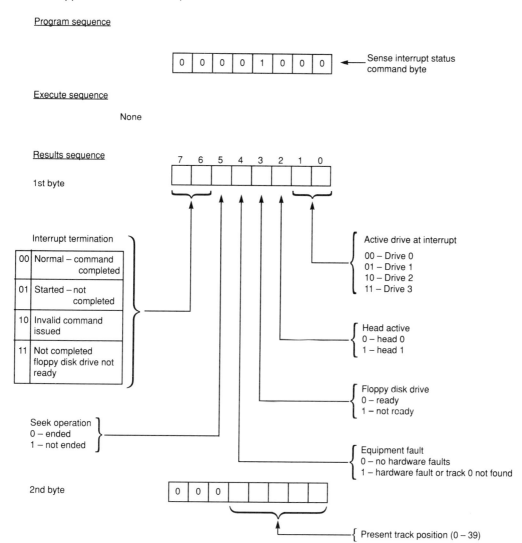

Figure 3.63 Sense interrupt command

Positioning the Head Over the Track (SEEK)

The calibrate command will only position the head over track 0, and an alternative command, called SEEK, is used to position the head over any selected track, including track 0. Some additional information is required by the SEEK operation; the head to be used, indicating which side of the disk, and the track to be moved to, called the **new track position** (NTP). These values were not required for calibrate as track 0 of side 0 is always assumed. These values form a three-byte command sequence, see *Figure 3.64* (overleaf), with a straightforward construction.

The execution phase of this command causes the head to move from its present track position to the designated new track position. Again, there are no result status bytes for this command and the sense interrupt status command is used to confirm that the seek command has correctly terminated.

It is important to remember that the position of the head is maintained internally in the FDC and is not a measurement of the physical position of the head over the track. If the physical position of the head were to become different from the value maintained by the FDC, then incorrect data would be transferred. Vibration caused by excessive physical movement can cause this

Command sequence

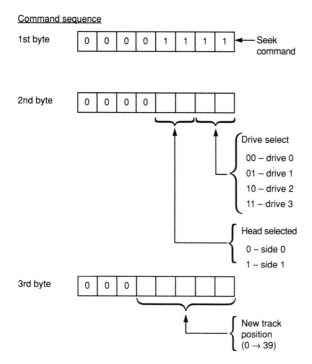

Execute phase
    The head is moved from the existing track to the new track

Result phase
    None

Figure 3.64   Seek command

to happen and this is one reason why floppy disk drives are only used on stationary computers. A more robust system can be obtained by performing a read track number command after the SEEK to ensure that the correct track is found. The syntax of this command can be found in the appropriate Intel data manual.

Example

The following algorithm indicates the sequence of actions required to perform a seek command:

(1) Check the FDC is not busy;
(2) Check direction is correct for programming the FDC;
(3) Send the SEEK command sequence of bytes;
(4) Check the head is positioned correctly;
(5) Check for any errors.

Assembly language program for seek.   The algorithm has been implemented in the following subroutine which makes use of two subroutines for the sense interrupt status command, and assumes the existence of the sense interrupt status subroutine. This subroutine is

called to check that the head is correctly positioned. To make the programs simpler, two subroutines will be used to write the command byte sequence, and read the result sequence of bytes.

Example program to transfer command bytes to the FDC.   This subroutine sends the byte value in the AH register to the data register of an FDC:

```
SEND_CMD:   PROC   NEAR
            MOV    DX, 03F4H
WAIT_RDY:   IN     AL, DX        ;Wait until ready for
            CMP    AL, 10000000B ;the next byte.
            JZ     WAIT_RDY
            ;
            MOV    DX, 03F5H     ;Write the command
            MOV    AL, ASH       ;byte in the AH
            OUT    DX, AL        ;register to the data
                                 ;register.
                                 ;
            RET                  ;The end of the
                                 ;subroutine.
```

Example

Subroutine to read a status byte from the data register after a command has terminated. The byte is returned in the AL register.

```
FETCH_STATUS:   PROC   NEAR
                MOV    DX, 03F4H
WAIT_RDY2:      IN     AL, DX        ;Wait until the next
                CMP    AL, 10000000B ;byte is ready.
                JZ     WAIT_RDY2
                ;
                MOV    DX, 03F5H     ;Read the status byte
                IN     AL, DX        ;from the data
                                     ;register to AL.
                ;
                RET                  ;The end of the
                                     ;subroutine.
                                     ;
```

These two small subroutines will now be incorporated into the procedure to execute the entire sense interrupt status command.

Example

This sense interrupt status command procedure first checks that the FDC is ready to be programmed. Then the command sequence of bytes is transferred, and finally the status byte sequence is obtained and checked for any errors.

```
SENSE_INT_STAT   PROC   NEAR
                 PUSH   BX        ;Save register
                 PUSH   CX        ;contents.
                 PUSH   DX
                 MOV    BX, 0000H ;Initialise error count
```

```
            MOV   DX, 03F4H    ;to zero.
                               Wait until not busy.
                               ;Step (1)
WAIT_BUSY:  IN    AL, DX       ;Read the status
            CMP   AL, 00010000B ;byte.
            JNZ   WAIT_BUSY
                               ;Wait for correct
                               ;direction. Step (2)
WAIT_DIR:   IN    AL, DX       ;Wait for correct
            CMP   AL, 01000000B ;direction.
            JNZ   WAIT_DIR
                               ;Send the sense
                               ;interrupt status
                               ;command. Step (3)
            MOV   AH, 08H      ;Interrupt status
            CALL  SEND_CMD     ;command.
                               ;Get the status bytes.
                               ;Step (4)
            CALL  FETCH_STATUS ;Get the first
            MOV   CL, AL       ;status byte.

            CALL  FETCH_STATUS ;Get the present
            MOV   CH, AL       ;head position.
                               ;Check for normal
                               ;command termi-
                               ;nation. Step (5)
            MOV   AL, CL       ;Perform the
            AND   AL, 11000000B ;tests for error
            JZ    NORMAL       ;free completion.
                               ;An error has been
                               ;detected, therefore
                               ;increment the error
            INC   BX           ;count.
                               ;Check that the disk
                               ;drive is ready.
                               ;Step (6)
NORMAL:     MOV AL,CL
            AND AL,00011000B   ;Check that the
            JZ  NO_ERRORS      ;equipment is OK
                               ;and that the disk
                               ;drive is ready.
                               ;If there is a hard-
                               ;ware error then
            INC BX             ;increment the
                               ;error count.
                               ;Save the detected
                               ;head position.
                               ;Step (7)
NO_ERRORS:  MOV AL,CH          ;Head position saved
                               ;in AL.
            MOV AH,BL          ;Number of detected
                               ;errors is saved in
                               ;AH.
            POP BX             ;Restore saved
            POP CX             ;register contents.
            POP DX
            RET
            ENDP
```

This would be performed immediately after a calibrate command to ensure that the head is positioned over track zero. The following program segment would implement this.

Using the Sense Interrupt Status Command

Program fragment to demonstrate how the sense interrupt command is used after a calibrate command:

```
          CALL CALIBRATE      ;Calibrate command.
          CALL SENSE_INT_STAT ;Sense interrupt
                              ;status command.
          AND  AH,0FFH        ;Check for any errors.
          JZ   NO_ERRORS
          CALL ERRORS
NO_ERRORS: AND AL,0FFH        ;Test for track 0 in
          JZ   TRACK_0        ;present track position
                              ;count.
          CALL NOT_TRACK_0;Error handling routine
                              ;for when not positioned
                              ;over track 0 after a
                              ;calibrate command.
TRACK_0:
                              ;The rest of the program.
                              ;would then be placed
                              ;here.
```

This procedure uses the seek command to correctly position the head before a read or write operation:

```
SEEK:       PROC NEAR          ;Required track in
            PUSH DX            ;the AL register.
            PUSH BX
            MOV  BH,AL         ;Move the track
                               ;position to the AH
                               ;register.
                               ;Check the FDC is not
                               ;busy. Step (1)
            MOV  DX,03F4H      ;Read the FDC status
                               ;register.
WAIT_BUSY:  IN   AL,DX
            CMP  AL,00010000B
            JNZ  WAIT_BUSY     ;Wait until not busy.
                               ;Check the direction
                               ;is correct for
                               ;programming.
                               ;Step (2)
WAIT_DIR:   IN   AL,DX         ;Wait for the
            CMP  AL,03000000B  ;correct direction.
            JNZ  WAIT_DIR
                               ;Send the seek
                               ;command sequence
                               ;of bytes. Step (3)
            MOV  AH,00FH
            CALL SEND_CMD

            MOV  AH,00H        ;Side 0, drive 0
            CALL SEND_CMD      ;assumed for
                               ;simplicity.

            MOV  AH,BH         ;Required track
                               ;position.
            CALL SEND_CMD
                               ;Check head is
                               ;correctly
                               ;positioned. Step (4)
```

```
        CALL  SENSE_INT_STATUS
                          ;Perform the sense
                          ;interrupt status
                          ;command.
                          ;Check for any
                          ;errors. Step (5)
        AND   AH,00FH
        JZ    NO_ERRORS
        CALL  ERRORS      ;Error handling
                          ;subroutine.
NO_ERRORS:  CMP   AL,BH   ;Is the track position
                          ;correct?
        JZ    CORRECT_TRACK
        CALL  WRONG_TRACK;No, then execute
                          ;the wrong track
                          ;error handler
                          ;subroutine.
CORRECT_TRACK:  POP  BX
                POP  DX
                RET
SEEK:       ENDP
```

The Read and Write Commands

The previous commands have been concerned with positioning the head over the required track. The read and write commands are used to transfer the data between the floppy disk and the microcomputer memory under DMA control, via the FDC. The read and write commands are the most complex of the FDC operations and have a 9-byte programming sequence and a 7-byte result and status sequence, see *Figure 3.65*. Only the initial command byte value varies from 066H for the read operation and 045H for the write operation. The status information obtained at the end of the operation is also the same, except that if the disk is write-protected, the write operation will not be performed and the appropriate status bits set.

The commands assume that the head is already correctly positioned so that a seek command to the selected track must first be executed. This is followed by the associated sense interrupt status command to ensure that the positioning of the head over the correct track was achieved.

The first byte of the read/write sequence of command bytes selects the read (066H) or the write (045H) operation. The following four bytes select the drive, track, head and the starting sector. The sixth byte selects the number of bytes per sector and *Table 3.2* contains some possible values used with the IBM PC. The seventh byte indicates the number of sectors per track and the eighth byte contains some technical information about how the data is laid out on the track. To be compatible with the IBM PC a value of 02AH is used. If the number of bytes per sector (byte six) is set to zero, the ninth byte must contain the number to be used. This is used in single

Command sequence

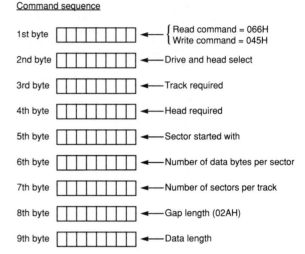

Execution phase
- The head is loaded (it must already be correctly positioned)
- The correct sector is identified (this information is contained on the track itself) and complete sectors are transfered until the DMA transfer is complete
- The head is unloaded after the transfer is completed

The results sequence

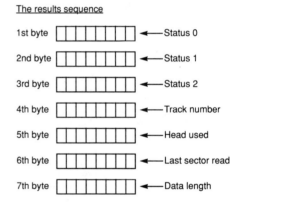

Figure 3.65   The read (and write) command structure

Table 3.2   Bytes per sector

N	Bytes per sector	(assuming 8 sectors per track)
02	512	
03	1024	
00	Number given in data length byte of programming sequence	

Note: Other values of N are possible but they relate to disks which have a different number of sectors per track sector transfers when a sector is being transferred which is not a complete sector. If a non-zero number of bytes per sector is selected the ninth byte is ignored, but it must still be sent.

Once the 9 bytes have been sequentially written to the data register, the programming phase is complete and the operation will begin to execute. The first action to be performed is to load the head, that is, press it against the floppy disk. The head will already have been positioned over the required track using a previous seek operation. A settling time of approximately 15 ms is allowed before data transfer begins, to allow any mechanical vibrations caused by the head movement to disappear.

Track information which identifies the track and the sector is then read and compared with that specified in the command and is used by the FDC to verify correct head positioning. If the head is not correctly positioned the operation is terminated and an error indicated.

If the track is correct the head continues to read the sector identifiers until the sector identified in the programming sequence is reached. The FDC then transfers data between the floppy disk and the the microprocessor, under DMA control, until the DMA controller indicates the transfer has been completed. The DMA controller must therefore be programmed with the amount of data to be transferred before the operation is started.

The FDC will identify if the head reads past the last sector on the track and signify an error in the status bytes when the operation terminates. However, the termination of the operation has to be performed by the DMA controller and an error in programming the DMA controller could lead to a locked-up system.

Transfer Times

The time a transfer requires to complete is largely determined by the mechanics of the disk drive, but is also affected by other factors such as the number of sectors to be transferred and the sector position under the head when the head is loaded. The maximum time required would occur when an 8-sector transfer was to be performed starting at sector 1 and the head was loaded just after sector 1 had passed. This would require a complete revolution before sector 1 was again reached and another revolution to read the 8 sectors of data. A typical disk speed is 300 r.p.m., so that 2 revolutions would take:

$$\frac{\text{Number of revolutions required}}{\text{Revolutions per minute}} \times 60 \text{ s} = \frac{2}{300} \times 60$$

$$= 400 \text{ ms}$$

Assuming that each sector contains 512 bytes then the achieved data transfer rate is:

$$\frac{\text{Number of bytes per sector} \times \text{Number of sectors}}{\text{Transfer period}}$$

$$= \frac{512 \times 8}{0.40} = 10\ 240 \text{ bytes per second}$$

The minimum time required for any data transfer would be for a single sector transfer which had the head loaded at the exact beginning of the specified sector. This would take only one ninth of a revolution to give a transfer time of:

$$\frac{\frac{1}{9}}{300} \times 60 = 22.2 \text{ ms}$$

and the achieved data transfer rate is:

$$\frac{512 \times 1}{0.0222} = 23\ 063 \text{ bytes per second}$$

which is more than twice that of the slowest 8-sector transfer. The data transfer rate specified for the floppy disk and the floppy disk drive will be much larger than this, typically 100 000 bytes per second. However, this is the transfer rate when considering individual bytes and not complete sectors.

After the read or write operation has completed the FDC will have the result status byte sequence available. This is a 7-byte sequence of which the first 3 bytes contain status information and the next 4 contain position and data information. The first status byte, called status 0, contains the same information as the status byte in the sense interrupt status command, refer to *Figure 3.63*. The remaining two status bytes called status 1 and status 2 contain information on 13 additional parameters, as outlined in *Figures 3.66 and 3.67* (overleaf), and if the operation is correctly executed both these status bytes will be zero. If the floppy disk is write-protected then the write protect bit, bit 1 of status 1, will be set to a logic 1 to indicate this for write operations and the operation will terminate without writing the data. Read operations on write-protected floppy disks are not affected. If more details of the other errors represented by these bytes are required, consult the appropriate Intel data manual. To simplify the example program which follows, these status bytes will be assumed to be zero for correct operations and any other values will indicate an error of some sort.

The last four bytes of the result status byte sequence contain information on the track accessed, the head last used and the last sector accessed. If the track accessed is different to that in the programming command byte sequence, an error will already have been flagged in the status bytes. The head last used should be the same as

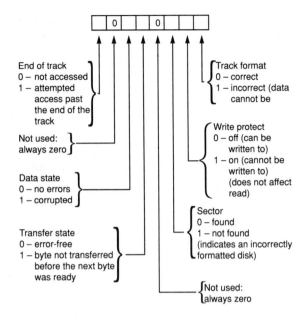

Figure 3.66 Status 1

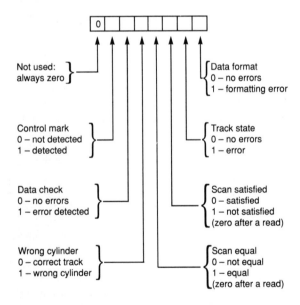

Figure 3.67 Status 2

that in the programming command byte sequence, but on double-sided disks it is possible to access sectors automatically from both sides of the disk. Normally this will not happen and the last head used will be the same as that programmed.

The last sector transferred is used to verify that a multi-sector operation has accessed the correct sectors.

Full programming information. The remaining FDC commands, how they are programmed, the execution and result stages and more detailed information on the commands discussed previously, can be obtained from the appropriate Intel data manuals.

Summary

Programming the FDC is a complex process and the programmer is encouraged to use the standard set of routines that are supplied with each computer, contained in the BIOS and DOS, to perform these actions. The **disk operating system** (DOS) is a useful set of routines for accessing the disk system of the microcomputer and is a complex piece of software which relies on having the basic FDC operations of multiple and single sector reads, writes and head positioning built into the boot program of the microcomputer. The basic FDC operations are contained in the **basic input/output system**, BIOS, which will initialise all the programmable peripherals to a known state and provide basic I/O functions, including floppy disk accesses. The DOS uses a defined standard method of accessing the hardware via the BIOS to perform the required functions.

Each manufacturer's computer requires a BIOS tailored to that computer but which still implements the standard BIOS interface to the DOS. There is then only one DOS required which can be used with all computers.

3.7 PROGRAMMABLE INTERVAL TIMER (PIT)

In microcontrollers and microcomputers there is often a requirement to produce outputs and signals at programmed periods. Two common types of time-programmable signals are a signal produced at a specified time after an external event has occured, called a **one-shot** and a periodic signal with a programmable frequency, often called a **clock signal**. Such signals can be produced by a **programmable interval timer** (PIT). A PIT usually consists of three 16-bit counters which can be made to count down from a programmed value to zero. The rate at which counting down occurs can be fixed by using the microprocessor system clock or some other external clock. A block diagram of a PIT is shown in *Figure 3.68* with two of the timers using the system clock to control decrementing and one as an alternative clock and provides an even greater flexibility when using the PIT, for producing programmable timer delays and programmable frequency signals.

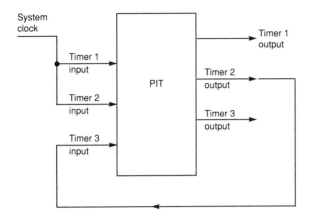

Figure 3.68 Block diagram of a PIT

The general programmer's model of the PIT consists of a command register for selecting the type of operation required from each timer and several timer count registers, usually 16 bits, into which is stored the initial count value. The general programmer's model of a PIT is shown in *Figure 3.69*.

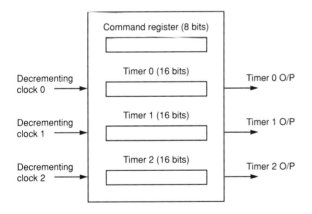

Figure 3.69 Programmer's model of a PIT

The smallest count value that can be loaded into a timer count register is 02H to allow the highest programmed frequency to be obtained, as the output is activated half way through the count. On decrementing from 02H to 01H the timer output is activated and at the next decrementing clock pulse the count is decremented to 00H and the timer output is returned to a logic 0. The timer count register is then automatically reloaded with the initial count value, in this instance 02H, and the process starts again. Loading a value of OFFFFH gives the largest count possible and produces the lowest programmed frequency. The rate at which

each counter is decremented is determined by the decrement clock, which has an input to each individual timer and will be provided by the hardware of the microcontroller.

Example of programmable one-shot. Assuming a hardware decrementing clock frequency of 1.193 18 MHz, which is the frequency used in the IBM PC, the highest possible programmable frequency output produced by the timer is:

$$\frac{\text{Decrementing clock frequency}}{\text{Count value}} = \frac{1.193\ 18}{2}$$

$$= 0.596\ 59\ \text{MHz}$$

The lowest possible programmable frequency output from the timer is obtained with the largest count value, which for a 16-bit register is 65 536. This produces a programmed frequency of 1.193 18/65 536 = 18.206 Hz.

In the one-shot mode, the programmable delay can be calculated from the following formula:-

$$\text{Programmed delay} = \frac{\text{Count value}}{\text{Decrementing clock frequency}}$$

Therefore the shortest possible delay is obtained when the count value = 01H which, for the same decrementing clock frequency used above, produces a programmed delay of $^-1/1.193\ 18 \times 10^6 = 0.838\ \mu\text{s}$.

The longest programmed delay is when the largest count value of 65 536 is used. The programmed delay is then:

$$\text{Programmed delay} = \frac{2^{16}}{1.193\ 18 \times 10^6} = 54.9\ \text{ms}$$

Example of a PIT, Intel 8253

The PIT that will be considered in detail is the Intel 8253 programmable interval timer, which has three 16-bit timers that can be used in a variety of modes. Only details on producing a programmable frequency output will be given, as the other modes are not often used. Full details of the operation and programming of this device can be obtained from the relevant Intel manuals.

Figure 3.70 (overleaf) shows the programmer's model of the Intel 8253 PIT. The base address of the timer will be taken as 040H to which is added the local address of the registers, to produce the final register address. Therefore, the command register with an offset of 03H has a final address of:

Command base + Offset = 040 + 03H = 043H

Timer 0 has an address 040 + 00H = 040H
Timer 1 has an address 040 + 01H = 041H
Timer 2 has an address 040 + 02H = 042H.

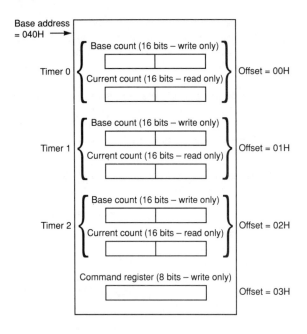

Figure 3.70   Programmer's model of the 8253 PIT

As the timer count registers are 16 bits and the data bus is only 8 bits, a special method is used to program the two bytes. This is used to program the least significant byte (LSB) and the most significant byte (MSB) separately.

Each of the timers has two registers associated with it at each offset. The initial count value, when transferred to the PIT, is stored in the **base-count register**, which is a write-only register. The value in the base count register is then available to be transferred into the **current-count register** at the beginning of a cycle. If the cycle is a programmable one-shot, the transfer from base-count to current-count registers takes place once at the beginning of the cycle. The value in the current count register is then decremented by the clock until zero is reached, when the output is activated and the cycle is completed.

If the timer is being used as a programmable frequency generator the beginning of the cycle is the same, but the rest of the cycle is different. When the halfway count value is reached the output is activated so that, when the zero count is reached, it can be de-activated to produce one complete clock cycle. The value in the base count register is then automatically reloaded into the current count register so that the entire cycle can be repeated. This produces a continuous clock signal from the timer output.

The timer base-count registers are write-only registers and it is not wise to attempt to read from them. Only under special circumstances is it possible to obtain

correct data during a read of these registers, see data book for full details. It is possible to read the current count register by sending a special instruction to the command register. It is not possible under any circumstances to obtain the original count value sent to the timer, as this is used as the base count and is available for auto-initialisation when it is loaded into the current count register at the end of every cycle.

Command Register

The command register is also write-only and if the program needs to know the state of the timer after it was programmed, the value should be saved somewhere in memory. There is no status register for the PIT and only the current count values for each timer can be read from the PIT by the microprocessor.

There are four parameters controlled by the command register, see *Figure 3.71:*

(1) Decrementing mode;
(2) Timer mode select;
(3) Operation selection;
(4) Timer select.

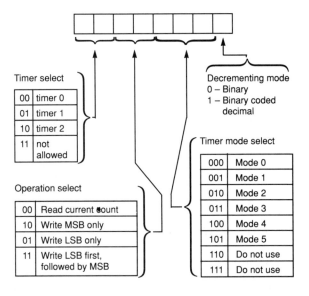

Figure 3.71   The command register

Timer select (bits 6 and 7).   The timer being programmed, 0, 1 or 2, is determined by the timer select bits, bits 6 and 7. The other parameters of the command byte then operate on the selected timer. This method enables the programming and reading of three 16-bit timers using only one 8-bit command register.

Decrementing mode (bit 0). The normal method of decrementing is to treat the value in the counter as a 16-bit binary number. This gives the maximum count of 2^{16} when count = 00000H as the counter is decremented before testing for zero. This requires bit 0 to be set to a logic 0.

However, it is possible to decrement the count value as if it were a binary coded decimal value. This is achieved by setting bit 0 to a logic 1 and gives a maximum count of 10 000. This mode is useful when using binary coded decimal numbers in the program. For example, it is possible to connect a sensor to the timer decrementing clock input which produces a single clock pulse every time an event is sensed. For example, this might detect the number of cars passing a sensor on a road. This would then count the number of cars that had passed and the value could then be read from the current count value. This mode is not often used.

Timer mode select (bits 1, 2 and 3). This particular timer has six different modes of operation and uses three bits of the command value to identify which one the selected timer is going to use. Each timer can be programmed for different modes of operation if required.

Programmable one-shot (mode 0). The first mode is the programmable one-shot used to produce an output when the current count reaches zero. The decrementing is started by an external hardware signal so that it can be synchronised to external events. This mode does not automatically restart and the count can only be de-activated by a new count value being loaded.

Re-triggerable programmable one-shot (mode 1). Mode 1 operation is similar to mode 0 operation except that it operates as a re-triggerable programmable one-shot. The timer is activated and starts decrementing after an external event, and the output is activated when the current count reaches zero. However, if a second event occurs before current count reaches zero, the base count is reloaded and decrementing starts from the original value, see *Figure 3.72*.

This type of function can be used as what is known as a **watch-dog timer** in a microcontroller to prevent the program becoming stuck in an infinite loop. This operates by programming a timer for re-triggerable programmable one-shot operation with a fixed program time of, for example, 10 ms. The output of the timer is connected to a non-maskable interrupt into the microprocessor and an I/O port bit is used to generate events, as illustrated in *Figure 3.73*. To prevent interrupts the program must generate an event at intervals less than

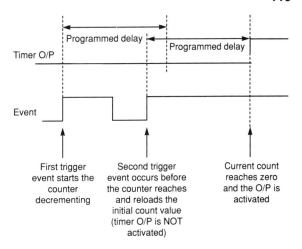

Figure 3.72 Retriggerable programmable one shot

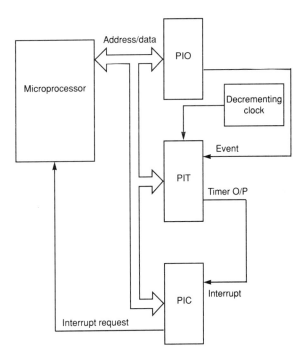

Figure 3.73 Watch-dog timer

10 ms. Then if an interrupt does occur it indicates that there is a program fault and error recovery procedures can be implemented.

Programmable pulse generator (mode 2). A programmable pulse generator can be produced by extending mode 0 operation so that it automatically reloads the base count value into the current-count register whenever the current count reaches zero. The timer output is then activated for only one decrementing clock pulse. Decrementing then restarts and continues until the timer is re-programmed.

Programmable square wave generator (mode 3).

A variation on the programmable pulse generator is the programmable square wave generator which is used to produce a square wave. The timer output is logic 0 for half the initial count value and then logic 1 for the remaining half. When the current count reaches zero, the initial value is reloaded from the base count register into the current count register to produce a fixed frequency square wave. This is the most common mode used.

Software-triggered programmable one-shot pulse (mode 4).

A software-triggered programmable one-shot can be produced by programming the PIT for mode 4 operation. This is similar to mode 1, except that decrementing starts immediately after the initial value is loaded, instead of waiting for an externally-generated event to occur. Also, the timer output is activated for only one decrementing clock pulse, rather than being left at a logic 1. This mode is re-triggerable.

Hardware-triggered programmable one-shot pulse (mode 5).

The last mode is similar to mode 4, except that an external event is used to start the counter decrementing. This mode is different to mode 0 operation, as when the current count reaches zero the timer output is activated for one decrementing clock pulse rather than being left at logic 1. This mode is also re-triggerable.

Operation selection (bits 4 and 5).

The means of writing the two 8-bit values, LSB and MSB, into the 16-bit timer count registers is provided by the operation selection bits. Two techniques can be used; either the bytes are written individually with a mode command in between each one, or a mode command is followed consecutively by the LSB and MSB bytes.

Example

The following algorithm and program illustrate how the two bytes, LSB and MSB, are transferred separately with individual mode commands. Timer 0 is being programmed to produce a square wave (mode 3 operation).

(1) Send a LSB load command to timer 0;
(2) Send the LSB to timer 0;
(3) Send a MSB load command to timer 0;
(4) Send a MSB to timer 0.

Programming an Intel 8253 PIT for timer 0 mode 3 operation, writing LSB and MSB separately:

```
                            ;Send a LSB load command
                            ;to timer 0. Step (1)
MOV DX, COMMAND   ;Write to the command register
MOV AL, 00010110B ;that a LSB load is to be
OUT DX, AL        ;made timer 0, mode 3.
                            ;Send the LSB to timer 0. Step (2)
MOV DX, TIMER_0   ;Output the LSB to
MOV AL, LSBYTE    ;timer 0.
OUT DX, AL

                            ;Send a MSB load command
                            ;to timer 0. Step (3)
MOV DX, COMMAND   ;Now write the MSB of the
MOV AL, 00100110B ;command.
OUT DX, AL

                            ;Send the MSB to timer 0. Step (4)
MOV DX, TIMER_0   ;Output the MSB to
MOV AL, MSBYTE    ;timer 0.
OUT DX, AL
```

The following algorithm illustrates consecutive byte writes to produce the same square wave:

(1) Send a consecutive byte write command to timer 0;
(2) Send the LSB to timer 0;
(3) Send the MSB to timer 0.

Writing the assembly program is left as an exercise for the reader.

Reading the Current-Count Register

The final operation that can be selected is to read the current count register of the selected timer. This operation copies the current count into an accessible read-only register with the same address as the timer current count register. When this command is issued, the decrementing mode and timer mode select bits are unused and their state is irrelevant.

The read operation of the 16-bit current count register is performed as two successive 8-bit read operations with the low byte, LSB, being transferred first, followed by the high byte, MSB.

Example

The following algorithm and program listing illustrate how to read the current-count value of timer 0. It is important to note that the value is transferred from the current-count register into the shadow current-count register while the decrementing is continuing, so that the value transferred will usually be larger than the actual current count at the timer of transfer.

(1) Send a timer 0 current-count register read command;
(2) Read the LSB of timer 0;
(3) Read the MSB of timer 0.

```
                              ;Perform a read of timer 0 current-
                              ;count register.
                              ;Send a timer 0 current-count
                              register read command. Step (1)
MOV   DX,COMMAND              ;Send the read to the current-
MOV   AL,00000000B            ;count register instruction.
OUT   DX,AL
                              ;Read the LSB of timer 0. Step (2)
MOV   DX,TIMER_0              ;Read the LSB of timer 0.
IN    AL,DX
MOV   CL,AL
                              ;Read the MSB of timer 0. Step (3)
IN    AL,DX                   ;Read the MSB of timer 0.
MOV   CH,AL                   ;Save the current-count value
                              ;in the CX register.
```

Example: Real-Time Clock

As an example of how a PIT can be used, **a real-time clock** will be maintained automatically with the time in seconds, minutes and hours, implemented for a PC. The layout of the circuit would be similar to that in *Figure 3.74* and requires a microprocessor, a PIT and a PIC. The PIC is required to handle the output from the timer which is to be used as an interrupt. This will enable the microprocessor to execute other programs which will be periodically interrupted by the timer output. The interrupt service subroutine will then correctly maintain the real-time values.

The decrementing clock frequency will be 1.19318 MHz, and timer 0 will be programmed as a programmable square wave generator (mode 3 operation). A maximum count value of 0000H will be loaded into the base count register and this will generate a square wave with a period of 54.9 ms. Each cycle of the square wave will be called a timer tick. Therefore:

1 sec requires	1000/54.9	= 18.2 timer ticks,
1 min requires	(60 × 1000)/54.9	= 1092.9 timer ticks,
1 h requires	(60 × 60 × 1000)/54.9	= 65 573.7 timer ticks.

As a second requires 18.2 timer ticks it is necessary to maintain separate independent counts for seconds, minutes and hours, which are incremented each timer tick, in order to maintain the accuracy. Then when the appropriate count value is reached, the location containing the second, minute or hour count can be incremented. While this does maintain the accuracy of the real-time clock it makes the program more complicated. The number of timer ticks each quantity requires (seconds, minutes or hours) will be rounded to the nearest integer for this example, so that:

1 sec = 18 timer ticks,
1 min = 1093 timer ticks,
1 h = 65 574 timer ticks.

In addition, just for this example, the hours timer ticks will be reduced to 65 536 so that it will fit into a 16-bit memory location and simplifies the program. The error introduced by this is very small but if this were used for a real-time clock that was designed to run for months then it would accumulate. If this were being implemented in a real PC an allowance would have to be made for this.

The interrupt used for the timer output is 08H, which has an interrupt vector address of 020H. The four bytes starting at memory address 020H then contain the address of the interrupt service subroutine.

Example

The algorithm for the interrupt service subroutine will be shown as this is the important part of the program.

(1) Save the registers, and re-enable higher priority interrupts;
(2) Increment the sub-second count;
(3) If the sub-second count is not 18 then go to step (6);
(4) Clear the sub-second count and increment the second count;
(5) If the second count is 60 then clear the second count;
(6) Increment the sub-minute count;
(7) If the sub-minute count is not 1093 then go to step (10);
(8) Clear the sub-minute count and increment the minute count;

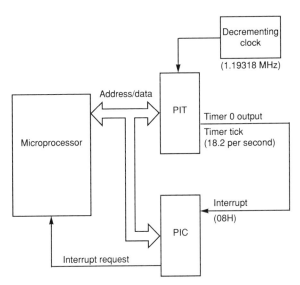

Figure 3.74   Real-time clock

(9) If the minute count is 60 then clear the second and minute counts;

(10) Increment the sub-hour count;

(11) If the sub-hour count is not 65 536 then go to step (14);

(12) Clear the sub-hour count and increment the hour count;

(13) If the hour count is 24 then clear the second, minute and hour counts;

(14) Restore the registers saved.

Summary

The programmable interval timer is a useful device which, once programmed, can be used to produce hardware-controlled one-shot or square-wave generators. Typical uses would be as a watch-dog timer or a periodic interrupt generator for a real-time clock.

It is normal for software to have only indirect control of these quantities, so that if a program malfunctions it is unlikely that items such as the real-time clock would be affected and the watch-dog timer can be used to restart and re-initialise a malfunctioning program automatically.

3.8 PERIPHERALS

The Visual Display Unit (VDU)

This is a piece of equipment which performs two functions; one is to display information from the computer in a manner understandable by the user, the other is to accept information from the user and convert it into a format compatible with the computer. The VDU and associated keyboard are each essentially output and input devices.

To enable any VDU to operate correctly with any computer, a **standard communication protocol** is used. There are two common types, serial and parallel. Serial, in the form of **RS232C**, is the most common, being simpler and operating over much longer distances. Parallel, however can be substantially quicker.

To complement the communication protocol, a set of **standard data characters** is also used, namely **ASCII**, or an equivalent. This restricts all data to being one of a limited character set. This simplifies the operation of the VDU. The computer program executing, and the user, then 'interpret' the combinations of characters in a specified manner. For example, when a word processor is executing, 'THEN' is a word, whereas if a BASIC editor is executing, 'THEN' becomes part of a program statement: IF true THEN GOTO 1000.

The VDU Screen

The normal VDU screen consists of a cathode ray tube operating in a similar way to a television. The difference is that the VDU operates at a much higher frequency, usually at least twice that of a television in order to obtain a higher resolution. This is why televisions do not make good VDUs. A beam of electrons is scanned in a symmetrical fashion across a phosphor-coated screen, see *Figure 3.75*.

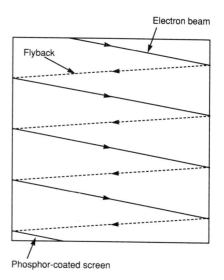

Figure 3.75 VDU screen scanning

A normal VDU will have 312 lines scanned from left to right, but variations on this are becoming more common as graphics terminals become popular. These terminals have a much higher scan rate to enable higher resolution graphics to be implemented.

The dotted line is called the flyback and returns the electron beam to the left-hand side ready for the next line. During flyback the beam is turned OFF so that the phosphor is not excited and no light is emitted. This means the flyback path cannot be seen. However, by turning the intensity control on the VDU to very high for a short period of time, it is possible to see a faint flyback signal. A line normally takes 64 μs to travel from left to right and the flyback takes approximately 6 μs. During a line the intensity of the electron beam and hence the light emitted by the phosphor, is modulated. The modulation normally takes the form of being completely ON (i.e. bright) or completely OFF (i.e. blank). Some VDUs allow intermediate variations in intensity for highlighting. The normal number of dots which is possible on any one line is usually $1\frac{1}{3} \times$ number of lines. For a 312-line VDU this means there will be 416 dots per line. Computers, such as the IBM PC/XT/AT tend to have slightly different scan rates and numbers of dots per line.

The line thickness is arranged such that there is a small overlap between adjacent lines on the phosphor, so that by turning ON two adjacent lines, a thicker line can be created. In the same way by altering which dots on each line are ON and OFF almost any curve can be displayed upon the screen.

Normal output is text using the defined set of character symbols, usually ASCII. Each character is composed of a block of dots, usually 15×11, which by illuminating various combinations, can represent all the symbols, see *Figure 3.76*. For text, only the first 9×7 dots are used, with the remaining 4 columns forming the intercharacter spacing, and the remaining 6 rows the line spacing. For graphics, the complete dot array can be used, although it is not normally separated into blocks but simply used as 418 dots per line, with 312 lines per screen.

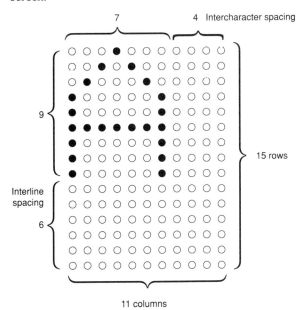

Figure 3.76 Illumination of VDU phospor dots

A VDU will normally display 23 lines of 80 characters, a total of 1840 characters per screen, and most VDUs have a 2 kbyte internal buffer so that once the characters have been sent to the VDU, the VDU will automatically maintain them on the screen. The **refresh rate** is 50 Hz to avoid screen flicker.

A row of text characters is displayed as a line of dots at a time, so that the first row of dots of each of the characters is displayed, then the second row of dots and so on, until all 15 rows have been displayed. This is then repeated for the next row of characters and so on until the end of the screen. All 1840 characters are displayed on every screen every time, so that to obtain a blank screen or blank parts of the screen, the blank characters are placed into the appropriate positions in the VDU internal buffer.

Cursor

The cursor is a flashing (2 Hz) block which indicates the position at which the next character received from the computer will be displayed. After each character is displayed, the cursor is automatically incremented one character position to the right, ready for the next character. Although the VDU screen is only 80 characters wide, the actual length of the line is considered to be 132 characters long to match wide carriage printers. Some VDUs automatically start on the next line when they get to the end, and this is called **word-wrap**. Others require special characters to move onto the next line called LINEFEED and CARRIAGE RETURN. Both these characters are required to get to the beginning of the next line of text. To move the cursor to the right without printing any characters, the space character is repeatedly sent until the cursor is correctly positioned.

X–Y addressing. If it is necessary to move the cursor to several different positions on the screen, there is normally a method of directly moving the cursor to any text position in any sequence, called X–Y addressing. First a special non-printable character is sent to the VDU which indicates that X–Y mode addressing of the screen is to be used. This character is followed by two more characters which indicate the position on the screen. The X direction is the number of characters along the line, usually 1–80 from left to right, and the second is the Y position in number of lines of text, 1–23 from top to bottom. The cursor is then moved automatically by the VDU to that position so that any printable characters now sent will appear at the new cursor position. This can be anywhere in the 80×23 grid of allowed character positions.

Keyboard

The second half of the VDU is the keyboard. This consists of an arrangement of simple switches, where each switch is assigned to mean an ASCII character if pressed. Normally, there is a maximum of 128 keys, although many keyboards have less, around 88. To reduce the number of I/O lines required to identify which key was pressed, a grid layout of switches is used, usually 8×7, see *Figure 3.77*. A scanning routine is then operated which puts a signal onto each of A_0–A_7 in turn, and then B_0–B_7 are all sampled simultaneously, until a keypress (closed switch) is detected. The values of A and B can then be combined to form the ASCII character. This is then transmitted back to the computer in serial form to confirm that the key has been pressed.

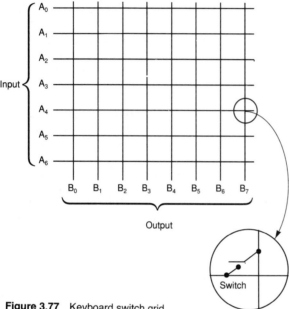

Figure 3.77   Keyboard switch grid

The keyboard has its own microcontroller and is usually independent of the operation of the VDU screen. The keyboard is scanned at a high rate so that multiple keypresses can be identified, and the order in which they were pressed, also determined. There is a standard layout of the alphanumeric keys on the keyboard, called QWERTY, as these are the first six characters of the top left-hand row of alphabetical characters. The remaining punctuation characters and other special characters can be in different places on the keyboard depending upon the manufacturers requirements. Usually the same special characters are present, although in different countries the currency sign will usually be different, for example, £ and $.

Full Duplex

There are two methods of transmitting data along the bi-directional serial links. One is called full duplex, if simultaneous transmission and reception of characters is

possible. If this method is being used, the computer connected to the VDU is expected to echo the character of the key pressed, back to the screen. This is used to indicate that the two-way serial communication link is operating correctly.

Half Duplex

The alternative method is called half duplex. In this instance, any time a key is pressed, the associated character is transmitted to the computer and an echo is not expected as simultaneous transmission is not possible and the rate at which characters could be sent would be much reduced. To enable the user to see what is happening, the character is automatically displayed onto the screen as well as being tranmitted. Therefore, in half duplex mode the appearance of characters on the screen cannot be used to verify that the serial communication link is operating correctly.

Graphics

A graphics option is often fitted into modern VDUs, and makes use of the dot display technique used to display text. When any text is displayed only the ASCII value is stored in the VDU display RAM. Then at the appropriate point on the display, a ROM is used as a decoder to convert the ASCII value into the full 15×11 dot array necessary to build up the character on the screen. For graphics, the state of each dot must be stored in RAM to determine whether each dot is ON or OFF. ROM is not used at all in graphics displays.

The number of dots is large and can be calculated from the number of possible character positions (number of lines × number of characters per line) multiplied by the number of dots per character position (15×11). This gives a maximum number of dots as 303 600 and assuming that each RAM location can hold the value of 8 dots, as it is 8 bits long, then 37 950 bytes of RAM are required. In addition, it is usual to add an additional processor to handle the graphics display, as the large number of possible dot locations slows down the display rate. Often, the number of graphic dots is reduced to 256×256 to give 65 536 dots, requiring only 8 kbytes of RAM, in order to simplify the graphic display electronics. In this instance, either the dot size is increased from that used to build text characters, or more probably, the size of the graphic display is limited to a fraction of the possible VDU screen display area.

Some very high resolution graphic displays use a much higher number of dots, typically 1024×1024. These give a much better resolution so that more detail can be shown. However, the amount of RAM required is much increased and special processors are used to maintain a reasonable display rate. This results in a considerable increase in cost and displays of this resolution are only used when absolutely necessary.

Printer Port

In addition, there is often a second communication port, again serial, which can be made to transmit everything that was displayed upon the screen. This could be from the computer connected to the VDU or from the keyboard of the VDU. This second serial port is designated the 'printer port' and is designed to be used to obtain hardcopy of the screen display. This can be altered from the VDU keyboard, or by sending special characters from the computer to the VDU, to print selected portions of the display, or everything. With the correct printer, the graphics mode of the VDU can also be made to print.

Impact Printer

With printers the aim is to transfer characters onto a permanent and readable material. The normal technique is to deposit an ink substance onto paper. Impact printers perform this action mechanically by forcing together under pressure, an ink-bearing material, and paper, as in *Figure 3.78*. Ink is then permanently transfered to the paper. By raising protrusions on the printhead, the ink transfer can be shaped to the desired character. Most printers of this type have a fixed character set, where each character is fixed on the printhead, and cannot be altered. Each character must then be moved to the correct position in the correct sequence, for printing.

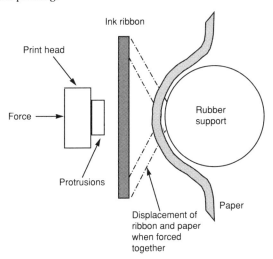

Figure 3.78 Impact printer mechanism

Daisywheel Printer

Each character is held on the end of a flexible spoke, see *Figure 3.79*, and when a particular character is required, it is rotated to the print position, and a solenoid-powered hammer presses the ink ribbon and paper together. The speed of printing is limited by the necessity to rotate to each new character, but the quality is very good. To move to the next print position, the entire carriage containing the paper is moved one character space to the left. Printing from right to left is often not available.

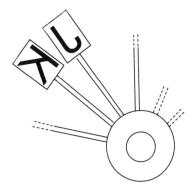

Figure 3.79 Daisywheel print head

Golfball Printer

This is an alternative to daisywheel which is now beginning to lose market share and is mainly restricted to typewriters, rather than computer-driven printers. All the characters are mounted in rows on a small globe, see *Figure 3.80*. The globe is then positioned in two axes, the height and the rotation, in order to present the correct character to the printing position. Quality of print is high and can be almost as fast as the daisywheel. The mechanical complexity required is greater which results in a higher capital cost than that for the daisywheel.

Figure 3.80 Golfball print head

Dot Matrix Printer

To avoid having to move each character outline to the printing position, and to move the paper after each character has been printer, the dot matrix printer was designed. The printhead consists of one or more columns of pins powered by solenoids, which can be individually selected. The pattern or matrix of pins is used to deposit pin-points of ink to build up the character a column at a time, see *Figure 3.81*. The arrangement of ink dots is similar to the characters formed on a VDU screen.

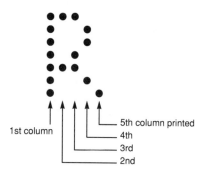

Figure 3.81 Dot matrix ink pattern

Printing speed is much faster as the printhead can be moved to the next printspace, left or right, rather than move the paper itself. The paper then only needs to be moved up or down to get to the next line. The mechanical alignment associated with moving the character and paper to the print position has been eliminated. Mechanically the printer is also much simpler and is therefore more reliable and cheaper. The only important part is the printhead itself, and these can be made in large quantities to reduce costs. Additionally, any character set can be printed, including special characters, and importantly, graphics. This is possible because the printspaces are adjacent, as on the VDU, and by careful control of the printhead, graphics printing can be achieved. This allows mixed text and graphics to be printed in one pass, and allows the images displayed on VDUs and graphics displays to be printed out or 'dumped' to a printer.

The disadvantage of dot matrix printers is that the print quality is poorer than any of the other types of printer. Often it will not photocopy satisfactorily and is not suitable for the production of final reports and letters. This problem can be compensated for by printing each character twice, the second time slightly displaced so that the dots are in a slightly different position to the first print. This fills out the characters and makes them a better quality. As each printhead usually has 8

pins in a column this effectively enables a 16-pin printhead to be simulated. The drawback is that two passes over the paper are required so that this mode, which is refered to as **near letter quality** (NLQ), takes much longer. Therefore dot matrix printers have a **draft mode**, when only one pass over the paper is made, to allow a quick print at reduced quality, and a NLQ mode, when two passes are made, for an improved quality.

To improve quality even more, and to allow the printing of Japanese characters, 24-pin printheads have been introduced. These have three columns of 8 pins, arranged so that the dots produced overlap to produce solid characters. The quality produced is good but is still not quite as good as daisywheel or golfball printers. Obviously three times as much information is required for each character, so that the ROM size holding the character dot patterns has been increased, and the complexity of the electronics and software also has been increased.

The increased resolution of 24-pin dot matrix printers has introduced the possibility of different fonts. A **font** is a particular style used to represent each character and is derived from the printing trade. This allows different styles and also different sizes of characters to be produced allowing more visually satisfying printouts to be produced. A dot matrix printer may now have several different fonts which can be printed at several different sizes controlled by the built-in microcomputer. In addition, there may be the opportunity to 'download' or transfer a new font from the computer into the printer if a special font or size is required which is not built-in to the printer. This enhances the usefulness of the printer and also maintains the useful life of the printer.

The result of all these possible variations is that print speed, quality, and special features vary between printers so that dot matrix printers are produced for almost any specification, and range in price from the cheapest printer available, to some of the most expensive.

Non-Impact Printer

Non-impact printers are becoming increasingly popular, as they can produce high quality output at higher speeds than the impact printers, albeit at a generally higher cost.

Disadvantages include:

(a) Cannot be used with multi-part stationary;
(b) More expensive;
(c) May require special paper or other consumerables such as ink powder.

Electrographic (Laser Printer)

The electrographic printer, more commonly known as a laser printer, uses a moving mirror, or rotating polygon, to direct a beam of laser light. This is then focused onto a moving belt or rotating drum which has a photoconductive surface. The beam is then modulated to produce a latent image on the surface. This is then passed over a toner, normally a powder ink, pressed onto the paper, and heat-fused to bond the ink and paper, see *Figure 3.82*. This is a very similar process to that used in photocopiers, and often the same mechanism can be used in both. A very high quality can be produced as the dot size can be made very small, and text and graphics can still be mixed. There is usually a much wider range of built-in font sizes and styles available with a large number of alternatives easily downloadable. Speed varies from approximately four pages per minute to several hundred pages a minute for the more expensive models.

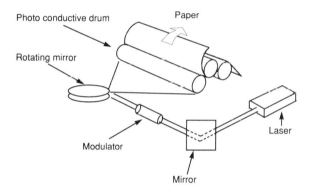

Figure 3.82 Laser printer mechanism

The main disadvantages are that continuous or multi-part stationary cannot be used and the printers are approximately two or three times more expensive than the equivalent dot matrix printer. Toner cartridges, costing about £70 will only produce between 2000 and 4000 pages before a refill is required.

The entire image to be transferred to the paper must be bit mapped because of the way that the laser printer operates. So that instead of obtaining the character dot layout from ROM whenever the character is to be printed, the dot layout is transferred to RAM, and an image of the entire page built up in the internal RAM. The page is then printed as a complete entity, after which the next page can be built up in memory. Due to this most laser printers have at least 0.5 Mbytes of built-in RAM as a minimum, which must almost invariably be increased to 2 Mbytes to obtain a reasonable print speed.

Thermal Printer

Thermal printers are similar to dot matrix printers except that the dot array is not mechanically activated. Instead each pin is an electrical heater and is used in conjunction with a thermally sensitive paper. The paper, or the paper surface, contains a chemical which alters when heat is applied. The two states of the chemical, before heat and after heat is applied, have different colours or reflective indexes, so that the characters can be recognised, and thereby forms a permanent print.

Speeds vary from 30 to 120 characters per second. The paper used is of a special type which is sensitive to heat, and is therefore more expensive. Also, the print fades with time as the thermal sensitivity is a chemical process which degrades with exposure to light. The print quality is low as only an 8-pin printhead is used. However, the main advantage thermal printers have is their relative cheapness because there are very few moving parts, as the printhead pins only produce spots of heat and do not move.

Thermal transfer. Similar to thermal except that special ribbons are used with normal paper. The ribbons have a wax coating which is melted by the spot heat produced by the printhead. The ink underneath is rolled onto the paper to form a permanent print. This method is often used when colour printing is required. Much the same characteristics as thermal except that ordinary paper can be used and the print does not degrade with exposure to light.

Electrosensitive Printer

This uses a special paper which has a metallic coating over a black background. As the printhead moves across the paper a voltage applied to the pins which are non-moving, burns away the metal on the paper to reveal the black underneath. Speeds vary from 160 to 6000 characters per second with much the same characteristics as the two thermal techniques, except that it can be quicker.

The advantages of this type of printer are that it is cheap and quick but the disadvantage is that the print quality and colouring are unattractive.

Ink Jet Printer

In ink jet printers small dots of ink are sprayed onto the paper to build up the characters. With a **continuous ink jet printer**, ink droplets are sprayed continuously out of the nozzles, whether a dot is required on the paper or not. Single nozzle printers produce a stream of electrostatically charged droplets that are directed at the paper through deflection plates that position the drop vertically on the paper. As the printhead moves either left or right, the characters are built up a column at a time. When ink is not required, the droplet is directed into a gutter for disposal. Multi-nozzle printers have a nozzle for each dot position.

As a liquid ink is used there is the possibility of the nozzles being blocked with dried ink. The continuous production of droplets helps to prevent this. The printers require ink to be added and the surplus to be disposed off, and this can be a very messy process. The print quality can be very good, as good as laser printers and high speeds can be attained. However, there is a tendency for the ink to soak into the paper to produce blurred images rather than the sharp edges required for good quality. Also, multi-part stationary cannot be used. However colour ink jet printers are likely to be very effective.

Drop on demand.   This type of ink-jet printer is similar to continuous except that no ink is sprayed when not printing, and hence requires no gutters, see *Figure 3.83*. The main problem is that during the periods of non-use, the ink can dry and block the nozzles. This often requires a higher pressure be used to expell the droplet of ink, in

order to break any dry ink blockages. Speeds vary between 90 to 400 characters per second for both types of ink jet printer.

Paper Feed Mechanisms

The majority of printers require continuous paper to be used, which is perforated on some standard page length, for example A4. Only the letter quality printers tend to use multi-sheet feeders. These are a separate mechanism fitted to the top of the printer to allow separate sheets of paper to be inserted into the printer without manual intervention. However, because of the improved quality, modern dot matrix printers are being used more often for office work and because of this, single sheet feeders for dot matrix printers are fairly common. These require every sheet of paper to be manually inserted but the printer will then correctly position it for printing. Multi-sheet feeders will soon become available for these printers.

Communication Protocols

Usually the communication link between the computer and the printer is RS232C for serial communication which occurs most often when printers are connected to the rear of VDUs. Most other printer configurations have standardised upon the *Centronics protocol*, which is a parallel protocol allowing the print data to be transferred at a much higher rate. This is important due to the rise in popularity of personal computers, as the computer cannot be performing other useful tasks whenever data is being transferred to the printer. Therefore, the shorter the period of time it takes to transfer the data to the printer the better, especially as most modern printers have large printer buffers. These enable most small documents and letters to be transferred in one burst, rather than having to break up the print data into several blocks, which are then transferred one at a time.

Print Buffers

As already mentioned, print buffers are often included to allow text to be transferred to the printer at a fast rate. This is usually much faster than it can be printed. Therefore, the buffer acts to convert the high speed transfer to the low print speed. This frees the computer for other tasks and increases the usage of the printer. Buffers vary in size from one character on older printers, to an average of 8 kbytes on most dot matrix printers and up to 2 Mbytes on the laser printers.

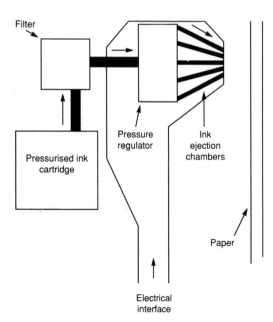

Figure 3.83   Ink jet printer

FOUR

Top-down
microcomputer design

4.1 MICROCOMPUTER SYSTEMS

In Chapter 1 the basic operation of a microcomputer and a microcontroller was considered. This chapter will consider the basic design technique of such systems in general terms and deduce the basic functional blocks required. A functional block design will be deduced for both a microcomputer and a microcontroller and the initialisation and system software will be outlined. These designs will make use of some of the peripherals detailed in chapter 3 and the programs will be written in 8086 assembly language. It should be easy to substitute alternative peripherals and microprocessor assembly languages if desired.

The Design Process

There are several different design techniques that can be used to create the microcontrollers and microcomputers required to implement a task specification. These techniques are designed to produce products which do what is required of them and also to do it with a minimum of error situations, as efficiently and cheaply as possible. Sometimes design is regarded as an art rather than an engineering discipline due to the difficulty of applying fixed laws to the process. However, it is usual to apply a set of guidelines to the design process which introduce those aspects considered to be good and attempt to exclude those that are considered to be bad. This process can never be 100 per cent successful as the majority of the design process is the selection of the optimum solution at every stage. The alternatives that might be used at each stage of a specific design are considered to ascertain the advantages and disadvantages of each. The alternative with the best combination of advantages and disadvantages is deemed to be the optimum. This usually means that the selected alterna-

tive has some disadvantages and some advantages; other solutions might have more advantages but they will also have more disadvantages and are therefore not as good.

The functional block-structured top-down design technique. A common technique for designing products is the functional block-structured top-down method. The functional block-structured approach separates common actions and functions into self-contained blocks with defined interfaces to the other blocks. Each block is then subjected to a **top-down design** which considers the actions required of each block. These actions are then broken down into smaller sub-actions which are effectively simpler blocks with simpler interfaces. These simpler blocks are then broken down into even simpler blocks. This process is repeated until the blocks being produced contain only single actions which can be implemented directly. As the blocks are completely defined and the interfaces between all the blocks are completely defined, by implementing the lowest level of blocks the product is also implemented completely.

In order to start reducing the block design, it has to be specified and the first part of any design technique is the creation of the **specification**. This is obtained by considering what actions are required of the product and then detailing all of them and their side-effects completely. The specification is then implemented. If there are any errors in the specification they will be implemented in the product, so it is very important to ensure that the specification is error-free. One method of producing the specification, is to consider what actions and functions the product should perform. Some will be directly defined by the nature of the product, others will have to be deduced. For example, a window may be considered to let the light in and keep the external temperature out. This does not explicitly indicate whether the window should be completely transparent or just translucent.

What does the product do? There are several basic functions that any programmable device such as a microcontroller or a microcomputer is required to perform:

(a) Executing user programs;
(b) Manipulating and saving data;
(c) Displaying results;
(d) Responding to user intervention.

These functions are common to both microcomputers and microcontrollers and no distinction between these two devices will be made.

Block-Structured Design

Where possible, operations and functions that are similar should be gathered together and a fixed boundary drawn around them. The functions can be separated into three blocks as illustrated in *Figure 4.1*, which are:

(a) User interface;
(b) Processing unit and execution memory;
(c) Program and data storage.

This matches the original design outlined in Chapter 1, *Figure 1.1*. There three operational units are gathered together to operate as a coherent whole by the operating system software.

In terms of a top-down design, the diagram in *Figure 4.2* would be more appropriate as each function has clearly defined boundaries and identifiable interfaces.

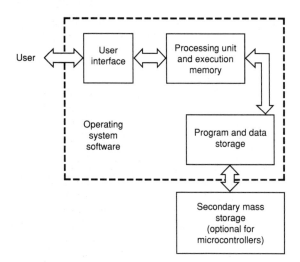

Figure 4.1 Operational blocks

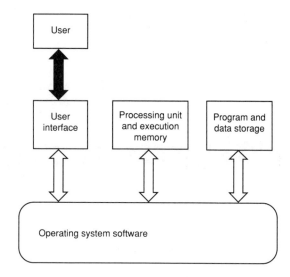

Figure 4.2 Top-down design

This diagram illustrates some important features of a block structured top-down design.

The functions inside the boundary are only allowed to communicate with functions outside the boundary through defined interfaces. An interface can be considered to be the connection between dissimilar systems and in this context it will be a combination of hardware and software. The use of interfaces enables the functions inside the boundary to be invisible to those outside so that the block functions can be specified in terms of the interfaces. A block may then be replaced at any time with an alternative block, provided the interface is maintained.

The interfaces contain error detection procedures to ensure that errors are not transmitted throughout the entire system and detected errors are handled in a specified and controlled manner. Testing can be reduced to testing at the interfaces to ensure that if correct data enters then correct solutions are produced and that incorrect data is detected and prevented from propagating throughout the entire system. If a system is found to be producing incorrect results it is only necessary to trace the erroneous data at the interfaces until the block which has an error-free input but a faulty output is detected. The error has then been isolated within that particular block.

It is important in block-structured designs to use only the defined interfaces so that the testing technique outlined can be applied. This means that global variables in programs and *ad hoc* communication links between functions, are not allowed. This may appear to produce an unnecessarily complex method of transferring data between functions but it is more reliable and makes testing much easier.

Assuming that the functions inside the boundary do not generate errors, then errors must enter via the interfaces. Therefore, to minimise the possibility of erroneous input, the number of interfaces per block in *Figure 4.2* should be minimised. In order to maintain block-to-block communication, the operating system block has to have several interfaces, one to each other block and this indicates that the operating system introduces errors into the system. Experience of personal computers seem to confirm this prediction.

The use of the operating system as the medium for inter-block communication has advantages, in that a common communication channel can be established and all block interfaces can be designed to match that standard. This allows blocks to be added or subtracted without having to re-design the system or the operating system. Due to the standardisation of the interfaces the operating system is able to perform more error detection operations on the data and messages being communicated than would be economical for individually designed interfaces, as illustrated in *Figure 4.3*.

Figure 4.2 illustrates how the user is buffered from the hardware and the operations of the microcomputer/microcontroller by the user interface which enables the user interface to remain constant even if the hardware or the operating system change.

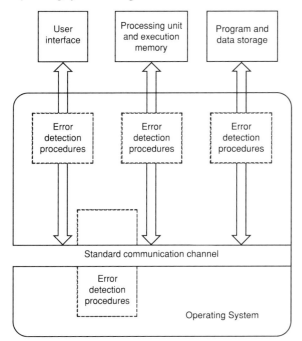

Figure 4.3 More detailed block system

Top-Down Design

In terms of the top-down design concept described earlier, the functions of the system in *Figure 4.2* can be represented as shown in *Figure 4.4* (overleaf), which identifies each operational block and the interfaces each requires. In this example, each of the blocks has a single interface to the operating system, except for the operating system which has three interfaces corresponding to the three blocks. Each block is complete in itself with the defined interfaces indicating the how, when and why of data and information communication with the other blocks. The interfaces are the only means of transferring data and information and can be hardware, software, or a combination of the two.

The lines joining each block to the top block indicate the parent block and show that the main block of a microcomputer or microcontroller has been separated into four discrete and simpler blocks, with defined interconnecting interfaces. Each of the simpler blocks then becomes the parent of a series of further simplified functional blocks, as illustrated in *Figure 4.5*. One of the simplified blocks handles the interface defined at the previous level, and the remaining blocks perform subfunctions which have simpler interfaces. All blocks must have at least one interface to enable them to be connected to the complete device.

Figure 4.5 shows that the user interface has been divided into four sub-functions which make up the operations of the **user interface**. The main sub-function is the link to the operating system, which is an interface defined at the previous level and three interfaces to specific I/O devices. In this way, the blocks can communicate in a structured way with the higher levels.

The user interface performs two basic operations, input of data and commands from the user which form one sub-function, and output of data and results as a second sub-function. As there are many forms of output, such as visual display units (VDUs) and printers, each of which needs to be handled in a different way, a block is required for each one. If there are several input devices, each one will require a separate sub-functional block.

Examples of input devices are keyboards, mice, digitising pads, and speech recognition devices; output devices are text displays, graphics displays, serial communication links and parallel printer ports. Each requires a separate block to control them correctly, but there is still the standard interface to the operating system. In the **MS-DOS operating system** this is accomplished by the DEVICE command which allows users to create their own sub-functional input or output blocks. MS-DOS has several built-in interfaces for keyboard, text, graphics, serial, printer port and floppy and

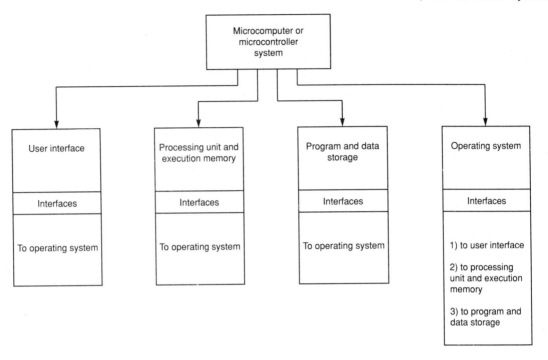

Figure 4.4   Top-down hardware design

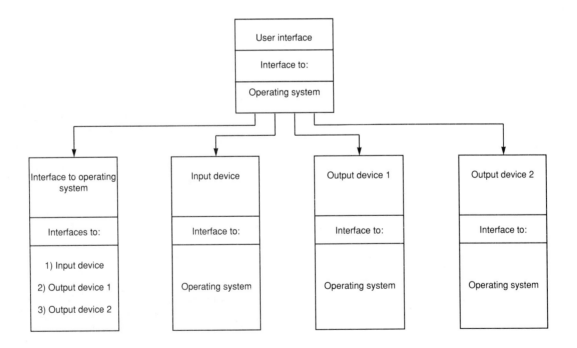

Figure 4.5   Next level of user interface

hard disk I/O functions, but these can be readily expanded with new ones by the DEVICE command.

To determine exactly what actions each block has to perform, a detailed specification has to be available so that the number and variety of output devices can be chosen. In this case study the specification stage was omitted to simplify the consideration of the general principles of top-down design. This prevents specific detail being added at this stage, but later sections detail the specification of a microcontroller and a microcomputer, with corresponding top-down designs leading to functional block circuit diagrams and assembly language programs.

If a sub-block has to communicate with the higher level, this is performed via the interface link defined at the same level. This achieves the error checking and correct formatting of data required, but unfortunately it also slows down the communication process as each additional interface takes a finite time to execute. This is one factor which has to be optimised for a particular design. The use of well-structured communication interfaces produces error free, robust and reliable links, but with the drawback that each level introduces additional delays. As a general rule the more levels the top-down design introduces the slower the communication process is. However, this is ameliorated by the interfaces lower down in the levels being implemented in hardware which is much faster. This is illustrated in *Figure 4.6* which also indicates that the higher levels are implemented mainly in software which is correspondingly slower. However, the data at the higher levels is more significant and there is less of it and this tends to reduce the impact of slow high level communication interfaces.

The reason the low level functions are implemented in hardware is that the interfaces become simpler and more easily implemented in hardware. As more levels are created in the design process, the additional delay in communication links increases significantly, as seen in *Figure 4.7*. This only applies to products containing both hardware and software, such as microcontrollers and microcomputers.

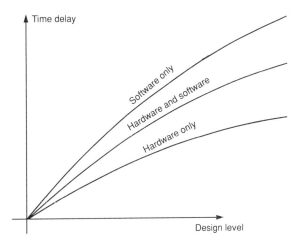

Figure 4.7 Interface time delay against design level

To determine the optimum combination of hardware/software interfaces the response time of the system is considered. This is known as the real-time response and a system can be said to have a **real-time response** when there is no user-perceivable delay from the initiation of an action to the response of the system with the desired data and/or results. This makes the assessment of real-time response subject to the user and different users may well view the same system in different ways. A user is not necessarily a person but can be other computers and hardware systems.

A communication link between a person and a computer is illustrated in *Figures 4.8* (overleaf). The computer always responds to the person pressing keys on the keyboard within a few hundred milliseconds. This is not perceivable by the user as a delayed response so the computer is operating with a real-time response. However, the time between the person pressing keys, even at a speed of ten keys per second, is relatively long as perceived by the computer. Therefore, the computer does not perceive the person as operating in real-time. However, the computer does not have any influence on the design of the system.

Even if a user does perceive a delay in the response it may be considered acceptable. There are various reasons for this; for example, it may not be possible to

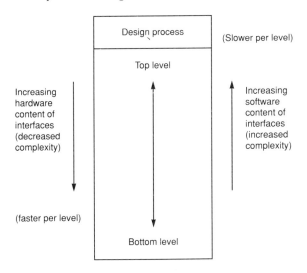

Figure 4.6 Hardware/software optimisation

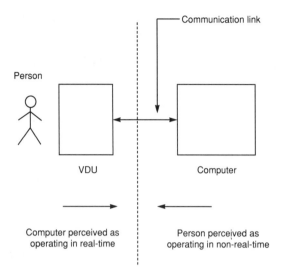

Figure 4.8 Real-time operation

obtain a faster response, or it may only occur infrequently. A floppy disk provides an illustration of infrequent slow use. Usually the disk is accessed relatively infrequently and the delay is accepted. If the disk is accessed frequently an alternative such as a hard disk or solid state disk is used.

The more levels used in the top-down design technique, the longer the interfaces take to communicate and the use of a real-time response enables a limit to be placed onto the interface execution time versus design level graph, as illustrated in *Figure 4.9*. The design level

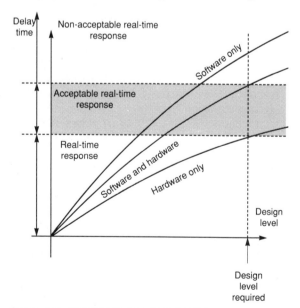

Figure 4.9 Limiting interface execution time

required is mainly determined by the complexity of the product as any product has to be reduced to similar simple blocks. The more complex a product the more levels are required, assuming compatible complexity of each level. Some variation in the number of levels is possible by increasing the number of blocks per level to achieve the individual block simplicity. This reduces the number of levels needed but it also reduces the advantage of using top-down design and an alternative design process may be required.

Once the design level and the interface execution times have been determined, a range of solutions from mostly hardware to mostly software can then be implemented.

If the response time cannot be achieved, it may be necessary to implement a special interface linking a low level functional block with a block much higher up in the design, as illustrated in *Figures 4.10*. This is acceptable, but not a preferred solution and can lead to difficulties later.

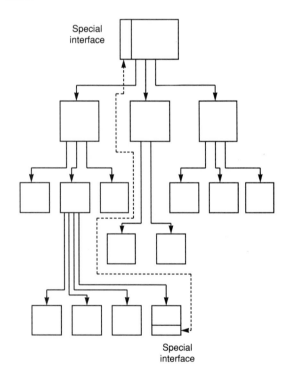

Figure 4.10 Special interfaces

A common illustration of this technique is found in computer games designed for early versions of the IBM PC. Because the early IBM PCs were not capable of fast response graphics output, particularly when the specified interface via the operating system was used, games designers implemented special links between the games software and the display hardware, by directly controlling the display. This avoids the specified interface and all its associated delays and achieves an acceptable graphics response. However, this is against the basic principle of top-down block-structured design and the games only execute correctly on the specific PCs they are designed for whereas later versions of the PCs with improved graphics hardware, are not always compatible with the early versions, and do not execute the games. This also illustrates how the concept of block-structured designs can be extremely beneficial as both the original software and hardware of the original IBM PC have changed significantly, but the interface has been maintained consistently. This means that any programs designed to execute on the early versions of the PC and its operating system software will still execute correctly on all the later versions. The main advantage of this is that it extends the life of the software, making it more worthwhile for customers to purchase it and also means that the product performance can be improved by implementing it on newer versions of the PC which execute programs faster. This advantage is so significant that all new software for the PC always uses the standard interfaces specified, even for games. The slowness of the interfaces has been overcome by the improved hardware which executes the software at a faster rate.

The nearer the top of the top-down design the more complex the interface links become and the more likely they are to be implemented using software. Software has the ability to implement complex functions relatively easily and can implement any changes by updating the software. This is a requirement as the more complex a link the more likely it will be that changes, upgrades and error removal will be necessary. If implemented in hardware, complex interface links are difficult to change. Low level links are suitable for implementing in hardware as they are simpler and stable, requiring few upgrades and can be used in a wide variety of applications.

Case Study

A design will now be considered for a microcontroller using the top-down process outlined previously. In order to be a useful demonstration of this technique rather than a detailed manual for a specific design, some parts of the design will be simplified and will use non-ideal solutions. This should enable the flow and function of the design processes to be seen and understood whilst still providing as much realistic detail as possible. Full working circuit diagrams will not be produced, although major components and their functions will be

identified and their inter-connection shown. The majority of the assembly language programs required to initialise these components and to implement several system functions will be given, but these will not necessarily be complete in every detail. Chapter 5 gives precise detail on the layout and design of programs for realistic assembly, linking and execution, and these can be used to update the listings given, so that they can be used in practical projects if desired.

4.2 MICROCONTROLLER DESIGN: BEDSIDE ALARM CLOCK

A simple alarm clock will be used to illustrate the design of a microcontroller and as the functional specification is relatively simple a nearly complete version can be written out in a few paragraphs. The practical implementation of the final design in terms of the power supply, printed circuit board and so on will not be considered.

Functional Specification

Display time function. A digital display will be used consisting of two groups of two digits separated by a colon, as illustrated in *Figure 4.11*. The left hand pair of digits will display the time in hours, using a 12-hour format and the right hand pair of digits will display the minutes. The colon will be capable of flashing a rate of 1 Hz which is once per second and will be visible for 0.5 seconds out of every second.

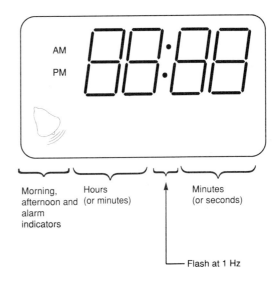

Figure 4.11   Clock display layout

As a 12-hour format is being used, a further indicator will be used to show whether it is morning using the AM symbol, or afternoon using the PM symbol. One of these symbols will always be displayed.

The seconds are displayed by pressing a button marked 'seconds', see *Figure 4.12*, which will display the current seconds time using the right hand pair of digits. The colon will still flash at a rate of 1 Hz, and the second count will be incremented at the beginning of the flash. The AM and PM indicators will not be visible during the seconds display.

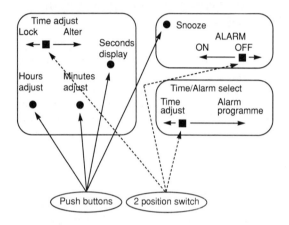

Figure 4.12   Switch layout for alarm clock

Alarm function.   The alarm function will enable a single time to be programmed into a memory location maintained by the clock, in terms of AM or PM, hours and minutes. The alarm time is deemed to have occurred immediately the AM/PM, hours and minutes values are correct and always assumes the seconds value to be zero.

When the programmed alarm time is the same as the displayed time, and the alarm function has been enabled by the alarm switch being in the ON position, (see *Figure 4.12*) the alarm output is started. This consists of flashing the alarm symbol, (*Figure 4.11*) at 1 Hz, in conjunction with the colon symbol, for 0.5 s visible and 0.5 s invisible. In addition, an audible tone will sound consisting of 8 bursts of a 1000 Hz tone, repeated at intervals of 2 seconds. Each tone burst lasts 0.1 s and is separated by 0.1 s of no tone from the next burst. This will separate each block of 8 bursts by 0.5 s of no tone, as illustrated in *Figure 4.13*. The tone will continue to sound and the alarm symbol to flash until either the snooze button is pressed or the alarm switch is set to the OFF position.

If the alarm switch is set to OFF after the alarm has sounded, the alarm function will be reset. The alarm will not start again until the alarm switch is set to ON and the

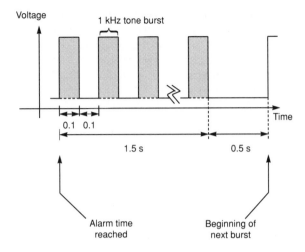

Figure 4.13   Audible alarm tone

programmed time is reached again. The alarm symbol will also cease to flash in the same manner. If the snooze button is pressed after the alarm has sounded, the audible tone will stop sounding for five minutes from when the button is released. The alarm symbol will continue to flash until the alarm switch is set to OFF. After 5 minutes the audible tone will restart until either the snooze button is pressed again or the alarm switch is set to OFF.

If the alarm switch is not set to OFF within 1 hour of the alarm initially sounding the alarm function automatically resets, the audible tone stops and the alarm symbol stops flashing. The alarm will start again when the programmed alarm time is reached in twenty-three hours if not re-programmed.

Set time/program alarm time functions.   The two different times that can be programmed into the clock, the current time value and the alarm time, are programmed in a similar manner. The time/alarm select switch is used to select whether the current time or the alarm time is being programmed.

Current time.   The time adjust switch is set to ALTER and the time/alarm switch to TIME to program the current time, with the present value of the current time displayed on the hours and minutes digits. Whenever the hour button in the time adjust panel is pressed, the current time displayed hours digits are incremented by one. Successive presses cause the hours to be incremented by one each time the hour button is pressed. When the hour is incremented past 11, the AM/PM indicator changes state. If AM was on it goes off and PM comes on and if the PM indicator is on it goes off and AM comes on. When the hours count is incremented past 12 it resets to a 1.

The same procedure is used to program the minutes value except that pressing the minutes button increments the minutes displayed. If the minutes display is incremented past 59 the display resets to 0. The hours display is not affected when this occurs to enable separate programming of the hours and minutes.

The lock/alter switch is then placed back to the lock position so that the current displayed time can no longer be altered. When this switch is set to the LOCK position the seconds count (which is not currently displayed) is reset to zero and begins to increment.

Current time display. When the seconds count reaches 59 the seconds count resets to zero and the minutes display is incremented. This continues until the minutes display reaches 60 when it resets to zero and the hours display is incremented. When the hours display is incremented from 11 to 12, the AM/PM indicator is reversed, as explained earlier. When the hours count is incremented to 13, it is reset to 1.

Programming the alarm time. To program the alarm time the time adjust switch is set to ALTER and the time/alarm switch to ALARM. The current programmed value of the time is then displayed consisting of the AM/PM indicator, the hours and the minutes. The separating colon is on but does not flash. Pressing the hours button increments the hours value and AM/PM indicators and pressing the minutes button increments the minutes display as described previously. The lock/alter switch is then set to the LOCK position to fix the alarm time and the time/alarm switch is set to the TIME position so that the current time will be re-displayed. The value of the current time is updated correctly throughout the alarm time programming sequence.

Power-up. When the power is first applied, the current time is set to 1.00 AM and the alarm time to 12.00 AM. It would normally be expected that the clock would be re-programmed at this time.

Implementation

As can be seen, the functional specification of this apparently simple product is long and complicated in order to achieve a correctly functioning alarm clock. All eventualities have been foreseen and a recommended course of action specified so that there are no unpredictable situations.

The physical specifications of the ergonomics, cost, and so on have not been specified in order to simplify

the overall specification. If the specification is not 100 per cent complete there is the possibility of the alarm clock, or any other product designed in this way, entering error states which produce unpredictable actions. These states can often be found on products by operating the input devices in unpredictable and illogical combinations. On the alarm clock for example, what happens if both the hours and minutes buttons are pressed simultaneously when programming the time? The specification does not indicate the required action so the result is unpredictable and depends on the implementation produced by the development engineer who creates the product from the specification.

Although a top-down block-structured design can often identify these faults in the specification and prevent the error situations occurring, it is not possible to eliminate them all. Therefore, the implementation should always be considering how to recover from error situations which should theoretically never occur. An example is the simple incrementing of the seconds count and resetting it to zero when 60 is reached. A naive approach would simply test for the seconds being equal to 60:

```
IF SECONDS = 60 THEN RESET(SECONDS)
ELSE
SECONDS := SECONDS + 1
```

If for some reason the seconds count is able to reach a value greater than 60, which is an error condition, this simple test for the end of the incrementing loop would never be successful. Therefore, a more robust implementation is:

```
IF SECONDS > 59 THEN RESET(SECONDS)
ELSE
SECONDS := SECONDS + 1
```

Block Design

From the specification, the functional blocks of the product which will meet it are deduced. This is where the experience and knowledge of the designer is important, so that the important functional blocks of the solution are identified. The solution presented here is not the only possible solution.

The four basic blocks of any solution, as outlined in *Figure 4.1*, can be applied although considerably simplified. There is no requirement for secondary storage as there are no data or programs to be saved and, as there is only one program to be executed, the program can be permanently stored in execution memory. The user interface is simple with the output consisting of the display digits and symbols shown in *Figure 4.11*, and the input of the switches shown in *Figure 4.12*. This results in

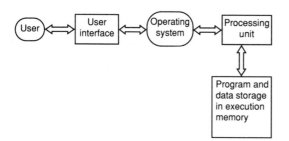

Figure 4.14   Alarm clock block diagram

a minimal operating system which produces the simplified block diagram shown in *Figure 4.14* and this will be used in the following design process.

The initial level of the top-down design is shown in *Figure 4.15* and this is slightly different to the general design illustrated in *Figure 4.4*, as there is a direct interface between the processing unit and the program and data storage. This avoids the use of the operating system to transfer the program as there is no need to change the program or its position in memory.

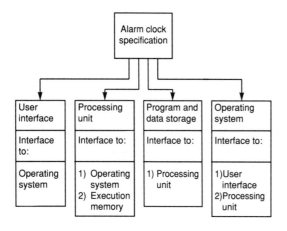

Figure 4.15   Top-down design of the alarm clock

The User Interface

The basic user interface design diagram initially shown in *Figure 4.5* is used as the basis for this design problem, see *Figure 4.16*.

The input and output blocks of this diagram are expanded first, in order to determine what information has to be transferred to and from the operating system. These blocks have been expanded in *Figures 4.17 and 4.18* (page 140) and show that one input device is required and two output devices. It is important to remember that only the lowest levels of the top-down design

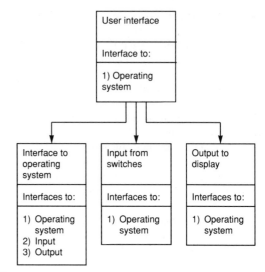

Figure 4.16   Alarm clock user interface

will be implemented. The higher levels are automatically implemented when the lower levels are implemented.

One criterion of top-down design is that each functional block is isolated from all other blocks, except for the specified interfaces. This enables the user interface to be implemented completely and tested before the rest of the design has been completed, by substituting dummy blocks which simulate the replaced block. It would be possible to expand each of the blocks further into separate diagrams adding more detail in each. However, for this case study a solution will be implemented from these diagrams.

The Interface to the Operating System

The interface to the operating system block receives information from the operating system to be passed to the output and returns values from the input. This means that this interface is influenced by the other two blocks at this level, input and output. Software-initiated interrupts will be used to perform the interface functions so that any changes to the hardware will not affect the main program. The interface between the operating system and the user is described in terms of the functions that each of the input and output interfaces has to perform, see *Figure 4.17*. The interface to the operating system itself is simply the initiation and end of the interrupt service subroutines.

The Interface to the Output

The interface to the output uses interrupt 021H and consists of five basic operations, each of which has

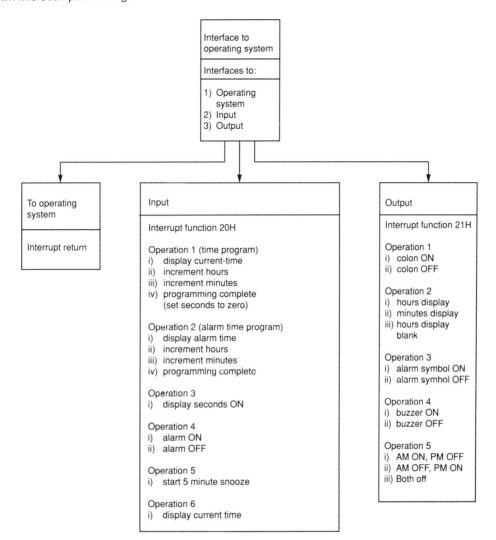

Figure 4.17 Interface to operating system

several parameters used to select which of the output displays is to be updated. The 8086 interrupt structure is used with the values transferred in selected registers. The AH register is used to select the operation as listed below with AL and BX containing additional information when required.

Colon symbol control AH = 01H. The values to be displayed are stored as Binary Coded Decimal (BCD) numbers with each digit stored in a separate register.

AL = 00H   Colon on display is turned ON
AL > 00H   Colon on display is turned OFF

Time display control AH = 02H. When AL = 01H then:

BL = Units of hours to be displayed
BH = Tens of hours to be displayed

When AL = 02H then:

BL = Units of minutes to be displayed
BH = Tens of minutes to be displayed

This operation is also used when the seconds value is to be displayed. When AL = 03H then the hours display is blanked and this operation is used when displaying seconds only.

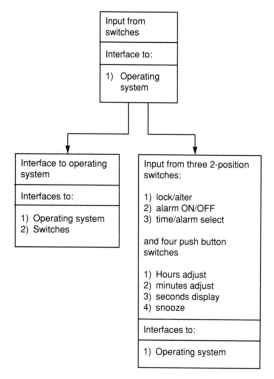

Figure 4.18 Input from switches

Alarm symbol control AH = 03H.

AL = 00H   Alarm symbol ON
AL > 00H   Alarm symbol OFF

Buzzer control AH = 04H.

AL = 00H   Buzzer tone ON
AL > 00H   Buzzer tone OFF

AM/PM symbol control AH = 05H.

AL = 01H   AM symbol ON, PM symbol OFF
AL = 02H   AM symbol OFF, PM symbol ON
AL = 03H   Both symbols OFF (used in seconds display)

Example

The following sample algorithm and program demonstrates how this interface is used to display a time of 3:32 PM. This will perform some initialisation operations that would not normally be required but these have been included to illustrate how the interface is used. The colon symbol is turned ON in this example but in the practical device this symbol would be care-

fully controlled to ensure that it flashes at exactly 1 Hz as part of the timing operation.

(1) Turn the alarm tone OFF;
(2) Turn the PM symbol ON;
(3) Update the hours display;
(4) Update the minutes display;
(5) Turn the colon symbol ON.

This then is an example program to demonstrate how the output interface is used to update the alarm clock display to the value 3:32 PM.

```
                    ;Turn the alarm tone OFF. Step (1)
MOV   AH,04H        ;Select buzzer control.
MOV   AL,0FFH       ;The buzzer OFF value.
INT   021H

                    ;Turn the PM symbol ON. Step (2)
MOV   AH,05H        ;Select PM symbol control.
MOV   AL,02H        ;Turn the symbol ON.
INT   021H

                    ;Update the hours display. Step (3)
MOV   AH,02H        ;Select time display control.
MOV   AL,01H        ;Update the hours digit
MOV   BL,03H        ;with the value 3.
MOV   BH,00H
INT   021H

                    ;Update the minutes display. Step (4)
MOV   AH,02H        ;Select time display control.
MOV   AL,02H        ;Update the minutes tens digit
MOV   BL,02H        ;with the value 3 and the minutes digit
MOV   BH,03H        ;with the value 2.
INT   021H

                    ;Turn the colon symbol ON. Step (5)
MOV   AH,01H        ;Select the colon ON operation.
MOV   AL,00H
INT   021H

                    ;The rest of the program.
```

The hardware and the software to implement these functions has not yet been implemented, but because the interface has been designed it is possible to write the programs which control them.

The Interface to the Input

This interface uses interrupt 020H and is required every time there is a change in the switch and button states. The change in switch states is determined by polling the switches at regular intervals to determine when there is a change in the switch states. When a change is detected, the input interface is initiated using INT 020H which returns with the values in the AX register to indicate the operation selected by the switch position combination. The selected operation can then be implemented by the remaining alarm clock program which uses the output interface to update any display symbols necessary. The seven possible operations and sub-operations selected by the switches are listed opposite.

Time is being programmed AH = 01H.

AL = 01H   Display the current hours and minutes

AL = 02H   Increment the hours value and update the hours display

AL = 03H   Increment the minutes value and update the minutes display

AL = 04H   Programming of time complete and set the seconds value to zero

Alarm time is being programmed AH = 02H.

AL = 01H   Display alarm time in hours and minutes

AL = 02H   Increment hours value and update hours display

AL = 03H   Increment minutes value and update minute display

AL = 04H   Programming of alarm time complete

Seconds display AH = 03H. Display seconds only ON.

Alarm control AH = 04H.

AL = 01H   Turn alarm checking ON

AL = 02H   Turn alarm checking OFF

Snooze function AH = 05H. Start a five minute snooze operation by turning off the audible alarm but leave the alarm symbol flashing.

Display current time AH = 06H. Display the current hours and minutes values and the AM or PM symbols.

No operation AH = 07H. No operation is performed. This is required for invalid switch combinations and prevents the wrong values from being displayed.

Example

The following algorithm and program illustrates how the input interface is used and assumes that the switches are selecting seconds display. The method of detecting that the switch settings have changed is not shown.

(1) Use input interface to identify which operation is being changed;
(2) If time programming, then update the time and go to step (8);

(3) If alarm time programming, then update the alarm time and go to step (8);
(4) If displaying seconds then display seconds and go to step (8);
(5) If altering the alarm state then alter alarm state and go to step (8);
(6) If snooze selected implement the snooze actions and go to step (8);
(7) Error condition;
(8) The rest of the program;

The sample program to illustrate how the input and output interfaces are combined. Use the input interface to identify which operation is being changed:

```
        INT   020H            ;What function is to be
                              ;performed? Step (1)
                              ;If time programming update
                              ;the time, then go to step (8).
        CMP   AH,01H          ;Is it programming? Step (2)
        JNZ   NOT_TIM_PROG    ;No, then check for another
                              ;function.
TIM_PROG:                     ;Yes, then perform time
                              ;programming.
                              ;(Time programming program
                              ;code is not included in order to
                              ;simplify this example.)
        JMP   CONTINUE
;
NOT_TIM_PROG:
                              ;If alarm programming update
                              ;the alarm time, then go to step
                              ;(8). Step (3)
        CMP   AH,02H          ;Is it alarm programming?
        JNZ   NOT_ALARM_PROG  ;No, then check for another
                              ;function.
;
ALARM_PROG:                   ;Yes, then execute
        JMP   CONTINUE        ;programming.
;
NOT_ALARM_PROG:
                              ;If seconds display then display
                              ;seconds, then go to step (8).
                              ;Step (4)
        CMP   AH,03H          ;Is it seconds display?
        JNZ   N_SECONDS       ;No, then check for another
                              ;function.
;
SECONDS:                      ;Yes, then execute seconds
                              ;display function.
                              ;The display seconds function
                              ;leaves the colon under flash
                              ;control.
```

```
        MOV   AX,0203H      ;Blank the hours display.
        INT   021H
;
        MOV   AX,03FFH       ;Turn the alarm symbol OFF.
        INT   021H

                            ;Turn the AM and PM symbols
                            ;OFF.
        MOV   AX,0503H       ;
        INT   021H
;
        MOV   BH,SEC_TENS    ;Display the seconds value on
                            ;the minutes digits.
        MOV   BL,SEC_UNITS
        MOV   AX,0202H
        INT   021H
        JMP   CONTINUE       ;Continue with the program.
;
N_SECONDS:

                            ;If altering alarm state, alter
                            ;alarm state and go to step (8).
                            ;Step (5)
        CMP   AH,04H         ;Is it the alarm function?
        JNZ   N_ALARM        ;No, then check for another
                            ;function.
;
ALARM:                      ;Yes, then execute alarm
                            ;function.

        JMP   CONTINUE
;
N_ALARM:

                            ;If snooze then implement the
                            ;snooze function, then go
                            ;to step (8). Step (6)
        CMP   AH,05H         ;Is it the snooze function?
        JNZ   N_SNOOZE       ;If not, then there has been an
                            ;error in the switch handling
                            ;routines.
;
SNOOZE:                     ;Yes, then execute snooze
                            ;function.

        JMP   CONTINUE
;
N_SNOOZE:

                            ;Error condition. Step (7)
        CALL  SWITCH_ERR;
                            ;The rest of the program.
                            ;Step (8)
CONTINUE:                   ;Rest of program
```

This is only a demonstration program for the input interface which also shows how the output interface can be used and does not necessarily represent the way in which the alarm clock function will be implemented.

The Input from the Switches

The interface between the switch inputs and the operating system has been described above. The software and hardware which comprise the switches must have exactly the same interface so that the two interconnect exactly.

Therefore, of the two blocks in *Figure 4.18,* only the input from switches needs some further explanation and is illustrated in *Figure 4.19.* The input operations are identified by the prioritised logic combination of switches to select which of the 12 possible actions is to be performed. Two switch parameters are used. The first is the guard condition to determine which basic function, alarm programming, time programming, seconds display, alarm control, snooze function and display current time, is to be altered. The second parameters identify which sub-function is being programmed and is determined by which switch has changed state. For example, when the seconds button is pressed its state changes from $\overline{\text{SECONDS}}$ to SECONDS. This is then used to identify a possible sub-function and the steady state of the guard switch is used to confirm the function to be performed.

In this example, to display seconds the time/alarm switch has to be in the TIME position and lock/alter in the LOCK position and these form the guard and the seconds switch goes from $\overline{\text{SECONDS}}$ to SECONDS. None of the other switches affect this function. Therefore, the seconds display function consists of the following guard and steady state conditions:

[TIME and LOCK] $\overline{\text{SECONDS}} \rightarrow$ SECONDS

and these will produce the input interface operation: after INT   20H has completed executing:

AH = 03H   Function 3 display seconds

It is an important part of the input function that any guard condition which is not matched or a guard condition which does not have a corresponding change does not alter the state of the display or any internal program operations.

The Hardware Required for Input

The only requirement of the input in terms of the programmable peripherals is one 8-bit input port as there are only seven switches, such as would be available from a programmable input and output (PIO) device, see *Figure 4.20.*

Output to the Display

The output function controls four seven-segment digit

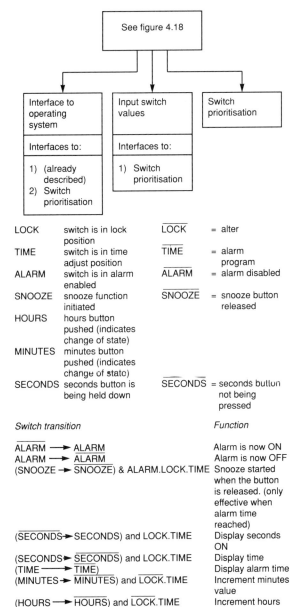

LOCK   switch is in lock position
TIME   switch is in time adjust position
ALARM   switch is in alarm enabled
SNOOZE   snooze function initiated
HOURS   hours button pushed (indicates change of state)
MINUTES   minutes button pushed (indicates change of state)
SECONDS   seconds button is being held down

$\overline{\text{LOCK}}$ = alter
$\overline{\text{TIME}}$ = alarm program
$\overline{\text{ALARM}}$ = alarm disabled
$\overline{\text{SNOOZE}}$ = snooze button released
$\overline{\text{SECONDS}}$ = seconds button not being pressed

Switch transition   *Function*

Switch transition	Function
ALARM → ALARM	Alarm is now ON
ALARM → $\overline{\text{ALARM}}$	Alarm is now OFF
(SNOOZE → $\overline{\text{SNOOZE}}$) & ALARM.LOCK.TIME	Snooze started when the button is released. (only effective when alarm time reached)
($\overline{\text{SECONDS}}$ → SECONDS) and LOCK.TIME	Display seconds ON
(SECONDS → $\overline{\text{SECONDS}}$) and LOCK.TIME	Display time
(TIME → $\overline{\text{TIME}}$)	Display alarm time
(MINUTES → $\overline{\text{MINUTES}}$) and $\overline{\text{LOCK}}$.TIME	Increment minutes value
(HOURS → $\overline{\text{HOURS}}$) and $\overline{\text{LOCK}}$.TIME	Increment hours value (including AM/PM)
(MINUTES → $\overline{\text{MINUTES}}$) and $\overline{\text{LOCK}}.\overline{\text{TIME}}$	Increment alarm minutes value
(HOURS → $\overline{\text{HOURS}}$) and $\overline{\text{LOCK}}.\overline{\text{TIME}}$	Increment alarm hours value
($\overline{\text{LOCK}}$ → LOCK) and TIME	Time programming completed, seconds value set to zero
($\overline{\text{LOCK}}$ → LOCK) and $\overline{\text{TIME}}$	Alarm time programming completed

Figure 4.19 Switch specification

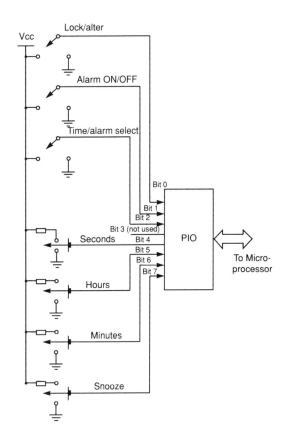

Figure 4.20 The PIO and switch inputs

displays, and the AM, PM, ALARM and COLON symbols, as illustrated in *Figure 4.11*. As the tens symbol for the hours display is only ever blank or a 1 as this is not a 24 hour clock, it can be treated as another symbol if necessary, so that there are effectively only three seven-segment digit displays to control.

There are several methods of producing the correct display on the seven-segment displays involving direct control of each segment of each display using binary to seven segment decoders, or time-multiplexed versions of same. Decoders are used to reduce the programming required if the controlling microprocessor has many other actions to control and time-multiplexing to reduce the power required by the display. Neither of these two points are important for this case study so the simplest method of direct control of each segment will be used. The individual display segment elements are controlled from the bits of an I/O port, as illustrated in *Figure 4.21* (overleaf). The seven segments of the display are numbered A to F and are controlled by the seven bits of the I/O port.

There are four 7-segment digits so four output ports

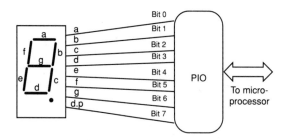

Figure 4.21   7-segment display

will be required plus an additional output port for the AM, PM, ALARM and colon symbols. Most PIOs only have three I/O ports so this will require two PIOs, as illustrated in *Figure 4.22*. The unused port is programmed for input and used as the switch states input port.

The Display Operations Required

There are effectively eleven different display functions required and these can be grouped into the five operations specified in the output to display interface, see *Figure 4.23* and these are listed below:

Alarm symbol
   a)   Symbol ON
   b)   Symbol OFF
Hours seven segment digit display
   a)   Tens digit OFF or a 1
   b)   Unit digits OFF or 0 to 9
Minutes seven segment digit display
   a)   Tens digit 0 to 5
   b)   Units digit 0 to 9

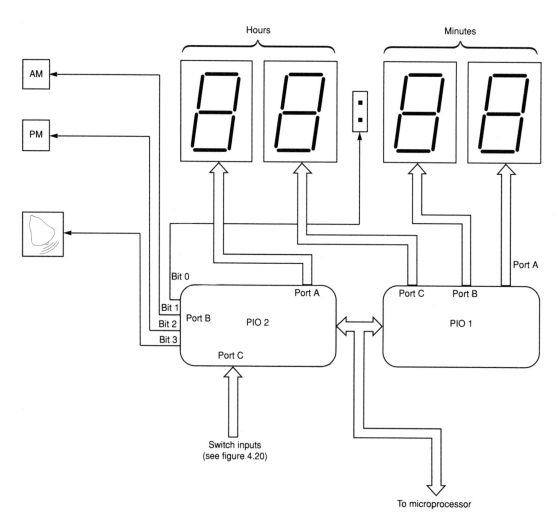

Figure 4.22   Complete display control

Colon symbol
  a) Colon symbol ON
  b) Colon symbol OFF
AM and PM symbols
  a) Both symbols OFF
  b) AM symbol ON and PM symbol OFF
  c) AM symbol OFF and PM symbol ON

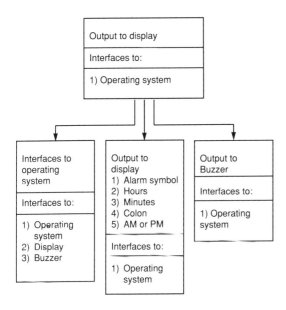

Figure 4.23 Output to display

The display updating is initiated in one of two ways, either a new status is produced by altering a switch position, or the new time in increments of seconds or minutes is to be displayed. The basic unit of time between display updates is 0.5 seconds and this is also the colon flash rate and the alarm symbol flash rate. The programs to perform the time update function are part of the processing unit functional block top-down design.

This technique provides an easy and direct control of symbols and switches but does require two PIO components. This increases the cost, size and power requirements and a realistic design would achieve control of the display and switches by using multiplexing, to reduce display power and the number of I/O ports required so that all those functions can be achieved by using only one PIO. This is a more difficult method to implement and will not be used in this case study as cost, size and power requirements are not being considered. Considering these aspects of design would produce a different solution that is more complex and would take longer to implement.

The Output to the Alarm Buzzer

The alarm buzzer has been treated as a separate output device because it is not a visual display device, but an audible one. There are two possible techniques for producing the required alarm buzzer tones using either hardware or software. The required alarm buzzer functions are listed below and form part of the output to the display interface illustrated in *Figure 4.23*.

The Alarm Buzzer Operations

(1) Turn the buzzer OFF. This stops the alarm buzzer at the beginning of the next 0.1s period.
(2) Turn the buzzer ON. This pulses a 1 kHz tone with ON periods of 0.1 s and OFF periods of 0.1 s, for 8 pulses, followed by 0.4 s OFF.

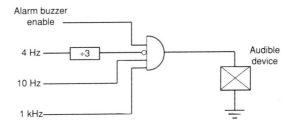

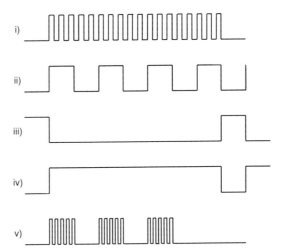

Figure 4.24 Buzzer hardware and waveforms

A possible hardware solution is illustrated in *Figure 4.24* which will implement this specification and consists of four timers programmed as programmable frequency generators with frequencies of 0.5 Hz, 4 Hz, 10 Hz and 1000 Hz, where each frequency generator acts as the output enable for the next higher frequency. This produces the waveform shown. This could be achieved by using two programmable interval timers (PITs), a divide by 3 and a 4-input AND gate. The alarm buzzer enable signal input to the AND gate is produced from one of the spare bits of the output port of the PIOs used to control the display symbols.

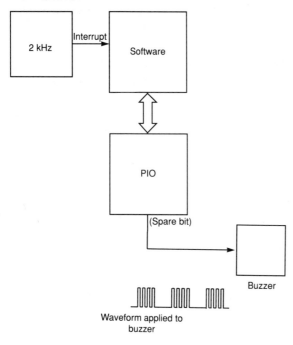

Figure 4.25   Software buzzer

The software-based alternative produces the same signal on one bit of the PIO as illustrated in *Figure 4.25*. This signal is best produced using an interrupt as this can also be used to provide the basic timing signal for the clock time-keeping. A 2 kHz interrupt will produce a 1 kHz square wave, see *Figure 4.26*, as well as forming the basic real-time interrupt for the current time counter values. This function is discussed later in the processing unit section. This case study will use the software technique for producing the buzzer alarm pulse waveform in order to eliminate the need for PITs.

This completes the design of the user interface block, and has produced a fairly complex design from what was apparently a simple problem. The user interface has been completely specified and a design implemented that will fulfil it.

The Processing Unit

The processing unit implements the main functions of the alarm clock. An interrupt will create the basic unit of

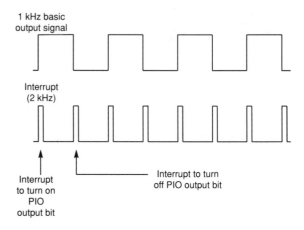

Figure 4.26   The interrupt signal

time on which the clock will be based, taken as a 2 kHz signal to be compatible with the buzzer interface. This will maintain the correct time counts for hours, minutes, seconds, alarm, colon symbol flashing and the alarm buzzer tone generator.

The four main functions of the processing unit are illustrated in *Figure 4.27* and consist of the interrupt

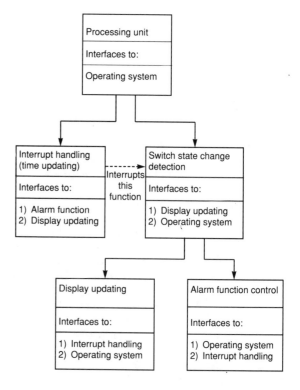

Figure 4.27   Processing Unit Functions

handling, display updating, alarm function control, and switch state change detection. The display updating interface has already been designed in the user interface block.

Table 4.1 Interrupt handling: update time function

Data variables	Range of values	Explanation
Buzzer	0, 1	1 kHz interrupt, toggled every interrupt to produce buzzer square wave
Buzzer pulse	0→99	on 100, reset to zero and increment buzzer pulse count
Buzzer pulse count	0→14 15→19	On 15, disable buzzer audible. On 20, reset to zero, enable buzzer audible
Pre$^1/_{100}$ seconds	0→19	Increment every interrrupt. On 20, reset to zero and increment one hundreths
One hundreths	0→49	On 50, reset to zero, and increment half second count. Toggle colon and alarm symbols
Colon alarm	0 (OFF) 1 (ON)	Toggled every $\frac{1}{2}$ second
Half second count	0→1	On 2, reset to zero and increment seconds unit. Update seconds display if being displayed
Seconds unit	0→9	On 10, reset to zero and increment seconds-tens. Update seconds display if being displayed
Seconds-tens	0→5	On 6, reset to zero and increment minutes units. Update minutes display if being displayed
Minutes units	0→9	On 10, reset to zero, increment hours. Update hours display if being displayed
Hours	1→12	On 10, set hours tens symbol to ON. On 13, reset to ome. Toggle AM/PM symbols. Update symbols and hours display if being displayed
AM symbol PM symbol	0 (OFF) 1 (ON)	Toggle on hours count going 12→1 (see above)

Table 4.2 Initiate alarm function

Data variables	Range of values	Explanation
Alarm hours AM or PM	1→12 AM = 0 PM = 1	If the present time matches this 'alarm' time, the alarm is turned ON
Alarm minutes units	0→9	
Alarm minutes tens	0→5	
Alarm enabled	0 (enabled) 1 (enabled)	This value is obtained directly from the alarm enable switch
Snooze		If greater than zero, then disable audible
Audible	0 (disabled) 1 (enabled)	
Alarm time valid	0 (valid) 1 (invalid)	The alarm time will be valid for all times less than 1 hour past the specified alarm time (see above)

The Interrupt Handling Function

The interrupt handling function will operate as illustrated in Tables 4.1, 4.2, and 4.3, by maintaining a series of data values which determine the internal status of the alarm clock function.

The interrupt operation has an influence on three functions:

(a) Maintaining a correct current time count which is not necessarily displayed;

Table 4.3 Initiate display function

Data variables	Range	Explanation
Seconds display	0	Display seconds only
	1	Display hours and minutes
Colon flash	0	constantly on
	1	Flashing enabled
Colon	0	Colon off
(see also Table 4.1)	1	Colon on
Alarm time display	0	Display alarm hours and minutes
	1	Use seconds display

(b) Initiating the alarm function by checking if the alarm needs sounding;

(c) Initiating the display function by checking if the display requires updating with a new set of values.

The display unit checks the current display mode to determine whether the time (hours/minutes) or seconds value is being displayed and if it needs updating because the value has changed. A change in the seconds count value only affects the display if in seconds mode unless it is from 59 to 60, when the the seconds value is reset, the minutes count incremented and checked to determine whether hours need updating.

These three functions are performed on every interrupt every 0.5 ms, after which the interrupt terminates and returns to the switch state change detection block illustrated in *Figure 4.27*.

The Switch State Change Detection

The heart of the processing unit function is the function which detects when a switch setting has been changed. When a change is detected the input function (INT 20H) of the user interface is initiated to update the necessary data variables shown in *Figures 4.28, 4.29* and *4.30* and an update display (INT 21H) made as required.

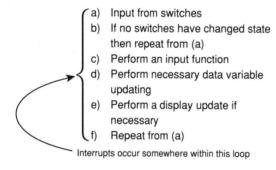

a) Input from switches
b) If no switches have changed state then repeat from (a)
c) Perform an input function
d) Perform necessary data variable updating
e) Perform a display update if necessary
f) Repeat from (a)

Interrupts occur somewhere within this loop

Figure 4.28   Main software loop

The 2 kHz signal is used to interrupt this process, see *Figure 4.28*, to perform the interrupt service subroutine. Once the interrupt service subroutine has completed, the main switch state change detection loop continues. Care is needed to ensure that the interrupt service subroutine executes in less time than the period between interrupts, as illustrated in *Figure 4.29*, otherwise the system will not operate correctly. There must also be sufficient time left between the end of the interrupt service subroutine and the next interrupt to allow a reasonable proportion of the main loop and associated input and output operations to be performed.

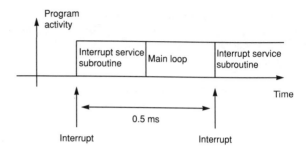

Figure 4.29   Interrupt service subroutine

The Main Switch State Change Detection Loop

A change in the switch state is detected by comparing the present state of the switches with the state when they were last sampled. If the two values are different the switch settings have been changed.

An algorithm and 8086 assembly language program which would implement the main loop are illustrated below.

Example

(1) Input the present switch state;
(2) If unchanged from the previous sampled states then repeat from step (1);
(3) Update the switch state store;
(4) Initiate the input interface.

This program detects when the alarm clock switches have been changed and then executes the input interface.

```
LAST_STATE  DB   OOH        ;Status of switches after last
                            ;change.
                            ;Input the present switch
                            ;states. Step (1)
        MOV  DX, SWITCH_PORT ;Get the switch settings
                            ;from the PIO.
MAIN_LOOP:
        IN   AL,DX

                            ;If unchanged repeat from
                            ;step (1). Step (2)
        CMP  AL,LAST_STATE   ;Test for any changes in the
        JZ   MAIN_LOOP       ;switch settings.
                            ;If no changes then repeat
                            ;the test.
                            ;Update the switch state
                            ;store. Step (3)
        MOV  AH,LAST_STATE   ;There has been a change so
        MOV  LAST_STATE,AL   ;find out what function is
                            ;required.
                            ;Initiate the input interface.
                            ;Step (4)
```

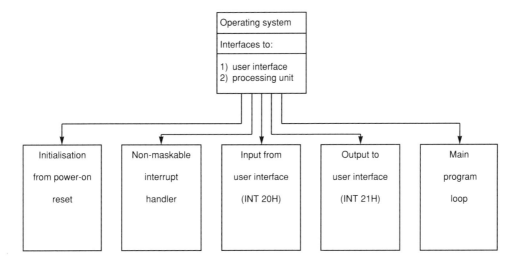

Figure 4.30 Operating system

```
INT    20H                    ;The state of the switches is
                              ;passed in AH, and the new
                              ;state in AL. The present
                              ;switch status is saved first.
                              ;The operation requested
                              ;by the switches is
                              ;performed here.
```

A handler for the results of the input interface, INT 20H, has been shown previously. This is incomplete, but demonstrates a partial solution which can be expanded to a full solution.

The Requirements of the Processing Unit

This completes the design of the processing unit at this level and consists of:

(a) A single hardware initiated interrupt;
(b) Some data variable memory locations;
(c) Some software modules.

The software function interfaces have been well defined and perform simple functions and there should be little difficulty in writing the programs. Fragments of the required code have been illustrated throughout this chapter and it would only require a small effort to put this together with the missing sections.

The remaining block to be designed concerns the operating system and this is a software-based function with no additional hardware required.

The Operating System

The remaining block of the top-down design is the operating system which has four main operations as illustrated in *Figure 4.30* and consists of:

(a) Initialisation from power-on-reset;
(b) The NMI interrupt handler;
(c) The input interface, INT 20H handler;
(d) The output interface, INT 21H handler.

The Initialisation from Power-On-Reset

This section of program is only performed when the power is first applied to the alarm clock and is required to program the peripherals for correct operation, to initialise all the data variables to the values in the specification and to perform any other initialisation tasks required.

Example

The initialise sequence for this design would be:

(1) Initialise the segment registers and the stack;
(2) Program PIO 1 for output;
(3) Program PIO 2 for ports A and B output, port C input;
(4) Initialise interrupt handlers;
(5) Set up data variables for switch setting using current time of 1.00 am and an alarm time of 12.00 pm;
(6) Execute the main program loop.

The following program will perform the necessary initialisation for the alarm clock power on:

```
                              ;Initialise the segment registers
                              ;and the stack. Step (1)
DATA     SEGMENT
;
DATA     ENDS
;
```

```
;STACK      SEGMENT
            DW   100 DUP (?)
STK_TOP   EQU *
STACK     ENDS
;
CODE      SEGMENT
          ASSUME     CS:CODE,DS:DATA,SS:STACK
          MOV   AX,STACK
          MOV   SS,AX
          MOV   SP,STK_TOP
          MOV   AX,DATA
          MOV   DS,AX
                          ;Program the first PIO. Step (2)
          MOV   DX,PIO1_CONT
          MOV   AL,PIO1_INIT
          OUT   DX,AL
                          ;Program the second PIO. Step (3)
          MOV   DX,PIO2_CONT
          MOV   AL,PIO2_INIT
          OUT   DX,AL
                          ;Initialise the interrupt
                          ;handlers. Step (4)
          MOV   AX,0000H
          MOV   ES,AX
          MOV   DI,NMI_VECTOR
          MOV   ES:[DI],OFFSET NMI
          MOV   ES:[DI + 2],SEG NMI
```

This is followed by step (5): set up the data variables to a current time of 1.00 am and an alarm time of 12.00 pm. Step (6) is: execute the main program loop.

The NMI Handler

The NMI has three functions to perform every interrupt:

(1) Maintain the correct time, see *Table 4.1*;
(2) Initiate the alarm function, see *Table 4.2*, if necessary;
(3) Initiate the display function, see *Table 4.3*, if necessary.

Example

The following program indicates one method of implementing this interrupt-initiated function, although only the program to maintain the correct time is shown. The program performs all the actions required by the interrupt to the NMI. Note that the buzzer signal is always produced even if it is not sounding. The alarm enable signal is used to produce the tone when the alarm time is reached and the alarm is active.

```
NMI        PROC  FAR
           MOV   AL,BUZZER2K
           INC   AL
           CMP   AL,02H
           JB    TOGGLE
           MOV   AL,00H
TOGGLE:    MOV   BUZZER1K,AL
;
```

```
           MOV   AL,BUZZ_PULSE;Increment the
           INC   AL           ;buzzer pulse length.
           CMP   AL,100       ;Has the tone burst
                              ;finished?
           JB    NO_CHANGE    ;No, then save the
                              ;value.
           MOV   AL,00H       ;Yes, then reset it to
                              ;zero.
NO_CHANGE: MOV   BUZZ_PULSE,AL
           JB    NO_INC       ;The flags are still set
           MOV   AL,PULSES    ;from the previous
                              ;test.
                              ;If reset then
                              ;increment the pulse
           INC   AL           ;count.
           CMP   AL,15        ;If the pulse count =
           MOV   PULSES,AL    ;15 then disable the
                              ;audible tone.
           JNE   NOT_EQUAL
           MOV   AL,AUDIBLE
           MOV   AL,00H       ;Disable audible
           MOV   AUDIBLE,AL   ;tone.
           MOV   AL,PULSES
NOT_EQUAL: CMP   AL,20        ;If the pulse count =
           JB    MORE_PULSES  ;20, then reset the
           MOV   AL,00H       ;pulse count to zero
                              ;and re-enable the
                              ;audible tone.
           MOV   PULSES,AL
           MOV   AL,0FFH      ;Enable audible tone.
           MOV   AUDIBLE
MORE_PULSES:
                              ;Maintain the correct
                              ;time. Step (1)
```

As the interrupts are occurring at the rate of 2000 per second then a division by 20 is required to produce a counter incrementing in 100ths of a second. This is performed by the PRE-100THS counter which on a count of 20 resets to zero and increments the 100THS of a second counter.

```
                              ;Increment the pre-
                              ;100 count.
           MOV   AL,PRE_100
           INC   AL
           MOV   PRE_100,AL
           CMP   AL,20        ;If the pre-100 count
           JB    NOT_100THS   ;= 20, then reset it
           MOV   AL,00H       ;to zero and
           MOV   PRE_100,AL   ;increment the
                              ;100ths count.
           MOV   AL,ONE_HUND  ;Increment the
           INC   AL           ;100ths count.
           MOV   ONE_HUND,AL
           CMP   AL,50        ;If the 100ths count
                              ;= 60, then
                              ;increment the ½
                              ;second count.
           JB    NOT_HALF     ;When this occurs,
           MOV   AL,COLON     ;toggle the colon and
           INC   AL           ;alarm symbols.
           MOV   COLON,AL
           CMP   AL,02H
```

```
          JB    NOT_COLON
          MOV   AL,00H
NOT_COLON: MOV  COLON,AL
;
          MOV   AL,ALARM_SYM  ;Toggle the alarm
          INC   AL            ;symbol.
          MOV   ALARM_SYM,AL
          CMP   AL,02H
          JB    NOT_ALARM
          MOV   AL,00H
NOT_ALARM: MOV  ALARM_SYM,AL
;
          MOV   AL,HALF_SEC   ;Increment the 1/2
          INC   AL            ;second count.
          MOV   HALF_SEC,AL
          CMP   AL,02H
          JB    NOT_HALF
          MOV   AL,00H        ;Reset the 1/2 second
NOT_HALF: MOV   HALF_SEC,AL   ;count to zero if it is
                              ;already 1. This
                              ;indicates when 1
                              ;second has elapsed.
          JB    NOT_SECOND    ;The flags are still
                              ;valid.
          MOV   AL,SEC_UNITS  ;Increment the
          INC   AL            ;seconds count.
          MOV   SEC_UNITS,AL
          CMP   AL,10         ;If 10 seconds then
          JB    NOT_SEC_UNITS ;reset the seconds to
                              ;zero and increment
          MOV   AL,00H        ;the tens of seconds
          MOV   SEC_UNITS,AL  ;count. This
                              ;maintains the
                              ;numbers as BCD.
;
          MOV   AL,SEC_TENS
          INC   AL
          MOV   SEC_TENS,AL
          CMP   AL,06H        ;Does the tens-of-
                              ;seconds count = 6?
                              ;(equivalent to 60
                              ;seconds).
          JB    NOT_SEC_TENS  ;No, then continue.
          MOV   AL,00H
          MOV   SEC_TENS,AL   ;Yes, then reset the
          MOV   AL,MINS_UNITS ;tens-of-seconds
                              ;count to zero, and
          INC   AL            ;increment the
          MOV   MINS_UNITS,AL ;minutes count.
          CMP   AL,10         ;Does the minutes
                              ;count = 10?
          JB    NOT_MINS_UNITS
          MOV   AL,00H        ;Yes, then reset the
          MOV   MINS_UNITS,AL ;minutes count to
          MOV   AL,MINS_TENS  ;zero and increment
          INC   AL            ;the tens-of-minutes.
          MOV   MINS_TENS,AL
          CMP   AL,06H        ;Does the tens-of-
                              ;minutes = 6?
                              ;This is equivalent to
                              ;60 minutes.
          JB    NOT_MINS_TENS ;No, then continue.
          MOV   AL,00H        ;Yes, then reset the
          MOV   MINS_TENS,AL  ;tens-of-minutes
          MOV   AL,HOURS      ;count to zero and
```

```
          INC   AL            ;increment the hours
                              ;count.
          MOV   HOURS,AL
          CMP   AL,13         ;Does the hours
                              ;count = 13?
          JB    NOT_AMPM      ;No, then skip the
                              ;AM/PM symbol
                              ;toggle.
          MOV   AL,00H        ;Yes, then reset the
          MOV   HOURS,AL      ;hours count to zero
                              ;and toggle the
          MOV   HOURS_TENS,AL ;AM/PM; symbols.
;
          MOV   AL,AM
          INC   AL            ;If AM symbol
          MOV   AM,AL         ;change to PM.
          CMP   AL,02H
          JB    NOT_AM
          MOV   AL,00H
NOT_AM:   MOV   AM,AL
;
          MOV   AL,PM         ;If PM symbol change
          INC   AL            ;to AM.
          MOV   PM,AL
          CMP   AL,02H
          JB    NOT_PM
          MOV   AL,00H
NOT_PM:   MOV   PM,AL
;
NOT_AMPM: MOV   AL,HOURS      ;Does the hours
          CMP   AL,10         ;count = 10?
          JNE   NOT_TENS      ;No, then continue.
          MOV   AL,HOURS_TENS ;Yes, then increment
          INC   AL            ;the tens-of-hours
          MOV   HOURS_TENS,AL ;count.
NOT_TENS:
NOT_HOURS:
NOT_MINS_TENS:
NOT_MINS_UNITS:
NOT_SEC_TENS:
NOT_SEC_UNITS:
NOT_100THS:
NO_INC:
                              ;Initiate the alarm
                              ;function if
                              ;necessary. Step (2)
                              ;Program code goes
                              ;here.
                              ;Initiate the display
                              ;function if
                              ;necessary Step (3)
                              ;Program code goes
                              ;here.
          IRET                ;End of interrupt.
;
NMI       ENDP
```

The instructions used illustrate the function of the program and are not designed to produce a fast executing program. A shorter program can be produced by directly incrementing memory and performing comparisons on memory, rather than using registers, so that instead of:

```
MOV   AL,COUNT
INC   AL
MOV   COUNT,AL
CMP   AL,10
JB    DO_NOTHING
```

this produces:

```
INC   COUNT
CMP   COUNT, 10
JB    DO_NOTHING
```

This would save a total of approximately 36 instructions out of 120.

Input and Output to User Interface

The program codes for the input (INT 20H) and the output (INT 21H) interrupt service subroutines for the user interface can be designed from the interfaces specified earlier and will be left as an exercise for the reader.

Summary

The hardware design of the alarm clock can be finalised and a block circuit diagram drawn, as illustrated in *Figure 4.31*. As only one hardware-initiated interrupt is used the **non maskable interrupt** (NMI) of the microprocessor will be used as this avoids the need for a programmable interrupt controller (PIC). The software method of creating the buzzer waveform using the time-keeping interrupt has removed the need for a PIT. It would have been possible to achieve a circuit using only one PIO but that would have made the software much more complicated. The block circuit diagram does not contain all the components to be used but merely identifies the main functional blocks. Address decoding, clock generating, address de-multiplexing and data buffering are not shown, but would be required.

The aim of this case study is to show how top-down functional block design works and simplifications have been made where necessary in order that the reasoning behind decisions and techniques be more clearly understood.

From the previous sections, it can be seen how the process of top-down functional block design is utilised. Unrelated functions are separated into different blocks with defined interfaces allowing the transfer of data and other information. This improves the structure of the solution, leading to error-free designs that are readily and easily expanded. It would be simple to add additional functions and operations to the input and output to the user interface. It also enables testing and verification of individual blocks to be performed before they are integrated into the complete product. However, the product is designed as a coherent complete whole, with all the component parts fitting together neatly.

It would have been easy to start writing a program which would implement the time-keeping function right from the beginning, as this would appear to be the main purpose of this design. However, this approach would soon have encountered difficulties due to incomplete analysis of the problem and would have led to an attempt to adapt the initial solution to fit in problems such as changing the current time value. These changes, even if successful, would destroy any structure that might have been present in the initial solution and the result would have been a series of patches to achieve the desired effect. Each patch would have had the possibility of introducing errors and unpredictable results into the solution.

The solution presented is not the optimum one as it was designed to illustrate the technique of top-down design, as well as introducing several useful design techniques such as interrupts and interfacing to operating systems. However, this solution is expected to perform to the specification given earlier and to provide a working product.

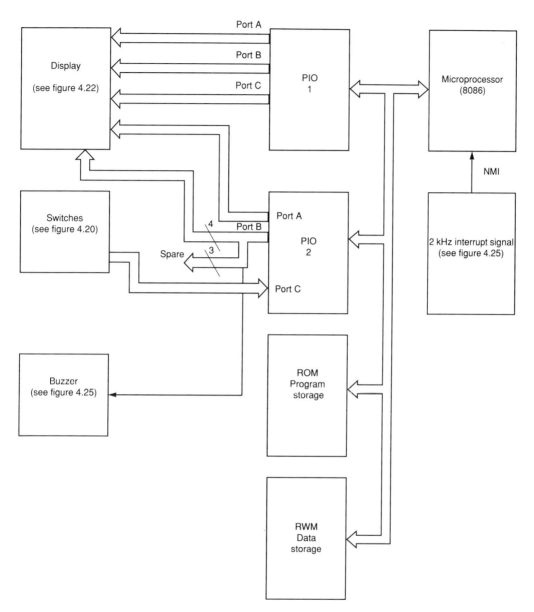

Figure 4.31   The alarm clock block circuit diagram

FIVE

Software Development

5.1 INTRODUCTION

Software can be considered to be the changeable, or 'soft' part of a computer-based control system and hardware can be considered to be the unchangeable, or 'hard' part. Some systems implement software as part of the hardware, for example, by using programmable memory components in such a way that changes in the software require changes in the hardware. An alternative name used for the software is program and these two terms are used interchangeably.

Software Design

The development of software can be considered to fall into three parts:

(a) Specification;
(b) Implementation of the specification;
(c) Testing.

Specification

The software specification describes the actions to be performed and the limitations imposed, such as accuracy. The operation of the software is outlined functionally using generalities and should be independent of the programming language. The specification may define the interfaces between different sections as this is helpful for modular techniques of design, but it will not contain any detailed descriptions of the implementation. The aim is to produce an error-free specification and if internal details are included which are hardware- or software-dependent, there may be problems at a later stage if the hardware or software is changed.

The aim of the specification is to produce a set of written documents which specify the complete program or software operation with all of the interfaces defined, before any programming is performed or the computer language selected. This allows all programmers working on a particular project to work to the same specific

defined standard, against which they can measure the operation and performance of their programs. Once the program has been completed, the specification is used as the basis of the tests devised to ensure its correct operation. A group of programmers working on a large program can use the specification to understand how their particular part contributes to the whole.

Implementation of the specification. The design of software can be considered to be three distinct but inter-related processes:

(a) Algorithm design;
(b) Flowchart or pseudo-code design;
(c) Program writing.

The first two sections should be independent of the computer and language being used. Various computers and languages can be used, each of which has advantages and disadvantages in solving categories of problems. Computers vary from those designated as microcomputers which contain a microprocessor as the central processing unit (CPU), through to mainframe computers which implement special architectures designed to increase the number of instructions executed per second. Languages also vary between the two main types, high level languages, (HLL), and low level languages, (LLL).

Although the design of algorithms and flowcharts should be independent of the computer language used, as a general guideline, assembly languages are better designed using flowcharts and high level languages using pseudo-code, but either process can be used for either type of language.

Algorithms

An algorithm is a short set of logical English-like statements which when executed sequentially will perform the required task. An example would be the tasks to be performed when walking through a closed door, as illustrated by the following algorithm.

(1) Approach the door;
(2) Turn the door handle and open the door;
(3) Go through the door;
(4) Turn and close the door;
(5) Continue journey.

The number of statements in the algorithm should be minimised and should never be more than 10 or 12. The statements themselves should make no reference to the hardware, or only general references, in order to make the solution as general purpose as possible. A general purpose solution is a sign of good programming as the solution can be applied to other similar problems without having to start the design process from the beginning. This leads to increased programmer output which in turn produces cheaper programs, and of a higher quality and reliability as the general solutions will have had previous testing and use.

The algorithm statements may contain decisions and/or jump conditions. These generally take the form of:

IF <condition> THEN <action1> ELSE <action2>

with the ELSE <action2> being optional. Using the example of passing through a closed door, if the door had already been open the initial algorithm would probably produce an error situation by attempting to open an already open door. This could be avoided by changing the second statement to a conditional statement:

(1) Approach the door;
(2) If the door is open then goto (3) else turn the door handle and open the door,
(3) Go through the door,
(4) Turn and close the door,
(5) Continue journey.

This solution will always leave the door closed which may be acceptable, but in some circumstances, it may be desirable to leave the door open if it was already open. This can be achieved by changing statement (4) to a conditional statement with no optional ELSE <action2>.

(1) Approach the door;
(2) If the door is open then goto (3) else turn the door handle and open the door;
(3) Go through the door;
(4) If the door was originally closed then turn and close the door;
(5) Continue journey.

The original algorithm has been improved by considering an increased set of initial conditions without increasing the number of statements. These form the input data to the problem and the increased set of possible conditions prevents situations from occurring which could cause the program to fail. Further consideration of the problem may introduce other conditions requiring alternative actions which may in turn introduce other problems. It is the programmer's responsibility to consider all the possible input conditions and design suitable responses to enable the program to continue executing correctly. The ability to continue executing for all input conditions is considered to be a measure of the program's reliability. The ability to produce 'useful' results for these situations is a measure of its robustness. For large programs which have complex data input situations, 50 per cent or more of the program may be concerned with checking the validity of the input conditions with the purpose of excluding those which are invalid and reorganising those that are correct into a more useful format. Of the remaining 50 per cent of the program, 45 per cent will be involved in coping with the special input data conditions which occur infrequently and in recovering from any errors caused by invalid inputs which have passed undetected through the previous input checking, or other errors caused by unknown situations. The remaining 5 per cent of the program will be concerned with implementing the basic function required by the specification. For example, consider the solution of the problem of controlling the entry and exit of cars in a multistorey car park.

5.2 SOFTWARE DESIGN: MULTI-STOREY CAR PARK

The car park has two entrances controlled by barriers and two exits also controlled by barriers where payment is made. The car park holds a maximum of 400 cars.

Detailed specification.
(a) Assume that the car park holds a known number of cars;
(b) Cars entering are added to the total;
(c) Cars leaving are subtracted from the total;
(d) Cars cannot enter if the car park is full;
(e) Cars cannot leave without payment;
(f) Display FULL sign if car park is full.

This specification can now be transformed into an algorithm.

Algorithm.
(1) If no action is required then goto step (1);
(2) If a car is leaving then extract payment and adjust the total;

(3) If a car is entering, check there is sufficient room and adjust total;

(4) goto step (1).

This is an example of a simple algorithm deduced from the specification. After some consideration this algorithm may be considered to be satisfactory in which case the next stage of the software design process, the design of the flowcharts, can be started. If the initial algorithm is unsatisfactory then rewrites are necessary. The algorithm will be used as the basic structure for the entire program and any unsatisfactory steps will filter through and produce unsatisfactory programs.

Flowcharts

Once a general solution has been produced it needs to be refined until it can be implemented directly in the selected computer language. A technique known as top-down design based upon flowcharts produces acceptable results for most problems. The aim of using flowcharts is to break down the problem into ever smaller and smaller sub-problems with defined boundary conditions, until the point is reached at which further subdivision would shed no further information on how to solve the problem. It is possible to continue using algorithms for this sub-problem design but flowcharts are more suitable because they have a visual structure which conveys more information then written algorithms. Therefore, once a satisfactory algorithm has been designed it is transferred to a series of flowcharts.

The simplest type of flowcharts consist of four basic structures:

(a) Start and stop boxes (appear only once in a program);

(b) Entry and exit boxes (occur once for every sub-flowchart);

(c) Action boxes (actions which will always be performed);

(d) Decision diamonds (conditional statements).

A sample flowchart is given in Figure 5.1. This contains a start box at the top indicating where program execution will always begin. There is a corresponding stop box at the bottom, indicating where the program will always end. Although it is possible to write software which has multiple start and/or stop points, it is not recommended as the structure can become difficult to follow and even more difficult to alter.

Following the start box are two action boxes. These indicate the actions to be performed using statements similar to those used in the algorithm. For example, 'approach the door'. Again there should be minimal

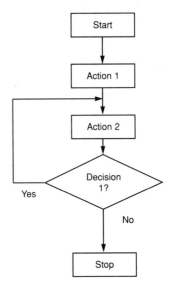

Figure 5.1   A simple flowchart

references to the actual hardware that the program is to be executed on. Following the action boxes is a decision diamond which would be based on some function or parameter controlled or altered by the previous action boxes, or possibly external actions. There are a variety of decision diamond configurations, as illustrated in *Figure 5.2,* each of which has one entry point at the top

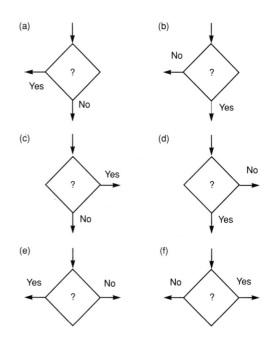

Figure 5.2   Possible decision diamond configuration

and two exit routes, which can be any two of the three remaining corners of the diamond. The test used in the decision diamond must result in a true or false answer for this structure to be used, usually designated by YES and NO answer. For example, if the decision was: is count A bigger than count B? the YES exit from the decision diamond would be taken if A was bigger than B or the NO exit if B was larger than or equal to A.

In addition, there should only be one **feedback loop** on any single flowchart but any number of feedforwards provided that none of the lines actually cross. A feedback loop is one where the flow of the program, indicated by the straight lines, returns to a point in the program which has been previously executed, see *Figure 5.3*. A feedforward always points to a section of program which has not yet been executed and is used to bypass sections of program which do not need to be executed for the particular set of input data conditions. The arrows on the lines indicate which direction the program flow will continue along. The program cannot flow both ways along a line so the arrow is used to indicate the valid direction. Multiple feedback loops are not allowed as they lead to unnecessary complexity.

A **feedforward loop**, shown in *Figure 5.4*, is usually used by a decision diamond to avoid an action box, so

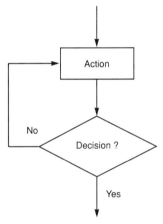

Figure 5.3   A feedback loop

that the action may or may not be executed depending on the result of a suitable test. For example, the decision diamond might be: 'is the door open?', and the action might then be: 'open the door'. Obviously if the door was already open it is not necessary, or even possible, to open it again.

One flowchart structure which is not allowed is to have an action box in the feedback or feed forward branch of a decision diamond. This is because it is not possible to write a program in assembly language which directly implements it. Even if it appears to be simpler to

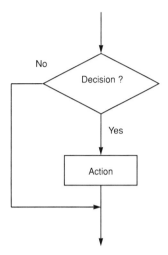

Figure 5.4   A feedforward loop

do this and it may even be possible to write some program code which will eventually perform the desired actions, it leads to unnecessary complexity. It is much better to redesign the flowchart to avoid this problem. The most common cause of this problem is what structure to use if, after a decision, only one of two or more possible actions is to be executed. The best solution is to provide a decision box for every action possible and then retest before each one, using feedforwards around unwanted actions as illustrated in *Figure 5.5* (overleaf). The same test can be used but with altered exit routes so only one of the actions will be performed. This technique does depend on the variables used in the decision diamonds remaining unchanged until after the second decision diamond.

Sub-Flowcharts

The algorithm is normally converted directly into the top level flowchart, designated FC 1.0 and given some short descriptive name such as 'car park controller'. Each statement from the algorithm can usually be converted into one action box or decision diamond using a shortened form of the English statements for simplicity. It may be useful occasionally to expand a single algorithm statement into two or more action boxes, or condense two or more statements into a single action box.

There is little additional information obtained from this first flowchart, but it does provide a better understanding of program flow than the algorithm. For non-trivial problems all the information cannot be contained in one flowchart and it is necessary to expand each action and possibly decision diamonds, into a complete new flowchart.

FC 1.0 Demo

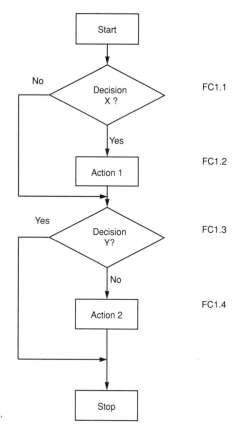

Figure 5.5 Using feedforwards to model IF . . . THEN . . . ELSE

FC 1.0 Car park controller

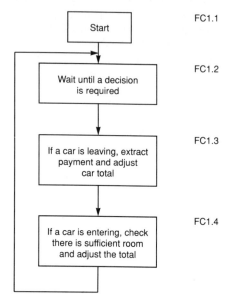

Figure 5.6 Main car park flowchart

Each of the new flowcharts is given a new number which indicates the 'parent' flowchart and a name which indicates the function of the flowchart. Each of the action boxes or decision diamonds is numbered starting from the top and this is added to the number for the complete flowchart separated by a decimal point as in *Figure 5.5.* Not all of the boxes may require further expansion and it is unlikely that any of the decision boxes will be expanded, but they are still included in the numbering system. In the expanded flowcharts the start and stop points are replaced by entry and exit boxes to show that there were previous program statements and that there are more program statements still to come. All sub-flowcharts must have only one entry point and one exit point.

As an example, the car park controller will be expanded into several sub-flowcharts to illustrate the process.

Flowcharts for the car park controller. The first flowchart, see *Figure 5.6*, implements the algorithm and is similar in content and information. The next step is to produce the flowchart for the following levels. The start box of FC1.0 is expanded into FC1.1, see *Figure 5.7*, and contains the initialisation procedures. Note that there is some reference to the hardware of the system, namely the barriers, but this is maintained as general as possible. The specific details of the hardware initialisation software will be produced at a later time and in a separate module, so that the same program could easily be transferred to a different car park controller.

The first action box of FC1.0 is expanded into FC1.2 which contains an example of a repeated loop, see *Figures 5.8.* Further expansion of this flowchart is not possible as it is hardware dependent and the hardware is unknown at the moment. The next two boxes of FC1.0 are expanded into FC1.3 and FC1.4 which have a similar structure of a decision diamond and a feed forward around the conditional action to be performed, see *Figures 5.9 and 5.10.* In *Figure 5.9* it can be seen that payment will only be made if the car is leaving and the action box of extract payment will require further expansion. Similarly for *Figure 5.10,* the action box, check sufficient room and open barrier, needs to be expanded further.

The expanded flowcharts, extract payment FC1.3.2, and check room FC1.4.2, *Figures 5.11* (page 160) *and 5.12* respectively, detail the steps necessary to perform

FC 1.1 Start

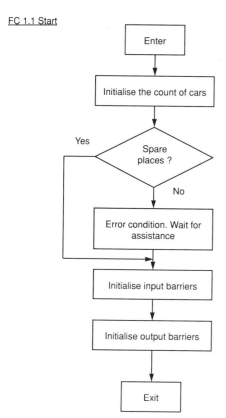

Figure 5.7 First sub-flowchart

FC 1.2 Wait

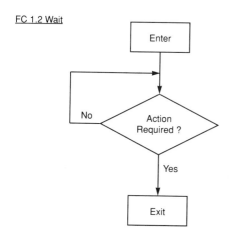

Figure 5.8 The second sub-flowchart

FC 1.3 Car leaving?

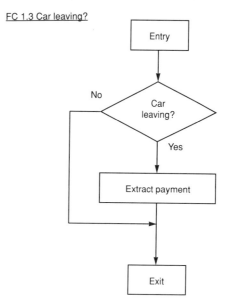

Figure 5.9 Another sub-flowchart

FC 1.4 Car entering?

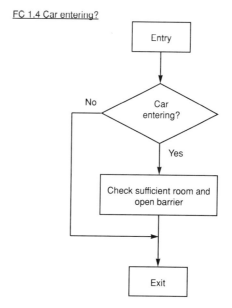

Figure 5.10 The last sub-flowchart

the specified actions. At this point in the program the real-time requirement of the program can be observed as the program must be able to allow cars to enter and leave simultaneously and not spend time waiting while the cars are entering or leaving. This is achieved by the use of the action flag which is set whenever a car is about

to enter or leave and it is not cleared until the desired action has been completed. During every loop that an action flag is set both input and output from car park are monitored until the required action is completed, at which point the action flag will be cleared. This may appear to be satisfactory but an error can be identified in

FC 1.3.2 Extract payment

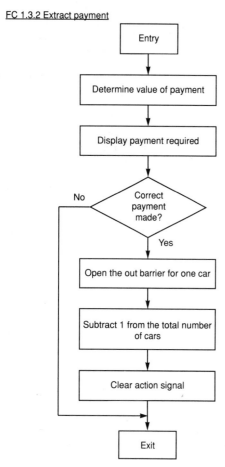

Figure 5.11   A sub-sub-flowchart

FC 1.4.2 Check room

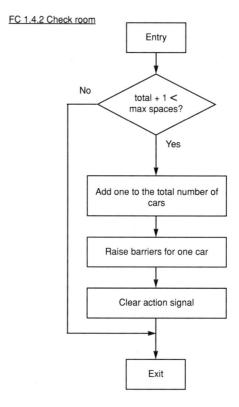

Figure 5.12   Another sub-sub-flowchart

that if a car is leaving and one is entering, whichever action terminates first will also cause the other action to terminate. This would be incorrect and a potentially disastrous error and some method of avoiding this must now be considered and introduced. The simplest solution is the use of two actions flags, one for entering and one for exiting. Now whenever a car is leaving or entering, the program will continue to loop until either the car has completely left or completely entered. This structure will also cope with the problem of a car waiting to enter when the car park is full, as the program will continue to loop until either a car leaves and there is space, or the car trying to enter goes away.

Choosing the Language

Once the solution to the problem has been developed using some symbolic structure this can now be transferred into the language selected. There are a variety of languages which have been developed for this pro-

cesses, each of which fulfils different specific needs. The simplest is machine code which converts the flowchart directly into the binary 0's and 1's that are directly executable by the microprocessor. This provides the greatest control over the hardware but the programs are extremely difficult to write and to change if a fault is discovered. A preferred alternative which is universally available for all computers, are **assembly languages** which replace the binary codes with English-like mnemonics representing the action required. These are then converted into the machine code by an **assembler**, which converts each mnemonic into a machine code. Because of this direct relationship between mnemonics and machine code, the reverse translation from machine code to mnemonics can also be performed, by a dis-assembler. Dis-assemblers are not often required as the original program source file should be available, but if this has been lost then a dis-assembler allows some of the original program text to be reproduced. Unfortunately because label names and comments are not converted into machine code these cannot be recovered and a program source file which does not contain labels or comments is difficult to understand.

The assembler uses the mnemonic instructions

contained in the source file as its input and produces a file containing only machine code as its output, called a relocatable file. Other files may also be produced which provide the programmer with additional information. The main additional file is the listing file which contains a copy of the original source file, but with additions such as the machine code produced, linked to the appropriate mnemonic instruction, the date, time and equipment used, lists of label names, locations and initial values.

Assembly languages allow a large degree of control over the hardware itself and like machine codes, are specific to each particular type of microprocessor and CPU. Because of this, the programs become hardware-specific and cannot be transferred easily to other types of computer.

As programs are expensive to write, languages which are more general purpose and independent of the hardware have been designed and these are generally known as **high level languages** (HLL). High level languages are based upon some mathematical concepts, ideas and sets of rules which are self-consistent. The following is a definition of a HLL.

> A high level programming language is a means of writing down, in formal terms, the steps that must be performed to process a given set of data in a uniquely defined way. It may bear no relation to any given computer but does assume that a computer is going to be used. [*High Level Languages for Microcomputer Projects*, Taylor and Morgan, NCC, 1980.]

The idea is to write the program in line with the restraints of the mathematical model of the language normally called the **syntax** so that an intermediate 'halfway code' is produced which cannot be executed but which is logical and simple. A second process called compiling is then applied which converts the mathematical model instructions into instructions for the microcomputer or computer being used. In this way, by simply changing the conversion program, it is possible for programs written to execute on one computer, to execute on a completely different type of computer. It is usual for modern **compilers** to contain both the syntax checker and compiler.

Compilers produce more than one machine code instruction from a single HLL instruction and may produce several tens of machine code instructions. Complex HLL instructions may produce several hundred machine code instructions. Also, compilers from different companies designed for the same language and for the same target microprocessors are likely to produce different sequences of machine code for exactly the same HLL instruction. This is due to the general purpose nature of HLL and the many ways in which the conversion process can be implemented by the compiler writer. This prevents the conversion of machine code instructions back into the original HLL so discompilers do not exist.

Table of advantages and disadvantages

Language	Advantages	Disadvantages
Machine code	Direct control of hardware.	Difficult to write. Difficult to understand. Difficult to change. No error detection.
Assembly language	English-like statements easier to understand. Some syntax checking. Easier to change. Quicker to produce.	Requires assembler. Control of hardware may be reduced slightly.
High Level	Independent of hardware. Syntax, run-time and I/O error checking increased. Quicker to write programs. More complex programs possible.	Program execution may be slower. Produces larger programs. Compiler required. Large memory and disk drives required.

Documentation

Every program that is written should be completely documented to ensure that the design is completed before program writing takes place and that the operation of the program can be understood by users who did not originally design the program. The algorithm and flowcharts provide some of that information but the majority of program information will be contained within the program source code as that is the only file which will be consistently maintained by all users and programmers. Therefore the following structure is advocated for all programs:

(a) Program header;
(b) Data definitions;
(c) Program code with explanations and subroutine/procedure headers.

Program Header

This section of the program consists purely of comments which do not contribute anything to the execution of the program itself, but provide information to the user and other programmers concerning the way it was written, executed, designed, tested, updated and what the program is designed to do. This will take the form of:

(a) Descriptive title (not Fred or Burt but a useful name);

(b) Author(s) name, title, and other relevant information;

(c) Where, when and on what equipment the program was written, and is to be executed upon;

(d) Revision updates, giving short explanations of the reasons for each new version;

(e) Program purpose;

(f) Program operation, and how it works. It is quite acceptable at this point to include the original algorithm, provided it is understandable.

Data definitions. Within the body of the program code, no explicit numbers, such as 027H, should be used, as informative names give additional information when 'reading' the program. They also enable any changes in constants, or numerical values to be easily made by only changing the definition at the beginning of the program, rather than trying to find the occurrences of say, 027H, which are relevant from those which are not, throughout the program listing.

There are four categories of data definitions that may be necessary:

(a) Global, those defined within a particular program which can be used by other programs;

(b) External, those defined in other programs, which are to be used in this particular program listing;

(c) Constants and labels which have a numeric value associated with them;

(d) Memory and I/O locations. These may be specific, such as those required for interrupt vector address, or general floating ones, such as those required for the temporary storage of arithmetic operations and should have labels associated with them.

There are two acceptable methods of defining data; the concentrated and distributed methods. With the concentrated method the data definitions for the complete program are maintained at the beginning of the program, just below the program header section. This gathers together everything into one tidy section but does have some disadvantages. Label names are not obviously associated with a particular part of a program and once changes start to be made it is easy for some labels to have no current use. This may just clutter up the program listing but if specifying memory and I/O locations, then actual memory locations may be reserved but never used. Also, once changes are made, the editing process has to swap continually between the top of the program for the data definitions and the section of the program where the data definitions are actually used. This is not a particularly efficient process and it can lead to difficulties if a large program is broken up into smaller modules. Smaller modules are best for

program production as each module can be separately developed and then linked together when correct. Any changes and updates then only require a small section of code to be re-assembled or re-compiled. For concentrated data definitions a problem occurs when a small section has 'grown' because of additions to the original program code and needs to be divided into two or more smaller modules. Deciding which data definition should go into each sub-module or sub-modules, can be difficult.

The alternative is to use distributed data definitions where all the data definitions required by each subroutine or equivalent are maintained between the subroutine header (see later) and the beginning of the subroutine program code. This reduces the problems of unused labels being undetected and of which labels are associated with which subroutine or module. However, it has the disadvantage that multiple copies of data definitions may have to be maintained so that updating can become a complex process, and some updates may be missed. With modern editors this is not so much of a problem as searches in the complete source code for similar character sequences can be made. The decision as to which technique to use is a consequence of the language and method of software design selected.

Program structure. Following the data definitions is the program code. If flowcharts have been used then it is best to implement each flowchart as a separate subroutine or procedure. This leads to 'nested' subroutines which are subroutines called from within subroutines which may contain other subroutines, and so on. **Nesting subroutines** and procedures do result in an increased program execution time due to subroutine entry and exit times. The use of nested subroutines does not contribute directly to the program operation, but for most programs the advantage of a good structure resulting in 'good' programs, outweighs the disadvantage of longer execution times.

Normally the subroutines or procedures are written in the same order as the flowcharts or pseudo-code, with the higher levels, which are more abstract, being near the top of the program code and those which are lower down in the hierarchy dealing with the details of the program execution, being near the bottom of the source code. This is not always possible with some languages such as Pascal, which require the lower levels to appear at the top of the source program and the higher levels to appear at the bottom. There is little difference between using the two methods except to ensure that the user knows which has been used when 'reading' the program source code.

Each of the subroutines can be considered to be a

mini-program requiring separate subroutine headers, data definitions (if distributed data definitions are being used) and then program code. The subroutine header need not be as comprehensive as the main program header as it is serving a different purpose. It should only contain two or possibly three sections as outlined below:

(a) Sub-routine operation description;
(b) Data passing information;
(c) Data definitions. This section may be absent if a concentrated data definition technique were adopted at the beginning of the program, see earlier.

A short description informing the reader of the operation of the subroutine is necessary, so that an assessment of its importance and usefulness can be made. It also enables the positions of any updates to be more easily identified. For example, if the data structure of a program is to be changed then the sub-routine header which contained the statement: 'sets up the data structure for the program' would be a better place to make changes than one which contained: 'interfaces with the user to display the date and time'.

To be a useful program, most of the subroutines will perform a data processing task which may be to output data only, to accept data only, or to accept and output data. Therefore the ways in which data is transferred between subroutines must be defined in the subroutine header so that any changes will not affect this process.

There are three main methods of passing data between subroutines or procedures which are dependent on the language being used:

(a) Memory locations;
(b) Registers;
(c) Stack.

If assembly languages only are being used all three techniques can be used, although passing via **the stack** would normally not be used as the other two techniques are much quicker but lead to a poor structure. If high level languages are used it is normal to pass parameters or data via the stack as this is the preferred method, being the most general purpose. However, it is possible to use all three methods from assembly language or from high level language programs.

If using memory locations then specific memory locations, normally identified by a label name, are known to the subroutine passing the information and the subroutine receiving the information and data transfer takes place via the memory location. The memory location could have a specified absolute location in the memory space although this is unusual as it can restrict the way the program is written. Alternatively, a location is allocated to a label after each assembly or compilation which is known to both processes. The data label could be global, external, local, etc., provided that both subroutines can access it.

When using registers to pass data the data is output from one subroutine in a specified CPU register and then input into another subroutine using the same register. This is a satisfactory method provided that the amount of data transferred is small as there is only a small number of registers. The specified register must not be used for anything else when it is used for transferring data and to aid the programmer to identify which registers are used by each subroutine, this information is contained in the subroutine headers, indicating which registers are used within a subroutine, their state on entry and on exit. This identifies which registers are used for data transfer and how the data is manipulated within the subroutine. This avoids the necessity of 'reading' all the subroutine program code to determine which registers can be used for data transfers and which are allocated to specific subroutines.

Data passing via the stack is an implicit technique used in high level languages although it can be used by assembly language programs as well. The stack is a continuous sequence of memory locations within the computer with a fixed bottom location, but with a variable top location called the top of stack pointed to by the stack pointer. Data is pushed, that is, transferred from a register or memory location to the top of stack memory location and the stack pointer altered to point to the next 'empty' stack memory location. When required, the stack pointer is returned to that specific location and the data popped, that is, transferred back from the indicated stack memory location to the specified register or alternative memory location. In this way data can be transferred from subroutine to subroutine without having to use specific registers or memory locations. Large amounts of data can be transferred in this way, limited only by the size of the stack, whereas the alternative techniques are not as flexible when the amount of data is large.

The Assembly Process

An **assembler** is a program which converts a file containing ASCII characters representing the mnemonics of the instructions into a different file containing the equivalent machine code representations. Several other files may also be produced at the same time.

Assembly Language

An assembly language program consists of lines of text with each line containing an instruction. The layout of each line is divided into four sections as indicated

| labels | operators | operands | comments

The order of these sections or 'fields' as they are known, cannot be changed but they can be omitted if they are not required. For example, it is not necessary to have a label on every line.

Labels. Labels are used to designate points in the program which will be referred to by operators, operands or comments at other parts of the program, before or after the defining position. Labels must begin in column 1, the first character position on the line and must start with an alphabetical character. Subsequent characters in the label can be alphabetical or numeric or some other special character. Spaces cannot be contained within a label as they are used to indicate the end of one field and the beginning of another and are called **delimiters**. Sometimes a limit is placed on the length of the labels and common maximum lengths are 6 and 8, although with modern assemblers there is effectively no limit. The minimum label length is one character. At the end of the label there is a delimiter (i.e. space) which indicates that the label has finished. Some assemblers use other characters such as a colon as a label delimiter. Below are examples of valid and invalid labels.

Valid labels	Invalid labels	Reason not valid
Here	22def:	Starts with a number
here	here	Doesn't start in the first column
D4455g:	$fit:	Starts with a non-letter character
delay5:	stop here	Contains spaces
multiply:		

Operators. Operators are used to describe symbolically the action performed by the computer at that point in the program and are specific to the microprocessor being used. Common types of operators are:

(a) Moves, from memory to memory, memory to I/O, or I/O to memory;
(b) Logical operations, i.e. Boolean;
(c) Arithmetic operations, binary and/or integer and decimal;
(d) CPU control, such as setting condition flags;
(e) Interrupts;
(f) Jumps, which change the next instruction to be executed from the following one to the one specified in the jump.

Operators are usually three characters long but can be 2, 4 or more and are an abbreviated representation of the operation to be performed. For example, for the 8086 microprocessor the following are examples of operators:

MOV	;Performs a move of data operation.
AND	;Performs the Boolean AND operation.
ADD	;Performs the binary addition operation.
INTO	;Interrupt on overflow operation.
JNZ	;Performs a jump to a different part of ;the program if the Z flag is not set.

Operands. Operands are separated from the operator by the delimiter which is again one or more space characters. Multiple spaces are used to allow the sections of each line to be aligned in the program source listing. Although alignment adds nothing to the execution of the program, it enables the user to obtain a better understanding of the text as the source program listing is clearer to read. The operands indicate the specific registers, data, memory or I/O locations that the operators are to perform on. The registers must be selected from those available for the particular operator. For example the 8086 instruction:

MOV   ax,bx

has an operator, MOV, which operates on the two operands 'ax' and 'bx'. When there are two operands as with the above example, the operator relates the right hand operand to the left hand operand. So for the example given above, the contents of the register bx, are transferred to the register ax. As the operands can be registers, data, or memory and I/O locations, a wide variety of actions can be performed with only a small selection of operators.

The Motorola assembly languages have the operands in a more logical order with the source operand being the one on the left and the destination operand the one on the right. For example:

MOV   d1,d2

transfers the contents of register d1 into register d2.

Some combinations of operations and operands are not possible as, for example, the transfer of the contents of a register to a data value; others are just not available. In addition, if the user is not familiar with the particular set of mnemonics being used it is possible to write instructions combining operators and operands which, although they assemble without errors, perform a different operation to that required. This is a particular problem if software for more than one type of microprocessor is being developed by one person, as operations possible with one microprocessor may not be possible in another, or may produce completely different results. An example of an invalid use of operands for the 8086 microprocessor is shown below:

    MOV   ax,bl

which is not valid as 'bl' represents an 8-bit register, and 'ax' a 16-bit register. This particular microprocessor does not allow movements of data between a source and destination which have different bit lengths.

Some instructions only have one operand which can be due to the operation only being applicable to one operand, such as:

    INC   ax

which increments the contents of the 'ax' register. Alternatively the second operand may be implied in the operator, such as the following instruction for the 8085 microprocessor:

    ADI   data

which adds the value represented by the label 'data' to the unspecified but implicit accumulator register. This is an implied register and is not specified in the operator or operand mnemonic.

Some assembly languages have the facility to combine three or more operands using only one operator although these tend to be for minicomputer and mainframe computer assembly languages which have complex structures. By allowing three or more operands the speed of execution is increased and the size of the program code decreased, which are important features for these particular computers. However, the complexity of the computer and hence its cost are increased.

There are two methods of accessing memory and I/O locations; direct and indirect addressing. In direct addressing the address of the memory location to be accessed is included in the instruction, while for indirect addressing which is an inherently more flexible although more complex technique, the address of the memory to be accessed is obtained using the operands rather than being directly specified. The operand acts as a pointer to the memory address or even as a pointer to a pointer, pointing to the memory location to be accessed. Depending on the microprocessor, the indirect addressing calculation can be simple or complex, using only one level of pointing or several. For example the following 8086 instruction:

    MOV   ax,word ptr value

uses the contents of the memory location indicated by the address represented by the label value, to transfer data into 'ax', rather than the memory address value itself.

Comment field. The final field of the line is the comment field which again is separated from the operands by a delimiter. The delimiter can be one or more spaces, which may or may not be terminated with a special character such as the semi-colon. Anything after the comment delimiter is information for the user explaining the operation of the program at that point. Alternatively, general comments concerning the operation of the program as a whole can be stored there. The assembler does not check any of the text after the comment delimiter, so that if necessary labels, operators and operands can be included in the text without causing any errors.

A well-commented program is essential for program maintenance and for continued understanding of the operation of the program being developed. Because of the modularity of programs and information hiding, it is easy for the programmer to forget exactly how a particular module operation was implemented. If this happens and a change has to be made, the comments contained in the program are often the only reliable indication of how the module works. Commenting a program as it is written is also the only reliable method of ensuring that comments are added. The intention expressed by any programmer to go back and add comments once the program is executing correctly, in order to save time typing comments which may later be changed or removed, is false. By the time the program is executing correctly, the programmer will have forgotten how the module operates or be more interested in the next problem to be solved.

Comments are always the last section on the line as they contribute nothing to the execution of the program. However, if some of the previous sections are absent from a line the comment start can be moved nearer to the left. Acceptable combinations are:

    | comments only |
    | label | comments
    | label | operator | comment |

Comment-only lines still require the special comment delimiter as the first non-space character on the line.

Where the operator must be one without any operands, such as below, operands are implied:

    INTO   ;interrupt on overflow

Further combinations are:

    | label | operator | operands | comments
    | | operator | comments
    | | operator | operands | comments

Labels may be absent but the label-operator delimiter must be present, usually one or more spaces.

Pseudo Operator Codes

As well as the mnemonics of the microprocessor instructions, assembly languages contain additional operators called pseudo operator codes, or pseudo op-codes. These do not directly affect program execution as they are not program instructions; instead pseudo op-codes are instructions to the assembler program itself. The following descriptions are based on Intel assembler pseudo op-codes and for different assemblers the spelling and general mnemonics may vary; however the basic operators and descriptions will be present in one form or another.

Equates.   Within an assembly program there is often the requirement to manipulate numbers, usually expressed as hexadecimal values (base 16) but sometimes in binary (base 2), octal (base 8), decimal (base 10), or as ASCII characters (bytes with values between 0 and 255 which represent the alphanumeric and special character set). To identify which particular base is being used a single letter either at the beginning or end of the number is used.

H or $ for hexadecimal.   Permissible characters from which all hexadecimal numbers are taken are the decimal numbers, 0, 1, 2, 3, 4, 5, 6, 7, 8 and 9 and the first six letters of the alphabet, A, B, C, D, E, F, representing the numbers 10, 11, 12, 13, 14 and 15 respectively. In order to differentiate between hexadecimal and labels, the first character of a hexadecimal number must be numeric and that of a label alphabetical. To ensure this it is strongly recommended that all hexadecimal numbers start with a leading 0. This is ignored when the number is assembled but serves to indicate that it is a number and is necessary because valid hexadecimal numbers starting with a letter have the same syntax as a label and cannot be distinguished. For example:-

    FFH   ;could be a label or the hex number 0FFH.

Motorola use the $ symbol at the beginning of the number rather than a H at the end, otherwise there is no difference between them.

    $0FF   ;Motorola hexadecimal number.

B for binary.   Permissible characters are the numbers 0 and 1. For example:

    0 0 1 0 1 0 1 0 0 1 B

O for octal.   Permissible characters are the numbers 0 to 7. For example: 023O.

Decimal.   If no letter is present the number is assumed to be decimal and must therefore contain no letters. For example: 2921.

ASCII.   Any ASCII characters enclosed within two single quotes are converted to hexadecimal. For example: 'ab' becomes 05152H where 051H is 'a' and 052H is 'b'. The program is more readable and understandable if all numbers are replaced with labels which give some indication of the purpose of the numeric value. It is also easier to change the value of a single label definition and consequently all its uses within a program than to find the position of every use of a particular number within a program listing. This is achieved by associating a label with a specific numeric value using the EQU pseudo op-code. A EQU operand associates the specified label with the number value but does not produce any executable code. For example:

    data: EQU   027H   ;Data label has a value of 027H.
                            ;associated to it.
    ioport: EQU   010H   ;Address of input/output port.
    initio: EQU   03H   ;Value used to initialise I/O
                            ;peripheral.

The values equated with the labels can themselves be labels or combinations of labels and simple arithmetic operations. For example:

    data: EQU   027H
    ioport: EQU   data-027H
    initio: EQU   ioport*data

All these three instructions result in valid data equates. The rule that is applied is that the labels used in equates must resolve at assembly time into a single numeric constant.

External and global.   Two of the important pseudo op-codes are EXT or external, and GLBL, or global, which enable the transfer of label addresses and values into and out of a module file. Normally the label fields for these two pseudo operators are empty as labels would serve no useful purpose. Also, each of the operators will have at least one operand and can have as many as will fit onto the line. The operands can be any valid labels defined or used within the module file.

The GLBL pseudo op-code is used to indicate labels which are defined within the module file but which will also be accessed by a different program file. The particular labels indicated in this way have a parameter associated with them, which can be a memory address or a data value. For example:

    GLBL   value

where 'value' is defined in the same program listing as:

```
value:   MOV   ax,bx   ;Save counter value
```

enables the label 'value' to be accessed by another program in a completely different file. In this example the label has an address associated with it which would not be known at the time of assembly. Only the offset from the last stated memory address or byte counter initialisation (explained later) is known. The absolute value of the address is supplied by the linker, also described later.

Alternatively the label may have a value explicitly associated with it by using EQU. For example:

```
value2:  EQU   0477FH   ;Associate a value with the
                        ;label value2.
```

To use a global definition of a label, the EXTernal operator is used in another program to indicate to the assembler that the specified label(s) are not defined within the file but that they can be used and that the appropriate associated value will be supplied at a later point by the linker. For example:

```
EXT   subr3
```

might be used in the following manner:-

```
cnz   subr3        ;If NZ flag set then call the
                   ;subroutine called subr3.
```

For the correct use of global and external labels, each label should have only one global definition, but may have one or more external definitions provided that each one is in a different file. This enables large programs to be split into smaller modules as recommended by the modular software design methodology but which still enables all of the required labels to be accessed from within any of the linked files.

Data Reservations

Within a program it is often necessary to set aside memory locations to perform certain tasks, such as counters or temporary variable stores. This can be achieved by using the data reservation pseudo-ops. These enable a byte, word, multi-byte or multi-word sequence of memory locations to be associated with labels and used as storage for variables, rather than as storage for program code.

DB and DBS. There are two data reservation pseudo op-codes available for byte or multi-byte reservations, examples of which are given below:

```
var1:  DB   00H     ;Reserves one byte, with the label var1
                    ;and the initial value 00H.
var2:  DBS  15      ;Reserves 15 bytes from the label var2
                    ;which are not initialised.
```

If the section of assembler program is destined for ROM which will not lose the data values even if the power is removed, then the initial value will be permanently saved and the label will always have that data value. Labels used in this way have two values associated with them, one is the address of the label within the program code (not known until after linking) and the second is the data value specified, in this case 00H.

Alternatively, if RWM is the destination for this particular instruction, then the initial value will only be present if the program is downloaded into the RWM every time before execution. This only occurs during the software development stages and as soon as the completed program is transferred into the micro-computer and executed the initial values will be lost. Therefore, it is recommended that any initial values must be set up during the program's initialisation sequence rather than relying on the assembler downloading initialisation. Methods of downloading programs will be considered later.

DBS enables a sequence of bytes to be reserved in memory starting at the address of the specified label but does not initialise them to a particular value. The byte locations can be accessed by adding the appropriate offset to the starting label. For example:

```
MOV   al,val2       ;Loads the contents of the byte
                    ;indicated by val2.
MOV   ah,val2+7     ;loads the contents of the 7th byte
                    ;down from val2.
```

This avoids the repetitive inclusion of instructions which only reserve one byte.

DW and DWS. DW and DWS are almost exactly the same as DB and DBS except that instead of reserving a byte or multiple bytes, DW reserves a single word of memory which is two consecutive bytes giving it an initial value and DWS reserves multiple consecutive words which are not initialised to a particular value.

Example

```
demo   DW   02727H  ;Reserves 1 word of memory (two
                    ;adjacent bytes) with the initial value
                    ;02727H.
demo2  DWS  027H    ;Reserves 39 consecutive words (027H
                    ;= 39) but does not give initial values.
```

DD and DDS. Not used as much as DB and DW reservations, DD reserves a double word, which is four consecutive bytes and allocates them an initial value. DDS reserves a number of consecutive double words without allocating any initial values. This type of data definition is useful for floating point numbers as one of the more common standards uses a 64-bit length number representation which can be accomplished by using a DD reservation.

Example

```
numb1    DD   37.34    ;The assembler converts the
                       ;floating point number into the
                       ;equivalent 64 bit represent.
many_dd  DDS  10       ;Reserves 10 consecutive double
                       ;words. (a total of 40 bytes) but
                       ;does not give them an initial value.
```

DC and DS. Motorola use slightly different pseudo operators for data reservations:

DS Define space which reserves the number of bytes specified but doesn't give them an initial value;

DC Define constant which reserves the number of bytes specified and gives them a fixed value.

Example

```
days   DC.B  7    ;Reserves one byte, with a value of 7.
hours  DS.W  1    ;Reserves one word (= 2 bytes) but
                  ;does not give them an initial value.
```

ORG. Programs residing in program memory are required to have specific starting addresses and the assembler has a method of specifying those addresses in the program using the ORG pseudo-op, short for origin. This initialises the byte counter used to allocate address offsets to labels to a specified value. Address offsets indicate the number of bytes from the beginning of the program that have been allocated to instructions or used as variable data reservations. The default value for the byte counter at the beginning of the program is zero. The ORG pseudo-op enables this to be changed to any required value, at the beginning or any position in the program. In this way programs can be written which will be placed at specific addresses and the internal operation of the program will already be suitable for those addresses. For example:

```
ORG  0100H    ;Start of the program is at 0100H in
              ;memory.
```

There can be multiple ORGs within a program listing and each time the byte counter is initialised to the specified value. If any of the blocks of program instruction addresses generated in this way overlap, the assembler will not detect it as this is considered to be the responsibility of the programmer. Overlapping program blocks corrupt the instructions in those blocks and means the program will not execute correctly.

It is recommended that ORGs are not used in structured modular programming as the modules containing ORGs are no longer relocatable. Being relocatable means that the program module can be linked into the main program starting at any address within the computer. To be relocatable the module program code must not allocate any instructions to specific memory or I/O locations. Instead, if sections of program code are to be placed at specific addresses then these sections must be placed into separate files, assembled and then linked into the correct position. If a program contains one or more ORG pseudo-ops that program will not be relocatable as the ORGs override the starting address values specified during linking.

END. The final pseudo-op of interest is the END operator. This indicates to the assembler that there are no more valid assembler instructions after the line containing the END statement. Most assemblers require an END statement to be present to indicate the last valid line, otherwise they generate an error message. It is important to remember that the END operator does not generate any executable microprocessor instructions and does not stop program execution. Instead, the computer will continue executing whatever subsequent values are contained in the program memory. These are usually of a random nature and will cause the microprocessor to perform some actions, even if they are undefined. This is often fatal to the program, causing the existing program instructions to be corrupted with undefined values, if the program is in RWM. With ROM-based program code the program instructions will not be changed but the operation of the microprocessor will be undefined.

An optional operand can be added to the END pseudo op-code which is used as the starting address for program execution. This can be different from the address at which instructions begin because the start of the program does not always occur at the first instruction. For example, the first few instructions might be data reservations and not executable instructions. Data definitions using EQU do not produce any instruction codes, so a program which only contains data definitions and no data reservations will begin execution at the first microprocessor instruction.

The use of an initial address specified by the END pseudo-op is only available if the program is to be downloaded into RWM memory. For programs which have been stored into ROM, alternative means are used to ensure that execution begins at the correct point. This may involve the use of an END statement with a specified starting address, but normally the linker is used to place the first instruction at the reset address of the microprocessor. This means that the program stored in ROM will automatically begin to execute after a reset operation. In programs consisting of several separate modules joined together by the linker, each file must have an END statement. However, only one of the files can specify a start address operand otherwise an error will be indicated by the linker.

Any statements occurring after the line containing the END statement will be ignored by the assembler and no executable code will be produced. Some assemblers do include these lines in the listing file and this may be of use occasionally if the bottom sections of a program do not require assembling. In these instances the END statement can be moved further up in the program file so that the assembled executable code is amended but the source file still contains the text of the unwanted instructions. If these statements are required at a later date, this can easily be achieved by altering the position of the END statement.

Example

An example of a program listing using the 8085 assembly language making use of most of the pseudo-operators mentioned above is given below:

```
;─────────────────────────────
;Assembler demo program
;written by Dr R C Seals
;24 July 1990
;using a Personal Computer
;version 1.0
;Updates: none so far
;─────────────────────────────

;The program operates by initialising an ioport, inputting
;values from it into an array maintained in memory.
;The algorithm is:

;(1) Initialise;
;(2) Get a value from ioport and save in array;
;(3) Repeat from (2) until the end of the array;
;(4) Stop.

forty:    equ 40        ;Number of values in array.
ioport:   equ 00H       ;Ioport address.
iodata:   equ 00H       ;Address of data port.
initio:   equ 03H       ;Value used to init io port.
counter:  db 00H        ;RWM location used as a counter.
array:    dbs forty     ;An array of 40 bytes.

start:    mvi a,initio  ;Set up ioport.
          out, ioport
          mvi a,forty   ;Set up array counter.
          sta counter
          lxi h,array   ;Set up memory ptr to array.
next:     in iodata     ;Get a value from ioport.
          mov m,a       ;Save in the array.
          inx h         ;Increment memory ptr to next.
                        ;position
          lda counter   ;Is it the last value?
          dcr a
```

```
          sta counter
          jnz next      ;No then repeat.
          hlt           ;Yes then stop executing
                        ;instructions.

          end start     ;Indicate beginning of program.
```

Symbol Table Listing

Because of the extensive use of labels within an assembly language program the assembler provides the option of producing an organised list of all the labels used within the source file, with their associated numeric value. This is called the symbol table listing. The labels are listed in alphabetical order, with EQUates having a data value, and addressable labels an offset address determined by the byte counter. GLoBal labels are indicated with an additional symbol, often the letter G, while EXTernal labels which have unknown values until after linking, are indicated by a series of question marks, ????, or similar special characters. Labelled data variables have two values associated with them; the offset address determined by the byte counter and the initial value. If the initial value is not specified the symbol table will use question marks to indicate this.

The symbol table may not appear to be of much interest to the programmer, being mainly used to check what labels are used within a program, their first occurrence, or the value of EQUates. However, if EXTernal or GLoBal labels are used then the symbol table provides the interface between the two or more different files which are to be combined into one executable object file by the linker. The linker uses the symbol tables from all the separately assembled modules to indicate where each label originates, whether it is a GLoBal or EXTernal and what its associated numeric value is. Linkers do not check the use of labels passed between files as this is considered to be the responsibility of the programmer. Because of this, it is easy to use a label defined as an address incorrectly as a data constant.

Local labels can be considered to be those in a particular file's symbol table which are not GLoBaLs or EXTernals and cannot be accessed outside of the file they are defined in. This is a simple error reduction technique designed to ensure that labels passed between files have been explicitly defined. In addition, it also allows the same label name to be used locally within different files which are going to be linked together into a single executable file, in different ways and with different numbers if desired. For large programs this is advantageous because it allows re-use of label names in different files as it becomes difficult to keep thinking of large numbers of meaningful label names.

Linkers

Programs output from assemblers are in a form called relocatable or relocatable object code files which means that the address values of labels within the files can be altered by the linker to relocate them to the desired absolute values. The linker accepts as input one or more assembled programs and outputs an executable program file called an absolute or object code file. This is necessary because the microprocessor can only execute absolute object code and not relocatable object code. Commands are input to the linker by the user indicating which relocatable object code files are to be linked together, the order in which they are to be linked, the starting address and any other special considerations to be applied.

An example of the operation of a linker is illustrated in *Figure 5.13*. The three relocatable object code files are designated by the file extension .ROC and are of different lengths. Each file has instructions starting at the address 0000H. The first instruction given to the linker is the starting address of the absolute code file which is also going to be 0000H, although any address could have been used. Following this, the order in which the .ROC files are to be linked is entered. The output from the linker is an absolute code file given the file extension .ABS, starting at the address 0000H, and ending at 05A9H. The value 05A9H is arrived at by adding together the number of bytes in the three separate .ROC files. The result of linking is that addresses within MODI.ROC have not been changed because the specified .ABS file starting address is also at 0000H but that the addresses of instructions within the last two of the files have been changed. Any EXT or GLB values will be different because the MOD3.ROC and MOD2.ROC local addresses do not start from an offset of 0000H and all address labels must have the appropriate offset added to them. This is the main operation of the linker.

Relocation of labels is achieved by the linker looking into the MOD3.ROC symbol table listing to find the relative positions of all local address labels and replacing them with the correct offsets, which can be calculated by the linker once the three files have been concatenated. Once this has been completed the same process can be repeated with the file MOD2.ROC but this time with a different starting offset address equal to the sum of files MODI.ROC and MOD3.ROC which in this example is 04A7H. The calculation of all the offsets and subsequent addition to the addresses of the local labels is called the first pass of the linker. The linker must go through every file and every symbol table to calculate and update all the local address labels. Once this has been completed the positions of the global labels can be

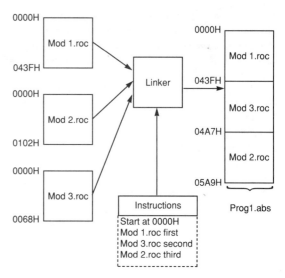

Figure 5.13 An example of linking

determined as the labels will have been given an absolute address value. Assigning absolute values to local labels is known as the second pass. When using some linkers, message outputs while the linker is operating may indicate that there has been a third pass. Three pass linkers are required if MACRO or LIBRARY facilities are allowed and these will be discussed at a later point.

During the second pass the global labels are replaced with the correct absolute address values calculated during the first pass, with the positions and values of the global labels being obtained from the symbol table listing. At the conclusion of the second pass or third pass for three-pass linkers, the linker outputs the absolute object code file containing the executable machine code. In addition, a file containing a list of the relocatable files, their absolute start address and absolute stop address can be output as an optional listing file, as can a cross-referenced listing of all the global labels used in all the relocatable files.

Example of linker operation. The three assembly files given below contain assembly language modules which are to be assembled and linked into a single executable absolute object code file.

Example

The initialise module is in a file called DEMO1.SRC.

EXT	START	;Externally defined address for ;the beginning of the main ;program.

```
GLB     BEGIN      ;Proper start address of the
                   ;program defined in this
                   ;module.
STK_TOP: EQU 02000H ;Top of stack in memory.
BEGIN:  lxi  sp,STK_TOP;Initialise stack
        JMP   START  ;and jump to start of main
                   ;program.
        END
```

Example

The subroutine module is in a file called DEM02.SRC. This demo file, contains a subroutine to count down to zero.

```
        GLB   CDOWN   ;Define CDOWN as a global
                     ;label.
COUNT:  EQU  0100H   ;Initial count value.
CDOWN:  lxi  d,COUNT ;Initialise count value.
delay:  dcx  d       ;Decrement count.
        mov  a,e     ;Is the count zero?
        ora  d
        jnz  delay   ;No, then repeat decrement.
        ret          ;Yes, then exit subroutine.
        END
```

Example

The main program module is in a file called DEM03.SRC. The demo program calls a subroutine which counts down to zero:

```
        EXT   CDOWN, BEGIN
        GLB   START    ;Label defining beginning of
                      ;main program defined as a
                      ;global label.
START:  Call  CDOWN   ;Execute the subroutine to
                      ;count down.
        hlt           ;Stop the microprocessor.
        END   BEGIN    ;Define starting point of
                      ;complete program.
```

When these three separate assembly language modules have been assembled the following symbol tables are produced:

Symbol table listing for DEM01.SRC

BEGIN   0000   G   START   ????   E   STK_TOP   2000

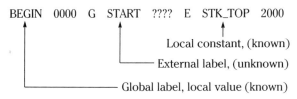

Local constant, (known)

External label, (unknown)

Global label, local value (known)

Symbol table listing for DEMO1. SRC

CDOWN   0000   G

Global label, local value (known)

Symbol table listing for file DEMO1. SRC

BEGIN   ????   E   CDOWN   ????   E   START   0000   G

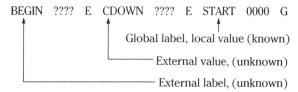

Global label, local value (known)

External value, (unknown)

External label, (unknown)

The following absolute memory positions for the three files are specified during the operation of the linker:

DEMO1 specified at 0000H
DEMO2 specified at 0100H followed by DEMO3

It is not necessary to specify the start address of DEMO3 because it follows on immediately after DEMO2. The file DEMO2 is specified to start at 0100H and leaves a considerable empty gap between the end of the file DEMO1 and the beginning of DEMO2. This is not necessary but was chosen to illustrate that each file can have its starting address specifically given, or it can default to the next available memory address as for DEMO3. The listing file output produced by the linker looks like:

Filename	Start	End	Comment
DEMO1	0000H	0005H	
DEMO2	0100H	0109H	
DEMO3	010AH	0113H	No errors

The symbol table listing looks like:

```
BEGIN    0000H
CDOWN    0100H
START    010AH
```

The starting address of DEMO3 appears directly after the end of the DEMO2 program code which in this particular example is 0109H. The linker automatically supplied this address after the end of pass 1 ready for the beginning of pass 2. The three files have only three global labels between them which have been listed out at the end of the linker listing output file.

This may not seem much of an advantage for this particular example but rather the opposite because of the extra effort involved in producing three separate files. It would have been possible to achieve the same effect using only one file, as shown below, which is a demo file only, containing a single module subroutine to count down to zero:

```
STK_TOP: EQU  02000H  ;Top of stack in memory.
         ORG  0000H   ;Initialise byte counter to
                     ;zero.
BEGIN:   lxi  sp,STK_TOP;Set up stack.
```

```
              jmp   START      ;Jump to beginning of program.
              ORG   0100H      ;Initialise byte counter 100H.
CDOWN:        lxi   d,COUNT    ;Initialise count value.
delay:        dcx   d          ;Decrement count.
              mov   a,e        ;Is the count zero?
              ora   d
              jnz   delay      ;No, then repeat decrement.
              ret              ;Yes, then exit subroutine.
START:        call  CDOWN      ;Execute the subroutine to
                               ;count down.
              hlt              ;Stop the microprocessor.
              END   START      ;Initialise program counter
                               ;to entry point.
```

However, if at a later stage it is decided to change the locations of BEGIN to 04000H and CDOWN to 06000H, then it would be necessary to re-edit and re-assemble the source file. For the modular files of DEMO1, DEMO2 and DEMO3 there would be no need to re-edit or to re-assemble, only to relink at the new specified addresses.

For these small example programs it still may not seem worthwhile to use a linker but when much longer files are used and there are many more of them, which may require some sections to be removed or others added, then it becomes much quicker and more cost effective. Once sections of program code have been written as self-contained modules with defined input and output interfaces (these were ignored for this example) and have been thoroughly tested, there is no need to rewrite them and they need only to be specified at link time. This idea of producing re-usable modules which have previously been assembled leads naturally into the concept of libraries.

Libraries

A library as used by a linker is a collection of already assembled modules which have been written to perform commonly required functions and have been saved as relocatable object codes. A special structure is used to store all of the individual relocatable object code modules as one large file rather than many small ones. These libraries may be supplied with the assembler to perform such functions as arithmetic routines and string handling routines. Alternatively they can be written by the users and incorporated into an existing or new library.

If the library concept is not used it is necessary to specify individually every module file name to be included into the final absolute code file, whereas if libraries are used only the name of the library containing the assembled modules needs to be given. In addition, only those modules specified are included in the absolute file at link time, identified from being specified as EXTernals, the rest are ignored. To achieve this the library has a 'list' of modules and when an EXTernal definition is

encountered on the first pass, the list is searched for a match. When a match is made, a copy of the relocatable assembly module is added to the absolute code file at that point. If no match is made, the linker searches through all the other specified relocatable assembly files looking for a match and only then if no match is found is an error flagged. This saves time and effort which would otherwise have been used to ensure that the correct modules were specified for each program. With libraries it is only necessary to specify the libraries which contain the modules.

To add relocatable assembly files into the library, a special process is executed which places the module name onto the library list and adds the relocatable code to the library itself. If the library becomes too large for efficient linking because there are a large number of modules which have been included in the list, unused or unwanted modules can be removed using the opposite process.

Downloading and Uploading

The absolute machine code output from the linker can be stored in the file as binary or hexadecimal values. Binary files contain directly executable machine code values and are preferred for transferring into the computer memory ready for execution. Alternatively, the binary file can be translated into a hexadecimal file which stores the absolute file as ASCII characters using a special format. ASCII characters are used so that the file can be transmitted along a standard serial communication link. A special format is necessary to ensure that both the transmitting and receiving stations know where the absolute machine code is to be placed into the computer memory. Before the absolute object file can be executed it has to be converted back to the binary file format. Transferring the hexadecimal file over a serial link and converting it into a binary file is known as downloading.

When downloading, an absolute file stored in the hexadecimal format is transmitted over a serial communication link to a **single board computer** (SBC) or equivalent. The SBC must be capable of performing two major functions; downloading programs using a monitor into RWM and then executing the program. A SBC is used to ensure that the hardware of the microcomputer will operate correctly and execute the programs. Often the SBC will have been purchased as a complete item rather than being designed and built by the user. Buying the SBC can be a cheaper alternative than a custom-designed and constructed microcomputer although its general purpose design can lead to inefficiencies and redundancy.

A portion of the RWM memory is allocated to executing programs that have been developed externally and downloaded. Sometimes this memory will be non-volatile so that when the power is removed the program code is not lost. This avoids having to download programs every time the power is connected to the SBC so that downloading only takes place when a new program is to be executed.

The *monitor* is a small program contained in non-volatile memory on the SBC which performs a small number of simple functions, similar to those listed below:

(a) Memory to memory movement of data;
(b) Changing memory contents;
(c) Viewing memory contents;
(d) Downloading and uploading.

The monitor will be able to receive absolute code files which have been converted in one of the standard formats. One of the most common is the Intel HEX format which was designed by Intel but which can be used with any microprocessor provided. The format used is as follows. The data is transmitted as lines of ASCII characters where each line can contain a maximum of 32 bytes of absolute machine code. Each byte of machine code consists of 8 bits which can be represented by the range of hexadecimal numbers between 00H and 0FFH. In the hexadecimal absolute file the data would look similar to that shown below:

Memory address	Machine code byte
02000H	000H
02001H	0F5H
02002H	048H
02003H	07BH

The beginning of each new line of ASCII code is indicated by the colon character which is followed by the number of bytes in the line, between 0 and 32. Each line is terminated by a checksum value and then a line feed and carriage return. The checksum is a simple method for identifying single errors in blocks of data transmitted over a serial communication link. It operates by adding together all the hexadecimal values in the data block and then appending the last two digits to the block as it is transmitted. This process is illustrated in the following example.

Example of checksum production. The hexadecimal absolute object file contains five bytes represented by:

000H
0F5H
048H
07BH
080H

When all these are added together, the result is 0238H. The last two digits, 38H, are now appended to the end of the hexadecimal absolute object file so that it becomes:

000H
0F5H
048H
07BH
080H
038H

If a single error now occurs in any of the first five data values as they are being transmitted it can be detected. The received data values have another checksum calculated as they are being received except that the last data value which is the previous checksum, is not included in this calculation:

001H this data value now has an error
0F5H
048H
07BH
080H
038H

The received checksum result is 0239H of which the last two digits, 039H, do not match the transmitted checksum value of 038H. Therefore at least one error, possibly more, has occurred. The use of checksum is guaranteed to detect single errors and is used because serial transmission links have a very low probability of two or more errors occurring within a small block of data, so this simple technique is all that is necessary.

There is a good probability that **multiple errors** will be detected but this cannot be guaranteed as they may cancel each other out as illustrated below:

Transmitted data	Received data	
000H	001H	error
0F5H	0F5H	
048H	048H	
07BH	07BH	
080H	07FH	error
038H	038H	

The transmitted and received checksum values are the same so the multiple error is not detected.

Each program transferred has two additional lines of information added which contain control information not executable instructions. The first line added at the very beginning indicates the position in RWM the program is to start at. The second line which is at the very end contains a more sophisticated error check for the entire file. There are various error checking codes available, one of the most common being the **cyclic redundancy check,** (CRC).

The system which is transmitting the file obtains the starting position and the length of the program from the absolute program code file produced by the linker. The formatter uses these two pieces of information and the checksums generated to construct the complete HEX file. Each of the bytes of program code can be represented as hexadecimal numbers between 00H and FFH which are then converted into two ASCII characters. For example 00110100, which is 52 in decimal, becomes 034H in hexadecimal which in turn becomes the characters '3' and '4' as leading zeros are ignored and the H is not transmitted. The absolute hexadecimal code file for the earlier examples of linker operation is as follows:

```
:2354345345
:12423434534534545645645645645646
:2332
```

The monitor program will decode the characters as they arrive with the initial line being used to initialise a memory pointer to the memory location specified as the beginning of the program. All the line start and finish characters are ignored as they are only used to separate the program into lines of text for transmission. The pairs of ASCII characters representing the hexadecimal data are converted into a single binary byte of data and placed into the memory location indicated by the memory pointer. The memory pointer is then incremented to be ready for the next byte and the checksum calculated. This process continues until the last line of data is received which is the transmitted checksum and this is compared with the generated check sum. If the two check sums are the same then the program is considered to have been transmitted without any errors. If there has been an error the SBC will indicate this on the user interface connected, which might be a VDU, some simple 7-segment LED's, or some lights. In addition, a message may be returned to the transmitting system to indicate that there was an error in transmission. If the transmitting and receiving systems have been programmed to implement it, subsequent attempts may be made to re-transmit the absolute program code file as an ASCII HEX file again. If a second attempt fails this would indicate to the user that the communication link is faulty at some point and further attempts to download would be pointless. Assuming the download-

ing is error free the monitor could be used to begin execution of the downloaded program.

The reverse operation of transferring files from the SBC to the computer can also be performed, although this is not used as much due to the difficulty of developing programs on a SBC. However, if the SBC was executing a program which gathered data requiring further processing then this could be uploaded to transfer the binary data from the SBC RAM into an absolute program code file on the development system.

Testing Programs

The final part of the software development process is the testing and debugging section which ensures that the program performs the functions defined by the specification and is free of all detectable errors. Most programmers would recognise that for any program larger than a few hundred lines, it is extremely difficult, perhaps even impossible, to eliminate all possible errors. Instead the aim is to eliminate as many errors as can be detected and then during the lifetime of the program, as more errors are detected, they are eliminated and updated versions of the program issued.

A more detailed explanation of the testing and debugging of programs is contained within Chapter 6 which deals with debugging, simulators and emulators.

5.3 DEVELOPMENT SYSTEMS

So far only the functions of software development have been discussed not the methods of performing them. Most of the functions are based upon computers or computer-controlled interfaces and hardware. The systems used to produce the software are called 'development systems' as they develop the software and the hardware. There are three main types available:

(a) Mainframe environments;
(b) Dedicated systems;
(c) Personal computer add-ons.

Mainframe Environments

Mainframe computers are essentially multi-user time-shared computers and tend only to be used for the development of software, as it is difficult to attach target system hardware. The range of functions that are available are:

(a) Editing of source files;
(b) Compiling of source files into relocatable files;

(c) The linking of relocatable files and library files to produce HEX files;

(d) Loading the HEX files into a simulator.

If the mainframe system does have connections for downloading the developed HEX files, then suitable target hardware is required. This could be a SBC with a monitor or a personal computer used as a dedicated development system.

Although it is possible to download from the mainframe to the target system it is not easy to transfer information back to the mainframe system. This may seem to indicate that mainframe development systems have a serious disadvantage. However, mainframe development systems have the significant advantage of providing simultaneous multi-user access to program development facilities. The program development activities available are of a high standard and usefulness and are particularly suited for the development of high level language programs. This is because HLLs are designed to be as independent of the target system hardware as possible and only to use general purpose I/O channels. Only the I/O channels need to be designed specifically for each different target system hardware arrangement and the programmer can be confident that the program will execute correctly.

Pascal is such a language and only requires the target hardware to provide:

(a) A continuous block of RWM of sufficient length to contain the program and the dynamic variables generated as the program is executing;

(b) The implementation of a file access interface;

(c) An interface to input and output ASCII characters to a VDU, often available as a specialised variation of the standard file interface of (b).

Apart from these three basic requirements, Pascal programs will execute correctly on any target hardware for which there is a compiler and often the development system being used will contain compilers for several different microprocessors. This type of compiler is termed a **cross-compiler** as it can generate absolute files for microprocessors other than the host computer.

The mainframe environment is ideal for Pascal program development as there is essentially an unlimited amount of RWM available for each user and the file interfaces are sophisticated with many fail-safe characteristics. For example, automatic backup copies of all files are made which can be retrieved if the original is corrupted. The number and size of files is essentially unlimited and there are achieving facilities for permanently saving files. For large numbers of users such as in a teaching environment, limitations on the amount of

RWM available to each user and the number and size of files may be enforced to obtain the efficient use of resources.

Pascal programs developed on the mainframe use the standard I/O file interfaces and when transferred to the target hardware some problems may arise as the compilers for specific microprocessors may not implement the same file interfaces in the same way. This is because the file interface is dependent on the actual hardware components of the target system being used and these may vary from system to system. The sections of the file interface which have not been implemented must then be supplied by the user and this can lead to the introduction of non-standard Pascal I/O interfaces, optimised for a particular configuration of hardware, or which make use of a variation in the standard Pascal syntax to include extra useful facilities.

Such customisations are satisfactory for the original target hardware but problems occur when attempting to transfer the program onto a different hardware configuration, or more importantly, using a different Pascal compiler for a different microprocessor. The inability to re-use existing programs without re-writing them leads to a higher product cost with a lower quality and reliability. It was to avoid such problems that languages like Pascal were developed and the use of non-standard file interfaces for these languages negates their advantages.

Once the program has been written and if possible verified on the mainframe environment, it can be transferred either to the target hardware using a download protocol such as **Kermit**, or loaded into a simulator. The operation of a simulator is described in the next chapter.

When downloading from a mainframe to a target system a **transfer protocol**, which provides additional facilities and error checking and correction options to those available from simple checksum tests, becomes desirable. This is because program files are often of considerable size, several thousand or even several hundreds of thousands of bytes. The communication links between mainframes and the user's terminal have error rates which lead to corruption of such large downloaded program files. The large size of programs means that it is preferable to transfer files to an intelligent terminal, such as a personal computer (PC) with terminal emulation, using a transfer protocol. The program can then be transferred from the PC to the target using an ordinary simple serial communication link without using a sophisticated transfer protocol. This is because the communication links between the mainframe and the user's terminal are more likely to corrupt data values due to electrical interface than communication links between the terminal and target. This is mainly due to the distances involved as the probability of the communication link containing errors is proportional to the distance between the transmitting and receiving points. The mainframe to terminal link can be from several hundred metres if in the same building, to many thousands of kilometres if situated in a different country. The normal distance between the terminal and the target hardware is less than 2 metres.

The downloading process is complex and requires a method of starting the transmission process, detecting the termination point and implementing some method of handshaking to ensure that the data has been transmitted and received correctly. Handshaking is necessary because other symbols which might be used to indicate the end of a file are valid data values. This can lead to difficulties in terminating the transfer and return control of the communication link to the user's VDU and mainframe.

The Kermit protocol provides the necessary encoding, transmitting, handshaking, error detection and correction operations to transfer files successfully. The operation of Kermit is virtually invisible to the user but does require complete control of the terminal. The user can no longer use the terminal to access the mainframe while the transfer protocol is operating and this has the disadvantage that if the transfer is halted for some reason it can be difficult to regain control of the terminal. However, this does not happen often.

The essential functions of a transfer protocol are that the file being transmitted is split into packets of data, for example 255 bytes long, plus additional codes designed to detect any errors that occur in the transmission process. The individual packets are transmitted one at a time with the receiver checking each packet as it is received for errors. At the end of each packet the receiver sends a message back to the transmitter and if an error is detected, the message returned to the transmitter indicates this. If an error is detected the transmitter will re-transmit the packet. If the re-transmitted packet still contains errors this process is repeated a specified number of times, after which the transmission of the rest of the file is aborted as the communication link is considered to be too unreliable. If there are no errors the transmitter sends the next packet and this is repeated until the end of the file is reached. Then the protocol sends a special message indicating the end of the file has occurred and the transmission process terminates, returning control of the terminal to the user.

Once the program file has been transferred, either to the mainframe-based simulator or to the target hardware, the verification of the program continues using the appropriate methods, as outlined later.

If the program is developed in assembler language the mainframe environment does not offer many advantages, other than providing a simultaneous multi-user environment. Programs can be produced using the same editor and then passed to an assembler and linker. Assembler program operation cannot be verified in the same way as for HLLs unless verified in the mainframe environment, through the use of a simulator.

Dedicated Development Systems

Because mainframes are used to perform many tasks other than producing embedded systems software and the hardware costs of a mainframe are large, an alternative is to use a system which has been especially designed for the purpose of software and hardware development. Such systems are termed dedicated development systems and generally provide only single-user environments. The editor, compilers, assemblers, linkers and emulators are available to the user as for the mainframe environment but only one of them can be in use at any one time.

It is unusual to provide dedicated development systems with a simulator as they already have emulators. **Emulators** are superior to simulators as they allow extensive I/O operations to be performed and assuming the target hardware is available, enable real-time operation and verification of the software and hardware combination. The verifications obtained using an emulator are considerably more reliable than those obtained with a simulator so there is no advantage in supplying a dedicated development system with a simulator.

Some dedicated development systems do allow additional work stations to be linked together via a communications network to form a simple **local area network** (LAN), so that some resources can be shared. The most common shared resources are printers, PROM programmers, and permanent file storage in the form of a hard disk drive. If a hard disk system is being used then the system software used by the development system is maintained on it and this enables the same version of the operating system software to be used by all users. This prevents the possibility of some users operating with outdated and possibly incompatible software development facilities.

The terminals of dedicated development systems are referred to as **work stations** as they are able to perform all the software development processes, such as compiling, assembling, linking, and emulation, independently of the rest of the LAN. The only requirement they have is to be able to access the hard disk to obtain copies of the appropriate programs, such as compilers. The work station contains a computer with sufficient RWM, ROM and I/O functions to execute the software development process. In addition, an emulator, logic analyser and PROM programmer will be available to perform hardware and combined hardware/software verification, see *Figure 5.14*. Generally a work station will be expandable and adaptable by the addition of new printed circuit boards to perform new functions.

The ability to change the printed circuit boards extends the useful life of the dedicated development system which is important as one of the disadvantages of this type of software development system is that it is aimed at specific types of microprocessors. The useful life of dedicated development systems can be extended by making the basic chassis as general purpose as possible and then installing suitable additions to perform the required functions. Such a work station will contain a SBC with a monitor, a memory board, an emulator board and a logic analyser board. In addition some of the work stations may contain a PROM

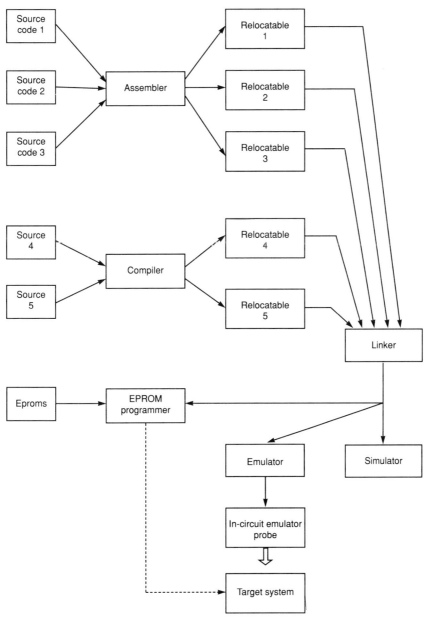

Figure 5.14 A development system structure

programmer for permanently storing programs in ROM and floppy disk drives for local storage of files. This helps to prevent the work station from becoming obsolete when new microprocessors become available.

Personal Computer Add-Ons

The third type of development system which can be used to overcome the problems of dedicated work stations is to use a general purpose computer such as a personal computer (PC), with some additional software and hardware. The software performs some of the development functions and the hardware performs the remainder connected to the PC via a standard communicaiton link such as a RS232C link.

The editing, compilation, assembly and linking are performed as software functions on a computer and operate in a very similar manner to those on the mainframe environment. Like the dedicated development work stations only one person can be using it at a time but the cost per user is much lower, because the PC is a more general purpose and hence cheaper computer. The compilation, assembling and linking can take longer than for mainframe and dedicated work station environments although if the mainframe has large numbers of terminals active its response time is considerably degraded and the PC may then be faster. With a PC the response time is constant as it is with dedicated work stations, but for mainframes the response time increases as the number of terminals in use increases.

The hardware interface added to the PC performs the emulation and logic analysis functions and is generally specific to a particular microprocessor. The basic operation of the emulator and logic analyser remain the same, such as single step, memory and register display and alteration, but some of the more sophisticated enhancements available on dedicated work stations, such as real-time tracing of program execution may be absent. This is due to the requirement to pass all information via the communication link and the simplicity of the hardware interface. The simplicity is necessary to lower the cost in order to compete with the dedicated work stations. However, a PC with an emulator and logic analyser add-on provides almost the same facilities as dedicated work stations, but at a much lower cost per user. In addition, the PC can be made available to perform other general purpose computer tasks when not being used as a development system.

Summary

If a mainframe environment is available as well as dedicated work stations or PCs with add-on interfaces, then utilisation of the available systems can be optimised. The mainframe environment provides multi-user access with good support for HLLs but only minimal support for assembly languages. The dedicated work stations and PCs with add-ons provide good HLL and assembly language development support, plus hardware development support but for a much more limited number of users. Therefore, where possible, programs should be written, developed and verified on the mainframe environment using a simulator and then downloaded via Kermit into the work stations or PCs. The program is then recompiled and/or re-assembled, re-linked and emulated on the target hardware, knowing that the operation of the program has already been verified. Only real-time verification whilst executing on the target hardware system remains and this is performed much more quickly than for programs that have been developed entirely on the PC. This enables the maximum use to made of all the existing systems and increases programmer productivity.

SIX

Program Testing

6.1 SINGLE STEP TESTING

When a program has been developed into the absolute program code file the process of design continues by testing the program to ensure that it performs correctly. If a structured modular top-down approach has been used the number of errors in the program structure will already have been minimised. Therefore any errors remaining within the program will probably be due to two factors: either the initial program specification was incorrect and the program can never perform correctly, or not all the input data conditions have been correctly dealt with. To validate the operation of the program a process of testing is necessary and there are several basic functions required of a system used to test software, which are listed below:

(a) The ability to detect when memory is accessed outside of the specified areas;
(b) The ability to single step through the program one instruction at a time, observing the contents of the registers;
(c) Tracing the contents of the registers when the program executes a section of code continuously which is necessary to detect faults in the program which only become apparent when the program is executing;
(d) To be able to execute sections of program code, starting and stopping at specified locations.

There are three systems capable of performing these tests which are a combination of special-purpose hardware and software. These are:

(1) Testing using the **monitor** on a **single board computer** (SBC);
(2) Testing using a **simulator**;
(3) Testing using an **emulator**.

Monitors

The SBC monitor, which enables the program produced by the linker to be downloaded into the SBC, also contains facilities to perform some verification operations during program execution. One of the functions of the SBC that can be of assistance is the **single step instruction** operation. Depending on the sophistication and complexity of the monitor, single stepping can be achieved either through software alone, as with the 8086, or through a combination of hardware and software, like the 8085. If single stepping is hardware controlled a suitable pulse is generated for every instruction to be executed, often produced by a special switch on the SBC or in some cases under the control of an I/O port signal.

A single step facility enables the program under test to be executed under the supervisory control of the monitor, one computer instruction at a time. After each instruction the monitor can be used to display the microprocessor registers and the contents of memory, so that the effect of the computer instructions can be observed in detail. This type of verification is best suited to assembly language programs because of their direct connection between a program instruction and a machine code binary instruction. For compiled languages which produce several assembler level instructions for every HLL instruction, single stepping through the assembler language program is not as useful.

An example where single stepping would be useful would be for a subroutine which added two numbers together that occasionally produced incorrect answers where the fault was that the carry bit was being ignored. By using the single step facility and observing the contents of all the microprocessor registers, it would be possible to identify this fault. The subroutine would then be re-written to correct this error, re-assembled, re-linked and re-downloaded. It would also be prudent to check that the alteration had in fact corrected the error by single stepping through the subroutine again.

The ability to check if memory locations which are outside of the specified ranges are accessed, is not included in SBCs as this would increase the complexity considerably.

Executing sections of the program code is possible on SBCs by the use of breakpoints provided that the program code is stored in RWM memory. Any subroutines contained in the SBC ROM memory area cannot be monitored using breakpoints as the process depends on replacing selected program instructions with alternative instructions which cause program execution to be stopped and control returned to the monitor. This can only be achieved if the program is in RWM. They are known as breakpoints as the execution of the program is 'broken' at the specified address. For the breakpoint to operate, the section of program code containing the breakpoint must be executed. To allow sections of program code containing conditional jumps to be tested in this way the monitor will normally be able to set at least three breakpoints at any one time. Once a breakpoint has been reached, control is returned to the monitor. At this point some monitors replace the breakpoints with the original instruction codes so that if the same section of program is to be tested in the same way again, the breakpoints must be reset. Once in the monitor, the states of the microprocessor registers and memory contents at the point the program was stopped, can be examined for errors.

If an error has been identified in the program and a solution proposed, an alteration to the program must be made. Sometimes it is possible just to change a few byte values using the monitor. For example, if the wrong initialisation values were used, these could be changed by using the monitor to access and change RWM memory contents. ROM memory contents cannot be changed in this way. It may also be possible to 'splice in' additional sections of program code by jumping to an unused RWM area, inserting the machine code instructions required, either by hand assembly or using a line assembler if the monitor contains one, and then jumping back to the original instruction. This is not recommended as a permanent solution as it leads to bad programs but is acceptable as a quick way of testing if a proposed alteration will solve a problem. If successful it would be necessary to change the original program and re-assemble. Program code which abruptly jumps about in memory is indicative of incorrect structuring. In addition, hand 'splices' would result in the code being executed being different from the assembly source file, making further changes difficult to make.

The best solution is to return to the editor, update the source code file, re-assemble, re-link and re-download, as illustrated in *Figure 6.1*. This process enables the source file to be kept as close as possible to the program executing. This is also one of the reasons why modular code is preferred, as once a module has been debugged there is no need to keep re-assembling it. Small modules are preferred as the program assembly time is approximately proportional to the number of lines of assembly source text.

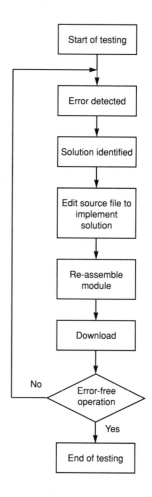

Figure 6.1   Correcting an error

If the assembling, linking, and downloading procedure is long or complex, is taking longer than 2 or 3 minutes and requiring more than 10 keystrokes, the programmer will start to use splices and hand assembly techniques to obtain a higher productivity and avoid long periods spent just waiting for updates to be processed. This should be avoided if at all possible.

Debuggers

If a computer complete with an operating system is being used, it is unlikely that a monitor will be built-in. However, many of the same facilities can be obtained through a software-only solution using a debugger. The name has little significance other than to distinguish it from monitors, emulators and simulators, as all of the techniques are designed to enable software and hardware combinations to be debugged. A bug is a jargon word used to describe a fault in a computer program and is often applied to hardware and hardware/software fault combinations as well. Debugging is then the process of identifying and correcting the fault so that the bug is removed. A debugger operates like any other program executed on a computer; when specified it is transferred from secondary mass storage into the computer main memory by the operating system and executed.

Basic debugger (and monitor) functions. There are thirteen basic functions required of debuggers and these are similar to those offered by the monitor. Most debuggers will provide all of them and probably several additional ones;

(1) Display and alteration of memory contents;
(2) Display and alteration of microprocessor registers;
(3) Display of blocks of memory contents;
(4) Execution of a program from the specified address;
(5) Single stepping (only possible with microprocessors which have this as a built-in feature, such as the 8086);
(6) Break point setting;
(7) Tracing program execution, either by recording register contents, memory contents or both;
(8) Copying contents of blocks of memory from one starting position to another;
(9) Filling a block of memory contents with the specified value (byte or word);

(10) Line assembler;
(11) Line disassembler;
(12) Loading a program (downloading);
(13) Saving a program (uploading).

With debuggers, the user is able to view the operation of the program at a low level, almost at machine code level.

Display and Alteration of Memory/ Register Contents

Often when testing programs there is a requirement to test the boundary conditions of part of the program. For example, a loop which will execute 100 times only really needs testing on the first loop, the last loop and somewhere in between. This could be achieved by executing the loop 100 times and testing the results of each one but this is time consuming. Alternatively, the program could be re-assembled, re-linked and executed with the loop counter at different values, say 100, 50 and 1, but again this is time consuming. A quicker solution is to use the memory alteration function to change the loop counter to the required value. The command operates by displaying the present contents of the specified memory location, with the options of leaving the value unchanged or of entering a new value which is then stored in the specified memory location.

If the loop counters are stored in one of the microprocessor registers then the register display and alteration command can be used; this allows the contents of any of the microprocessor registers to be displayed and altered if necessary.

Displaying/altering memory blocks. A common requirement during program testing is to display a block of memory, usually as data values rather than as disassembled instructions. It can be used to assess how the

```
-
-
-
-d 0:500
0000:0500  00 00 4D 42 00 00 20 20-43 4F 4D 27 00 00 00 00   ..MB..  COM'....
0000:0510  00 00 00 00 00 00 00 60-1A 11 02 00 20 5F 00 00   ....... .... _..
0000:0520  49 42 DF 02 25 02 12 1B-FF 54 F6 01 08 00 00 00   IB..%....T......
0000:0530  00 00 00 00 00 00 00 00-1A 11 08 00 B0 75 00 00   .............u..
0000:0540  43 4F 4D 4D 41 4E 44 20-43 4F 4D 20 00 00 00 00   COMMAND COM ....
0000:0550  00 00 00 00 00 00 00 60-1A 11 10 00 DC 62 00 00   ....... .....b..
0000:0560  44 4F 53 20 20 20 20 20-20 20 10 00 00 00 00 00   DOS      .....
0000:0570  00 00 00 00 00 00 62 96-58 12 17 00 00 00 00 00   ......b.X.......
-
-
-
```

Figure 6.2   A memory dump

program is transforming a specific set of data values into the new values. The display is usually in two formats, the left hand side displaying the memory contents as hexadecimal values and the right hand side displaying the same block as the equivalent ASCII characters, as illustrated in *Figure 6.2* (previous page). This makes it easier to identify text strings using the right hand side and specific numeric sequences using the left hand side.

In addition to displaying a block of memory contents, it is useful to be able to copy a block of memory contents from one location to another, particularly if the program being tested contains a block move sequence and there is a requirement to test it several times to verify its operation. If a block move command is not available, the only alternative is to keep re-loading the program, which is time consuming. Finally, a block fill command is useful as it allows the user to identify which memory locations a program is using. For example, by filling what is to be used as the stack block with zeros and then executing the program, the amount of the stack actually used can be determined, as illustrated in *Figure 6.3*.

Program Execution

In a debugger, sections of the software are tested by specifying the start memory address of the first instruction and the stop address. One method of achieving this is by using the alter register command to change the program counter (or instruction pointer) of the microprocessor to the desired value and then issuing a go command. Usually however, the go command allows one or more parameters to be specified, the first one being the start address and the second and third being stop addresses as illustrated below:

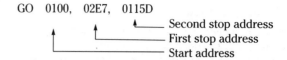

Two or more stop addresses are needed when testing conditional statements which branch to one of two or more different memory addresses depending upon the result of the test.

Temporary breakpoints used with commands such as GO operate in the same way as breakpoints except that they are automatically removed whenever any one of them is reached. Semi-permanent breakpoints can be inserted by using the breakpoint function which leaves the breakpoint in place even after it has been reached. Semi-permanent breakpoints can be removed using the breakpoint delete function. Temporary breakpoints are useful for tracking down a problem in a program by allowing consecutive sections of the program to be executed using the GO command without having to delete the breakpoints every time. Once the faulty section of program has been identified, a semi-permanent breakpoint can be inserted to allow the section of program to be repeatedly executed while the problem is being investigated. Once the fault is rectified the breakpoint can be removed.

Tracing

Sometimes it is necessary to compare the operation of a program at two different points, or with two different sets of input data. This is difficult to achieve using the debugger in real-time. Instead, the debugger has the ability to trace the operation of a program by saving the

```
-
-
-
-d 300
165E:0300  27 00 31 01 35 01 36 01-36 01 39 01 0E FF 36 01    '.1.5.6.6.9...6.
165E:0310  0A FF 28 00 00 FF 00 00-00 00 00 00 00 00 00 00    ..(.............
165E:0320  00 00 00 00 00 00 00 00-00 00 00 00 00 00 00 00    ................
165E:0330  00 00 00 00 00 00 00 00-00 00 00 00 00 00 00 00    ................
165E:0340  00 00 00 00 00 00 00 00-00 00 00 00 00 00 00 00    ................
165E:0350  00 00 00 00 00 00 00 00-00 00 00 00 00 00 00 00    ................
165E:0360  00 00 00 00 00 00 00 00-00 00 00 00 00 00 00 00    ................
165E:0370  00 00 00 00 00 00 00 00-00 00 00 00 00 00 00 00    ................
-
-
-
-
-
```

Figure 6.3   A stack block filled with zeros and then the program executed

```
-
-
-
-t=0 4

AX=0000  BX=0000  CX=0023  DX=0000  SP=0000  BP=0000  SI=0000  DI=0000
DS=167A  ES=167A  SS=168A  CS=168B  IP=0006   NV UP EI PL NZ NA PO NC
168B:0006 81260200FF7F  AND      WORD PTR [0002],7FFF                DS:0002=2000

AX=0000  BX=0000  CX=0023  DX=0000  SP=0000  BP=0000  SI=0000  DI=0000
DS=167A  ES=167A  SS=168A  CS=168B  IP=000C   NV UP EI PL NZ NA PE NC
168B:000C A10200        MOV      AX,[0002]                          DS:0002=2000

AX=2000  BX=0000  CX=0023  DX=0000  SP=0000  BP=0000  SI=0000  DI=0000
DS=167A  ES=167A  SS=168A  CS=168B  IP=000F   NV UP EI PL NZ NA PE NC
168B:000F 01060000      ADD      [0000],AX                          DS:0000=60CD

AX=2000  BX=0000  CX=0023  DX=0000  SP=0000  BP=0000  SI=0000  DI=0000
DS=167A  ES=167A  SS=168A  CS=168B  IP=0013   OV UP EI NG NZ NA PO NC
168B:0013 0000          ADD      [BX+SI],AL                         DS:0000=CD
```

Figure 6.4   Trace listing

contents of registers and specified memory locations after each instruction, in a file for future reference. This is only possible if the microprocessor has the ability to single step under software control. *Figure 6.4* shows a trace listing of part of a program execution. The traces from different parts of the program or with two different sets of input data can then be compared using printouts.

Assembler and Disassembler

In order to be able to make sense of the machine code program during the debugging process, a **line disassembler** is used to convert the machine code back into assembler mnemonics. The line disassembler cannot re-assemble labels so absolute addresses and values are produced. The user must then have a listing of the disassembled program nearby in order to follow program operation. *Figures 6.5 and 6.6* illustrate the difference between a disassembled program listing and the original program.

The line assembler is used to avoid the need to re-assemble, re-link and then re-enter the debugger, to test the effectiveness of minor changes. It operates by converting the microprocessor mnemonic instructions typed in a line at a time, into the equivalent machine code program. Labels cannot be used and all memory

```
;test file demonstrating CISC philosophy
;
;ORs msb of two numbers and then adds them together.
data_seg         segment
mem1    dw       01020h
mem2    dw       01042h
mem3    dw       0000h
data_seg         ends
;
code_seg         segment
                 assume  cs:code_seg,ds:data_seg
start:  and      word ptr mem1,07fffh
        and      word ptr mem2,07fffh
        mov      ax,word ptr mem2
        add      word ptr mem1,ax
code_seg         ends
        end      start
```

Figure 6.5   Assembly language program

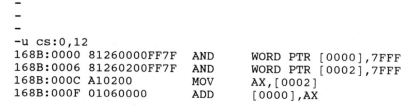

```
-
-
-
-
-u cs:0,12
168B:0000 81260000FF7F   AND    WORD PTR [0000],7FFF
168B:0006 81260200FF7F   AND    WORD PTR [0002],7FFF
168B:000C A10200         MOV    AX,[0002]
168B:000F 01060000       ADD    [0000],AX
```

Figure 6.6 Disassembled assembly language program

addresses and data values must be absolute hexadecimal values. Any changes made using the line assembler are not automatically made in the original source program listing and the user must return to the editor to update the listing, re-assemble and re-link, once the alteration has been shown to be satisfactory. Making permanent changes to the machine code version of a program using a debugger and not to the original source program is extremely poor programming style as it renders that program completely unmaintainable, as no one will have an accurate record of the program listing or its operation.

Downloading and Uploading

Transferring a copy of the program from secondary mass storage to the main computer memory is called downloading. If the reverse is possible, where blocks of memory contents are transferred from main computer memory to secondary mass storage, it is called uploading. Uploading is useful if a temporary halt to a debugging session is made as it allows a permanent copy of the partially debugged program to be made, so that it can be returned to at a later time. However, this is not the best solution as the user may forget some of the changes that have been made and it would be better to make the required changes to the original program before ending the debugging session.

The following is a brief outline of the main commands available to the DEBUG program supplied with MS-DOS.

DEBUG command	Operation
A aaaa	Start line assembler and store machine code starting at the address aaaa.
D ssss, ffff	Display the contents of the block of memory starting at the address ssss and finishing at ffff.
E aaaa, dd	Enter the data value dd into the memory at address aaaa.

DEBUG command	Operation
F ssss, ffff, dd	Fill the block of memory starting at the address ssss and finishing at the address ffff, with the data value dd.
G aaaa, bbbb	Go to the memory address aaaa and start executing the instructions there, until the breakpoint at address bbbb is reached (or the end of the program). Note: multiple, breakpoint addresses up to 10 can be added, separated by commas.
L aaaa, filename	Load the file called 'filename' from secondary mass storage into main memory starting at the memory address aaaa.
M ssss, ffff, nnnn	Move the block of memory contents starting at address ssss and finishing at the address ffff, to the new block of memory starting at address nnnn.
Q	Quit the debug program and return to MS-DOS.
R rr	The contents of the register called rr are displayed and may be altered.
T aaaa, nn	Traces the execution of the instructions starting at the memory address aaaa for nn instructions.
U ssss, ffff	Unassemble the machine instructions starting at memory address ssss and finishing at ffff.
W aaaa, bb	Write (or upload) the contents of the block of memory starting at address aaaa and of size bb to the default (but specified) file name.

This particular debugging program is now quite old. It is considered part of the operating system software and is supplied with most PCs. It does not have a very good or friendly user interface. It is also relatively unsophisticated and should not really be used with the more advanced versions of the 8086, such as the 80386 and 80486. However, it does have a major advantage that whenever there is a PC executing the MS-DOS operating system, a copy of DEBUG is usually available.

Much more sophisticated and user-friendly debuggers are available now, particularly for use with HLL where debugging at machine code level is not at all easy.

HLL Debuggers

HLL debuggers have all the features of a LLL debugger such as DEBUG plus much more. The user interface is more user-friendly, relying on windows and menus during command selection, rather than on command line execution of terse statements. It is also possible to single step individual HLL statements rather than the many individual machine code instructions that they produce and this simplifies the debugging process. HLL debuggers also allow a mixture of debugging to be taking place with LLL instructions (assembler) being debugged in one place and HLL instructions (compiled) in another.

The main additional functions provided by a HLL debugger over those of a LLL debugger are listed below:

Tracing. Execute programs one HLL statement at a time, with the option of stepping over procedures or functions. Stepping over means that the procedure or function is executed completely, without single stepping. This speeds up debugging considerably when single stepping.

Viewing. Viewing allows specified variables to be displayed on the screen and this can also be applied to many other activities to view the stack, data files, memory, registers and so on.

Inspecting. Similar to viewing but allows the values of complex data structures to be inspected, without having to use special techniques.

Changing. Allows named variables in a program to be changed without having to identify its memory address.

Watching. Similar to viewing except that it allows the contents of variables to be watched in real-time as the program is executing.

In addition, a sophisticated debugger will be integrated with the editor, compiler and linker to create an **integrated programming support environment** (IPSE). These enable the HLL program to be altered from within the debugger and then automatically recompiled, re-linked, downloaded and executed to the same point. This enables fixes to be made to a faulty program using the debugger to be automatically reflected in the original HLL source code program listing.

6.2 EMULATORS

The preferred solution to the software debug phase of program development is to use an **in-circuit emulator**, (ICE). This consists of a probe which is used to replace the microprocessor in the SBC, see *Figure 6.7*. The probe is connected to an interface which simulates the electrical characteristics of the microprocessor but which is under the control of a separate computer. When executing a program the emulator provides a means of directly monitoring the operation of the (emulated) microprocessor registers and memory without having to use any hardware or software located on the SBC. This allows a much wider range of SBCs to be used for program development as monitor programs are not required.

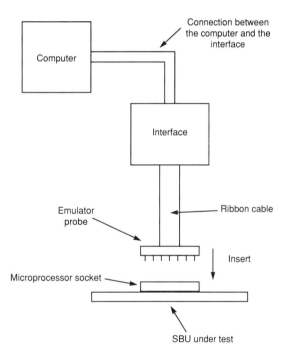

Figure 6.7 An in-circuit emulator (ICE)

Because the microprocessor electrical characteristics are emulated by the ICE probe, the memory address ranges accessed and the types of memory, ROM, RWM, and invalid, can be specified from the computer controlling the emulator. The emulator can access all the memory contained on the target SBC, both RWM and ROM. The only difference between them is that the ROM is read only, and the RWM is read or write. It is the responsibility of the user to ensure that a correct selection of memory ranges and types is made when setting up the emulator for the particular SBC connected. There are no fail-safe checks which detect if memory type and ranges have been correctly specified and memory designated as RWM will attempt to perform read and write operations even if the physical memory is ROM, and vice versa. The emulator will indicate an error has occurred if an attempt is made to write to ROM or unspecified memory address ranges and some emulators will also check that write operations change the memory locations to the specified values.

Additionally, the emulator provides two internal memory types, host RWM and host ROM, and if an access is made to this memory the internal memory of the emulator is accessed, not the target memory. The target memory address and data signals remain inactive during these accesses, so that if physical memory does exist on the SBC in the specified memory ·address ranges, it will not be accessed. This allows memory components that are not working correctly or are not present, to be emulated. This is useful for systems where the program code will eventually be stored in ROM components as during development host ROM is used to store the program rather then target ROM. This avoids having to program the ROM every time a change is made in the program. All that is necessary is to change the program code in the emulator.

Program code can be transferred into the specified memory address if the memory is target RWM or via the emulator ICE probe into host RWM or ROM. Trying to perform this operation on target ROM will cause an error. It is possible to download into host ROM as this memory is under the direct control of the emulator. However, once loaded the memory can only be read.

If memory is specified as 'unused' the memory address ranges indicated are considered not to exist in the target or host systems. The use of all the different types of memory addressing specification is illustrated in *Figure 6.8*. Accessing any of these locations will cause an error message and termination of the program as it indicates a fatal program error. Some SBC designs which make use of memory images to access the same locations using two or more different addresses may cause this error but new designs developed using emulators should not have this problem.

The full range of facilities available to the SBC monitor program are available as built-in functions of the emulator, such as:

(a) Single step;
(b) Starting execution from a specified address;
(c) Altering memory or register contents during the course of a program execution;
(d) Stopping execution when specific addresses or address ranges are accessed, when specific types of accesses are made, or for I/O reads or writes.

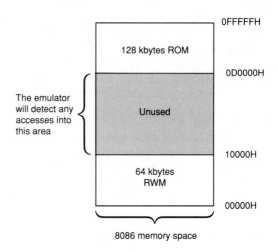

Figure 6.8 Specifying memory types

In addition, there is the trace function which maintains a record of the microprocessor registers after each instruction for a section of code with a maximum length of between 255 and 1000 instructions executed. The instructions can be single stepped or executed continuously. The range of facilities is extensive and varies between emulators but most will provide all the necessary functions to examine the operation of the program in detail as it executes.

There are some drawbacks to the use of an emulator; one is the cost of the interface, controlling computer and associated software, another is that most emulators do not usually execute programs in real-time so that time-critical functions are still difficult to verify. A lack of real-time verification can be caused by two factors; the crystal used or emulator control.

The **crystal** used is the source of the microprocessor timing and most emulators have two options; to use the crystal contained on the target SBC when individual instructions execute in real-time, or to use the emulator internal crystal. The emulator internal crystal has one value chosen so that the programs will execute at the fastest speed possible for that particular microprocessor and this may be different from that used on the target system. It is preferred to use the target crystal if possible so that the programs will execute at speeds as close as possible to the completed system. A problem with this is that some crystal/ICE probe combinations do not correctly drive the simulated microprocessor crystal oscillator inputs due to the long lengths of ribbon cable used to connect the ICE probe to the interface. To avoid this problem, either a more powerful crystal oscillator is used or a crystal of the same type and frequency as the target system is used but which is connected directly to the emulator interface. In this way the correct frequency can be obtained and the correct oscillation conditions obtained.

The internal crystal is designed to be used when the hardware of the SBC is not available but the program is to be tested. By using the internal crystal and host RWM and ROM, the majority of program instructions can be executed by the emulator. If the program requires specific hardware I/O operations, such as inputting data from a keyboard or outputting a value to a parallel output port, these functions are not available. Some emulators provide the option of simulating I/O operations by setting up files within the emulator computer which contain simulated values for the hardware I/O functions. For example, if reading from a keyboard, assuming a serial link was used, the codes to be received by the USART could be placed into a file. All accesses to the keyboard I/O port are replaced automatically by the emulator with equivalent instructions which access the data file instead. In this way the majority of the hardware functions can be simulated even if the hardware is not available. Although the hardware simulations are not 100 per cent accurate, particularly with respect to the real-time operation, they do allow more functions of the program to be verified when the hardware is not available.

The second reason why programs do not execute in real-time is due to the way the emulator is controlled as some emulators 'interrupt' the microprocessor to access the internal registers, monitor address and data values, or to perform other tasks. Therefore while these emulator control tasks are being performed the program is not executing and program execution is not in real-time. Programs can be executed in real-time using this type of emulator by disabling all the functions of the emulator which cause the interrupts to occur but unfortunately this disables most of the emulator functions. The method of obtaining real-time execution is to monitor program execution in near real-time (that is, with emulator interrupts enabled) to ensure that incorrect operations such as accessing invalid memory are avoided. Then when executing satisfactorily, the emulator functions are disabled, so that program execution takes place in real-time but with no debugging facilities available. The successful execution of the program can be monitored if necessary, by using additional equipment. This could be monitoring the SBC itself performing the required task such as controlling 7-segment displays, or by using equipment to monitor the digital signals in real-time.

Such equipment is known as a **logic analyser** and the basic operation of a logic analyser is outlined in *Figure 6.9*, consisting of threshold detectors, digital compara-

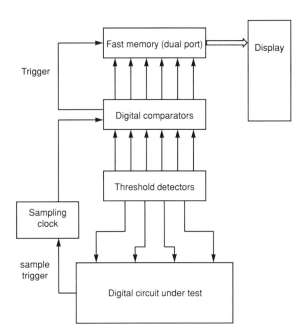

Figure 6.9 A logic analyser

tors and fast memory storage. The threshold detectors determine if signals are at logic 0 or logic 1. These values are passed to the comparators to determine if the value is to be saved when it is written into the fast memory. Logic analysers cannot be controlled directly by a microprocessor as the speed of sampling is at least 20 MHz and can be up to 100 MHz or greater. The maximum speed of execution of most microprocessors is 1–3 MHz and several instructions would be required to perform all the sampling and saving operations outlined. Therefore the logic analyser is 'hardwired', so that specific hardware functions perform the actions required. In this way the very fast sampling speeds required can be obtained.

The digital values saved can vary from one bit to as many as the logic analyser can store, often 16 and 32 bits, sometimes up to 64 bits or more. Logic analysers have many similarities to the trace function available in emulators, as the most common method of tracing is to specify a trigger signal which when detected, saves all the following data values until the memory has been filled. Data values can be stored prior to the trigger signal, or before and after by continuously saving the data values while a program is executing. The memory available is limited so that values are saved starting at the beginning of the memory and over-writing the existing data with new data. When the end of the memory is reached, it continues saving data from the beginning of the memory again. Therefore the trigger signal can occur at any time and it is only necessary to save the remaining number of values required. Once the trigger state has been detected, a marker is left and the remaining number of data values saved. The positioning of the trigger signal is denoted by a percentage pre-trigger or a percentage post-trigger so that it is independent of the actual size of memory inside the logic analyser.

Once the trigger signal has been generated and the data values saved the logic analyser changes to the display mode, which can be under the control of a microprocessor as this is not such a high speed operation. The data values can be displayed in a variety of ways depending on the type of data gathered. Blocks of 8 or 16 signals, depending on the size of the display screen, can be displayed as oscilloscope-like traces of logic values against time. The time-scale of the display can be altered to observe the detail of a particular sequence of signals, or to obtain a larger perspective. Alternatively, the data values can be displayed as logic 0s and 1s although this mode is not often used as it is not as informative as the previous mode.

As shown in *Figure 6.9*, the sampling of the digital data is performed at intervals controlled by the sampling clock. The sampling signal can be obtained from two alternative sources, either a signal from the system being monitored by the logic analyser or by using an asynchronous clock generated by the logic analyser itself. Both types of sampling clock have specific advantages. If the data values being monitored are essentially asynchronous then the internal asynchronous clock is preferred as this operates at the maximum sampling rate of the logic analyser. This may cause some problems if the data values being monitored do not change at the clock frequencies close to the sampling frequency as the memory will soon be filled with excess values. For example, if signals of 2 MHz are being investigated and the internal 100 MHz asynchronous sampling clock is used, then each change in data value occupies at least 50 memory locations and the available memory will soon fill up. This may occur before all the test variations in data values have occurred. This problem can be overcome by using an external asynchronous sampling clock with a frequency nearer to the signals being sampled. For the previous example of 2 MHz signals, a sampling clock of between 4 and 8 MHz would be used. The external asynchronous sampling clock is supplied by the user.

For microprocessor systems this may be the system clock and data samples will be taken for every pulse to save the internal states, known as 'machine' or 'T' states. Other useful signal sampling signals might be the read, write or address latch enable (ALE) signals as these occur once per microprocessor instruction. By using

these signals, the data values obtained contain information about the operation of the program and the use of a suitable decoding program allows the data values to be displayed as microprocessor instructions, allowing the operation of the program to be monitored in real-time.

If the signals being investigated are very short duration pulses which occur infrequently neither method outlined previously will detect them satisfactorily. This type of signal is known as a 'glitch' and is generated by faults in the digital designs causing error conditions to occur momentarily. They are not intentionally produced but are a by-product of the difference between the model of digital devices used to design the circuits and the physical devices. For example, the circuit in *Figure 6.10* would apparently never produce an output because one of the AND gate inputs will always be a zero. However, in the physical device the NOT gate has a small propagation delay of typically 10-20 ns. This may be sufficient to produce a small pulse at the AND gate output whenever the input signal changes from a logic 0 to a logic 1, or from a logic 1 to a logic 0. This signal would be extremely difficult to detect because it has a very narrow pulse width which implies a very high frequency bandwidth and may not occur regularly. Because of their high bandwidth these signals often cannot be detected by relatively low frequency instruments such as oscilloscopes. Logic analysers contain specialised circuits known as **glitch detectors** especially to detect very narrow pulses.

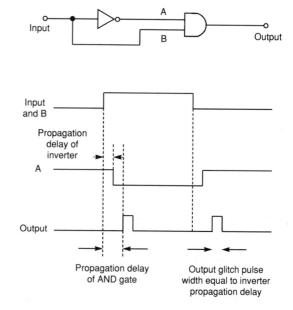

Figure 6.10   Glitch-producing circuit and waveforms

Emulator Logic Analysers

The trace operation of most emulators is obtained using a simplified version of the logic analyser hardware with the target clock signal as the sampling signal. Some sophisticated modern emulators contain a logic analyser optimised for operation with microprocessors and this combination enables real-time execution of programs and retains all the functions of the emulator and logic analyser. The disadvantage is that these systems are more expensive. However, the use of custom components is reducing the price of such systems and the majority of modern emulators allow real-time program operation under emulator control.

6.3 SIMULATORS

Simulators provide many of the functions available to emulators except that there is no ICE probe, but the microprocessor is simulated by a computer program. Because there is no hardware involved simulators can only be used to develop software and not any of the hardware. The simulation operates by implementing the programmer's model of the microprocessor which consists of the registers, how they are used and the instructions that can be executed. The input to the simulator is the same machine code program the physical microprocessor would execute, so that the same software development process can be used for a simulator or emulator.

The input to the simulator is the same file downloaded to the emulator or SBC with a common format being the Intel HEX format or the Motorola S format. The simulator provides all the required program debugging functions, such as single step, memory display and alteration, program trace and register display. These functions allow the operation of the program to be verified using the same techniques as outlined for the emulator and SBC with monitor.

Because there is no target hardware involved the range of I/O operations simulated is limited and generally separates into two categories:

(a) Built-in I/O functions;
(b) Simulated I/O functions using files.

As the majority of the software verification process involves the display of data values, some simulators provide specialised built-in functions for performing input and output operations to access the screen and keyboard of the computer. If the program produces data values to be output to a port, they are output to the screen port and any input required while the program is executing can be input from the VDU keyboard. The data values obtained this way are 8 bits, which is not a great problem as most I/O are 8 bits, but the data values are treated as ASCII characters as they need to be transferred to the VDU which only recognises ASCII characters. This requires the translation of the ASCII characters into hexadecimal values and vice versa, depending on the direction of data transfer. This I/O port connection is most useful when the data values being transferred are already ASCII characters as for example, would be obtained from a USART. Alternatively, the program may contain some instructions to convert the 8-bit data values into displayable ASCII hexadecimal representations. This is easily achieved if modular programming techniques are used in the program design by writing two different I/O transfer subroutines. One is used when the target system hardware is being used and the second performs the ASCII/hex translation when the simulator is used. Then, when the linking process is taking place, the module containing the subroutine with the data translations would be included when the simulator is being used, and the module containing the I/O subroutines without the data translations would be included when the target system hardware is being used. The only requirement is that the two subroutines should have the same label names. In this way, no changes at all to the program need be made when switching between target and simulator systems, illustrating the advantages of modular programming.

If modular programming is not used, for example, if the program is small, the translation subroutines could be included in the source file when using the simulator and removed when using the target hardware. This requires a re-assembly every time the execution system is changed, but with small programs this is more productive than using two alternative subroutines, selectable at link time.

If the target system hardware has a wide variety of different I/O port transfers, the alternative technique of simulating the I/O ports using computer files can be used, as outlined for emulators without target system hardware. This technique is not recommended due to the difficulty of producing satisfactory file contents to simulate the operation of I/O ports. Time spent producing these files may be wasted if they are not sufficiently accurate and a better technique may be to write a section of program which will produce suitable values from within the simulated program.

As the simulator is a model of the microprocessor then it cannot execute programs in real-time. However, some simulators will provide an indication of the execution time calculated at the specified crystal frequency. The simulator maintains a record of the elapsed time from some designated starting point in the program and displays the predicted time taken from that point to another selected point. This provides some indication of the elapsed time of program execution but if there are time critical sections of program code, there is no real alternative to using an emulator operating in real-time mode, or a SBC and monitor.

Comparison of Monitors, Debuggers, Emulators and Simulators

Each type of fault finding technique has its own particular characteristics, advantages and disadvantages and these have been summarised below.

Monitors. *Characteristics*: contained in ROM. *Advantages*: do not require operating system. Suitable for single board computers (SBC). Low cost. Small program size. *Disadvantages*: Limited functionality due to limited program size. Can only debug software. Limited to programs executed by SBC. Only work with LLLs. Poor user interface. Difficult to control interrupts.

Debuggers. *Characteristics*: Stored in secondary mass storage. *Advantages*: Can be used to debug a wide range of programs. Can be enhanced to debug HLL programs. Relatively low cost. Improved user interface. *Disadvantages*: May have limited functionality. Can only debug software. Cannot easily be used on single board computers. Single step is not hardware controlled and it is difficult to control I/O and interrupts.

Emulators. *Characteristics*: Combination of hardware and software. *Advantages*: Hardware control of single stepping and program execution. Program execution (almost) in real-time. Usually contains a logic analyser for debugging hardware as well as software. Improved user interface. Good control of I/O. *Disadvantages*: Expensive and complex. Require a separate computer to control them. Each different type of microprocessor requires a new emulator. Difficult to control interrupts.

Simulators. *Characteristics*: Software only. *Advantages*: Relatively low cost. Can debug software under complete control. Executing times can be calculated. Can develop software without target systems. Can be used on a different type of computer such as mainframe to provide good multi-user software development environment. Easily upgradeable to cope with improvements in the microprocessor. *Disadvantages*: Usually used for debugging LLL programs but simulators suitable for debugging HLL programs do exist. Do not execute programs in real-time. Poor I/O simulation.

Summary

The methods and techniques of detecting and rectifying faults in software are similar and independent of the product used:

(a) Monitor;
(b) Debugger;
(c) Emulator;
(d) Simulator.

They have the ability to control program execution, to display the contents of computer memory and register contents and to relate these to the programs being tested. There is little difference between debugging a LLL program and a HLL program other than in the level of sophistication required by the hardware/software package.

SEVEN

System Testing

7.1 TESTING AND EVALUATING TEST RESULTS AGAINST DESIGN CRITERIA

The testing of microcomputer systems is a complex task which has many facets that can be considered individually or as related groups. There are three main areas of testing:

(a) Hardware;
(b) Software;
(c) Hardware/software interaction

which can be approached in similar ways using similar techniques and equipment, although in each category the specific details will vary.

A comprehensive analysis and discussion of hardware testing is beyond the scope of this book. Instead, the testing of the hardware will be restricted to the testing of single board computers or complete computer systems hardware through brief general guidelines. This chapter will consider the different aspects of software testing and the testing of hardware/software combinations and finishes with a consideration of common causes of faults in Pascal and C HLLs and assembler languages.

Stage Testing

The techniques of testing alters depending on which stage of production a product is at: prototyping to specification, or testing for manufacture.

The majority of these sections will consider prototyping to the specification and the tests required as this is of most interest to the designer. Only when testing for manufacture has an effect on the design will the second stage of testing be considered.

Steps to testing.　There are two main steps involved in the testing of a product:

(a) Verification;
(b) Failure diagnosis.

Verification is usually designed to determine whether the product is operating as defined by the specification and is 'go or no go'. That is, the test works perfectly or it does not work at all. If the correct answers are supplied then the product is considered to be correct. If the wrong answer is produced then the product has failed and there is little information to indicate where the fault is. This is where failure diagnosis becomes important. Further verification tests are performed, designed to ensure that all possible parts of the product are exercised and produce the correct results. The tests are designed purely on input and output data, whereas failure diagnosis usually requires some form of intervention in the product itself in order to produce intermediate test results that can be used to identify the fault position and nature.

Test Strategy

The two steps to testing which enable a test strategy to be produced, are illustrated in *Figure 7.1*. The strategy begins with the design of the product which has to take into account the debugging techniques being used, which in turn is governed by the technology and the economics of the project. Technology covers such

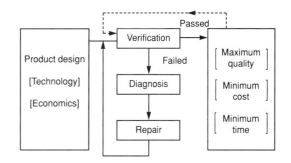

Figure 7.1　A test strategy

191

areas as whether a LLL such as assembler or a HLL such as Pascal is going to be used and whether a monitor, debugger, emulator or simulator will be used during testing and fault diagnosis. Economics dictate how much resource such as man-hours, money, time, equipment, is available for the project and this determines the level of sophistication of the program and the testing performed.

Once the design has been completed it should be fully verified using a complete set of test data. If the product fails verification it enters a diagnostic stage where the causes and reasons for the failure are determined. Following this the product is repaired to remove the error-causing functions and passed back to be verified again. This process is repeated until the verification is passed.

The final product can be analysed in terms of three quantities:

(a) Quality;
(b) Cost;
(c) Time allowed.

Each has an influence on the verification process. If a product must be of high quality then maximum testing via verification is required. If the cost is to be minimised then testing and verification (and also design) have to be reduced to a minimum. Finally, the time required to produce the finished item influences the verification and design stages with more time allowing better design and verification. These three quantities are difficult to predict accurately at the beginning of the project unless the specification is correct, fully detailed and not subject to change.

The optimum test strategy will produce a product with the maximum amount of quality with the minimum cost in the minimum time. Unfortunately, many projects, even quite small ones, are of poor quality, cost a great deal to produce and are past the deadline.

Test as soon as possible. In order to reduce the cost and avoid wasting time on unnecessary testing, the product should be tested as early as possible. *Figure 7.2* illustrates the relative costs of testing for a fault at the four stages of a product's life:

(a) Design;
(b) Procedure or component level;
(c) Program or product level;
(d) Post installation.

The design fault is the easiest to correct at the design stage as there is very little that has been produced and it is easily changed. Errors detected are referred back to the design stage to determine if they were a design fault

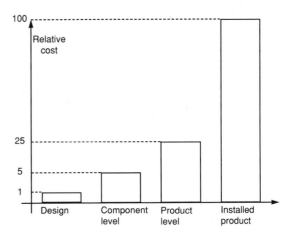

Figure 7.2   The cost of testing

requiring a change to the design or an implementation fault which required no design changes.

Total Program Cost

The total cost of a product is not just the cost of producing it but also the cost of maintaining it as illustrated in *Figure 7.3.*. The production costs cease to increase after the release date, which is the date the product actually becomes available to users and forms a constant block of cost against time. However, the maintenance costs, which are zero before the release date, increase with time.

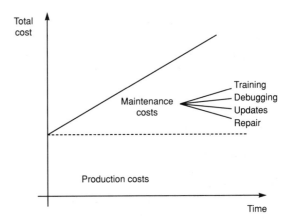

Figure 7.3   Cost has two elements

Maintenance for a software program is different from the maintenance of hardware as hardware wears with time, so that periodically parts have to be replaced. Programs do not wear in the same way, as a program will always execute in exactly the same way, no matter how many times it is executed or how long it is after the release date. What may change is the hardware the program is executed on and the data being used as input. Any new hardware/input data combination may produce new circumstances the program has not encountered previously and may not have been tested for. In those situations there is a relatively high probability that a fault will be uncovered during program execution. This must then be identified by debugging, a repair made and updates issued. To be able to effect repairs efficiently it will be necessary to maintain the programmer's skills by training, both in how to use the program and how to identify and correct faults. Training is necessary to understand the operation and function of the entire program so that suitable tests can be produced and the data produced by them correctly analysed. Testing at procedure level is relatively easy as the operation of the procedure can be determined from the listing itself. Understanding the operation of the entire program requires an understanding of the purpose of the program, which can only be obtained through testing. The four maintenance areas are: training, debugging, repairing and updates, and require continuous expenditure, indicating why the maintenance cost is always increasing.

Analysing Testing

The analysis of the type of tests required and the subsequent test results produced is a cyclical process, listed below:

(a) Know what needs to be tested;
(b) Identify suitable methods of testing;
(c) Analyse the cost of each method of testing;
(d) Test and use test results to update the product and test analysis;
(e) Repeat from step (a).

It is better to identify what needs testing and only test in those areas rather than test for everything. This requires an understanding of the operation and function of the product so that critical points can be identified. Once these are identified methods of testing can be considered and an optimum test produced to perform the necessary parts of the test with the minimum cost.

Having obtained test results it is necessary to analyse them to understand what they indicate. The test values are compared with the expected values derived from the detailed specification and differences identified. The reasons for the differences are deduced and the related sections of the program listing analysed. Probable causes for the fault are deduced and further tests implemented if necessary to verify the deductions. Once the specific sections have been identified, suitable repairs are made and the tests re-executed to confirm that the fault has been eradicated.

This sounds simple, but the reality is much more different. Sometimes the faulty section may not be identified correctly so that at best the repair is ineffective. A more likely result is that an unnecessary repair will introduce additional faults, making it difficult to assess whether the original fault has been cleared and another one uncovered or a new fault introduced.

For new products the number of faults appears to increase during the fault finding process rather than decrease, although usually they are easy to fix. This is illustrated in *Figure 7.4*. It is also true that as each fault is fixed it invariably takes longer and longer to find and repair the next one. In reality, the number of faults should not increase, which is illustrated by the dashed line, provided that no mistakes are made in the fault correcting process. However, note that there are always more faults than are detected and a product can never be considered to be fault-free. A point is reached at which further fault finding is considered uneconomic, unproductive and a waste of further time.

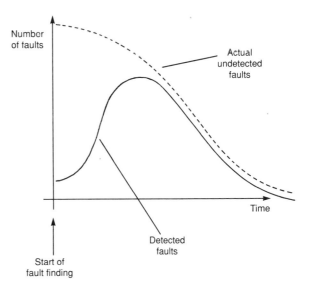

Figure 7.4 The number of faults in a product

Spectrum of Software Faults

The spectrum of faults in a software product can be categorised into three groups, as listed below:

(a) Language/compiler faults;
(b) Procedure faults;
(c) Operational faults.

Language and **compiler faults** are not caused by the programmer but by either an incomplete or incorrect programming language specification, or by a faulty compiler (or assembler) which does not correctly implement the language specification. These faults are rare but when they do occur they will be obtuse and difficult to identify as language specifications and compilers undergo a great deal of testing before they are released. To illustrate that compilers have faults, with most compiler programs there will be some documentation which lists the known defects. This is because it is uneconomic to update compilers every time a minor fault is uncovered. Instead, the compiler manufacturers wait until there are many small faults, several large ones and/or some major improvements to the compiler operation are required. When this occurs a completely new, or a revised version of the compiler can be introduced which will correct all known faults, but will in turn introduce its own new ones.

Confidence in a particular compiler can be gained by prior experience or by using a compiler that has been verified against a known standard. Standards for most major programming languages do exist although verifying a compiler is time consuming and expensive. Many compiler manufacturers do not bother with compiler verification to reduce costs but also because many of them contain extensions to the language specification which would not be verified anyway.

Procedure faults are faults in the use of the programming language itself, so that what the procedure does when executed is not what is required. This is called a procedure fault to emphasise that **structured program design** techniques should be used, resulting in the use of procedures which will therefore contain the majority of faults. These faults are all caused by the programmer.

The final category of fault is the operational fault which is a fault discovered in the entire program and its operation. The program does not work as expected but the fault cannot be traced to a specific procedure. It is more likely to be an incorrect or incomplete specification or the incorrect use of procedures. If the specification is perfectly correct and there are no procedure faults, there should not be any operational faults.

7.2 TYPICAL FAULTS (HARDWARE)

An overview of typical hardware faults has been included.

Component failure. Inputs may be open circuit, short circuited or connected to each other internally. Outputs may be stuck at high or low logic levels. Internal faults

may cause incorrect operation (often these are known). Incorrect use of a component by trying to achieve something it was not designed for, such as operating too fast or too slow. Adjacent components such as integrated circuits, capacitors, resistors, etc., may be faulty or incorrectly connected. Faulty components or peripherals causing excessive loading.

Open and short circuits. Connections may not be soldered or incorrectly soldered, leading to intermittent connections. Edge connectors may be faulty, misaligned or dirty. Switches may have dirty contacts. Cables may be broken by bending and twisting to produce open or short circuits especially at connectors.

External interference. Faults in the power supply may provide a voltage which is too large, too small, or unstable, or insufficient current. Mains interference may be picked up on digital or analogue signals and superimpose erroneous states. Sharp fluctuations in mains voltage may be transmitted through the computer power supply and cause intermittent faults, e.g. fridges, coffee machines when turning off or on. Cross coupling between adjacent or crossing signal paths can corrupt and interfere with both signals. Cosmic radiation can affect the data values stored in dynamic RWM, particularly as storage density increases. This is called a soft fault as there is no permanent fault or damage. Unspecified transient faults which may occur randomly with time and are extremely difficult to identify.

Fault Finding Techniques for Microprocessor System Hardware

Once a paper design has been converted into a prototype, a logical process of testing should be performed, which can be categorised into three groups:

(a) DC tests;
(b) AC tests;
(c) Tests with an emulator.

Tests performed without an in-circuit emulator (DC tests). Check power supply values when no integrated circuits (IC) are present. Voltages should be within given tolerances, i.e. 5 per cent. Insert all ICs and recheck power supply voltages are within given tolerances.

If possible, check that the crystal is oscillating. Note: an oscilloscope probe capacitance may short out the crystal and an alternative test instrument may be advisable. Check that the system clock is present directly, or indirectly via a function signal such as address latch enable (ALE) or address strobe (AS).

Check the operation of the RESET switch for correct voltages and timing.

If possible, ensure that all data and address lines are floating, at approximately 1.4 V when in the tri-state mode. Ensure that you know which signals are not tri-state.

Ensure that all interrupt signals are prevented from being activated. The correct operation of interrupts is difficult to verify using any method.

Test the operation of the READ signal by using a logic probe with a pulse stretcher. After a RESET, this will be the first signal produced by the microprocessor.

All tests must have written documentation indicating the tests performed and the results obtained. These results provide clues if faults are present and can also be used at a later date to ensure that there has been no deterioration. These results can also be useful when testing production versions of the product.

Memory and address decoding (AC tests).

At this point, tests on the operation of the functions of the microprocessor can begin. A test program which has been previously saved in ROM is required, normally of the form:

```
START:   JMP START
```

This is used to check that the memory read operation is correct and that instructions can be fetched from memory. When the program is executing some of the DC and AC checks need to be repeated.

Check that the power supplies are still within the given tolerances. This ensures that execution of programs does not cause a problem with the power supplies.

Check for the presence of the chip select (CS) signal to the ROM by using a logic probe. This is usually active low, that is, a logic 0. It may not be possible to verify that the timing of this signal is correct unless a high speed digital storage oscilloscope is available. Look for the presence of the READ signal at the ROM using a logic probe.

Ensure that data appears on the output pins of the memory and is correctly transferred to the data input pins of the microprocessor. Any intervening buffers and latches should also be checked for correct operation. Check latches and buffers receive the correct signals and operate correctly.

Check that the test program saved in ROM executes correctly. Use an oscilloscope to look for the repeated data patterns on the address and data buses.

At this point further tests are performed by the execution of test programs as detailed below. These tests can be easily monitored by the use of an **in-circuit emulator** (ICE), but the same tests can be performed by the

use of programmed ROMs in conjunction with an oscilloscope or logic analyser. These have the drawback that more skill is required and it takes longer to complete the tests.

Using an In-Circuit Emulator in the Test Process

An ICE replaces the microprocessor in the system under test with a probe which is electrically and functionally the same, but with the probe under the control of the development system. Commands can be entered via the keyboard and results displayed on the screen. Programs can be single stepped, or sections of programs executed, or the results of programs inspected in memory locations and microprocessor registers. Any errors detected can then be rectified directly if they are simple or the original source code can be edited, when re-compiling, or re-assembling, re-linking and reloading is necessary. Such a system is presently one of the quickest methods of producing error-free code.

The most important parts remaining to be tested are the I/O devices. Each component has a series of tests performed on it to exercise all the facilities available.

Example

The 8155 I/O component contains:

(a) 256 bytes RAM;
(b) 2 × 8 bit, 1 × 6 bit I/O ports;
(c) 14-bit timer counter.

Test 1. Test programs are required that will write 0FFH to all RWM locations, read them back and check that they have changed to the correct value. This checks that all the bits will go to logic 1. Repeat this test with 00H. This checks that all the bits will go to logic 0. Repeat this test with data values having a combination of logic 0s and logic 1s, usually 01010101B. Although the previous two tests show that all the bits can be made to change between logic 0s and logic 1s, it will not detect if any of the bits are shorted together. This can be detected by using a pattern of logic 0s and 1s. It is unusual to test every possible combination of bits for cross connection as most designs maintain the data bus signals in parallel and these data values cover most of the expected problem areas. An exhaustive test of all possible fault conditions is not feasible as it would take a long time.

Test 2. Further programs are required to test the I/O ports for correct operation. Test output 0FFH to all ports and check that the data is present using a logic probe. Repeat the test with 00H. Repeat the test with a pattern of logic 1s and logic 0s. These tests perform the same test function on the I/O as the previous tests did on the RWM.

Test 3. Finally, programs are required to test the timer/counter and these are more complex as it can be programmed for a wide range of different functions. To test all of them would take a long time. Instead, it is usual to test only those functions that are going to be used by the prototype product. Typical tests might be to supply a clock input then set the timer an initial value and monitor the output for the end-of-count signal. Test the event counter then test the period measurement function. Any faults discovered should be isolated and repaired before proceeding onto the next test.

Functional Testing

Once the components have been tested, the sub-functions and functions can be tested until the complete product has been functionally tested.

Example

Assuming that a product has a set of switches connected to one port and a set of LEDs to another port:

(a) Test that the input from the switches is correct;
(b) Test that the output to the LEDs is operating;
(c) Combine tests (a) and (b) so that the LEDs are controlled by the switches.

This could now start to include more complex functions, such as contact bounce which could be either software or hardware implemented. At this point the distinction between testing the hardware and testing the software starts to blur. The tests are being performed upon an interactive combination of both the hardware and the software.

Test Data

If some of the tests require data from other functions which have not yet been implemented, simulated test data should be produced. It will require additional software to create and present the test data in the correct manner to the function being tested.

Use of test data. An experienced engineer will be able to use the test data results to identify the general area of any detected faults and possibly even the fault itself. Test data provides a standard to which subsequent models can be compared and differences and faults identified. Test data is vital for future development of the product and for the training of engineers new to the project.

Software Diagnostics

The use of software diagnostics in computer systems to check the hardware of the computer for faults is becoming increasingly common as the computers become more and more complex. These can be separated into two categories:

(a) Power-on self test (POST);
(b) Run time diagnostics.

Power-on self test software is resident on the computer hardware in non-volatile ROM and is executed as soon as the power is turned on. This software tests the hardware, starting with the most basic and important components and increasing in test complexity until the majority of the hardware has been tested. As the tests continue various diagnostic indicators are produced which can be used by repair technicians to identify the faulty functional area and sometimes the actual component. The tests performed are not exhaustive but if successful they do indicate that the hardware seems to be working. An example of a POST is illustrated in *Table 7.1* (over), which describes the operation of the IBM PC POST and lists the indicators which allow the user to identify faulty areas.

Run time diagnostics are similar to the POST programs except that they are maintained in secondary mass storage instead of in ROM and may be executed any time after the operating system has been loaded. Because they are stored in secondary mass storage the programs can be larger and more comprehensive and sophisticated. Usually menus are used to guide the user through various choices and tests with the tests being more exhaustive.

Other Software Diagnostics

In addition to complete programs designed to test the hardware of the entire computer there are simpler programs designed to execute in collaboration with test instruments such as logic analysers and oscilloscopes. The four common tests are listed below:

(a) Free running;
(b) I/O tests;
(c) RWM tests;
(d) ROM tests.

In order to test the dynamic operation of the computer hardware rather than just the static DC characteristics, in a controlled manner, it is necessary to cycle through all of the memory addresses sequentially. This can be achieved by free running the microprocessor which emulates the actions of a program occupying the entire

Table 7.1 Power-on self-test example

POST	Indicator
Power good signal from the power supply	Fan running
ROM-BIOS self test	
Initialise DMA controllers	
Read and write tests to base 64 kbytes of dynamic RWM	
Initialise interrupt controllers	
Read system hardware setup information (This is the information altered by the setup program)	
Initialise display controller	
Display cursor	Cursor may appear
Read and write test of interrupt controllers	
Initialise interval controller	
Keyboard test and reset	Keyboard lights flash
Expansion box test	
Read and write tests on remaining RWM	Increment count on display
Check for additional ROMs	EGA and VGA cursors may appear
Check for floppy disk drive	Floppy LED activates
Reset floppies found	Floppy LED activates for a second time
Speaker beeps	Sequence of beeps can be used to indicate error free test results, or identify the faulty area and may be accompanied by an error message on the display

Table 7.2 RWM test data values

Data value	Tests for
000H	Bits stuck at logic 1
0FFH	Bits stuck at logic 0
0AAH	Adjacent bits stuck together (0AAH = 010101010B)

ROM tests are different as it is not possible to write data values, only to read them. So tests involving reading are used, the simplest of which is the checksum test implemented in the setup program. This sums the contents of all the memory locations and compares the result with a value stored in the ROM. Single errors which occur in the ROM contents are guaranteed to be detected but multiple errors may cancel each other out. More sophisticated checks such as cyclic redundancy checks (CRC) can be used which give a very high probability of detecting multiple errors.

7.3 TYPICAL FAULTS (SOFTWARE)

The range of software faults is more limited than the range of hardware faults and can be categorised into four areas:

(a) Software corruption
(b) External interference
(c) Design faults
(d) User errors.

Once a program is executing correctly, it will never wear out and the only reason for incorrect operation of a program that has previously been executing correctly is the corruption of the program. This can occur in a number of ways such as electromagnetic interference, cosmic radiation, or other electrical noise, which induce a change in the machine code instructions comprising the program. This could be a temporary change if the program is executing in the main memory and can be rectified by re-loading the program from secondary mass storage. Alternatively, if the stored version of the program is corrupted this is permanent and a new copy must be obtained. This is the reason why original copies of programs should never be used but back-up copies made and these used. This allows the original to remain uncorrupted and to be available when required for restoring corrupted copies.

External interference ranges from:

(a) Changes to the hardware of the computer;
(b) The incorrect use of the setup program to indicate the wrong type number of the hard disk;

memory area consisting of no operations, (NOP). NOPs have a useful function in that they cause the instruction pointer to increment by one, incrementing the memory address but performing no other actions. Therefore, the microprocessor will start at the reset memory address and cycle through every address in turn. Measuring instruments connected to the microprocessor and other parts of the microcomputer hardware can check the timing and correctness of signals.

I/O tests enable data values to be input from input ports, checked and data values to be output and checked, using suitable measuring instruments.

RWM tests have been discussed in POST and run-time diagnostics and are often produced as separate programs. These programs seek to identify faulty memory locations through a series of tests which first write and then read back data values. A minimum series of data values is outlined in *Table 7.2* indicating what test they are checking for.

(c) Malicious intent through programs such as 'viruses' which are designed specifically to corrupt programs.

Design faults are essentially caused by errors in the specification or errors in the implementation of the specification, which are not detected by the tests performed on the software before it was issued. These external interferences are generally caused by using the program in a novel way or through inputting novel data values. The program itself remains perfectly usable in other situations except for the novel uses and data which have to be avoided.

Avoiding user faults. The most common cause of error in any microcomputer system is user error, either the hardware of the computer is incorrectly set up or used, or the user does not follow the instructions given in the manuals.

Not reading the manual is a common source of user error but there is a body of opinion that says if the program is well designed and robust, any user can learn how to use it from actually using it without having to read the manuals. This is achieved by a good user interface, good menus, a logical structure and extensive checking on the data entered by the user, coupled with the ability to recover from all erroneous data input. Many modern programs come with a tutorial as a separate program and help screens built into the program itself. The reason for this approach is that manuals are often lost or stolen so they cannot be referred to and that the training of new users is made considerably easier as they require reduced guidance.

Fault Logging

One area of testing that is overlooked is that of fault logging, where faults uncovered are documented and copies sent to the designer. This is helpful in the five areas listed below:

(1) Feedback of information to the designers as to how the program is being used.
(2) Gives an early warning for users of the same or similar programs.
(3) Identifies the source of errors.
(4) Provides useful information to service engineers which enables an informed guess to be made as to probable error situations.
(5) Identifies weaknesses in the design, particularly in the hardware/software interaction area, that were previously unknown.

All this information is most useful in the design of new versions of old programs as well as in new programs so that the same or similar faults can be avoided. It also provides the designers with information on the usefulness of the testing techniques used in the original design to determine how effective they were and how they might be improved.

Debugging Techniques

Debugging techniques can be separated into two categories which correspond with the two areas of the total cost of a program, that is design testing (which is part of design costs) and runtime testing (part of maintenance costs). Once the specification has been completed the design testing can begin and this can be further separated into two categories: debugging as part of the design and accuracy testing.

It is possible to design products so that a great deal of testing is incorporated, but this has the disadvantage of making the product larger and more expensive. This can be condensed into the two statements listed below:

A large amount of built-in testing will produce a robust, reliable product but it will be larger than absolutely necessary and cost more.

The minimum of checking will produce the smallest product, but it will be easily upset by faulty input data.

A compromise between these two extremes is to provide maximum testing on all input data. This helps to prevent faulty data propagating through the product and increases reliability. Only minimal checking is incorporated into the remaining parts of the product as the data being processed is assumed to have a high probability of being correct. This approach produces the optimum solution of a program with the minimum size, but is still robust and reliable.

Accuracy testing is performed when the product is nominally complete and is designed to ensure than it implements the specification. This is mainly achieved by using input test data, divided into three groups:

(a) Boundary and limiting case tests;
(b) Faulty input data tests;
(c) Empty data set input tests.

All products have boundary conditions or limiting conditions where the product is more vulnerable to failure. By testing all these a high degree of confidence can be obtained. Boundary conditions can be illustrated by the simple Pascal program listed below:

```
for index:= 1 to 10 do
    something (index);
```

The boundary conditions are when index = 1 and index = 10 and these would be tested for correct operation. It is also normal to test for at least one no-boundary condition such as index = 6 to ensure that the program also executes correctly when not at the boundary condition.

Testing for the correct response to faulty input data is a little more difficult as it relies on being able to identify what constitutes faulty data. In some cases, such as the matrix multiplication program, it is easy to identify faulty data. The program expects integer numbers to be input and any non-integer input such as a real number or a character string will cause the program to fail. However, for the following program it is more difficult to identify the faulty input data.

```
var
    ch:char;
    choice:integer;
begin
    readln (ch);
    choice:= ord(ch) – ord('0');
    case choice of
        0: action_0;
        1: action_1;
        2: action_2;
    end;
end;
```

All the inputs are treated as characters so that whatever key is pressed the input routine will execute correctly. The character, which should be '0', '1' or '2' is converted into the corresponding integer before being used in the case statement. Faulty data would be any key other than '0', '1' or '2' but this can only be identified by looking further down the program from the read statement to the case statement. Testing the

```
readln(ch);
```

statement would not uncover any faulty input data values.

This faulty piece of code only needs the 'else' extension to the case statement to ensure that it will always execute, as illustrated below:

```
begin
    readln (ch);
    choice:= ord(ch) – ord('0');
    case choice of
        0: action_0;
        1: action_1;
        2: action_2;
        else;
    end;
end;
```

This prevents the case statement from failing but may still allow the faulty data to propagate through the program. A better solution would be to execute an error routine when the else option is executed as illustrated below:

```
begin
    readln(ch);
    choice:= ord(ch) – ord('0');
    case choice of
        0: action_0;
        1: action_1;
        2: action_2;
        else error_routine;
    end;
end;
```

A common test situation not tested for is the empty data set. This can be achieved on keyboard data entry by just pressing the return key instead of alphanumeric keys. A more likely source of empty data set errors is when a program accesses files. An empty file would cause an I/O error and should be checked for to prevent this.

The market for the product will also determine the amount of testing that is performed. A product such as the word processor used to produce this book would have an extensive set of input test data designed to test every facet of its operation.

Run time testing is the term used to identify testing performed after a product has been issued, that is, in the maintenance stage of its life. This type of testing will only be initiated if a fault is discovered while it is being used, which will have been passed on through the fault logging methods used. The aim of run time testing, as with all testing, is to:

(a) Identify the fault position;
(b) Identify the faulty code;
(c) Make a repair;
(d) Check that the repair corrects the fault and does not affect the operation of the rest of the product.

When faced with the problem of identifying the position of a fault, particularly within a large program, there are two important 'dont's': DON'T panic; DON'T try random tests. Any large problem when faced in its entirety will always appear overwhelming and the method of successfully solving it is to break the program into smaller problems. Random tests are not made as this is unlikely to be productive. Instead, as with all engineering, a methodical, structured and systematic approach is taken until the solution is found, by following the steps listed below:

(a) Divide and conquer;

(b) Think about the symptoms;
(c) Make assumptions and then test them.

First the position of the fault has to be identified and unless there are some obvious clues, the best technique is called 'divide and conquer'. The entire problem is first divided into two and then one half is tested. If that half is not faulty then the fault must be in the second half. The faulty half is then divided into two again and each of these halves is tested. This process is repeated until the faulty item is identified and sometimes even the faulty component or connection.

Once the fault position has been identified, the symptoms of the fault are considered and the cause of the fault deduced. A repair which will rectify the deduced fault is proposed, implemented and the tests executed again. If the fault was correctly identified and there are no other faults and the repair was the correct one to make, then the fault will have disappeared.

Types of Software Bugs

There are many types of software bugs and it would be impossible to describe them all in this chapter. They can be roughly divided into two groups, language-specific bugs and bugs common to all software. Bugs, or faults, common to all software have been described previously. This section will briefly outline some of the language-specific bugs for C, Pascal and assembler.

C-specific bugs. *Using un-initialised auto-variables.* The variable m in the example below has no specific value before it is passed to the function do_something and any value, perhaps not even an integer number, will be passed.

```
int m;
    do_something(m);
```

Confusing assignment (=) with the test for equality (==). A = B; copies contents of B into A whereas A == B tests for A equal to B and returns the answer true or false.

Confusing operator precedence. A = B * C + D is actually equivalent to A = (B * C) + D and not A = B * (C + D).

Bad pointer arithmetic.

Unexpected sign extensions. This is usually caused when converting from byte to word and requires an understanding of binary arithmetic.

Unexpected truncation. Usually caused when converting to byte from word and requires a knowledge of binary arithmetic to understand.

Superfluous semi-colon. The semi-colon is used as the end of statement marker and if incorrectly placed will cause problems. For example:

```
if (A=B);
{
do_something();
}
```

The semi-colon after [if (A = B);] terminates the 'if' statement and the do_something function will always be executed.

Macros with side effects.

Repeated autovariables names. This occurs because of the ability to keep defining variables.

```
auto int;
while (A=B)
   {auto int;
      auto=27;
   }
```

Which of the two variables called 'auto' is actually used in the statement [auto = 27;]?

Undefined function return values. In C all functions must have a return value, even if it is not used.

Misuse of break keyword to get out of a loop. This is similar to the GOTO command and is considered to be bad programming style and should not be used.

Errors, usually due to typing. Code has no effect but is syntactically correct so it will compile and execute. For example, A = A instead of A + = A;.

Forgetting to pass addresses of variables instead of the variables themselves, a common fault with scanf().

Omitting the open and close brackets, (), on functions with no parameters, as all C functions must have these.

Indexing multi-dimensional arrays incorrectly. For example:

```
B = matrix[x,y];
```

is incorrect and should be:

```
B = matrix[x][y];
```

Forgetting that C is case sensitive, particularly with variable names. For instance:

```
matrix [A][B] = 27;
```

is not the same as:

```
matrix [a][b] = 27;.
```

Pascal-specific bugs. *No initialisation.* All variables in Pascal must be initialised before they are used, otherwise the compiler does not allocate them memory locations. For example:

```
var
parameter: integer;
begin
    do_something (parameter);
end;
```

This code will compile and execute, but the value of 'parameter' passed to 'do_something' could be anything.

Dangling pointers are common in Pascal as the pointer structure can be made very complex.

Scope confusion, which is similar to C bug 'repeated auto-variable names' and effectively mixes up local and global variables with the same name. For example:

```
procedure demo_1;
var
param1:integer;
procedure demo_2;
var
param1:integer;
begin
    param1:=27;
end; {demo_2}
begin
    param1:=32;
    demo_2;
end; {demo_1}
```

What is the value of param1 after this is executed?

Superfluous semi-colons and has a similar effect to the C bug.

```
if (A = B) then;
    do_something;
```

The IF statement will accomplish nothing and the procedure 'do_something' will always be executed.

Undefined function return values are similar to uninitialised variables, the actual value returned could be anything. Example:

```
function demo_2 (A, B:integer):integer;
begin
    A:=B;
end; {demo_2}

begin
    A:=2; B:=3;
    C:= demo_2 (A,B);
end;
```

The value of C could be anything.

Decrementing byte or word variables past zero, or incrementing past the maximum value. Byte and word variables are treated as always being positive numbers with wrap-around. So, for example, a byte incremented

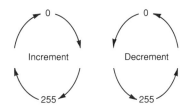

Figure 7.5 Byte wrap-around

past 255 becomes zero and decrementing past zero becomes 255, as illustrated in *Figure 7.5*.

Ignoring boundary or special cases is another common bug that can be difficult to track down. For example:

```
count:=0;
repeat
    do_something (count);
    count:=count+1;
    until count = 10;
```

If 'count = 10' is a valid parameter to pass to 'do_something' then a different conditional repeat terminator is required, such as:

```
until count > 10;
```

Range errors, usually in case statements but in integer arithmetic as well:

```
begin
    A:=32000; ←{valid integer}
    B:=32000; ←{valid integer}
    C:=A*B; ←{invalid integer result}
end;
```

Assembler-specific bugs. Assembler-specific bugs are a little more difficult to categorise as they are dependent upon the specific microprocessor. The following were derived from a study of the 8086 assembler language to give some idea of the type and range of bugs.

Forgetting to return to the operating system at the end of the program. This does not apply to embedded systems which do not have operating systems.

Forgetting to put returns (RET) at the end of subroutines.

Using the wrong type of return at the end of subroutines (should be RET) and interrupt service routines (should be IRET).

Reversing operands. 8086 assembler language is an example of a language where destination operands are given before the source:

```
MOV   AX,BX          ;copies contents BX into AX
```

68000 assembler language puts the source operand first:

    MOV   A5,D6   ;copies contents A5 into D6.

Forgetting about the stack or allocating a stack that is too small for the program.

Register contents being altered by subroutines when the original values are needed later, hence the importance of subroutine headers.

Using the wrong type of conditional jump after a flag is altered. For example:

    JE   loop   or   JNE loop?

Forgetting about instruction quirks, such as INC not affecting the carry flag.

Setting the auto increment/decrement flag to the wrong direction to that required by the program.

Using the wrong sense of an instruction, for example:

    Rotate arithmetic right

is not exactly the same as:

    Rotate logic right

although they are similar.

Forgetting about default addresses, for example, segment defaults.

Forgetting that multiplication always creates a result longer then the two original operands which will over-write the contents of another register other than those explicitly identified in the instruction.

Forgetting that string instructions, which must have source and destination memory pointers, will alter multiple register contents.

Expecting the carry flag to be altered by an instruction when it is not, as in INC.

Not using a flag state soon enough in a program, so that later instructions over-write with a new and unwanted value.

Confusing memory and immediate versions of instructions.

Forgetting that segments wrap around at the beginning and end of the segment and do not increment the segment registers.

Failing to save everything in an interrupt service routine so that it cannot be correctly restored.

Summary

The testing of software and hardware products is a complex problem which requires consideration from the moment the design is started until the time the last copy of the issued program is erased. Many factors influence the type, range of tests and the testing techniques used, ranging from the timescale available through to what specific programming language is going to be used to implement the program.

Index